Marjorie Cohn is a professor at Thomas Jefferson School of Law in San Diego, former president of the National Lawyers Guild, and deputy secretary general of the International Association of Democratic Lawyers. Her books include *Cowboy Republic: Six Ways the Bush Gang Has Defied the Law*; *Rules of Disengagement: The Politics and Honor of Military Dissent* (with Kathleen Gilberd); and the edited volume, *The United States and Torture: Interrogation, Incarceration and Abuse*. Cohn is a recipient of the Peace Scholar of the Year Award from the Peace and Justice Studies Association. She testified before Congress about the Bush torture policy.

ADVANCE PRAISE FOR *DRONES AND TARGETED KILLING*

"This book provides much-needed analysis of why America's targeted killing program is illegal, immoral and unwise."
—**from the foreword by Archbishop Desmond Tutu**

"Armed unmanned drones have radically reduced the practical constraints on the use of force, and in so doing present challenging legal, political and moral issues. This hard-hitting collection offers multiple critiques of drone targeting, raising—if not resolving—many of the questions that must be asked as nations increasingly develop and deploy unarmed drones as a security tool."
—**David Cole, Georgetown University Law Center**

"Just weeks before 9/11, U.S. Ambassador to Israel, Martin Indyk, told the Israelis: 'The United States government is very clearly on the record as against targeted assassinations. They are extrajudicial killings, and we do not support that.' This extraordinary collection shows how two presidents abandoned that principled stand and, more importantly, the need to reclaim it."
—**Mary Ellen O'Connell, Professor of Law, University of Notre Dame**

D11132229

DRONES AND TARGETED KILLING

LEGAL, MORAL, AND GEOPOLITICAL ISSUES

EDITED BY MARJORIE COHN

WITH A FOREWORD BY ARCHBISHOP DESMOND TUTU

OLIVE
BRANCH
PRESS

An imprint of Interlink Publishing Group, Inc.
www.interlinkbooks.com

First published in 2015 by
OLIVE BRANCH PRESS
An imprint of Interlink Publishing Group, inc
46 Crosby Street
Northampton, Massachusetts 01060
www.interlinkbooks.com

Library of Congress Cataloging-in-Publication Data
Drones and targeted killing : legal, moral, and geopolitical issues / edited by
Marjorie Cohn ; foreword by Archbishop Desmond Tutu. -- First American
edition.
    pages cm.
ISBN 978-1-56656-989-7
1. Drone aircraft--United States. 2. Drone aircraft--Moral and ethical aspects--
United States. 3. Drone aircraft--Government policy--United States. 4. United
States--Foreign relations--1989- 5. Geopolitics--United States. I. Cohn,
Marjorie, 1948-, editor.
UG1242.D7D76 2014
358.4--dc23
                          2014033926

Printed and bound in the United States of America

To request our 48-page, full color catalog, please call us toll free at
1-800-238-LINK, visit our website: www.interlinkbooks.com,
or send us an email: info@interlinbooks.com

For Jerry, Victor, and Nicolas

CONTENTS

PART IV THE FUTURE OF TARGETED KILLING

APPENDIX A

APPENDIX B

ACKNOWLEDGMENTS

I thank Archbishop Desmond Tutu and the other wonderful contributors to this collection, whose critical work has been instrumental in shedding light on a dark new weapon of war. My heartfelt gratitude to my assistants, Michael Klitzke and Lisa Scarpa, without whom this book could not have been published. Michel Moushabeck, David Klein, and Pam Fontes-May from Interlink Publishing believed in this project and provided invaluable editorial assistance; I am grateful to Olive Branch Press for publishing and promoting the book.

Dean Thomas Guernsey, former Dean Rudy Hasl, and my colleagues at the Thomas Jefferson School of Law provided crucial assistance as the book took shape. I also wish to acknowledge my book group—Carol, Deborah, Donna, Kate, Lindy, and Lynne—for their ongoing support. My family and friends—Mom, Victor, Nicolas, Gary, Sherril, Nancy, Susan, Terri, David, John, Dan, Pedro, Luis, Susana, Josefa, Gustavo, Emilio, Lenin, Vaughdean, Claire, Chuck, Dean, Joan, Jeanne F, Jeanne M, Dorothy, Christa, Josie, and Anne—are my best fan club. My father, who died during the writing of this book, would have been proud, as he always was. Jerry Wallingford, my husband, editor, and life partner, continues to be my main source of inspiration. Finally, my deep appreciation goes to the courageous people struggling to stop US wars of aggression. We will prevail someday.

FOREWORD

Archbishop Desmond Tutu

A terrible thing happened on September 11, 2001, when 19 men committed suicide and took 3,000 innocents with them. That was a crime against humanity. People around the world expressed solidarity with Americans. We have all suffered painful repercussions since that awful day.

After the United States and its coalition partners invaded Afghanistan, hundreds of men were taken prisoner, most of them innocent of any terrorist activity, and sent to Guantánamo. There they have been detained indefinitely with no charges, much like what the apartheid government did in South Africa. Guantánamo has become the symbol of American hypocrisy on human rights. Unknown numbers of men have been tortured there, as well as in Iraq, Afghanistan, and the secret CIA black sites. George W. Bush and Tony Blair, claiming that Saddam Hussein had weapons of mass destruction, invaded Iraq. It was a lie and they knew it. Many people were killed, wounded, and tortured.

But different standards are applied to leaders in the West and those in Africa. Although Bush and Blair committed war crimes, by starting an unnecessary and deadly war, only African leaders have been tried in the International Criminal Court.

The "war on terror" continues. Unfortunately, Barack Obama has failed to close Guantánamo and his government is trying men in the military commissions with a reduced level of due process. And Obama's drones have been killing thousands of people with no due process at all.

When it was revealed that the Obama government might kill American citizens on US soil, many people in the United States called for a special court so that judges could rule on those decisions. But the outrage they expressed was limited to the killing of Americans. Thus, I wrote in the *New York Times*:

> Do the United States and its people really want to tell those of us who live in the rest of the world that our lives are not of the same value as yours? That President Obama can sign off on a decision to kill us with less worry about judicial scrutiny than if the target is an American? Would your Supreme Court really want to tell humankind that we, like the slave Dred Scott in the 19th century, are not as human as you are? I cannot believe it.
>
> I used to say of apartheid that it dehumanized its perpetrators as much as, if not more than, its victims. Your response as a society to Osama bin Laden and his followers threatens to undermine your moral standards and your humanity.

There is a Xhosa word, *Ubuntu*. It means human beings need each other in order to survive and thrive. *Ubuntu* is the essence of being human. We are all interrelated. We cannot exist in isolation. Our well-being depends on our interconnectedness, our relationships with other people. When anyone is diminished, we are all diminished. When anyone is humiliated, or tortured, or killed by a drone, we are all harmed.

The system of apartheid in South Africa was based upon hatred of the other. In order to maintain the vast inequality and injustice, those in power objectified all black people. Nazi propaganda likewise objectified all Jewish people. Anti-Japanese prejudice led to the internment of thousands during World War II. Racism is evil. When we dehumanize our enemies, it becomes more palatable to mistreat and kill them. But when this happens, both the perpetrator and the victim suffer. We are all God's children—the Africans, the Whites, the Christians, the Arabs and the Muslims. None of us is better than any other. The torch of freedom does not burn only for Americans.

American college students demonstrated *Ubuntu* in the 1980s when they boycotted their classes to protest apartheid by opposing US investment in South Africa. Black South Africans were moved by the actions of the students, who took on our struggle as their own. During the 1950s and 1960s, Americans had marched and many gave their lives during the US civil rights movement. And in the 1960s and 1970s, other college students joined Americans from all walks of life in protesting the Vietnam War. They were all participating in *Ubuntu*. Not all Americans place US lives over others who are killed by drones. The day after my letter was published in the *Times*, nine people, including a Catholic priest and Catholic workers, peacefully blocked the entrance to the Hancock Field Air National Guard Base in upstate New York. They were demonstrating against the hub for the Reaper drones that have killed people in Pakistan and Afghanistan. The protesters issued this statement:

"We come to Hancock Airfield, home of the National Reaper Drone Maintenance and Training Center, this Ash Wednesday to remember the victims of drone strikes and to ask God's forgiveness for the killing of other human beings, most especially children."

Barack Obama won the Nobel Peace Prize. I have said, and I continue to say, "Become what you are." Become a peacemaker.

This book provides much-needed analysis of why America's targeted killing program is illegal, immoral, and unwise.

1•INTRODUCTION
A FRIGHTENING NEW WAY OF WAR
Marjorie Cohn

In his 2009 acceptance speech for the Nobel Peace Prize, President Barack Obama declared, "Where force is necessary, we have a moral and strategic interest in binding ourselves to certain rules of conduct. And even as we confront a vicious adversary that abides by no rules, I believe the United States of America must remain a standard bearer in the conduct of war."[1] By the time Obama accepted the award, one year into his presidency, he had ordered more drone strikes than George W. Bush had authorized during his two presidential terms.[2]

The Bush administration detained and tortured suspected terrorists.[3] The Obama administration has chosen to illegally assassinate them, often with the use of drones. The continued indefinite detention of men at Guantánamo belies Obama's pledge two days after his first inauguration to close the prison camp there. However, Obama has added only one detainee to the Guantánamo roster. "This government has decided that instead of detaining members of al-Qaeda [at Guantánamo] they are going to kill them," according to John Bellinger, who formulated the Bush administration's drone policy.[4]

On "Terror Tuesdays," Obama and John Brennan, Obama's former counterterrorism adviser, now CIA director, go through the "kill list" to identify which individuals should be assassinated that week.[5] The Obama administration has developed a creative method to count the civilian casualties from these assassinations. All military-age men killed in a drone strike zone are considered to be combatants "unless there is explicit intelligence posthumously proving them innocent."[6] Brennan falsely claimed in 2011 that no civilians had been killed in drone strikes in nearly a year.[7]

Obama orders two different types of drone attacks: *personality strikes,* which target "named, high-value terrorists," and *signature strikes,* which target training camps and "suspicious compounds in areas controlled by militants."[8] In the signature strikes, sometimes called "crowd killings," the Obama administration often doesn't even know who it is killing. "But ," write Jo Becker and Scott Shane in the *New York Times,* "some State Department officials have complained to the White House that the criteria used by the CIA for identifying a terrorist 'signature' were too lax. The joke was that when the CIA sees 'three guys doing jumping jacks,' the agency thinks it is a terrorist training camp, said one senior official. Men loading a truck with fertilizer could be bombmakers—but they might also be farmers, skeptics argued."[9]

The Due Process Clause of the US Constitution[10] requires that, before taking the life of a person off the battlefield, the government must arrest a suspect, inform him of the charges against him, and provide him with a fair trial. But like his predecessor, Obama defines virtually the entire world as a battlefield, ostensibly obviating the necessity to provide due process before execution. Moreover, in a 2012 speech, Attorney General Eric Holder drew a curious distinction between "due process" and "judicial process": "'Due process' and 'judicial process' are not one and the same, particularly when it comes to national security," he said. "The Constitution guarantees due process, not judicial process."[11]

The Bush administration took the position that neither the criminal law nor international humanitarian law—which comes from the Hague and Geneva Conventions and governs the conduct of war—protected the targets of the "war on terror."[12] They existed in a legal "black hole."[13] Obama has apparently adopted the same position, although he has replaced the moniker "war on terror" with "war on al-Qaeda." But "there is not a distinct entity called al-Qaeda that provides a sound basis for defining and delimiting an authorized use of military force," according to Paul Pillar, former deputy director of the CIA's Counterterrorism Center.[14]

Both administrations have justified their targeted killing policies with reference to the Authorization for the Use of Military Force (AUMF), which Congress passed a week after 9/11. It authorizes the president:

[t]o use all necessary and appropriate force against those nations, organizations, or persons he determines *planned, authorized, committed, or aided the terrorist attacks that occurred on September 11, 2001, or harbored* such organizations or persons, in order to prevent any future acts of international terrorism against the United States by such nations, organizations or persons.[15]

This authorization is limited to groups and countries that supported the 9/11 attacks. Congress rejected the Bush administration's request for open-ended military authority "to deter and preempt any future acts of terrorism or aggression against the United States."[16] But deterrence and preemption are exactly what Obama is trying to accomplish by sending robots to kill "suspected militants."

Obama has extended his battlefield beyond Iraq and Afghanistan to Pakistan, Yemen, Somalia, and Libya, even though the United States is not at war with those countries. US drones fly from allied bases in Saudi Arabia, Turkey, Italy, Qatar, the Philippines, and the United Arab Emirates. Expanding into West Africa, the United States has built a major drone hub in Djibouti.[17]

Armed drones are operated by "pilots" located thousands of miles from their targets. Before launching its payload, the drone hovers above the area. It emits a buzzing sound that terrorizes communities. "The drones were terrifying," observed *New York Times* journalist David Rohde, who was captured by the Taliban in Afghanistan in 2008 and later escaped. "From the ground, it is impossible to determine who or what they are tracking as they circle overhead.

The buzz of a distant propeller is a constant reminder of imminent death. Drones fire missiles that travel faster than the speed of sound. A drone's victim never hears the missile that kills him."[18]

After the drone drops a bomb on its target, a second strike often bombs people rescuing the wounded from the first strike. And frequently, a third strike targets mourners at funerals for those felled by the prior strikes. This is called a "double tap," although it is more accurately a "triple tap." US drones have killed children, rescuers, and funeral processions "on multiple occasions," according to a report written by Micah Zenko for the Council on Foreign Relations (CFR).[19]

Obama's administration has killed at least as many people in targeted killings as died on 9/11. But of the estimated 3,000 people killed by drones, "the vast majority were neither al-Qaeda nor Taliban leaders," CFR reported. "Instead, most were low-level, anonymous suspected militants who were predominantly engaged in insurgent or terrorist operations against their governments, rather than in active international terrorist plots."[20]

Although more than 95 percent of all non-battlefield targeted killings have been carried out by drones, the killer robots are not the only medium used to conduct targeted killings. The United States also employs Joint Special Operations Command (JSOC) to conduct raids, as well as AC-130 gunships, and cruise missiles launched offshore by air or sea.[21]

Drones are Obama's weapon of choice because, unlike piloted fighter aircraft, they don't jeopardize the lives of US pilots. There are claims that the use of drones results in fewer civilian casualties than manned bombers. However, a study based on classified military data, conducted by Larry Lewis from the Center for Naval Analyses and Sarah Holewinski of the Center for Civilians in Conflict, found that the use of drones in Afghanistan has caused ten times more civilian deaths than manned fighter aircraft.[22]

"In the United States, the dominant narrative about the use of drones in Pakistan is of a surgically precise and effective tool that makes the US safer by enabling 'targeted killing' of terrorists with minimal downsides or collateral impacts. This narrative is false," according to the comprehensive report *Living Under Drones* issued by Stanford Law School and NYU Law School.[23] Many killed by drones are civilians, or, in the administration's parlance, "bug splat," referring to the "collateral damage" estimate methodology the US military and the CIA employ.[24]

Targeted killing with drones is counterproductive. General Stanley McChrystal, architect of the US counterinsurgency strategy in Afghanistan, declared that drones are "hated on a visceral level" and contribute to a "perception of American arrogance."[25] Kurt Volker, former US ambassador to NATO, concurs. "Drone strikes . . . do not solve our terrorist problem," he noted. "In fact, drone use may prolong it. Even though there is no immediate retaliation, in the long run the contributions to radicalization through drone use may put more American lives at risk."[26] Mullah Zabara, a southern tribal sheikh from Yemen, told Jeremy Scahill, "The US sees al Qaeda as terrorism, and we consider the drones terrorism. The drones are flying day and night, frightening women and children, disturbing sleeping people. This is terrorism."[27] The CFR reported a "strong correlation" in Yemen between stepped-up targeted killings since December 2009 and "heightened anger toward the United States and sympathy with or allegiance to AQAP [al-Qaeda in the Arabian Peninsula]."[28]

Drone strikes breed increased resentment against the United States and lead to the recruitment of more terrorists. "Drones have replaced Guantánamo as the recruiting tool of choice for militants," according to Becker and Shane. They quoted Faisal Shahzad, who, while pleading guilty to trying to detonate a bomb in Times Square, told the judge, "When the drones hit, they don't see children."[29] Pakistani ambassador Zamir Akram said the drone attacks are illegal and violate the sovereignty of Pakistan, "not to mention being counter-productive." He added, "thousands of innocent people, including women and children, have been murdered in these indiscriminate attacks."[30] In May 2013, Chief Justice Dost Muhammad Khan of the High Court of Peshawar in Pakistan ruled that US drone strikes in the region were illegal.[31]

The Bush administration's 2002 drone strike in Yemen that killed, among others, US citizen Ahmed Hijazi, also known as Kamal Derwish, was the first publicly confirmed US targeted killing outside a battlefield since President Gerald Ford signed a ban on political assassinations in 1976.[32] "It means the rules of engagement have changed," a former CIA official with knowledge about special operations told the *Los Angeles Times* after the strike in Yemen. "That would be the first time that they have started doing this kind of thing."[33]

It wouldn't be the last. Scahill writes, "The secret war in Pakistan became largely a drone bombing campaign, described by CIA officers at the US Embassy in Islamabad as 'boys with toys.'"[34] By the end of Obama's first year as president, he "and his new counterterrorism team would begin building the infrastructure for a formalized US assassination program,"[35] Scahill added, with "an aggressive embrace of assassination as a centerpiece of US national security policy."[36] In December 2009, Admiral William McRaven, JSOC commander, authorized JSOC to carry out a "series of targeted killings" in Yemen.[37]

The United States uses two types of armed drones—the Predator, which cost $4.5 million each, and the Reaper, valued at $15 million; both are produced by General Atomics Aeronautical Systems of San Diego.[38] The Reaper houses up to four Hellfire missiles and two 500-pound bombs. It can fly to heights of 21,000 feet for up to 22 hours. Its cameras enable the "pilots" operating the drone 7,500 miles away to see the faces of their targets on the computer screen "as the bomb hits."[39]

Tom Dispatch has identified sixty bases used in US drone operations, although there could be more, as there is a "cloak of secrecy" surrounding our drone warfare program.[40] The drone industry doesn't like to refer to their killer robots as "drones" because of the negative connotation of these machines droning above communities. They prefer to call them Unmanned Aerial Vehicles (UAV) or Unmanned Aerial Systems (UAS).

Targeted killing, which "is just the death penalty without due process," Clive Stafford Smith told the *Guardian*,[41] is an example of American exceptionalism, reflecting the view that people in the United States are somehow superior to those in other countries. In his 2013 speech to the United Nations (UN) General Assembly, Obama stated, "Some may disagree, but I believe that America is exceptional—in part because we have shown a willingness, through the sacrifice of blood and treasure, to stand up not only for our own narrow self-interest, but for the interests of all."[42] But in addition to the US soldiers killed in Iraq and Afghanistan, hundreds of thousands of people in those countries have been killed and untold numbers wounded. And the four to six trillion dollars we spent on those wars could have been put to much better use in this country.

Time columnist Joe Klein, considered by many to be a liberal, bought into American exceptionalism in a disturbing way in a 2012 interview by Joe Scarborough on MSNBC's *Morning Joe*. Scarborough observed, "You have four-year-old girls being blown to bits because we have a policy that says, 'You know what, instead of trying to go in, take the risk, get the terrorists out of hiding . . . we're just going to blow up everyone around them,'" and he mentioned "collateral damage." Klein retorted, "The bottom line, in the end, is: Whose four-year-old gets killed? What we're doing is limiting the possibility that four-year-olds here are going to get killed by indiscriminate acts of terror."[43] So it's preferable that foreign little girls get killed in order to protect American little girls?

American exceptionalism also reared its head after the February 2013 leak of a Department of Justice (DoJ) White Paper that describes circumstances under which the President could order the targeted killing of US citizens.[44] There had been little public concern in the United States about drone strikes killing people in other countries. But when it was revealed that US citizens might be targeted, Americas were outraged. This was exemplified by Senator Rand Paul's thirteen-hour filibuster of John Brennan's nomination for CIA director.

It is this double standard that motivated Nobel Peace Prize winner Archbishop Desmond Tutu to pen a compelling letter to the editor of the *New York Times*, in which he asked, "Do the United States and its people really want to tell those of us who live in the rest of the world that our lives are not of the same value as yours?"[45] The archbishop elaborates on that observation in the foreword to this collection.

In May 2013, as international criticism targeted Obama's drone policy and the continued indefinite detention at Guantánamo where detainees were starving themselves to death and military guards were violently force-feeding them, the president delivered a speech at the National Defense University.[46] He explained that "the United States is at war with al-Qaeda, the Taliban, and their associated forces," without defining who those "associated forces" are. Although he defended his use of drones and targeted killing, Obama proclaimed, "America does not take strikes when we have the ability to capture individual terrorists—our preference is always to detain, interrogate and prosecute them."

Obama referred to the killing of Osama bin Laden as exceptional because "capture, although our preference, was remote." Yet it was clear when the US soldiers arrived at bin Laden's compound that the people there were unarmed and bin Laden could have been captured. Obama admitted, "The cost to our relationship with Pakistan—and the backlash among the Pakistani public over encroachment on their territory—was so severe that we are now just beginning to rebuild this important partnership." In view of Pakistan's considerable arsenal of nuclear weapons, Obama took a substantial risk to our national security in breaching Pakistan's sovereignty by his assassination operation.

The month before Obama gave his speech, McClatchy reported that the administration had been misrepresenting the types of groups and individuals it was targeting with drones in Afghanistan and Pakistan. Citing classified US intelligence reports, the McClatchy piece said that contrary to the administration's claims that it had deployed drones only against known senior leaders of al-Qaeda and allied groups, it had in fact targeted and killed hundreds of suspected low-level Afghan, Pakistani, and "other" militants in scores of strikes in Pakistan.[47] At times, "the CIA killed people who only were suspected, associated with, or who probably belonged to militant groups." Micah Zenko, author of the CFR report cited earlier, said that McClatchy's findings indicate the administration is "misleading the public about the scope of who can legitimately be targeted."[48]

Obama's claim of vast executive power to kill anyone he wants with no judicial involvement is precisely what the founding fathers feared when they wrote three co-equal branches of government into the Constitution to check and balance one another. It is only Congress that has the power to declare war. Indeed, Georgetown University law professor Rosa Brooks testified at a congressional hearing: "[W]hen a government claims for itself the unreviewable power to kill anyone, anywhere on earth, at any time, based on secret criteria and secret information discussed in a secret process by largely unnamed individuals, it undermines the rule of law."[49]

Generals involved in the US overseas drone program are being tapped by the Department of Homeland Security (DHS) to develop and direct our domestic drone program. This is emblematic of "the increasing merger of the post-9/11 homeland security/border security complex with the military-industrial complex," in the words of Tom Barry,[50] a senior policy analyst at the Center for International Policy.

The Pentagon is slated to spend $5.78 billion in 2013 for research and procurement of drone systems, and DHS is spending millions of dollars in contracts with drone manufacturers, including General Atomics. As Congress considers immigration reform, Senator John McCain observed that the "Border Security Economic Opportunity, and Immigration Modernization Act," which the Senate passed, would make the US-Mexico border the "most militarized border since the fall of the Berlin Wall."[51] This raises troubling issues regarding the morality and wisdom of our national priorities.

Another disturbing issue is that the unlawful precedent the United States is setting with its use of killer drones and other forms of targeted killing not only undermines the rule of law. It also will prevent the United States from reasonably objecting when other countries that obtain drone technology develop "kill lists" of persons those countries believe represent threats to them.

In this interdisciplinary collection, human rights and political activists, policy analysts, lawyers and legal scholars, a philosopher, a journalist, and a sociologist examine different aspects of the US policy of targeted killing with drones and other methods. These contributors explore legality, morality, and geopolitical considerations, and evaluate the impact on relations between the United States and the countries affected by targeted killings.

The book includes the documentation of civilian casualties by the leading non-governmental organization in this area; stories of civilians victimized by the drones; an analysis of the first US targeted killing lawsuit by the lawyer who brought the case, as well as a discussion of the targeted killing cases in Israel by the director of The Public Committee Against Torture (PCATI), which filed one of the lawsuits; the domestic use of drones; and the immorality of drones using just war principles.

International legal scholar Richard Falk explains in Chapter Two why weaponized drones pose a greater threat than nuclear weapons to international law and world order. He notes that nuclear weapons have not been used since 1945 except for deterrence and coercive diplomacy as the countries of the world have established regimes of constraint on their use through arms control agreements and nonproliferation. Drones, however, are unconstrained by any system of regulation. They will likely remain unregulated as "the logic of dirty wars" continues to drive US national security policy.

In Chapter Three, policy analyst Phyllis Bennis describes assassination as central to US war strategy due to the militarization of our foreign policy. She traces the program of assassination to the post-Vietnam era "Salvador option," in which CIA and Special Forces developed assassination teams and death squads to avoid American casualties. Moving into the modern era, Bennis details how the war strategy shifted from counterinsurgency, with large numbers of US troops, to counterterrorism and targeted killing, using drones as the preferred weapon.

Chapter Four is an article published by journalist Jane Mayer in *The New Yorker* in 2009. This article was the first comprehensive exposé about the Obama administration's escalation of drone use for targeted killing. It is also one of the earliest efforts at documenting civilian casualties from the use of drones. Mayer raises the legal, political, and tactical ramifications of drone warfare and asks troubling questions about possible unintended consequences of this new weapon.

In Chapter Five, sociology professor Tom Reifer examines America's embrace of a global assassination program using the Joint Special Operations Command and the CIA, which he calls "a paramilitary arm of the President." He focuses on the effects of drone strikes on persons and targeted communities, as well as the drone pilots themselves.

Political activist Medea Benjamin, in Chapter Six, humanizes the victims of lethal drone strikes, particularly in Pakistan and Yemen. She includes personal stories about some of the victims and their family members. Benjamin describes how the drones, in addition to killing many innocent people, terrorize entire populations and destroy the fabric of local communities.

Chapter Seven is a comprehensive report by Alice K. Ross, of the Bureau of Investigative Journalism, documenting civilian casualties of the drone strikes. She underlines the critical importance of publishing contemporaneous information on all casualties, civilian or militant, in a transparent, incident-by-incident manner—even where the information might be limited due to ongoing hostilities. Without such detail, Ross writes, it is impossible to effectively challenge casualty claims by officials and for victims of drone strikes to claim compensation.

The United States' targeted killing through the use of drones and other methods violates international and US law, human rights attorney Jeanne Mirer explains in Chapter Eight. Extrajudicial killing is not illegal in the context of a legally declared war on a battlefield. However, the United States wrongfully claims that "self-defense" gives it the right to execute anyone in any country, regardless of citizenship and regardless of the existence of a legal war. Mirer analyzes how the United States is violating International Human Rights Law and International Humanitarian Law.

In Chapter Nine, philosopher Harry van der Linden analyzes whether targeted killing by drones in non-battlefield zones can be justified on the basis of just war theory, applying traditional *jus ad bellum* (justice in resort to war) and *jus in bello* (justice in execution of war) principles. He asks if proliferation and expansion of combat drones in war will be an obstacle to initiating or executing wars in a just manner in the future, utilizing principles of "just military preparedness," or *jus ante bellum* (justice before war), a new category of just war thinking. Van der Linden concludes that an international ban on weaponizing drones is morally imperative and, at a minimum, that an international treaty against autonomous lethal weapons should be adopted.

In Chapter Ten, Center for Constitutional Rights attorney Pardiss Kebriaei discusses the first legal challenge to the US targeted killing program in *Al-Aulaqi v. Obama*. That case involved the Obama administration's authorization of the targeted killing of a US citizen in Yemen. She cites the imperative for accountability, including through judicial review, and discusses the obstacles constructed by the Obama administration that have effectively precluded judicial review thus far.

PCATI executive director Ishai Menuchin, in Chapter Eleven, contrasts the discourse in Israel about the elimination of terrorists and preemptive action with the Palestinian discourse of "day-to-day acts of Israeli state-terror and repression." He wonders how extrajudicial execution became official Israeli policy since Israel does not have the death penalty. Menuchin examines assassination petitions filed in the Israeli High Court of Justice, including the "Targeted Killing" case, *PCATI v. Government of Israel*, and he laments Israel's lack of accountability.

Legal scholar John Quigley analyzes in Chapter Twelve the impact of the policy of using lethal pilotless aircraft on relations between the United States and the countries in which the affected populations are located, in the context of a history of resentment against US interventions and interference. He suggests that the policy redounds to the detriment of the United States by engendering resentment and the use of violence against the United States and its personnel. The chapter suggests that the Obama administration is aware of these risks but continues its policy in spite of them.

In Chapter Thirteen, Jay Stanley, from the ACLU, discusses policy issues surrounding the imminent arrival of domestic drones in US airspace. The main concern is privacy. Stanley asks how the technology is likely to evolve, and how the First Amendment "right to photography" interacts with serious privacy issues implicated by drones. The national discourse about drone deployment has opened up a space for privacy activists and others to create a genuine public discussion of the issue before it is widely deployed.

Finally, in Chapter Fourteen, political activist Tom Hayden places the advent of the Drone Age into a historical context of US military invasions and occupations. He discusses political and strategic considerations that animate the evolution of the military policies of President Obama, who is "in grave danger of leaving a new imperial presidency as his legacy." Hayden advocates a transparent set of policies to rein in the use of drones and cyber warfare, while protecting democracy.

Drones and targeted killing will not solve the problem of terrorism. "If you use the drone and the selected killings, and do nothing else on the other side, then you get rid of individuals. But the root causes are still there," former Somali foreign minister Ismail Mahmoud "Buubaa" Hurre, told Scahill. "The root causes are not security. The root causes are political and economic."[52]

A Pentagon study conducted during the Bush administration[53] concluded, "Muslims do not 'hate our freedom,' but rather, they hate our policies." It identified "American direct intervention in the Muslim world," through the US's "one sided support in favor of Israel," support for Islamic tyrannical regimes in Egypt and Saudi Arabia, and, primarily, "the American occupation of Iraq and Afghanistan." These policies, which are rationalized to stop terrorism, "paradoxically elevate the stature of and support for Islamic radicals."

Becker and Shane sounded an alarm about the ramifications of drone strikes on the future of US relations with Muslim countries. They noted, "[Obama's] focus on strikes has made it impossible to forge, for now, the new relationship with the Muslim world that he had envisioned. Both Pakistan and Yemen are arguably less stable and more hostile to the United States than when Mr. Obama became president. Justly or not, drones have become a provocative symbol of American power, running roughshod over national sovereignty and killing innocents."[54] We ignore this admonition at our peril. Until we stop invading countries with Muslim populations, occupying their lands, torturing their people, and killing them with drones, we will never be safe from terrorism.

It is my hope that this volume will provide information that can be marshaled to halt the illegal, immoral, unwise US policy of assassination.

NOTES

1   Barack Obama, President, United States, Remarks by the President at the Acceptance of the Nobel Peace Prize (Dec. 10, 2009), *available at* www.whitehouse.gov/the-press-office/remarks-president-acceptance-nobel-peace-prize.

2   *See* Daniel Klaidman, *Drones: The Silent Killers*, NEWSWEEK (Oct. 1, 2012), www.newsweek.com/drones-silent-killers-64909; Alice K.Ross, *Covert Drone War-The Complete Data Sets*, BUREAU OF INVESTIGATIVE JOURNALISM (last visited Sept. 24, 2013), www.thebureauinvestigates.com/2012/09/06/covert-drone-war-the-complete-datasets/.

3   *See generally,* THE UNITED STATES AND TORTURE: INTERROGATION, INCARCERATION, AND ABUSE (Marjorie Cohn, ed., NYU Press 2011).

4   Dan Roberts, *US drone strikes being used as alternative to Guantánamo, lawyer says,* GUARDIAN (May 2, 2013), www.theguardian.com/world/2013/may/02/us-drone-strikes-guantanamo.

5   Jo Becker & Scott Shane, *Secret 'Kill List' Proves a Test of Obama's Principles and Will,* N.Y. TIMES (May 29, 2012), www.nytimes.com/2012/05/29/world/obamas-leadership-in-war-on-al-qaeda.html?pagewanted=all.

6   *Id.*

7   Jack Serle & Chris Woods, *Secret US documents show Brennan's 'no civilian drone deaths' claim was false*, BUREAU OF INVESTIGATIVE JOURNALISM (Apr. 11, 2013), www.thebureauinvestigates.com/blog/2013/04/11/secret-us-documents-show-brennans-no-civilian-drone-deaths-claim-was-false/.

8   Becker & Shane, *supra* note 5

9   *Id.*

10 US CONST. amend. V.

11 *See* Eric Holder, Attorney General, US Dept. of Just., Speech at Northwestern Univ. School of Law (Mar. 5, 2012), *available at* www.justice.gov/iso/opa/ag/speeches/2012/ag-speech-1203051.html.

12 "War on Terror" is a misnomer as terrorism is a tactic, not an enemy. A country cannot declare war on a tactic.

13 *See* Leila Nadya Sadat, *America's Drone Wars*, 45 CASE W. RES. J. INT'L L. 215, 221 (2012).

14 Paul R. Pillar, *The Limitless Global War*, THE NAT'L INTEREST (June 19, 2012), nationalinterest.org/blog/paul-pillar/the-limitless-global-war-7094.

15 Authorization for Use of Military Force, 115 Stat 224 (2001) (emphasis added).

16 Bruce Ackerman, *President Obama: Don't go there,* WASH. POST (Apr. 20, 2012), articles.washingtonpost.com/2012-04-20/opinions/35452574_1_terrorist-group-terrorist-attacks-terrorist-threat.

17 Craig Whitlock, *Drone base in Niger gives U.S. a strategic foothold in West Africa*, WASH. POST (Mar. 21, 2013), articles.washingtonpost.com/2013-03-21/world/37905284_1_drone-bases-unarmed-predator-drones-surveillance-drones.

18 David Rohde, *The Drone War*, REUTERS (Jan. 26, 2012), www.reuters.com/article/2012/01/26/us-davos-reutersmagazine-dronewar-idUSTRE80P19R20120126.

19 Micah Zenko, *Reforming U.S. Drone Strike Policies, Council Special Report No. 65*, COUNCIL ON FOREIGN RELATIONS CTR. 14 (Jan. 2013), i.cfr.org/content/publications/attachments/Drones_CSR65.pdf.

20 *Id.* 10.

21 *Id.* at 8.

22 Spencer Ackerman, *US drone strikes more deadly to Afghan civilians than manned aircraft – adviser*, GUARDIAN (July 2, 2013), www.theguardian.com/world/2013/jul/02/us-drone-strikes-afghan-civilians.

23 Stanford Law Sch.& New York Univ. Sch. of Law, Living Under Drones: Death Injury, and Trauma to Civilians from US Drone Practices in Pakistan

v (2012), available at http://www.livingunderdrones.org/wp-content/uploads/2013/10/Stanford-NYU-Living-Under-Drones.pdf

[24] Zenko, *supra* note 19, at 12.

[25] Robert F. Worth, Mark Mazzetti & Scott Shane, *Drone Strikes' Risks to Get Rare Moment in the Public Eye*, N.Y. TIMES (Feb. 5, 2013), www.nytimes.com/2013/02/06/world/middleeast/with-brennan-pick-a-light-on-drone-strikes-hazards.html?pagewanted=all.

[26] Kurt Volker, *What the U.S. risks by relying on drones*, WASH. POST (Oct. 26, 2012), www.washingtonpost.com/opinions/we-need-a-rule-book-for-drones/2012/10/26/957312ae-1f8d-11e2-9cd5-b55c38388962_story.html.

[27] *See* JEREMY SCAHILL, DIRTY WARS 465–466 (Nation Books 2013).

[28] Zenko, *supra* note 19, at 11.

[29] Becker & Shane, *supra* note 5.

[30] Common Dreams staff, *Common Dreams, UN Investigator Blasts US Drone Program* June 19, 2012), www.commondreams.org/headline/2012/06/19-0.

[31] Daniel Mullen, *Pakistan court declares US drone strikes illegal*, JURIST (May 9, 2013), jurist.org/paperchase/2013/05/pakistan-court-declares-drone-strikes-illegal-directs-foreign-ministry-to-introduce-resolution-in-un.php.

[32] Scahill, *supra* note 27, at 75–77.

[33] Greg Miller & Josh Meyer, *CIA Missile in Yemen Kills 6 Terror Suspects*, L.A. TIMES (Nov. 5, 2002), articles.latimes.com/2002/nov/05/world/fg-yemen05/2.

[34] Scahill, *supra* note 27, at 177.

[35] *Id.* at 253.

[36] *Id.* at 353.

[37] *Id.* at 303.

[38] *See* NICK TURSE & TOM ENGELHARDT, TERMINATOR PLANET: THE FIRST HISTORY OF DRONE WARFARE 2001–2050, 9 (Dispatch Books 2012).

[39] *Id.* at 10, 74.

[40] *Id.* at 72.

[41] Mehdi Hasan, *Iran's nuclear scientists are not being assassinated. They are being murdered*, Guardian (Jan. 16, 2102), www.theguardian.com/commentisfree/2012/jan/16/iran-scientists-state-sponsored-murder.

[42] Barack Obama, President, United States, Obama's Speech at the U.N. (Sept. 24, 2013), *available at* www.nytimes.com/2013/09/25/us/politics/text-of-obamas-speech-at-the-un.html?pagewanted=all&_r=0.

43 Peter Hart, *Morning Joe's Drone Debate: Whose Four-Year-Old Girls Should be Killed?*, FAIR (Oct. 23, 2012), www.fair.org/blog/2012/10/23/morning-joes-drone-debate-whose-four-year-old-girls-should-be-killed/.

44 Lawfulness of a Lethal Operation Directed Against a U.S. Citizen Who Is a Senior Operational Leader of Al-Qa'ida or An Associated Force, at 8-9 (Nov. 8, 2011), [Hereinafter White Paper]; *see* Appendix A.

45 Desmond M. Tutu, *Drones, Kill Lists and Machiavelli*, N.Y. TIMES (Feb. 12, 2013), www.nytimes.com/2013/02/13/opinion/drones-kill-lists-and-machiavelli.html?_r=0.

46 Barack Obama, President, United States, Remarks by the President at the National Defense University (May 23, 2013), *available at* www.whitehouse.gov/the-press-office/2013/05/23/remarks-president-national-defense-university.

47 By Jonathan S. Landay, *Obama's drone war kills 'others,' not just al Qaida leaders*, McCLATCHY (Apr. 9, 2013), www.mcclatchydc.com/2013/04/09/188062/obamas-drone-war-kills-others.html#.UkXmFmSDQXw.

48 *Id.*

49 *The Constitutional and Counterterrorism Implications of Targeted Killing: Hearing Before the Senate Judiciary Subcomm. on the Constitution, Civil Rights, and Human Rights of the S. Comm. on the Judiciary*, 113th Cong. 19-20 (Apr. 23, 2013), www.judiciary.senate.gov/pdf/04-23-13BrooksTestimony.pdf.

50 Tom Barry, *Homeland Security Taps Generals to Run Domestic Drone Program: The Rise of Predators at Home*, TRUTHOUT (Aug. 7, 2013), www.truth-out.org/news/item/17995-homeland-security-taps-generals-to-run-domestic-drone-program-the-rise-of-predators-at-home.

51 *Id.*

52 Scahill, *supra* note 26, at 494.

53 Glenn Greenwald, *A Rumsfeld-era reminder about what causes Terrorism*, SALON (Oct. 20, 2009), www.salon.com/2009/10/20/terrorism_6/.

54 Becker & Shane, *supra* note 5.

PART I
THE UNITED STATES AND DRONE WARFARE

2

WHY DRONES ARE MORE DANGEROUS THAN NUCLEAR WEAPONS

Richard Falk

THREATS TO INTERNATIONAL LAW AND WORLD ORDER

Weaponized drones are probably the most troublesome weapon added to the arsenal of war making since the atomic bomb, *and from the perspective of world order*, may turn out to be even more dangerous in its implications. This may seem an odd, alarmist, and inflated statement of concern. After all, the atomic bomb in its initial use showed itself capable of destroying entire cities, threatening the future of civilization, and even apocalyptically menacing the survival of the species. It changed drastically the nature of strategic warfare, and will continue to haunt the human future until the end of time. Yet, despite the irrationality and war mentality that explains the diabolical unwillingness of political leaders to work conscientiously toward the elimination of nuclear weapons, it is a weapon that has not been used in the intervening sixty-nine years since it was first unleashed on the hapless residents of Hiroshima and Nagasaki, and achieving non-use has been a constant legal, moral, and prudential priority of leaders and war planners ever since the first bomb inflicted unspeakable horror and suffering on the ill-fated Japanese who happened to be present on that day in those doomed cities.

The *second-order constraints* imposed over the intervening decades to avoid nuclear war, or at least to minimize the risk of its occurrence, although far from foolproof, and likely not sustainable over the long term, were at least compatible with a world order system that has evolved to serve the principal shared interests of territorial states.[1] Instead of reserving this ultimate weaponry of mass destruction for battlefield advantage and military victory, nuclear weapons have been confined in their roles to deterrence and coercive diplomacy, which although unlawful, morally problematic, and militarily dubious, presupposes that the framework of major international conflict is limited to the belligerent interaction of territorial sovereign states.[2]

Reinforcing these constraints are the complementary adjustments achieved by way of arms control agreements and nonproliferation. Arms control based on the mutual interests of the principal nuclear weapons states, the United States and Russia, seeks increased stability by restricting the number of nuclear weapons, forgoing destabilizing innovations, and avoiding overly expensive weapons systems that do not confer any major deterrent advantage.[3] In contrast to arms control, nonproliferation presupposes and reinforces the vertical dimension of world order, legitimating a dual legal structure superimposed on the juridical and horizontal notion of the equality of states. The nonproliferation regime has allowed a small, slowly expanding group of states to possess and develop nuclear weapons, and even make nuclear threats, while forbidding the remaining 186 or so states from acquiring them, or even acquiring the threshold capacity to produce nuclear weaponry.[4] This nonproliferation ethos is further compromised by linkages to geopolitics, giving rise to double standards, selective enforcement, and arbitrary membership procedures, as is evident by the preventive war rationale relied upon in relation to Iraq and now Iran, and the comfort zone of silence accorded to Israel's known, yet unacknowledged, arsenal of nuclear weapons.

This experience with nuclear weaponry tells several things about international law and world order that establish a helpful background for considering the quite different array of challenges and frightening temptations arising from the rapid evolution of military drones. First of all, the unwillingness and/or inability of dominant governments—the vertical Westphalian states—to eliminate these ultimate weapons of mass destruction and achieve a world without nuclear weapons despite their apocalyptic implications. The requisite political will has never formed, and has over time actually receded.[5] There have been many explanations given for this inability to rid humanity of this Achilles' Heel of world order, ranging from the fear of cheating, the inability to disinvent the technology, the claim of superior security when deterrence is compared to disarmament, a hedge against the emergence of an evil and suicidal enemy, an intoxicating sense of ultimate power, and the prestige that comes with belonging to the most exclusive club joining together dominant sovereign states.[6]

Secondly, ideas of deterrence and nonproliferation can be reconciled with the virtues and thinking that has dominated the tradition of political realism that remains descriptive of the manner in which governmental elites think and act throughout the history of state-centric world order.[7] International law is not effective in regulating the strategic ambitions and behavior of stronger states, but can often be effectively imposed on the rest of states for the sake of geopolitical goals, which include systemic stability. Thirdly, the international law of war has consistently accommodated new weapons and tactics that confer significant military advantages on a sovereign state, being rationalized by invoking 'security' and 'military necessity' to move aside whatever legal and moral obstacles stand in the way.[8] Fourthly, due to the pervasiveness of distrust, security is calibrated to deal with worst case or near worst case scenarios, which is itself a major cause of *insecurity*. These four sets of generalizations, although lacking nuance and example, provide a background understanding as to why the efforts over the centuries to regulate the recourse to war, weaponry, and the conduct of hostility have had such disappointing results, despite highly persuasive prudential and normative arguments supportive of much stricter limitations on the war system.[9]

CONTRADICTORY NARRATIVES: CHIAROSCURO GEOPOLITICS[10]

Drones, as new weapons systems responding to contemporary security threats, have a number of features that make them seem particularly difficult to regulate, given the shape of contemporary political conflict. This especially includes the threats posed by non-state actors, development of terrorist tactics that threaten the capability of even the largest states to uphold territorial security, and the inability or unwillingness of many governments to prevent their territory from being used to launch transnational terrorist attacks on even the most powerful country. From the standpoint of a state considering its military alternatives within the present global setting, drones appear particularly attractive, and the incentives for possession, development, and use are far greater than in relation to nuclear weaponry. Drones are relatively inexpensive in their current forms as compared to manned fighter aircraft, they almost totally eliminate any risk of casualties to the attacker, especially in relation to warfare against non-state actors, they have the capacity to strike with precision even the most remote and inaccessible targets, they can target accurately on the basis of reliable information gathered through the use of surveillance drones with remarkable sensing abilities, their use can be *politically* controlled to ensure restraint and a new version of due process that vets the appropriateness of targets in procedures of assessments carried on behind closed doors, and the casualties inflicted by drones are miniscule as compared to other methods of counterterrorist warfare. In effect, why should not the use of drones by a morally sensitive, prudent, and legitimate leadership of the sort that controls American counter-terrorist policy be endorsed rather than criticized and lamented?[11]

There are two contradictory narratives, with many variations for each, analyzing the essential normative (law, morality) quality of drone warfare, and its dominant recent role in implementing the tactics of targeted killing of designated persons. On one side of the dialogue are the "children of light," who claim to be doing their very best to minimize the costs and scale of war while protecting American society against the violence of extremists whose mission is to use violence to kill as many civilians as possible. On the other side are the "children of darkness," who are portrayed as engaged in criminal behavior of the most reprehensible kind to kill specific individuals, including American citizens, without any pretense of accountability for errors of judgment and excesses of attack. In effect, both narratives present warfare as a discretionary form of serial killing under state auspices, officially sanctioned summary executions without charges or with no explanation or accountability even when the target is an American citizen.[12]

The comparison of drone use with nuclear weapons is revealing in this setting, as well. There never was an attempt by any Western political leaders to endorse the civilizing role that could be enacted through threats and uses of nuclear weapons, beyond the contention, which can never be demonstrated, that their mere existence had prevented the Cold War from becoming World War III. Such a claim, to be credible at all, rested on the amoral belief that their actual use would be catastrophic for both sides, including the users, while the threat of use was justifiable to discourage risk taking and provocation by an adversary.[13] In contrast, with drones, the positive case for legitimating the weaponry is associated exclusively with actual use as compared to the alternatives of conventional war tactics of aerial bombardment or ground attack.

"CHILDREN OF LIGHT"

The children of light version of drone warfare was given canonical status by President Barack Obama's speech delivered, appropriately enough, at the National Defense University, on May 23, 2013.[14] Obama anchored his remarks on the guidance provided to the government over the course of two centuries in which the nature of war has changed dramatically on several occasions but not the constitutional framework within which war is prosecuted. In Obama's view, the founding principles of the republic enshrined in the Constitution continue to provide authoritative and prudent guidance to political leaders, having "served as our compass through every type of change. . . . From the Civil War to our struggle against fascism, on through the long twilight struggle of the Cold War, battlefields have changed and technology has evolved. But our commitment to constitutional principles has weathered every war, and every war has come to an end."

Against this background, Obama continues the unfortunate discourse inherited from the Bush presidency, that the 9/11 attacks initiated a *war* rather than constituted a massive *crime*. In his words, "This was a different kind of war. No armies came to our shores, and our military was not the principal target. Instead, a group of terrorists came to kill as many civilians as they could." There is no attempt to confront the question of why this provocation might have better been treated as a crime, which would have worked against launching the disastrous pre-9/11 wars against Afghanistan and Iraq. Instead, Obama offers the bland, and rather disingenuous claim that the challenge was to "align our policies with the rule of law."

According to Obama, the threat posed by al-Qaeda a decade ago has greatly diminished, although not disappeared, making it "the moment to ask ourselves hard questions—about the nature of today's threats and how we should meet them." Of course, it is revealing that the crowning achievement of this type of warfare was not a battlefield victory or territorial occupation, but the execution in 2011 of the iconic al-Qaeda leader, Osama bin Laden, in a non-combat setting that was essentially a hideaway with little operational significance in the broader counterterrorist campaign. Obama expressed this sense of accomplishment in terms of striking names from a kill list: "Today, Osama bin Laden is dead, and so are most of his top lieutenants." This outcome is not a result, as in past wars, of military encounters, but rather a consequence of targeted killing programs.

It is in this setting that the speech turns to the controversy generated by the reliance on drones, which has increased dramatically since Obama came to the White House. He affirms in vague and abstract language that "the decisions that we are making now will define the type of nation—and world—that we leave to our children. . . . So America is at a crossroads. We must define the nature and scope of this struggle, or else it will define us." In an effort to refocus the struggle against global terrorism, Obama offers some welcome downsizing language: ". . . we must define our effort not as a boundless 'global war on terror,' but rather as a series of persistent, targeted efforts to dismantle the specific networks of violent extremists that threaten America." Yet there is no explanation offered as to why the struggles for political control in far-flung places such as Yemen, Somalia, Mali, even the Philippines should be considered combat zones from the perspective of American security. Surely, to introduce American military power in what appear to be struggles to control the internal political life of a series of countries does not create grounds in international law for recourse to war.

It is not that Obama is rhetorically insensitive to these concerns,[15] but it is his steadfast unwillingness to examine the concrete realities of what is being done in the name of America that makes his rosy picture of drone warfare so disturbing and misleading. Obama asserts that "[a]s was true in previous armed conflicts, this new technology raises profound questions—about who is targeted, and why, about civilian casualties, and the risk of creating new enemies; about the legality of such strikes under US law and international law; about accountability and morality."[16] Yes, these are some of the issues, but the responses given are little better than bland evasions of the legal and moral concerns raised. The basic argument put forward is that drone warfare has been *effective* and *legal*. Both contentions are subject to severe doubts that are never addressed in concrete terms that would be appropriate if Obama really meant what he said about confronting hard questions.[17]

His defense of legality is typical of the overall approach. Congress gave the Executive broad, virtually unrestricted authority to use all necessary force to address the threats unleashed after the 9/11 attacks, thus satisfying domestic constitutional requirements of separation of powers. Internationally, Obama sets forth some arguments about the right of the United States to defend itself before asserting, "So this is a just war—a war waged proportionally, in last resort, and in self-defense." It was here that he could have raised some skeptical questions about the attacks on the World Trade Center and Pentagon as being regarded as 'acts of war' rather than crimes of such severity as to be 'crimes against humanity.' There were alternatives to recourse to war accompanied by a claim of self-defense against the transnational terrorist network that al-Qaeda appeared to be that might have been explored, if not adopted, back in 2001. Such a reclassification of the security effort as of 2013 could have re-raised the fundamental question or, more modestly, de-escalated the counterterrorist undertaking from war to a fight against transnational crime.

Obama failed to seize such an opportunity. Instead, he presented a deceptively abstract set of responses to the main public criticisms of drone warfare as concept and practice. Obama claims, despite the growing body of evidence to the contrary, that drone use is constrained by "a framework that governs our use of force against terrorists—insisting upon clear guidelines, oversight and accountability that is now codified in Presidential Policy Guidance."

It followed similar lines to those taken by John Brennan in a talk at the Harvard Law School a year or so earlier. Brennan was then serving as Obama's chief counterterrorism advisor. He stressed the dedication by the US government to adherence to the rule of law and democratic values that have given American society its distinctive shape: "I've developed a profound appreciation for the role that our values, especially the rule of law, play in keeping our country safe."[18] Brennan, while claiming to do all that can be done to protect the American people against these threats from without and within, reassured his law school audience but in a manner that includes "adhering to the rule of law" in all undertakings, with explicit mention of "covert actions." But what is meant here is clearly not to refrain from uses of force prohibited by international law, but only that the covert undertakings that have become so much a part of Obama's "war on terror" do not exceed "authorities provided to us by Congress." In a rather sly sleight of mind, Brennan identifies the rule of law only with *domestic* legal authority while seeming to rationalize uses of force in various foreign countries. When it comes to the relevance of international law, Brennan relies on self-serving constructions of legal reasonableness to contend that a person can be targeted if viewed as a threat even if far from the so-called hot battlefield, that is, anywhere in the world is potentially part of the legitimate war zone.[19] Such a claim is deeply deceptive, as drone use in countries such as Yemen and Somalia are not only far from the hot battlefield; their conflicts are essentially entirely disconnected.

The claim of the Obama presidency is that drones target only those who pose a threat, that great care is taken to avoid collateral civilian damage, and that such a procedure produces fewer casualties and devastation than would result from prior approaches that rely on the cruder technologies of manned aircraft and boots on the ground. Obama addressed the awkward question of whether it is within this mandate to target American citizens who are acting politically while resident in a foreign country. Obama used the case of Anwar al-Aulaqi, the Islamic preacher, to justify the decision to kill him, pointing to his alleged connections with several failed attempted terrorist acts in the United States: ". . . when a US citizen goes abroad to wage war against America . . . citizenship should no more serve as a shield than a sniper shooting down on an innocent crowd should be protected from a SWAT team."[20] Yet such an explanation does not respond to critics as to why prior to the assassination no charges against al-Aulaqi were put before some sort of judicial body, allowing for a court-appointed defense, to ensure that 'due process' within the group deciding on targets was not just a rubber stamp for CIA and Pentagon recommendations, and certainly why there cannot be a full post-facto disclosure of evidence and rationale.[21]

More disturbing, because it suggests bad faith, was Obama's failure to bring up the much more problematic drone targeting of a group of young people in a different part of Yemen from where the drone stuck Anwar al-Aulaqi. The targeted ground included Aulaqi's sixteen-year-old son, Abdulrahman al-Aulaqi, a cousin, and five other children while they were preparing an open air barbecue on October 14, 2011, three weeks after the drone killed Abdulrahman's father. The grandfather of Abdulrahman, an eminent Yemeni who was a former cabinet minister and university president, tells of his frustrating efforts to challenge in American courts the reliance on such hit lists and the absence of accountability even in such extreme cases.[22] It is this sort of incident that highlights why the whole claim of effectiveness of drones is under such a *dark* cloud of incredulity. The younger al-Aulaqi seems to have been the victim of what military jargon calls a 'signature strike,' that is, a hit list directed not at designated individuals, but at a group that CIA or Pentagon analysts find sufficiently suspicious to justify their lethal elimination. Notably, Obama never mentioned signature strikes in his talk, much less committed the government to end such targeting. This undermines his whole claim that targeting is responsibly conducted under his personal direction and done in an extremely prudent manner that limited targets to so-called high-value individuals posing direct threats to US security and to arranging any attack so as to eliminate to the extent possible indirect damage to civilians. This whole line of rationalization is deceptive, as drone strikes, by their nature, cause deep fears to the whole community, and thus even if only the single targeted individual is killed or wounded, the impact of the strike is felt much more widely in space and for a long duration.

There are two other matters in the Obama speech that bear mention. His central logic is one of giving priority to protecting the American people against all threats, including the homegrown ones of the sort illustrated by the Fort Hood shooting and Boston Marathon bombings, and yet he affirms that no American president should ever "deploy armed drones over US soil."[23] First of all, what if there is a protection or enforcement imperative? Secondly, there is a seeming approval given, at least tacitly, to unarmed drones, which means surveillance from the air of domestic activities. Also dubious is Obama's way of acknowledging that American diplomats face security threats that exceed those faced by other countries, explaining that "[t]his is the price of being the world's most powerful nation, particularly as a war of change washes over the Arab world." Again the vague abstraction never yields to the concrete: Why are American diplomats singled out? Are there legitimate grievances against the United States, which if removed, would enhance American security even more than by making embassies into fortresses and carrying out drone attacks anywhere on the planet provided only that the president signs off? Are America's imperial claims relevant? What about the global surveillance program disclosed in the government documents released by Edward Snowden? Again the abstractions are fine, sometimes even clarifying, on their own detached plane of discourse, unless and until compared with the concrete enactments of policies, which are enveloped in darkness, that is, deprived of light. In encouraging tones, after providing a rationale for continuing a wartime approach, Obama does observe at the end of his speech that this war "like all wars, must end. That's what history advises, that's what our democracy demands." He finishes with an obligatory patriotic flourish: "That's who the American people are—determined, and not to be messed with." Brennan chose almost identical words in ending his Harvard Law School speech: "As a people, as a nation, we cannot—and must not—succumb to the temptation to set aside our laws and values when we face threats to our security . . . We're better than that. We're Americans."[24] The sad point is that the abstractions are decoys. Sadly, precisely what we have done is what Obama and Brennan say we must never do in relation to law and values.

"CHILDREN OF DARKNESS"

Turning to the counter-narrative in which the reality of drone warfare is presented in an entirely different mode does not necessarily imply a total repudiation of drone warfare, but it does insist that such tactics and their current implementation are not fairly or honestly reported, and as such, cannot be readily reconciled with constitutional or international law or with prevailing moral standards. The critics of the mainstream Washington discourse can be faulted for tending to presume that there is no way to scale back reliance on drones in a manner that is sensitive to the limitations of law and morality rather than to dwell only on the abusive and dangerously dysfunctional ways in which drones have been and are being used by the US government. In other words, if the basic fallacy of the pro-drone children of light discourse is to keep the focus on an abstract level that ignores the existential challenges by the actual and potential patterns of use, the complementary fallacy of the children of darkness scenario is to limit this commentary to the concrete level that neglects the legitimate security pressures that motivate reliance on drones and their counterparts in the domain of 'special operations' with a lineage that can be traced back to World War II, if not earlier. An appropriate discourse on drones would involve a synthesis that combined an assessment of their utility as weapons given the sorts of conflicts that are present in today's world and adherence to principles of law and morality that are supposed to set limits on how force is used for the sake of national and international security. As always in such an inquiry, security justifications and normative principles of law and morality should seek some sort of dynamic balance that takes account of the complexities involved. It would have been helpful if Obama had rejected the hypothesis of how to conduct a borderless war and instead defined the threat posed by political extremism as one of borderless crime. He also should have worried more about the implications of this American decision to validate its reliance on robotic approaches to conflict, especially as a precedent for others to follow.

This is undoubtedly what Dick Cheney meant when he said that for the United States to be effective in a post-9/11 world it would have to act on "the dark side." The initial disseminators of the children of darkness discourse were actually unabashed in their embrace of this imagery and accompanying policies. Indeed, it was Cheney himself who articulated the positive rationale in a September 16, 2001, interview on *Meet the Press*: "We also have to work, though, sort of the dark side, if you will. We've got to spend time in the shadows of the intelligence world . . . That's the world these folks operate in, and so it's going to be vital for us to use any means at our disposal, basically, to achieve our objective."[25] What this meant in real time was reliance on torture and kill lists, and either the sidelining of legal constraints or warping them out of shape to validate policies.[26] It meant reliance on "black sites" in a series of countries that would allow the CIA to operate their own secret interrogation centers, and would not raise questions. It led to 'extraordinary rendition,' transferring suspects to governments that would engage in torture beyond what was evidently acceptable under direct American auspices. Donald Rumsfeld's motivations in a vast expansion of the Pentagon Special Access Program for Joint Special Operations Command (JSOC) was partly to avoid further dependence on the CIA because dark side initiatives were, in his words, being "lawyered to death."[27] When the PBS TV documentary series *Frontline* presented its depiction of the "war on terror" associated with the neoconservative presidency of George W. Bush in 2008, it chose the title "The Dark Side," as did Jane Mayer in her searing critique of the tactics employed by the Cheney/Rumsfeld designers of the governmental response to 9/11.[28] It is not surprising that Cheney even seemed comfortable with being cast as the personification of evil in the popular culture by way of the *Star Wars* character Darth Vader.[29]

As is well known by now, 9/11 facilitated a prior resolve by Cheney and Rumsfeld to concentrate war powers in the presidency and to project American power globally on the basis of post-Cold War strategic opportunity and priorities, without regard for limitations of sovereignty or the restraints of international law. Their goal was to preside over a revolution in military affairs that would bring warfare into the 21st century, which meant minimizing conventional weapons and tactics, which produced casualties and domestic political resistance to an aggressive foreign policy and meant relying on technological and tactical innovations that would have surgically precise capacities to defeat any enemy anywhere on the planet. September 11th was at first a puzzle as the neocon grand strategy was devised to achieve quick and cheap victories against hostile foreign governments on the model of the Gulf War in 1991, but with an increased willingness to be politically ambitious in imposing the kind of political outcomes that would enhance US global dominance. What had not been anticipated, however, and struck fear in many hearts, was that the main hostile political actors would turn out to be non-state actors whose forces were dispersed in many places. Adapting to that kind of security threat is what brought the dark side tactics front and center; as human intelligence was indispensable, the main perpetrators could hide anywhere, including within the United States. Because their presence was often intermingled with the civilian population, there would either have to be indiscriminate violence or precision attained through targeted killing. It was here that special operations, such as the killing of Osama bin Laden, and drone warfare became the tactics and means of choice. And it is here that the counter-terrorist, despite being shrouded in a cloak of darkness, becomes a deadly species of terrorist. The political extremist who blows up public buildings is not essentially different from the governmental operative who launches a drone or goes on a kill mission, although the extremist makes no claim of targeting precision and appears to accept no responsibility for indiscriminate killing.

In reaction to the degree of continuity exhibited by the Obama presidency, despite its reliance on the children of light discourse, liberal critics have tended to focus on the *behavior* of the state as characterized by its reliance on dark side tactics. Authors such as Jeremy Scahill and Mark Mazetti discuss the degree to which the essential features of the Cheney/Rumsfeld worldview have been sustained, even extended, during the Obama presidency: a war in the shadows; a global battlefield; surveillance of suspects who are defined to include anyone, everywhere; conception of imminent threat as potentially anyone (including American citizens) within or without the country; accelerated reliance on drone strikes as authorized by the president; and targeted killing as "the battlefield" acknowledged by Obama pointing to the execution of Osama bin Laden as the high point of his success in the war against al-Qaeda and its affiliates. There are some refinements in the conduct of the war on terror: The emphasis is placed on non-state adversaries, and the regime-changing warfare against state actors is terminated; torture as a tactic is pushed deeper into the darkness, meaning it is repudiated but not eliminated (e.g., force-feeding controversy at Guantánamo). In other words, the children of darkness still control "the real" conflict, dramatically confirmed by the treatment of such whistleblowers as Bradley (Chelsea) Manning and Edward Snowden. The liberal discourse of the children of light calms American society but evades the fundamental challenges being directed at international law and world order by the ongoing tactics of the Obama approach to a continuing war in response to 9/11 (that is, to date, implicitly sharing the Cheney view that it would be a gross mistake to treat "terrorism" as a crime rather than as "war").

DRONES AND THE FUTURE OF WORLD ORDER

The central debate about drone warfare focuses on issues of style and secrecy, and downplays matters of substance. Both children of light (representing the Obama presidency and liberal supporters) and children of darkness (the Cheney/ Rumsfeld cabal) are unapologetic advocates of the military use of drones, ignoring the problems of such weaponry and tactics from the perspectives of international law and world order. To underscore this contention, the introductory references to nuclear weapons are relevant. For drones, the idea of first-order constraints of drones based on unconditional prohibition and disarmament to ensure non-possession seems outside the scope of debate. Given the rise of non-state political actors with transnational agendas, the military utility of drones is so great that any project seeking their prohibition would be implausible.

The same situation pertains to second-order constraints associated with controls on their dissemination comparable to the nonproliferation approach. Already drones are too widely possessed, the technology too familiar, and the practical uses for a range of states too great to suppose that any significant sovereign state would forgo the advantages associated with the possession of drones, although the deployment of attack drones may lag for a period of time depending on the perception of security threats by various governments. Therefore, the best that can be hoped for at this time are certain agreed-upon guidelines relating to use, what might be called third-order constraints similar to the way in which the law of war has affected the conduct of hostilities in a manner that gives way to the perceived requirements of 'military necessity.'

The world order issues have also been evaded in the unfolding debate on the use of drones, never being mentioned in the Obama speech of May 23 and only acknowledged indirectly in the Cheney/Rumsfeld view of the post-9/11 terrain of warfare. In short, the treatment of the 9/11 attacks as "acts of war" rather than "crimes" has more enduring significance than the attacks themselves. It leads almost thoughtlessly to viewing the world as a global battlefield, and to a war that has no true end point, as has been the case in past wars. In effect, it submits to the logic of perpetual war, and the related acceptance of the idea that everyone, including citizens and residents, are potential enemies. Since the suspicion is fueled by intelligence gathering, which is done secretly, the primacy given to protecting the nation and its population gives to political leaders and unaccountable bureaucracies a license to kill, to impose extrajudicial capital punishment without the intervening due process steps of indictment, prosecution, and trial. As time passes, this authoritarian nexus of governmental power as it becomes normalized undermines both the possibility of "peace" and "democracy," and necessarily institutionalizes "the deep state" as standard operating procedure for contemporary governance. If linked to the consolidation of capital and finance in plutocratic patterns of influence, the advent of new variants of fascism becomes almost inevitable, whatever the shape of the global security system.[30] In other words, drones reinforce other trends in world order that are destructive of human rights, global justice, and the protection of human interests of global scope. These trends include large investments in secret global surveillance systems that scrutinize the private lives of citizens at home, a wide range of persons abroad, and even the diplomatic maneuverings of foreign governments on a basis more extensive and intrusive than traditional espionage.

DRONE WARFARE AND INTERNATIONAL LAW: DIMINISHING RETURNS

There are certain specific effects of drone warfare that exert a strain on the efforts of international law to constrain uses of force and regulate the conduct of war. Some children of light critics of the official policies have raised questions as to the scope of permissible use of drones, not challenging drones, per se, but their mode of authorization and the rules of engagement pertaining to their use.

Recourse to War

A prime effort of modern international law has been to discourage recourse to war to resolve international conflicts that emerge between sovereign states. In many respects, that undertaking has been successful in the relations among major states with respect to *international* wars as distinct from *internal* wars. The destructiveness of war, the diminishing importance of territorial expansion, and the rise of a globalized economy have made this idea of war as a last resort an important achievement of the latest phase of state-centric world order. Such an achievement is now at risk due to the rise of non-state transnational violence and the response by way of drones and special forces that operate without regard to borders. What this means is that international warfare becomes more and more dysfunctional, and the war mentality is shifted to the new wars waged by a global state against non-state political actors. And these wars, which are largely conducted behind a thick veil of secrecy, and with low risks of casualties on the side relying on drone attacks, make recourse to war much less problematic: the public does not have to be convinced, congressional approval can be achieved in secret sessions, and there are no likely US military casualties or vast diversions of resources. Such wars become cheap and easy.

State Terror

There had always been some tendency for the tactics of warfare to involve explicit reliance on state terror, that is, military force directed at the civilian population. The indiscriminate bombing of German and Japanese cities during the last stages of World War II was one of the most extreme instances, but the German blockades of Soviet cities, rockets fired at English cities, and the rise of submarine warfare against ships carrying food and humanitarian supplies to civilian populations were other prominent examples. Yet the type of "dirty wars" undertaken after 9/11 embraced state terror as the essence of the dark side conduct of the effort to destroy the al-Qaeda network, and indeed undertake the destruction of so-called terror networks of global reach. As American operations in Yemen and Somalia suggest, the notion of "global reach" has been replaced by armed movements or groups with an Islamic identity even if the scope of their ambitions is confined to national borders, posing no threat, imminent or otherwise, to American national security. This tension, between treating anti-state "terrorism" as the worst form of criminality—one that suspends legal protections to those accused—while claiming to engage in comparable forms of violence, serves to deprive international law of its normative authority, which is based on some degree of ethical parity with respect to behavioral standards. Until the Cheney/Rumsfeld embrace of secret war by assassination, the United States did not follow Israel's adoption of terror to fight terror, which had evolved from the shadows of Israeli policy to an outright avowal of legality in 2000 (after years of disavowal). In addition to the tactical adoption of a terrorist approach to weakening the enemy, there is the terrorizing of the society as a whole that results from experiencing repeated drone attacks. That is, it is not only the targeted individual or group, but the experience of having such drone strikes that creates acute anxiety and severe disruption within the communities that have been attacked.[31]

Targeted Killing

Both the international human rights law and the international law of war prohibit extrajudicial executions. There is insistence that such targeting is legal if the threat is perceived as substantial and imminent, as determined by secret procedures, not subject to post-facto procedures of investigation and potential accountability. The reliance on such a process for the legalization of practices associated with drone warfare and special operations does two types of damage to international law: (1) it situates targeted killing beyond the reach of law, and is dependent on the non-reviewable discretion of government officials, including the subjective appreciation of threats (such a rationale is basically one of "trust us"); and (2) it substantially erodes the prohibition on targeting civilians not engaged in combat operations, and at the same time eliminates the due process arguments that those charged with crimes are entitled to a presumption of innocence and right of defense. As a result, both the customary international law distinctions between military and non-military targets is weakened and the human rights effort to protect civilian innocence is completely disregarded. Also, the underlying contention that extra-judicial targeted killing is done sparingly and in the face of imminent threat as underpinning the claim of "reasonableness" is unreviewable because of the secrecy surrounding these uses of drones, and the critical independent assessments of actual patterns of use do not support government claims of responsible behavior. That is, even if the argument is accepted that the law of war and human rights law must bend in relation to imminent security threats, there is no indication that such constraints have been or will be observed in practice. The criterion of imminence, even if interpreted in good faith, is notoriously subjective.

Expanding Self-Defense

The most fundamental argument with respect to drone warfare is that given the nature of the threats posed by political extremists pursuing transnational agendas and situated anywhere and everywhere, preemptive tactics must be authorized as components of the inherent right of self-defense. Reactive tactics based on retaliation in the event that deterrence fails are not effective, and since the destructive capabilities of non-state actors pose credible major threats to peace and security of even the strongest of states, preemptive strikes are necessary and reasonable. Such subjectivity surrounding threat perception, as applied in relation to drone warfare, undermines the entire effort to limit international uses of force to objectively determined defensive claims that can be reviewed as to reasonableness. This was the central claim of the United Nations Charter, and its abandonment represents a return to an essentially discretionary approach to uses of force and recourse to war.

The Logic of Reciprocity

An essential feature of the law of war is the idea of precedent and the acceptance of the reciprocity principle that what is claimed as legal by a dominant state cannot be denied to a weaker state for clear exposition of the logic of reciprocity.[32] The United States established such a precedent by recourse to atmospheric testing of nuclear weapons, and was not able to complain when other countries, including France, Soviet Union, and China, later tested their own weapons, although by that time the United States was limiting its own testing to underground sites with less damaging environmental effects. With patterns of drone use, however, the world would be chaotic if what the United States is claiming is lawful for its undertakings with drones is undertaken by other states. It is only an imperial relation of the United States regarding uses of force that can be projected into the future as a sustainable basis of world order, and as such, it implies a repudiation of Westphalian notions of the juridical equality of states. The drone debate has been embedded in a legal culture that takes American exceptionalism for granted.

The Global Battlefield

In significant respects, the Cold War converted the world into a global battlefield, with the CIA managing covert operations in foreign countries as part of the struggle against the spread of Communist influence ("warriors without borders"). After 9/11, this globalization of conflict was renewed in a more explicit form, and directed particularly at the security threats posed by the al-Qaeda network that was declared to exist in as many as sixty countries. As the threats emanated from non-territorial bases of operations, secret intelligence, sophisticated surveillance, and identification of dangerous individuals living as civilians amid civilian society became the prime focus of interest. Foreign governments, most notably Pakistan and Yemen, were induced to give their confidential consent for drone strikes within their own territory, which were the subject of explicit rebuke and protest. Such patterns of "consent" eroded the autonomy of many sovereign states, and generated intense distrust in the relations between the state and the people. It also raises questions about whether this muffled form of consent provides adequate justification for such erosions of the political independence of sovereign states.

The American claim has been that it has the legal option to use drones against targets that pose a threat if the foreign government is unwilling or unable to take action on its own to remove the threat, with the underlying legal presupposition being that a government has an obligation not to allow its territory to be used as a launching pad for transnational violence. What becomes clear, however, is that both the globalizing of conflict, and of threats and responses, are incompatible with a state-centric structure of law. If a legal order is to persist under these conditions, it must be globalized, as well, but there is an insufficient political will to establish and empower global procedures and institutions with such effective authority. As a result, the only alternatives seem to be an inchoate imperial regime of the sort that presently prevails, or an explicit global imperial regime that repudiates in explicit form the logic of reciprocity. This has not yet happened.

One-Sided Warfare

Drone warfare carries forward various tactics of warfare that are virtually without human risk for the more technologically powerful and sophisticated side in an armed conflict, and has assumed recent prominence due to the tactics and weaponry employed by Israel and the United States. A pattern of one-sided warfare has resulted that shifts the burdens of warfare to the adversary to the extent possible. To a degree, such a shift reflects the nature of warfare that seeks to protect one's own side to the extent possible from death and destruction, while inflicting maximum damage on the other side. What is distinctive in the recent instances of military intervention and counterterrorism, the two main theaters of combat, is the one-sidedness of the casualty figures. A series of military operations is illustrative of this pattern: Gulf War(1991); NATO Kosovo War(1999); Iraq Invasion (2003); NATO Libya War (2011); and Israeli military operations against Lebanon and Gaza (2006; 2008–09; 2012; 2014). The increasing use of attack drones in Afghanistan is a culminating example of one-sided warfare, removing the drone operational crew from the battlefield altogether, and executing strikes by commands issued from remote operational headquarters (e.g., in Nevada). The repudiation of torture as an acceptable tactic of war or law enforcement partly reflects the one-sidedness of the relationship between the torturer and the victim as morally and legally objectionable, aside from liberal arguments contending that torture is ineffective.[33] An analogous set of reactions to drone warfare exists, including the liberal contention that the rage and resentment of a population subject to drone attack encourages the very kind of political extremism that drones are deployed against, as well as alienating foreign governments.

Futuristic Drone Warfare

While the politicians are preoccupied with responding to immediate threats, the arms makers and Pentagon advance planners are exploring the technological frontiers of drone warfare. These frontiers are synonymous with science fiction accounts of robotic warfare with ultra-sophisticated weaponry and massive killing machines. There are possibilities of drone fleets that can conduct belligerent operations with minimal human agency, communicating with one another to coordinate lethal strikes on an enemy, which may also be armed with defensive drones. The reliance on drones in current patterns of warfare has the inevitable effect of devoting attention to what can be done to improve performance and to develop new military missions. Whether the technological momentum that has been released can be controlled or confined seems doubtful, and again the comparison with nuclear military technology is instructive. Yet it is important to keep in mind that drones are considered usable weapons, including for legal and moral reasons, while so far nuclear weapons are treated as non-usable except conceivably in ultimate survival situations.

A CONCLUDING NOTE

Four lines of conclusion emerge from this overall assessment of the impact of drone warfare, as practiced by the United States, on international law and world order. First, it is not plausible to eliminate drones from the warfare so long as the security of states is based on a military self-help system. As a weapons system, given the current threats posed by non-state actors and the memories of 9/11, drones are too effective. In any event, the technological momentum and commercial incentives are too great to halt.[34] As a result, such first-order international law constraints, as an unconditional prohibition as adopted in relation to biological and chemical weapons, and proposed in relation to nuclear weapons, is not plausible.

Secondly, the debate on the legality of drone warfare has been carried on within an American context in which the risks of setting precedents and the dangers of future technological developments is accorded minimal attention. This debate has been further trivialized by being conducted mainly between those who would cast aside international law and those who stretch it to serve changing national security priorities of American foreign policy.

Thirdly, the debate on drones seems oblivious to the world order dimensions of creating a global battlefield and coercing the consent of foreign governments.

Fourthly, the embrace of state terror to fight against non-state actors makes war into a species of terror and tends toward making limits on force seem arbitrary, if not absurd.

It is against this background that the counter-intuitive argument is put forward seriously to the effect that drone warfare is, and is likely to become, more destructive of international law and world order than is nuclear warfare. Such a contention is not meant to suggest that reliance on nuclear weapons would somehow be better for the human future than the acceptance of the logic of drone use. It is only to say that so far, at any rate, international law and world order have been able to figure out some regimes of constraint for nuclear weapons that have kept the peace, but have not been able to do so for drones, and will be unlikely to do so as long as the logic of dirty wars is allowed to control the shaping of national security policy in the United States.

NOTES

[1]   On the workings of the state-centric world order, *see* HEDLEY BULL, THE ANARCHICAL SOCIETY: A STUDY OF ORDER IN WORLD POLITICS (Columbia Univ. Press, 2d ed., 1995); ROBERT O. KEOHANE, AFTER HEGEMONY: COOPERATION AND DISCORD IN THE WORLD POLITICAL ECONOMY (Princeton Univ. Press, 1984); the vertical axis of world order reflects the inequality of states, and the special role played by dominant states; the

horizontal axis embodies the juridical logic of equality among states that is the foundation of the international rule of law. First-order constraints would entail the prohibition of nuclear weaponry and a phased and verified disarmament process that eliminated nuclear weapons. For critiques of the failures of diplomacy to achieve first-order constraints, *see* RICHARD FALK & DAVID KRIEGER, THE PATH TO ZERO: DIALOGUES ON NUCLEAR DANGERS (Paradigm, 2012); RICHARD FALK & ROBERT JAY LIFTON, INDEFENSIBLE WEAPONS: THE PSYCHOLOGICAL AND POLITICAL CASE AGAINST NUCLEARISM (Basic Books, 1982); JONATHAN SCHELL, THE FATE OF THE EARTH (Knopf, 1982); E.P. THOMPSON, BEYOND THE COLD WAR: A NEW ARMS RACE AND NUCLEAR ANNIHILATION (Pantheon,1982).

[2] The standard rationale of the deterrence doctrine credits it with maintaining stability during the Cold War, and John Mearsheimer even credits deterrence with preventing World War III. For the worldview that endorses such extreme political realism, *see* MEARSHEIMER, THE TRAGEDY OF GREAT POWER POLITICS (Norton, 2001); *see also* Mearsheimer, *Back to the Future*, International Security 15 (No. 1):5–56 (1990). It is true that for certain isolated smaller and medium-size states, nuclear weapons can operate as an equalizer and offset the vertical dimension of world order. There is also a role played by nuclear weapons in threat diplomacy that has been explored by many authors. *See* ALEXANDER GEORGE & WILLIAM SIMONS, EDS., LIMITS OF COERCIVE DIPLOMACY, (Westview Press, 2nd ed., 1994). Other authors pushed rationality to frightening extremes so as to find ways to take practical advantage of American superiority in nuclear weaponry. *See* HENRY KISSINGER, NUCLEAR WEAPONS AND FOREIGN POLICY (Doubleday, 1958); HERMAN KAHN, ON THERMONUCLEAR WAR (Princeton Univ. Press, 1960).

[3] The arms control regime, despite its managerial rationale, has always rejected any prohibition on first-strike options, and thus casts doubt on the morality and practical contributions of such second-order constraints.

[4] The nonproliferation regime, embodied in the Nuclear Nonproliferation Treaty (NPT) (729 U.N.T.S. 10485), is a prime instance of a vertical arrangement, allowing only the dominant states to retain nuclear weapons, and is the main form that second-order constraints have taken. It is relevant to note that the International Court of Justice, in its important Advisory Opinion of 1996, offered the view in its majority opinion that a use of nuclear weapons might be lawful, but only if the survival of the state was credibly at stake. In what seems a futile gesture, the judges were united in their belief that the nuclear weapons states had a clear legal obligation in Article VI of the NPT to engage in good-faith disarmament negotiations, suggesting a legalistic horizontal element that is likely to have no behavioral impacts. The nuclear weapons states, above all the United States, have treated this authoritative statement of the bearing of international law as essentially irrelevant to their attitude toward the role of nuclear weapons in national security policy.

5   Early in his presidency President Obama gave hope to those who had long sought the elimination of nuclear weapons when he spoke in favor of a world without nuclear weapons, but hedged his visionary statement with subtle qualifications that made it unlikely to proceed very far. *See* President Barack Obama, Remarks by President Barack Obama in Prague (April 5, 2009); the liberal-realist view insists that nuclear disarmament is a desirable goal, but must not occur in the face of unresolved international conflicts. It is never made clear when the time will be right, which has the quality of a utopian precondition that precludes the morally, legally, and politically compelling arguments for nuclear disarmament. For a typical statement of such a mainstream liberal outlook, *see* MICHAEL O'HANLON, SKEPTIC'S CASE FOR NUCLEAR DISARMAMENT (Brookings, 2010).

6   Among others, *see* ROBERT JAY LIFTON, SUPERPOWER SYNDROME: AMERICA'S APOCALYPTIC CONFRONTATION WITH THE WORLD (Nation Books, 2002); for a reluctant endorsement of the nuclear weapons status quo, *see* JOSEPH NYE, NUCLEAR ETHICS (Free Press, 1986).

7   There are two extreme orientations toward normativity in world politics— the Kantian tradition of skepticism about international law, but affirmation of international morality, versus the Machiavellian tradition of calculative and self-interested behavior that rejects moral as well as legal authority in the conduct of state politics. A contemporary master of the Machiavellian approach was Henry Kissinger, an approach he proudly acknowledged in KISSINGER, DIPLOMACY (Simon & Schuster, 1994).

8   Despite their increased participation in all aspects of international life, non-state actors remain on the outside of the circle of Westphalian political actors, who limit membership in the United Nations and most international institutions to sovereign states.

9   For views that international humanitarian law and the law of war generally are dubious contributions to human well-being, as they tend to make war an acceptable social institution, *see* RICHARD WASSERSTROM, ED., WAR AND MORALITY (Wadsworth, 1970); *see also* RAYMOND ARON, PEACE AND WAR: A THEORY OF INTERNATIONAL RELATIONS (Weidenfeld & Nicolson, 1966); RICHARD FALK, LEGAL ORDER IN A VIOLENT WORLD (Princeton Univ. Press, 1968).

10   Chiaroscuro is usually defined as the treatment of light and darkness in painting; in the sense used here, it refers to the contrasts of light and dark in the perceptions of the American global role.

11   The political leadership of states is legitimized by free elections, law and order, development as measured by growth rates, and executive political skills, including communication with the public, and only secondarily by fidelity to law and morality. Such an observation is even more accurate when applied to foreign policy, and more so yet if a state of war prevails.

[12] For classic exposition, *see* REINHOLD NIEBUHR, CHILDREN OF LIGHT AND CHILDREN OF DARKNESS (Scribners, 1960).

[13] *See* Kissinger & Kahn, *supra* Note 2, who, among others, contended in Cold War contexts that nuclear weapons were needed to offset the alleged conventional superiority of the Soviet Union in the defense of Europe, and that the human and physical costs of a regional nuclear war were an acceptable price to pay. This illustrates the extremes to which realist thinkers have been prepared to go on behalf of strategic goals.

[14] President Barack Obama, Remarks by the President at the National Defense University (May 23, 2013) (transcript available at www.whitehouse.gov/the-press-office/2013/05/23/remarks-president-national-defense-university).

[15] Lisa Hajjar, *Anatomy of the US Targeted Killing Policy*, MER 264 (2012).

[16] Obama, *supra* note 14.

[17] For instance, there is no consideration of the disruption of tribal society, as in Pakistan, through the use of drones or the "blowback" in countries such as Pakistan from what appear to the public to be flagrant violations of national sovereignty. For important depiction of impact of drone warfare on tribal societies, *see* AKBAR AHMED, THE THISTLE AND THE DRONE: HOW AMERICA'S WAR ON TERROR BECAME A GLOBAL WAR ON TRIBAL ISLAM (Brookings Inst. Press, 2013); for general assessment of blowback costs of relying on drones, *see* JEREMY SCAHILL, DIRTY WARS: THE WORLD AS A BATTLEFIELD (Nation Books, 2013); along similar lines, *see* MARK MAZZETTI, THE WAY OF THE KNIFE: THE CIA, A SECRET ARMY, AND A WAR AT THE ENDS OF THE EARTH (Penguin, 2013).

[18] Before Brennan, it was Harold Koh, Legal Advisor to the Secretary of State, who set forth a legal rationale for reliance on drones in an address given at the American Society of International Law, March 25, 2010.

[19] John Brennan, Assistant to the President, Homeland Security, Strengthening Our Security by Adhering to Our Values and Laws (Sept. 16, 2011), www. whitehouse.gov/the-press-office/2011/09/16/remarks-john-o-brennan-strengthening-our-security-adhering-our-values-an.

[20] Obama, *supra* note 14.

[21] *See* Jeremy Scahill, *supra* note 17 (discussing the non-indictment of al-Aulaqi.)

[22] *See Kebriaei* chapter 10.

[23] Obama, *supra* note 14.

[24] Brennan, *supra* note 19.

[25] *Meet the Press: Dick Cheney* (NBC television broadcast Sept. 16, 2001), www. fromthewilderness.com/timeline/2001/meetthepress091601.html.

26 For texts and commentary on torture during the Bush presidency, *see* DAVID COLE, ED., THE TORTURE MEMOS: RATIONALIZING THE UNTHINKABLE (New Press, 2009).

27 *See* Scahill, *supra* note 17, at 1551.

28 JANE MAYER, THE DARK SIDE (Doubleday, 2008); *see also* LALEH KHALILI, TIME IN THE SHADOWS: CONFINEMENT IN COUNTERINSURGENCIES (Stanford Univ. Press, 2013).

29 In this connection, it is worth noting that Richard Perle, the intellectual standout in the Lilliputian world of neocons, was dubbed "the prince of darkness," which was treated in the media as part comedy, part opprobrium, and part honorific in view of his influence.

30 For an analysis along these lines, *see* SHELDON WOLIN, DEMOCRACY INCORPORATED: MANAGED DEMOCRACY AND THE SPECTER OF TOTALITARIANISM (Princeton Univ. Press, 2008).

31 For detailed documentation, *see* Ahmed, *supra* note 17.

32 *See* David Cole, *A Secret License to Kill*, NYR BLOG (Sept 19, 2011, 5:30 PM), www.nybooks.com/blogs/nyrblog/2011/sep/19/secret-license-kill/.

33 For elaboration, *see* Richard Falk, *Torture, War, and the Limits of Liberal Legality*, *in* THE UNITED STATES AND TORTURE: INTERROGATION, INCARCERATION, AND ABUSE 119 (Marjorie Cohn ed., NYU Press, 2011).

34 For useful discussion and documentation, *see* MEDEA BENJAMIN, DRONE WARFARE: KILLING BY REMOTE CONTROL (Verso, rev. ed., 2013).

3

DRONES AND ASSASSINATION IN THE US'S PERMANENT WAR

Phyllis Bennis

Just before the end of the Vietnam War, a small theater in Los Angeles premiered a new play. Ostensibly about a hallucinogenic trip, *The Hashish Club* depicted five friends gathered for a night of stoned camaraderie that quickly deteriorated into brutality and madness. Its turn toward violence and issues of power linked it inextricably to Vietnam and to war.

The connection was evident not only in the story but from the origins of the word "hashish" itself, which has the same etymological roots as "assassin." The linkage was not what we might assume today—the role of drugs in fueling wars—but rather the historical connection between an ancient Persian warrior sect and its members' assumed reliance on drugs to elevate their religious fervor enough to carry out directed killings at the order of their leader.

That history, much of it grounded in Orientalist fantasy, is contested. But it remains true that assassins are often drugged with power, impunity, and extremist visions of patriotic or religious belief. And today the existence of bands of stealthy warriors, some linked to invisible killings from the sky, prowling the same lands of the Middle East, committing acts of targeted assassination, murder, and mayhem, is no longer a myth. The difference is that today's warriors, in the lands now known as West Asia or the Middle East, are teams of US Special Forces backed by armed drones.

As the 30,000 remaining US troops in Afghanistan are slowly withdrawn and deployment of additional ground forces in the region moves closer to political untenability, the role of those drones and Special Forces troops comes into clearer focus. In May 2013, there were 10,000 US Special Operations troops in Afghanistan (plus about 1,700 more from other NATO countries). Those 10,000 will be the core of the US forces remaining in Afghanistan after the "draw-down" of most combat troops by the end of 2014.[1]

For decades, Special Operations troops were linked to counterinsurgency strategies. But counterinsurgency, according to the old-fashioned (and quite mythical) definition of "winning hearts and minds" of the population through protecting villages and defending civilians from ruthless enemies with the goal of building support for a recognized, legitimate national government, is over. Counterterrorism (though the term is rarely acknowledged to be a replacement for counterinsurgency) is the new normal. A counterterrorism strategy is much simpler: go after those you define as terrorists, pretty much regardless of what happens to the vast majority of people not [yet] on your list.

That narrow mission makes the job of Special Forces—the Army's Green Berets, Delta Force, Navy SEALs, and Marine special forces teams, all operating within the Joint Special Operations Command (JSOC)—very clear and very specific: to kill people. To kill Afghans, Pakistanis, Yemenis, Somalis, and Malians. Sometimes to kill Iraqis or Saudis or Syrians. And on occasion, to kill Americans. Jeremy Scahill, writing in *The Nation*, quoted Col. Patrick Lang, a retired Special Forces officer, describing JSOC as "sort of like Murder, Incorporated. . . . Their business is killing al-Qaeda personnel. That's their business. They're not in the business of converting anybody to our goals or anything like that."[2]

Some of those killed will be identified and their names will appear on lists of "violent jihadis." A few—very few—will be trumpeted as "high-value" targets who someone will claim to be leaders of al-Qaeda or the Taliban or some other organization. In Afghanistan in particular this category is getting smaller and smaller. Back in 2009, officials admitted there were "less than 100 al-Qaeda terrorists" left there. By 2010, then CIA director Leon Panetta said it was "less than fifty." Many of those killed will be accused, at most, of being low-level supporters of one or another group fighting against US and NATO troops and/or the governments those troops back. Some will be killed in a house where unnamed and unknown troops kick down the door for a late-night assassination raid. Many will be targeted when their names are not even known, aimed at, and killed by drones programmed to carry out "signature strikes" based solely on an action—driving toward a certain house or gathering under a certain tree in a particular village—deemed sufficient evidence of evil-doing to be targeted and killed. The "action" need not have any military component.

And many more will be ordinary people—children, women, and men— whom no one even claims have committed any act of resistance except perhaps being an Afghan or a Yemeni or a Pakistani, living in their own country, sitting in their neighbor's house or riding in their cousin's car. They will be the "collateral damage." Their deaths will rarely be acknowledged; even rarer will an apology or compensation be offered. But with or without apology, their deaths, always, will quickly be forgotten by those who killed them and by those who armed, trained, and sent the killers. They will be forgotten by everyone except their families, their friends, their co-workers, their village, their tribe, their country. Those will be the people who remember.

VIETNAM, IRAQ, AND THE "SALVADOR OPTION"

After the US lost its decade-long war in Vietnam, public anger at its failure, exhaustion with the [US] casualties, and years of anti-war organizing led to widespread rejection of anything that remotely resembled the Indochina war. The military draft had already been cancelled. Other consequences included new military doctrines to fight the anti-Soviet Cold War largely through warm-to-hot proxy wars across the Global South, from Central America to Central Asia, from southern Africa to the southern cone of South America, always avoiding large-scale US troop deployments. The option of a major ground war, deploying thousands of troops, was off the table. The military brass were among the strongest backers of the new approach. Nevertheless, for many policymakers and war supporters, the change was evidence less of an appropriate reconfiguring of strategy than of a national pathology—quickly dubbed the "Post-Vietnam Syndrome."

The proxy wars in Afghanistan and Guatemala, Mozambique and El Salvador, Angola and Nicaragua and beyond, killed hundreds of thousands of people. US soldiers, along with copious amounts of US money, were deployed in small numbers, as "advisers" and "trainers" for the US-backed national armies or US-backed guerrilla opposition forces. The local casualties in each of these brutal wars escalated, but hardly any US soldiers died—so they became known in the US as "low-intensity" conflicts. For the Afghans, Angolans, Nicaraguans, and others who lived through them, of course, there was nothing low-intensity about them.

Years later, when the end of the Cold War had set the stage for resolving those derivative proxy wars, the core of that strategy became publicly known as the "Salvador option." It took the form of sending CIA and Special Forces operatives to create, arm, train and finance assassination teams and death squads, to avoid the risk of high US casualties and US public opposition to sending ground troops. The tactics themselves were not new. The United States had used assassination and torture and had turned whole villages into concentration camps dubbed "strategic hamlets" in Vietnam—actions carried out both directly by US troops and by Washington's South Vietnamese proxies. For the fifteen years between the end of the Vietnam War in 1975 and the first Gulf War in 1991, US strategy still rejected significant troop deployments into war zones, but continued to carry out assassination, "snatch" or capture operations and other military attacks. The United States executed those operations and attacks partly itself and partly by training and assisting local armies or guerrillas, while relying on only small numbers of US forces.

It wasn't until 1990–91, when the Soviet Union's defeat in Afghanistan was followed by its collapse and the final end of the Cold War, that the notion of a major deployment of US ground and air forces was reconsidered. In what would become the first US Gulf War against Iraq, Operation Desert Storm became, for almost a decade in the United States, the model of what a "good" war should look like—clear victory, with the expulsion of Iraqi troops from Kuwait, and very few US casualties.

In fact, throughout the 1990s in a constant reminder of what remained unfinished in anti-war education, asking young people in seminars how many people died in the Gulf War would result in a slew of hands waving in the air with proud cries of "I know, I know—it was 358." That was the number of US troops killed in the war. The tens of thousands of Iraqis killed directly during Operation Desert Storm, not to mention the hundreds of thousands, the million or more Iraqis, especially children, killed in the next decade as a result of US-led economic sanctions, were not known, so they did not figure in official US casualty counts.

In the aftermath of 2001's September 11th attacks, the last remnants of the war queasiness collapsed. Suddenly the massive deployment of US troops, in an old-fashioned though updated and ultra-modern air and ground assault and occupation, seemed (other than to the relatively small but soon-to-be influential anti-war forces immediately mobilizing against the coming war) perfectly acceptable. The large-scale air and ground battle in Afghanistan was immediately dubbed the "good war," anointed with red-white-and-blue patriotic legitimacy. From the beginning, part of Washington's official Afghan war strategy was to identify and assassinate those alleged to be "high-value" al-Qaeda and Taliban leaders. Part of the *operative* Afghan war strategy was to kill a whole lot of low-level supporters and a whole lot of ordinary Afghans who just happened to be in the wrong place at the wrong time.

When the US military focus shifted from Afghanistan to Iraq in 2003, the strategic value of the Salvador option inside the context of a major ground war was rolled out once again. The Iraq war, with regime change and US occupation, was always the primary strategic goal of the Bush administration and its neo-conservative supporters—not Afghanistan. President George W. Bush, Vice President Dick Cheney, and Secretary of Defense Donald Rumsfeld thought the war would be a "cakewalk." Iraqis would welcome the conquering troops as heroes with sweets and flowers in the streets, the oil revenue of the "new Iraq" would quickly pay for whatever small amount the war cost—and thus it would be easy to fight the war with a relatively small footprint.

One of the first, and among the most memorable, weapons of the US propaganda war in Iraq was the infamous deck of cards identifying the fifty-two top "wanted" Iraqis. Linked to bounties designed to appeal to impoverished and desperate Iraqis, the cards made clear that assassination was now a key component of US war strategy. And that was even before the full-scale military resistance that rose to challenge US occupation a year or so after the invasion.

By early 2005, with the resistance engaged and a full-scale war under way, *Newsweek* magazine provided an inside look at the internal debate within Bush's White House, Pentagon, and CIA:

DRONES AND TARGETED KILLING: LEGAL, MORAL, AND
GEOPOLITICAL ISSUES; ED. BY MARJORIE COHN.
                                Paper   TWAIN,
NORTHAMPTON: OLIVE BRANCH PRESS, 2015

AN AP PLUS! BOOK. ED: THOMAS JEFFERSON SCHOOL OF
LAW. COLLECTION OF NEW ESSAYS. TLS 6/12/15.
  LCCN 2014033926
  ISBN 1566569893   **Library PO#** FIRM ORDERS
                                List   25.00 USD
   8395 NATIONAL UNIVERSITY LIBRAR   **Disc**   .0%
   App. Date 11/11/15   GEN   8214-08 **Net**   25.00 USD

SUBJ: 1. DRONE AIRCRAFT--U.S. 2. DRONE AIRCRAFT--
GOVT. POL.--U.S.

CLASS UG1242   DEWEY# UTH.OR: LEVEL GEN-AC

YBP Library Services

DRONES AND TARGETED KILLING: LEGAL, MORAL, AND
GEOPOLITICAL ISSUES; ED. BY MARJORIE COHN.
                                Paper   TWAIN,
NORTHAMPTON: OLIVE BRANCH PRESS, 2015

AN AP PLUS! BOOK. ED: THOMAS JEFFERSON SCHOOL OF
LAW. COLLECTION OF NEW ESSAYS. TLS 6/12/15.
  LCCN 2014033926
  ISBN 1566569893   **Library PO#** FIRM ORDERS
                                List   25.00 USD
   8395 NATIONAL UNIVERSITY LIBRAR   **Disc**   .0%
   App. Date 11/11/15   GEN   8214-08 **Net**   25.00 USD

SUBJ: 1. DRONE AIRCRAFT--U.S. 2. DRONE AIRCRAFT--
GOVT. POL.--U.S.

CLASS UG1242   DEWEY# UTH.OR: LEVEL GEN-AC

What to do about the deepening quagmire of Iraq? The Pentagon's latest approach is being called "the Salvador option"--and the fact that it is being discussed at all is a measure of just how worried Donald Rumsfeld really is. … Now, *Newsweek* has learned, the Pentagon is intensively debating an option that dates back to a still-secret strategy in the Reagan administration's battle against the leftist guerrilla insurgency in El Salvador in the early 1980s. Then, faced with a losing war against Salvadoran rebels, the US government funded or supported "nationalist" forces that allegedly included so-called death squads directed to hunt down and kill rebel leaders and sympathizers. Eventually the insurgency was quelled, and many US conservatives consider the policy to have been a success--despite the deaths of innocent civilians and the subsequent Iran-Contra arms-for-hostages scandal. . . .

Following that model, one Pentagon proposal would send Special Forces teams to advise, support and possibly train Iraqi squads, most likely hand-picked Kurdish Peshmerga fighters and Shiite militiamen, to target Sunni insurgents and their sympathizers, even across the border into Syria, according to military insiders familiar with the discussions. It remains unclear, however, whether this would be a policy of assassination or so-called "snatch" operations, in which the targets are sent to secret facilities for interrogation.[3]

By 2006, as the Iraq war began its transition into a full-blown sectarian conflict internal to Iraq, even as the war against the US occupation continued, reliance on Special Forces and those specially trained Iraqi squads was stronger than ever. Night raids, in small towns and villages across Iraq, were the norm, with frequent assassination and "snatch" operations.

By 2007, Bush and his team had settled on a "surge" plan. Beyond the 30,000 additional US troops, key components of the strategy had far less to do with troop numbers and far more with buying off much of the Iraqi opposition. The main target was the predominantly Sunni militias who had been waging war against the US-backed Shi'a-dominated government and its supporters across Iraq. Over the next couple of years, by distributing huge amounts of cash in what became known as the "Sunni Awakening" process, the United States was able to flip a large percentage of those former opponents, and recruit them into newly created US-controlled pro-government militias. That, along with the horrific reality that much of the ethnic cleansing had indeed achieved its lethal goal—most formerly multiethnic, multi-religious towns and neighborhoods were now populated by only one sect or group—meant that the worst of the sectarian fighting was over.

But the emphasis on assassination as a strategic component of US war planning continued. With the inauguration of Barack Obama in 2009, direct US war fighting in Iraq began to wind down, even as the Afghan war escalated. His commitment to end what he called the "dumb war" in Iraq was implemented slowly and grudgingly. Only after the Iraqi parliament refused to authorize immunity for any war crimes that US troops might commit, was the pull-out plan broadened to include all the troops.

Despite the slow pace of the Iraq withdrawal, the Obama administration immediately pivoted from Iraq toward Afghanistan, beginning with President Obama's decision to send 17,000 additional troops to Afghanistan just two months into his presidency. The White House then initiated a nine-month internal debate on what the administration's Afghanistan war policy should be. Facing the combination of widespread and growing public opposition to the wars, a military seriously stretched by multiple deployments for so many years, and the budget constraints of a major economic crisis, there was some hope that a quick and total withdrawal from Afghanistan might be possible.

COUNTERINSURGENCY OR COUNTERTERRORISM?

But the fighting over war strategy was not only about numbers of troops. Proponents of counterinsurgency claimed their campaign would protect Afghan civilians, provide services, help create functional governance, build a viable military force to win public support for the US-backed government in the impoverished country, and oh yeah, wipe out al-Qaeda and the Taliban in the meantime. Supporters of counterterrorism, on the other hand, called for far fewer troops because they essentially just planned to go in and kill bad guys.

A few anti-war voices were invited to White House outreach sessions on Afghan war strategy. But actual participation was severely limited and those voices were essentially ignored. In the internal debate, administration and Pentagon advocates of a quick troop reduction, even for counterterrorism purposes, were defeated. Instead, on December 1, 2009, Obama announced plans for a major troop escalation, sending 33,000 more troops to Afghanistan, paralleled by talk of a "draw-down" of combat troops over five years or more.

With more than 100,000 US and about 40,000 more NATO troops occupying the country, counterinsurgency characterized the Afghan war for the next eighteen months or so. To few people's surprise, it didn't work very well. In June 2009, the *New York Times* reported that

> The commander of a secretive branch of America's Special Operations forces last month ordered a halt to most commando missions in Afghanistan, reflecting a growing concern that civilian deaths caused by American firepower are jeopardizing broader goals there. The halt, which lasted about two weeks, came after a series of nighttime raids by Special Operations troops in recent months killed women and children, and after months of mounting outrage in Afghanistan about civilians killed in air and ground strikes. The order covered all commando missions except those against the highest-ranking leaders of the Taliban and Al Qaeda, military officials said.
>
> American commanders in Afghanistan rely on the commando units to carry out some of the most delicate operations against militant leaders, and the missions of the Army's Delta Force and classified Navy Seals units are never publicly acknowledged. But the units sometimes carry out dozens of operations

each week, so any decision to halt their missions is a sign of just how worried military officials are that the fallout from civilian casualties is putting in peril the overall American mission in Afghanistan, including an effort to drain the Taliban of popular support.[4]

The raids began again after the temporary halt, but that evidence of counterinsurgency goals failing because of continuing counterterrorism tactics, so early in the Obama presidency, presaged even greater problems ahead. The combination approach—a counterinsurgency strategy with escalating counterterrorism attacks—continued until June 2011, when President Obama announced plans for withdrawal. Ten thousand of the 33,000 "surge" troops would be out by the end of that year, he said, with the remaining 23,000 gone by summer 2012. From then on, with about 60,000 US and 27,000 NATO troops remaining at least through the fall of 2013, dropping to about 30,000 by summer 2014, the myth of a broadly defined counterinsurgency strategy would continue. But the idea that the US war was really designed to shore up an Afghan government widely resented throughout the country, known equally for corruption and incompetence, with Afghan President Hamid Karzai barely on speaking terms with anyone in Washington and making regular public condemnations of US war strategy, was more legend than reality. The illusion that the US military occupation was somehow building support for a legitimate national government had long since begun to evaporate.

ASSASSINATION: WEAPON OF CHOICE

The reality behind the myth was that of continuing assassinations—via drone strikes and via special forces teams on the ground—with a concomitant rise in civilian deaths. US troops were coming home, however slowly, with many facing serious mental as well as physical injury. US military deaths were low, but Afghan casualties continued to rise. During the Bush years, when Afghanistan was kept in a distant second place to the priorities of the Iraq war, US policy in Afghanistan had included assassination. But it was during the Obama years that the assassination in US war strategy became the tactic of choice.

In a *New York Times* article entitled "Targeted Killing Comes to Define War on Terror," the *Times* almost casually described how "though no official will publicly acknowledge it, the bottom line is clear: killing is more convenient than capture for both the United States and the foreign countries where the strikes occur."[5] The *Times* was referring particularly to drone strikes—but the same could be said about assassinations carried out by US special forces or by the specialized killing teams they train.

Killing is not only "more convenient;" it's also, in certain ways, cheaper. In terms of hard cash, it costs less to assassinate a suspect and be done with it, than it might cost for the evacuations, surgery, years of health care, and insurance for any US soldier injured in an arrest operation. It costs a lot less to train soldiers to fire drones or missiles or to kick in a door and shoot everyone in sight, than it would to train soldiers to speak local languages, to understand local cultures, and to put the protection of local civilians *ahead* of their own safety. Afghanistan, for example, remains the centerpiece of the Obama administration's global war on terror. But despite the hundreds of billions of tax-payer dollars spent and the tens of thousands of troops who rotated through during the years of US occupation, money and expertise were both insufficient to have carried out anything close to a real national counterinsurgency campaign. It would have taken hundreds of thousands of troops and hundreds of billions of dollars more. And it bears noting that it still wouldn't have worked, not least because Afghanistan (unlike Iraq) doesn't have a history of strong central government on which to build. The impertinent labeling of Afghan President Karzai as the "mayor of Kabul" resulted not only from his own failings and inability to govern, but from the reality that most Afghans historically have been affected by and identified first with their extended family and village, then somewhat the region, and only a little bit, if at all, with what's going on in their nation's capital.

In terms of political costs, while drone strikes and, to a lesser extent, assassination in general are starting to engender more opposition in the US public discourse, the consequences of arresting potential suspects complicate what is already a much greater political challenge facing the Obama administration—the continuing existence of Guantánamo and its 149 illegally held prisoners. The growing movement to oppose drone strikes becomes particularly important when we look at the current public opinion in the United States. In March 2013, a Gallup poll found 65 percent support for drone strikes to kill "suspected foreign terrorists," with only 28 percent opposed. Reporting that poll, the *New York Times* asserted that "if Americans died trying to catch a midlevel militant—when drones were available but went unused—there would be a huge public outcry, most officials believe."[6]

On May 23, 2013, President Obama gave a much-anticipated speech on drones, assassination policy, Guantánamo, and the global war on terror. He raised some of the critical issues that the administration had previously refused to talk about, and tacitly acknowledged some of the key criticisms—that the endless borderless limitless "global war on terror" would in fact have to end. The president quoted James Madison, saying, "No nation could preserve its freedom in the midst of continual warfare." And he admitted that US counterterrorism strategy had indeed resulted in civilian casualties, that "any US military action in foreign lands risks creating more enemies" and that "those deaths will haunt us." He even conceded that the United States has to address "the underlying grievances and conflicts that feed extremism—from North Africa to South Asia" because "force alone cannot make us safe."[7]

That was all good. The problem, though, as is so often the case, is that the strong statements of principle collapsed into weak and uncertain policy proposals. His principles never actually set the terms of a new policy qualitatively different from his existing strategy.

President Obama described what he would like to do, what he would like his legacy to be—close Guantánamo, prefer capture to killing suspected insurgents, kill fewer civilians, limit excessive executive power—while never actually committing himself to specific actions to accomplish any of those goals. He spoke of lifting the moratorium he imposed on allowing Guantánamo's Yemeni prisoners already cleared for release to return home—but only to review them (again!) on a case-by-case basis. And he mentioned nothing about the other thirty prisoners also cleared for release. He also never acknowledged the dramatic prisoner hunger strike still under way at Guantánamo as he spoke—with his silence making unmistakably clear that the brutal force-feeding of hunger strikers would continue.

The president said he wants to capture more and kill fewer "terrorists." But there was no indication that as commander-in-chief he would be prepared either to end the war immediately or to order troops into harm's way to avoid killing either targets or the large numbers of civilian "collateral damage." His speech never mentioned the Tuesday morning White House meetings where new names are added to the "kill list."

President Obama was apparently ruminating about the eventual need to repeal the Authorization for the Use of Military Force (AUMF), but there was no indication of a plan to actually bring a real proposal to Congress to repeal the AUMF or to limit in any way the vast expansion of executive power he has taken advantage of since taking office. The AUMF was passed three days after the 9/11 attacks, authorizing the use of force against those who committed those attacks (al-Qaeda) or harbored them (the Taliban). It was used to justify Bush's invasion of Afghanistan and efforts to kill al-Qaeda leaders, but also to legitimize actions far beyond its original definition—everything from the Iraq war to the drone war to the entire "global war on terror."

Obama referred in his speech to a new Presidential Policy Guidance setting out new—or maybe not so new—rules for drone strikes, assassinations, killing those on the kill list, and more. But the actual content of the policy guidance remained classified. The usual frustration with Obama speeches remained—they identify great goals, but the president's insistence on bipartisan support, and his refusal to really fight for his goals, have rendered those goals moot.

As the *New York Times* described the speech:

> Even as he set new standards, a debate broke out about what they actually meant and what would actually change. For now, officials said, "signature strikes" targeting groups of unidentified armed men presumed to be extremists will continue in the Pakistani tribal areas. Even as he talked about transparency, he never uttered the word "C.I.A." or acknowledged he was redefining its role. He

made no mention that a drone strike had killed an American teenager in error. While he pledged again to close the Guantánamo prison, he offered little reason to think he might be more successful this time.[8]

Ultimately, President Obama's speech demonstrated his intention to amend, to reform, and to narrow his failing war on terror, with all the drone strikes, assassinations, and illegal detentions inherent in it, but not to end it. The rising US debate on drones (though only to a small degree on the broader question of assassination-as-US policy) reflects increasing strategic cautions among military and political elites as well as growing public outrage. The elite unease stems largely from the concern that the drone strikes and assassinations are creating so much antagonism in the countries involved that their "value" to the war on terror is lost. There is no question that the political cost of drone strikes and assassinations is very high. Maintaining good relations with governments is inordinately difficult when unaccountable US drone or missile attacks are launched at targets the CIA or Pentagon identifies as "terrorist threats," but which may not be viewed as such by the Afghan, Pakistani, Yemeni, Somali, or other governments. Those governments face escalating domestic pressures resulting from their decisions to allow, stand silent, or, in the case of Yemen, quietly approve such strikes.

It should hardly be surprising that, as a *New York Times* sub-head describes it, the "CIA Air War in Pakistan Began With Quid Pro Quo Killing of Rebel." The reference was to the CIA's agreement to kill Nek Muhammad, using a Predator drone, at the request of the Pakistani government. Muhammad wasn't an enemy of the United States—he wasn't an al-Qaeda leader or even a member. He was, allegedly, an ally of the Pakistani Taliban whom the Pakistani government wanted dead. As the *Times* described it, "[I]n a secret deal, the C.I.A. had agreed to kill him in exchange for access to airspace it had long sought so it could use drones to hunt down its own enemies."[9]

MILITARIZING FOREIGN POLICY

The centrality of assassination in US war strategy is also a consequence of the broader militarization of foreign policy. With declining economic and political spending on diplomacy, the State Department's budget—and arguably, influence— declining, the Pentagon and more recently the CIA have taken on more and more of the work once assigned to the foreign service. The State Department oversees (officially, at least) the military contractors it hires and pays in war zones. But no one even claims that State has any oversight or control of any of the Pentagon, CIA, and private military contractor-run assassination teams that have become the central actors in US foreign policy in crucial arenas around the world.

In a respectful but cautious analysis of the military's Special Operations Command and its chief, Admiral William McRaven, the *Washington Post*'s David Ignatius described the broadening role for special forces:

To fight the small wars, McRaven offers his agile, stealthy and highly lethal network of commandoes. Often their missions will involve training and partnering with other nations, rather than shooting. Sometimes, their activities may look like USAID development assistance or CIA political action.

McRaven's global network would help fill a vacuum in US foreign policy. As America retreats from its costly and unpopular wars, it needs ways to influence a world shaken by what former national security adviser Zbigniew Brzezinski calls the "global political awakening."[10]

But what those "highly lethal" commandoes actually do is remembered around the world far more in the context of assassination than partnering. Even Ignatius had to acknowledge that:

> The idea of filling the power gap with special forces is appealing, but I come away with this caution: The world is wary of forward-deployed U.S. commandoes, no matter how important the mission. A decade ago, a Pentagon plan to spread special forces abroad as 'military liaison elements' created a firestorm of protest. McRaven may promise that his network won't act anywhere without the approval of the U.S. ambassador, but the State Department will still have the jitters, not to mention foreign governments.[11]

The problem now is that State Department jitters, let alone those of foreign governments whose own sovereignty is at stake, are hardly likely to result in real opposition.

Maintaining assassination as a central component of US military strategy has already created a host of problems—moral, political, legal, and strategic. Legally, there is no justification in international law for killing anyone away from the battlefield who is not engaged in hostile action. President Obama defended lethal drone killings by saying they would

> have to be a target that is authorized by our laws. It has to be a threat that is serious and not speculative. It has to be a situation in which we can't capture the individual before they move forward on some sort of operational plot against the United States.

The problem, of course, is that far too many of the assassinations and other drone attacks killing targeted individuals, as well as civilians, *have* been speculative, *have* been in a situation where capture is possible even if there is a risk to soldiers, and had no connection to any "operational plot against the United States." And most important, even if a target is "authorized by our laws," such killings are prohibited by international law.[12] The reality is that the US assassinations are the actions of a rogue state.

President Obama, in September 2012, talked with CNN about lethal drone attacks, but his words apply to broader US reliance on assassination as well. He described it as "something you have to struggle with. . . . If you don't, then it's very easy to slip into a situation in which you end up bending rules thinking that the ends always justify the means, . . . That's not been our tradition. That's not who we are as a country."[13]

But President Obama was wrong. Bending rules, including ignoring international law, and operating on a "might makes right" assumption that the ends justify the means, including with the use of assassination as a policy of war, has exactly been our tradition. As much as ever, under President Obama, it is exactly who we are as a country.

NOTES

[1] Thom Shanker, *Special Operations Step Up in Afghanistan*, N.Y. Times, May 15, 2013, at A4.

[2] Jeremy Scahill, *JSOC: The Black Ops Force That Took Down Bin Laden*, The Nation (May 2, 2011), www.thenation.com/blog/160332/jsoc-black-ops-force-took-down-bin-laden#; *See also* Jeremy Scahill, Dirty Wars: The World is a Battlefield (Nation Books 2013).

[3] John Barry & Michael Hirsh, *The Salvador Option*, Newsweek (January 7, 2005), www.thedailybeast.com/newsweek/2005/01/07/the-salvador-option.html.

[4] Mark Mazzetti & Eric Schmitt, *U.S. Halted Some Raids in Afghanistan*, N.Y. Times (March 9, 2009), www.nytimes.com/2009/03/10/world/asia/10terror.html.

[5] Scott Shane, *Targeted Killing Comes to Define War on Terror*, N.Y. Times, April 8, 2013, at A1.

[6] *Id.*

[7] Barack Obama, President, United States, Remarks by the President at the National Defense University (May 23, 2013) (transcript available at www.whitehouse.gov/the-press-office/2013/05/23/remarks-president-national-defense-university).

[8] Peter Baker, *In Terror Shift, Obama Took a Long Path*, N.Y. Times (May 27, 2013), www.nytimes.com/2013/05/28/us/politics/in-terror-shift-obama-took-a-long-path.html?pagewanted=all&_r=0.

[9] Mark Mazzetti, *A Secret Deal on Drones, Sealed in Blood*, N.Y. Times, April 7, 2013, at A1.

[10] David Ignatius, *Drawing Down, but Still Projecting Power*, Wash. Post (March 29, 2013), articles.washingtonpost.com/2013-03-29/opinions/38124062_1_small-wars-usaid-global-network.

[11] *Id.*

[12] *See Mirer* chapter 8.

[13] CNN Wire Staff, *Drone Strikes Kill, Maim and Traumatize Too Many Civilians, U.S. study says*, CNN (September 25, 2012), www.cnn.com/2012/09/25/world/asia/pakistan-us-drone-strikes (internal quotation marks omitted).

4

THE PREDATOR WAR

Jane Mayer

On August 5th, 2009, officials at the Central Intelligence Agency, in Langley, Virginia, watched a live video feed relaying close-up footage of one of the most wanted terrorists in Pakistan. Baitullah Mehsud, the leader of the Taliban in Pakistan, could be seen reclining on the rooftop of his father-in-law's house, in Zanghara, a hamlet in South Waziristan. It was a hot summer night, and he was joined outside by his wife and his uncle, a medic; at one point, the remarkably crisp images showed that Mehsud, who suffered from diabetes and a kidney ailment, was receiving an intravenous drip.

The video was being captured by the infrared camera of a Predator drone, a remotely controlled, unmanned plane that had been hovering, undetected, two miles or so above the house. Pakistan's interior minister, A. Rehman Malik, told me that Mehsud was resting on his back. Malik, using his hands to make a picture frame, explained that the Predator's targeters could see Mehsud's entire body, not just the top of his head. "It was a perfect picture," Malik, who watched the videotape later, said. "We used to see James Bond movies where he talked into his shoe or his watch. We thought it was a fairy tale. But this was fact!" The image remained just as stable when the CIA remotely launched two Hellfire missiles from the Predator. Authorities watched the fiery blast in real time. After the dust cloud dissipated, all that remained of Mehsud was a detached torso. Eleven others died: his wife, his father-in-law, his mother-in-law, a lieutenant, and seven bodyguards.

Pakistan's government considered Mehsud its top enemy, holding him responsible for the vast majority of recent terrorist attacks inside the country, including the assassination of former prime minister Benazir Bhutto, in December, 2007, and the bombing, in September 2009, of the Marriott Hotel in Islamabad, which killed more than fifty people. Mehsud was also thought to have helped his Afghan confederates attack American and coalition troops across the border. Roger Cressey, a former counterterrorism official on the National Security Council, who is now a partner at Good Harbor, a consulting firm, told me, "Mehsud was someone both we and Pakistan were happy to see go up in smoke." Indeed, there was no controversy when, a few days after the missile strike, CNN reported that President Barack Obama had authorized it.

However, at about the same time, there was widespread anger after the *Wall Street Journal* revealed that during the Bush administration the CIA had considered setting up hit squads to capture or kill al-Qaeda operatives around the world. The furor grew when the *New York Times* reported that the CIA had turned to a private contractor to help with this highly sensitive operation: the controversial firm Blackwater, now known as Academi. Members of the Senate and House intelligence committees demanded investigations of the program, which, they said, had been hidden from them. And many legal experts argued that, had the program become fully operational, it would have violated a 1976 executive order, signed by President Gerald R. Ford, banning American intelligence forces from engaging in assassination.

Hina Shamsi, a human rights lawyer at the New York University School of Law, was struck by the inconsistency of the public's responses. "We got so upset about a targeted-killing program that didn't happen," she told me. "But the drone program *exists*." She said of the Predator program, "These are targeted international killings by the state." The program, as it happens, also uses private contractors for a variety of tasks, including flying the drones. Employees of Academi maintain and load the Hellfire missiles on the aircraft. Vicki Divoll, a former CIA lawyer, who now teaches at the US Naval Academy, in Annapolis, observed, "People are a lot more comfortable with a Predator strike that kills many people than with a throat-slitting that kills one." But, she added, "mechanized killing is still killing."

The US government runs two drone programs. The military's version, which is publicly acknowledged, operates in the recognized war zones of Afghanistan and Iraq, and targets enemies of US troops stationed there. As such, it is an extension of conventional warfare. The CIA's program is aimed at terror suspects around the world, including in countries where US troops are not based. It was initiated by the Bush administration and, according to Juan Zarate, a counterterrorism adviser in the Bush White House, Obama has left in place virtually all the key personnel. The program is classified as covert, and the intelligence agency declines to provide any information to the public about where it operates, how it selects targets, who is in charge, or how many people have been killed.

Nevertheless, reports of fatal air strikes in Pakistan emerge every few days. Such stories are often secondhand and difficult to confirm, as the Pakistani government and the military have tried to wall off the tribal areas from journalists. But, even if a precise account is elusive, the outlines are clear: the CIA has joined the Pakistani intelligence service in an aggressive campaign to eradicate local and foreign militants, who have taken refuge in some of the most inaccessible parts of the country.

The first two CIA air strikes of the Obama Administration took place on the morning of January 23, 2009—the president's third day in office. Within hours, it was clear that the morning's bombings in Pakistan had killed an estimated twenty people. In one strike, four Arabs, all likely affiliated with al-Qaeda, died.

But in the second strike a drone targeted the wrong house, hitting the residence of a pro-government tribal leader six miles outside the town of Wana, in South Waziristan. The blast killed the tribal leader's entire family, including three children, one of them five years old. In keeping with US policy, there was no official acknowledgment of either strike.

Since then, the CIA bombardments have continued at a rapid pace. According to a study by the New America Foundation, the number of drone strikes has risen dramatically since Obama became president. During his first nine and a half months in office, he authorized as many CIA aerial attacks in Pakistan as George W. Bush did in his final three years in office. The study's authors, Peter Bergen and Katherine Tiedemann, report that the Obama administration sanctioned at least forty-one CIA missile strikes in Pakistan in the first nine months of his first term—a rate of approximately one bombing a week. By October 2009, various estimates suggest, the CIA attacks have killed between 326 and 538 people. Critics say that many of the victims have been innocent bystanders, including children.

In the last week of September 2009 alone, there were reportedly four such attacks—three of them in one twenty-four-hour period. At any given moment, a former White House counterterrorism official says, the CIA has multiple drones flying over Pakistan, scouting for targets. According to the official, "there are so many drones" in the air that arguments have erupted over which remote operators can claim which targets, provoking "command-and-control issues."

General Atomics Aeronautical Systems, the defense contractor that manufactures the Predator and its more heavily armed sibling, the Reaper, can barely keep up with the government's demand. The Air Force's fleet grew from some 50 drones in 2001 to nearly 200 in 2009; the CIA will not divulge how many drones it operates. The government plans to commission hundreds more, including new generations of tiny "nano" drones, which can fly after their prey like a killer bee through an open window.

With public disenchantment mounting over the US troop deployment in Afghanistan, and the Obama Administration divided over whether to escalate the American military presence there, many in Washington support an even greater reliance on Predator strikes. In this view, the US, rather than trying to stabilize Afghanistan by waging a counterinsurgency operation against Taliban forces, should focus purely on counterterrorism, and use the latest technology to surgically eliminate al-Qaeda leaders and their allies. In September 2009, the conservative pundit George Will published an influential column in the *Washington Post*, "Time to Get Out of Afghanistan," arguing that "America should do only what can be done from offshore, using intelligence, drones, cruise missiles, air strikes and small, potent Special Forces units, concentrating on the porous 1,500-mile border with Pakistan, a nation that actually matters." Vice President Joseph Biden reportedly holds a similar view.

It's easy to understand the appeal of a "push-button" approach to fighting al-Qaeda, but the embrace of the Predator program has occurred with remarkably little public discussion, given that it represents a radically new and geographically unbounded use of state-sanctioned lethal force. And, because of the CIA program's secrecy, there is no visible system of accountability in place, despite the fact that the agency has killed many civilians inside a politically fragile, nuclear-armed country with which the US is not at war. Should something go wrong in the CIA's program—in September 2009, the Air Force lost control of a drone and had to shoot it down over Afghanistan—it's unclear what the consequences would be.

The Predators in the CIA program are "flown" by civilians, both intelligence officers and private contractors. According to a former counterterrorism official, the contractors are "seasoned professionals—often retired military and intelligence officials." (The intelligence agency outsources a significant portion of its work.) Within the CIA, control of the unmanned vehicles is split among several teams. One set of pilots and operators works abroad, near hidden airfields in Afghanistan and Pakistan, handling takeoffs and landings. Once the drones are aloft, the former counterterrorism official said, the controls are electronically "slewed over" to a set of "reachback operators," in Langley. Using joysticks that resemble video-game controls, the reachback operators—who don't need conventional flight training—sit next to intelligence officers and watch, on large flat-screen monitors, a live video feed from the drone's camera. From their suburban redoubt, they can turn the plane, zoom in on the landscape below, and decide whether to lock onto a target. A stream of additional "signal" intelligence, sent to Langley by the National Security Agency, provides electronic means of corroborating that a target has been correctly identified. The White House has delegated trigger authority to CIA officials, including the head of the Counter-Terrorist Center, whose identity remains veiled from the public because the agency has placed him under cover.

People who have seen an air strike live on a monitor described it as both awe-inspiring and horrifying. "You could see these little figures scurrying, and the explosion going off, and when the smoke cleared there was just rubble and charred stuff," a former CIA officer who was based in Afghanistan after September 11th says of one attack. (He watched the carnage on a small monitor in the field.) Human beings running for cover are such a common sight that they have inspired a slang term: "squirters."

Peter W. Singer, the author of *Wired for War*, a book about the robotics revolution in modern combat, argues that the drone technology is worryingly "seductive," because it creates the perception that war can be "costless." Cut off from the realities of the bombings in Pakistan, Americans have been insulated from the human toll, as well as from the political and the moral consequences. Nearly all the victims have remained faceless, and the damage caused by the bombings has remained unseen. In contrast to Gaza, where the targeted killing of Hamas fighters by the Israeli military has been extensively documented—making clear that the collateral damage, and the loss of civilian life, can be severe—Pakistan's tribal areas have become largely forbidden territory for media organizations. As a result, no videos of a drone attack in progress have been released, and only a few photographs of the immediate aftermath of a Predator strike have been published.

The seeming unreality of the Predator enterprise is also felt by the pilots. Some of them reportedly wear flight suits when they operate a drone's remote controls. When their shifts end, of course, these cubicle warriors can drive home to have dinner with their families. Critics have suggested that unmanned systems, by sparing these combatants from danger and sacrifice, are creating what Sir Brian Burridge, a former British Air Chief Marshal in Iraq, has called "a virtueless war," requiring neither courage nor heroism. According to Singer, some Predator pilots suffer from combat stress that equals, or exceeds, that of pilots in the battlefield. This suggests that virtual killing, for all its sterile trappings, is a discomfiting form of warfare. Meanwhile, some social critics, such as Mary Dudziak, a professor at the University of Southern California's Gould School of Law, argue that the Predator strategy has a larger political cost. As she puts it, "Drones are a technological step that further isolates the American people from military action, undermining political checks on . . . endless war."

The advent of the Predator targeted-killing program "is really a sea change," says Gary Solis, who teaches at Georgetown University's Law Center and retired from running the law program at the US Military Academy. "Not only would we have expressed abhorrence of such a policy a few years ago; we did." In July, 2001, two months before al-Qaeda's attacks on New York and Washington profoundly altered America's mind-set, the US denounced Israel's use of targeted killing against Palestinian terrorists. The American Ambassador to Israel, Martin Indyk, said at the time, "The United States government is very clearly on record as against targeted assassinations. . . . They are extrajudicial killings, and we do not support that."

Before September 11th, the CIA, which had been chastened by past assassination scandals, refused to deploy the Predator for anything other than surveillance. Daniel Benjamin, the State Department's counterterrorism director, and Steven Simon, a former counterterrorism adviser, report in their 2002 book, *The Age of Sacred Terror,* that the week before al-Qaeda attacked the US, George Tenet, then the agency's director, argued that it would be "a terrible mistake" for "the Director of Central Intelligence to fire a weapon like this."

Yet once America had suffered terrorist attacks on its own soil the agency's posture changed, and it petitioned the White House for new authority. Within days, President Bush had signed a secret Memorandum of Notification, giving the CIA the right to kill members of al-Qaeda and their confederates virtually anywhere in the world. Congress endorsed this policy, passing a bill called the Authorization for Use of Military Force. Bush's legal advisers modeled their rationale on Israel's position against terrorism, arguing that the US government had the right to use lethal force against suspected terrorists in "anticipatory" self-defense. By classifying terrorism as an act of war, rather than as a crime, the Bush Administration reasoned that it was no longer bound by legal constraints requiring the government to give suspected terrorists due process.

In November, 2002, top Bush administration officials publicly announced a successful Predator strike against an al-Qaeda target, Qaed Salim Sinan al-Harethi, a suspect in the 2000 bombing of the U.S.S. Cole. Harethi was killed after a Hellfire missile vaporized the car in which he and five other passengers were riding, on a desert road in Yemen. Paul Wolfowitz, then the Deputy Defense Secretary, praised the new tactic, telling CNN, "One hopes each time that you get a success like that, not only to have gotten rid of somebody dangerous but to have imposed changes in their tactics, operations, and procedures."

At first, some intelligence experts were uneasy about drone attacks. In 2002, Jeffrey Smith, a former CIA general counsel, told Seymour M. Hersh, for an article in *The New Yorker*, "If they're dead, they're not talking to you, and you create more martyrs." And, in an interview with the *Washington Post*, Smith said that ongoing drone attacks could "suggest that it's acceptable behavior to assassinate people. . . . Assassination as a norm of international conduct exposes American leaders and Americans overseas."

Twelve years later, there is no longer any doubt that targeted killing has become official US policy. "The things we were complaining about from Israel a few years ago we now embrace," Solis says. Now, he notes, nobody in the government calls it assassination.

The Predator program is described by many in the intelligence world as America's single most effective weapon against al-Qaeda. In May 2009, Leon Panetta, then CIA director, referred to the Predator program as "the only game in town" in an unguarded moment after a public lecture. Counterterrorism officials credit drones with having killed more than a dozen senior al-Qaeda leaders and their allies in 2009, eliminating more than half of the CIA's twenty most wanted "high-value" targets. In addition to Baitullah Mehsud, the list includes Nazimuddin Zalalov, a former lieutenant of Osama bin Laden; Ilyas Kashmiri, al-Qaeda's chief of paramilitary operations in Pakistan; Saad bin Laden, Osama's eldest son; Abu Sulayman al-Jazairi, an Algerian al-Qaeda planner who is believed to have helped train operatives for attacks in Europe and the United States; and Osama al-Kini and Sheikh Ahmed Salim Swedan, al-Qaeda operatives who are thought to have played central roles in the 1998 bombings of American embassies in East Africa.

Juan Zarate, the Bush counterterrorism adviser, believes that "[al-Qaeda] is on its heels" partly because "so many bigwigs" have been killed by drones. Though he acknowledged that Osama bin Laden and Ayman al-Zawahiri, the group's top leaders, remained at large, he estimated in 2009 that no more than fifty members of al-Qaeda's senior leadership still exist, along with two to three hundred senior members outside the terror organization's "inner core."

Zarate and other supporters of the Predator program argue that it has had positive ripple effects. Surviving militants are forced to operate far more cautiously, which diverts their energy from planning new attacks. And there is evidence that the drone strikes, which depend on local informants for targeting information, have caused debilitating suspicion and discord within the ranks. Four Europeans who were captured in December 2008 after trying to join al-Qaeda in Pakistan described a life of constant fear and distrust among the militants, whose obsession with drone strikes had led them to communicate only with elaborate secrecy and to leave their squalid hideouts only at night. As the *Times* has reported, militants have been so unnerved by the drone program that they have released a video showing the execution of accused informants. Pakistanis have also been gripped by rumors that paid CIA informants have been planting tiny silicon-chip homing devices for the drones in the tribal areas.

The drone program, for all its tactical successes, has stirred deep ethical concerns. Michael Walzer, a political philosopher and the author of the book *Just and Unjust Wars*, says that he is unsettled by the notion of an intelligence agency wielding such lethal power in secret. "Under what code does the CIA operate?" he asks. "I don't know. The military operates under a legal code, and it has judicial mechanisms." He said of the CIA's drone program, "There should be a limited, finite group of people who are targets, and that list should be publicly defensible and available. Instead, it's not being publicly defended. People are being killed, and we generally require some public justification when we go about killing people."

Since 2004, Philip Alston, an Australian human rights lawyer who has served as the United Nations Special Rapporteur on extrajudicial, summary or arbitrary executions, has repeatedly tried, but failed, to get a response to basic questions about the CIA's program—first from the Bush administration, and now from Obama's. When he asked, in formal correspondence, for the CIA's legal justifications for targeted killings, he says, "they blew me off." (A CIA spokesperson told me that the agency "uses lawful, highly accurate, and effective tools and tactics to take the fight to al-Qaeda and its violent allies. That careful, precise approach has brought major success against a very dangerous and deadly enemy.") Alston then presented a critical report on the drone program to the UN Human Rights Council, but, he says, the US representatives ignored his concerns.

Alston describes the CIA program as operating in "an accountability void," adding, "It's a lot like the torture issue. You start by saying we'll just go after the handful of 9/11 masterminds. But, once you've put the regimen for waterboarding and other techniques in place, you use it much more indiscriminately. It becomes standard operating procedure. It becomes all too easy. Planners start saying, 'Let's use drones in a broader context.' Once you use targeting less stringently, it can become indiscriminate."

Under international law, in order for the US government to legally target civilian terror suspects abroad it has to define a terrorist group as one engaging in armed conflict, and the use of force must be a "military necessity." There must be no reasonable alternative to killing, such as capture, and to warrant death the target must be "directly participating in hostilities." The use of force has to be considered "proportionate" to the threat. Finally, the foreign nation in which such targeted killing takes place has to give its permission.

Some lawyers who have looked at America's drone program in Pakistan believe that it meets these basic legal tests. But they are nevertheless troubled, as the US government keeps broadening the definition of acceptable high-value targets. In March 2008, the Obama administration made an unannounced decision to win support for the drone program inside Pakistan by giving President Asif Ali Zardari more control over whom to target. "A lot of the targets are nominated by the Pakistanis—it's part of the bargain of getting Pakistani cooperation," says Bruce Riedel, a former CIA officer who has served as an adviser to the Obama administration on Afghanistan and Pakistan. According to the New America Foundation's study, only six of the forty-one CIA drone strikes conducted by the Obama administration in Pakistan have targeted al-Qaeda members. Eighteen were directed at Taliban targets in Pakistan, and fifteen were aimed specifically at Baitullah Mehsud. Talat Masood, a retired Pakistani lieutenant general and an authority on security issues, says that the US's tactical shift, along with the elimination of Mehsud, quieted some of the Pakistani criticism of the American air strikes, although the bombings are still seen as undercutting the country's sovereignty. But, given that many of the targeted Pakistani Taliban figures were obscure in US counterterrorism circles, some critics have wondered whether they were legitimate targets for a Predator strike. "These strikes are killing a lot of low-level militants, which raises the question of whether they are going beyond the authorization to kill leaders," Peter Bergen told me. Roger Cressey, the former National Security Council official, who remains a strong supporter of the drone program, says, "The debate is that we've been doing this so long we're now bombing low-level guys who don't deserve a Hellfire missile up their ass." (In his view, "Not every target has to be a rock star.")

The Obama administration has also widened the scope of authorized drone attacks in Afghanistan. An August 2009 report by the Senate Foreign Relations Committee disclosed that the Joint Integrated Prioritized Target List—the Pentagon's roster of approved terrorist targets, containing 367 in 2009—was expanded to include some 50 Afghan drug lords who were suspected of giving money to help finance the Taliban. These targets are a step removed from al-Qaeda. According to the Senate report, "There is no evidence that any significant amount of the drug proceeds goes to al-Qaeda." The inclusion of Afghan narcotics traffickers on the US target list could prove awkward, some observers say, given that President Hamid Karzai's running mate, Marshal Mohammad Qasim Fahim, and the president's brother, Ahmed Wali Karzai, are strongly suspected of involvement in narcotics. Andrew Bacevich, a professor of history and international relations at Boston University, who has written extensively on military matters, said, "Are they going to target Karzai's brother?" He went on, "We should be very careful about who we define as the enemy we have to kill. Leaders of al-Qaeda, of course. But you can't kill people on Tuesday and negotiate with them on Wednesday."

Defining who is and who is not too tangential for the US to kill can be difficult. John Radsan, a former lawyer in the CIA's office of general counsel, who is now a professor at William Mitchell College of Law, in St. Paul, Minnesota, says, "You can't target someone just because he visited an al-Qaeda website. But you also don't want to wait until they're about to detonate a bomb. It's a sliding scale." Equally fraught is the question of how many civilian deaths can be justified. "If it's Osama bin Laden in a house with a four-year-old, most people will say go ahead," Radsan says. "But if it's three or four children? Some say that's too many. And if he's in a school? Many say don't do it." Such judgment calls are being made daily by the CIA, which, Radsan points out, "doesn't have much experience with killing. Traditionally, the agency that does that is the Department of Defense."

Though the CIA's methodology remains unknown, the Pentagon has created elaborate formulas to help the military make such lethal calculations. A top military expert, who declined to be named, spoke of the military's system, saying, "There's a whole taxonomy of targets." Some people are approved for killing on sight. For others, additional permission is needed. A target's location enters the equation, too. If a school, hospital, or mosque is within the likely blast radius of a missile, that, too, is weighed by a computer algorithm before a lethal strike is authorized. According to a 2009 Senate Foreign Relations Committee report, the US military places no name on its targeting list until there are "two verifiable human sources" and "substantial additional evidence" that the person is an enemy.

In Israel, which conducts unmanned air strikes in the Palestinian territories, the process of identifying targets, in theory at least, is even more exacting. Military lawyers have to be convinced that the target can't reasonably be captured, and that he poses a threat to national security. Military specialists in Arab culture also have to be convinced that the hit will do more good than harm. "You have to be incredibly cautious," Amos Guiora, a law professor at the University of Utah, says. From 1994 to 1997, he advised Israeli commanders on targeted killings in the Gaza Strip. "Not everyone is at the level appropriate for targeted killing," he says.

"You want a leader, the hub with many spokes." Guiora, who follows the Predator program closely, fears that national-security officials here lack a clear policy and a firm definition of success. "Once you start targeted killing, you better make damn sure there's a policy guiding it," he says. "It can't be just catch-as-catch-can."

Daniel Byman, the director of Georgetown University's Center for Peace and Security Studies, argues that, when possible, "it's almost always better to arrest terrorists than to kill them. You get intelligence then. Dead men tell no tales." The CIA's killing of Saad bin Laden, Osama's son, provides a case in point. By the time that Saad bin Laden had reached Pakistan's tribal areas, in 2008, there was little chance that any law-enforcement authority could capture him alive. But, according to Hillary Mann Leverett, an adviser to the National Security Council between 2001 and 2003, the Bush administration would have had several opportunities to interrogate Saad bin Laden earlier, if it had been willing to make a deal with Iran, where, according to US intelligence, he lived occasionally after September 11th. "The Iranians offered to work out an international framework for transferring terror suspects, but the Bush administration refused," she said. In December, 2008, Saad bin Laden left Iran for Pakistan; within months, according to NPR, a Predator missile had ended his life. "We absolutely did not get the most we could," Leverett said. "Saad bin Laden would have been very, very valuable in terms of what he knew. He probably would have been a gold mine."

Byman wrote a book about Israel's experiences with counterterrorism, including targeted killing. Though the strikes there have weakened the Palestinian leadership, he said, "if you use these tools wrong, you can lose the moral high ground, which is going to hurt you. Inevitably, some of the intelligence is going to be wrong, so you're always rolling the dice. That's the reality of real-time intelligence."

Indeed, the history of targeted killing is marked by errors. In 1973, for example, Israeli intelligence agents murdered a Moroccan waiter by mistake. They thought that he was a terrorist who had been involved in slaughtering Israeli athletes at the Munich Olympics a year earlier. And in 1986, the Reagan administration attempted to retaliate against the Libyan leader Muammar el-Qaddafi for his suspected role in the deadly bombing of a disco frequented by American servicemen in Germany. The US launched an air strike on Qaddafi's household. The bombs missed him, but they did kill his fifteen-month-old daughter.

The CIA's early attempts at targeting Osama bin Laden were also problematic. After al-Qaeda blew up the US Embassies in Tanzania and Kenya in August 1998, President Bill Clinton retaliated by launching seventy-five Tomahawk cruise missiles at a site in Afghanistan where bin Laden was expected to attend a summit meeting. According to reports, the bombardment killed some twenty Pakistani militants, but missed bin Laden, who had left the scene hours earlier.

The development of the Predator, in the early nineteen nineties, was supposed to help eliminate such mistakes. The drones can hover above a target for up to forty hours before refueling, and the precise video footage makes it much easier to identify targets. But the strikes are only as accurate as the intelligence that goes into them. Tips from informants on the ground are subject to error, as is the interpretation of video images. Not long before September 11, 2001, for instance, several US counterterrorism officials became certain that a drone had captured footage of bin Laden in a locale he was known to frequent in Afghanistan. The video showed a tall man in robes, surrounded by armed bodyguards in a diamond formation. At that point, drones were unarmed and were used only for surveillance. "The optics were not great, but it was him," Henry Crumpton, then the CIA's top covert-operations officer for the region, told *Time* magazine. But two other former CIA officers, who also saw the footage, have doubts. "It's like an urban legend," one of them told me. "They just jumped to conclusions. You couldn't see his face. It could have been Joe Schmo. Believe me, no tall man with a beard is safe anywhere in Southwest Asia." In February 2002, along the mountainous eastern border of Afghanistan, a Predator reportedly followed and killed three suspicious Afghans, including a tall man in robes who was thought to be bin Laden. The victims turned out to be innocent villagers gathering scrap metal.

In Afghanistan and Pakistan, the local informants, who also serve as confirming witnesses for the air strikes, are notoriously unreliable. A former CIA officer who was based in Afghanistan after September 11th told me that an Afghan source had once sworn to him that one of al-Qaeda's top leaders was being treated in a nearby clinic. The former officer said that he could barely hold off an air strike after he passed on the tip to his superiors. "They scrambled together an elite team," he recalled. "We caught hell from headquarters. They said, 'Why aren't you moving on it?' when we insisted on checking it out first." It turned out to be an intentionally false lead. "Sometimes you're dealing with tribal chiefs," the former officer said. "Often, they say an enemy of theirs is al-Qaeda because they just want to get rid of somebody. Or they made crap up because they wanted to prove they were valuable, so that they could make money. You couldn't take their word."

The consequences of bad ground intelligence can be tragic. In September 2009, a NATO air strike in Afghanistan killed between 70 and 125 people, many of them civilians, who were taking fuel from two stranded oil trucks; they had been mistaken for Taliban insurgents. (The incident was investigated by NATO.) According to a reporter for *The Guardian*, the bomb strike, by an F-15E fighter plane, left such a tangle of body parts that village elders resorted to handing out pieces of unidentifiable corpses to the grieving families, so that they could have something to bury. One Afghan villager told the newspaper, "I took a piece of flesh with me home and I called it my son."

Predator drones, with their superior surveillance abilities, have a better track record for accuracy than fighter jets, according to intelligence officials. Also, the drone's smaller Hellfire missiles are said to cause far less collateral damage. Still, the campaign to kill Baitullah Mehsud offers a sobering case study of the hazards of robotic warfare. It appears to have taken sixteen missile strikes, and fourteen months, before the CIA succeeded in killing him. During this hunt, between 207 and 321 additional people were killed, depending on which news accounts you rely upon. It's all but impossible to get a complete picture of whom the CIA killed during this campaign, which took place largely in Waziristan. Not only has the Pakistani government closed off the region to the outside press; it has also shut out international humanitarian organizations like the International Committee of the Red Cross and Doctors Without Borders. "We can't get within a hundred kilometers of Waziristan," Brice de la Vingne, the operational coordinator for Doctors Without Borders in Pakistan, told me. "We tried to set up an emergency room, but the authorities wouldn't give us authorization."

A few Pakistani and international news stories, most of which rely on secondhand sources rather than on eyewitness accounts, offer the basic details. On June 14, 2008, a CIA drone strike on Mehsud's home town, Makeen, killed an unidentified person. On January 2, 2009, four more unidentified people were killed. On February 14, 2009, more than thirty people were killed, twenty-five of whom were apparently members of al-Qaeda and the Taliban, though none were identified as major leaders. On April 1, 2009, a drone attack on Mehsud's deputy, Hakimullah Mehsud, killed ten to twelve of his followers instead. On April 29, 2009, missiles fired from drones killed between six and ten more people, one of whom was believed to be an al-Qaeda leader. On May 9, 2009, five to ten more unidentified people were killed; on May 12, 2009, as many as eight people died. On June 14, 2009, three to eight more people were killed by drone attacks. On June 23, 2009, the CIA reportedly killed between two and six unidentified militants outside Makeen, and then killed dozens more people—possibly as many as eighty-six—during funeral prayers for the earlier casualties. An account in the Pakistani publication *The News* described ten of the dead as children. Four were identified as elderly tribal leaders. One eyewitness, who lost his right leg during the bombing, told Agence France-Presse that the mourners suspected what was coming: "After the prayers ended, people were asking each other to leave the area, as drones were hovering." The drones, which make a buzzing noise, are nicknamed *machay* ("wasps") by the Pashtun natives, and can sometimes be seen and heard, depending on weather conditions. Before the mourners could clear out, the eyewitness said, two drones started firing into the crowd. "It created havoc," he said. "There was smoke and dust everywhere. Injured people were crying and asking for help." Then a third missile hit. "I fell to the ground," he said.

The local population was clearly angered at the Pakistani government for allowing the US to target a funeral. (Intelligence had suggested that Mehsud would be among the mourners.) An editorial in *The News* denounced the strike as sinking to the level of the terrorists. The Urdu newspaper *Jang* declared that Obama was "shutting his ears to the screams of thousands of women whom your drones have turned into dust." US officials were undeterred, continuing drone strikes in the region until Mehsud was killed.

After such attacks, the Taliban, attempting to stir up anti-American sentiment in the region, routinely claimed, falsely, that the victims were all innocent civilians. In several Pakistani cities, large protests have been held to decry the drone program. And, in the past year, perpetrators of terrorist bombings in Pakistan have begun presenting their acts as "revenge for the drone attacks." In 2009, a rash of bloody assaults on Pakistani government strongholds has raised the specter that formerly unaligned militant groups have joined together against the Zardari administration.

David Kilcullen, a counterinsurgency warfare expert who advised General David Petraeus in Iraq, said that the propaganda costs of drone attacks have been disastrously high. Militants have used the drone strikes to denounce the Zardari government—a shaky and unpopular regime—as little more than an American puppet. A study that Kilcullen co-wrote for the Center for New American Security, a think tank, argues, "Every one of these dead non-combatants represents an alienated family, a new revenge feud, and more recruits for a militant movement that has grown exponentially even as drone strikes have increased." His co-writer, Andrew Exum, a former Army Ranger who has advised General Stanley McChrystal in Afghanistan, told me, "Neither Kilcullen nor I is a fundamentalist—we're not saying drones are not part of the strategy. But we are saying that right now they are part of the problem. If we use tactics that are killing people's brothers and sons, not to mention their sisters and wives, we can work at cross-purposes with ensuring that the tribal population doesn't side with the militants. Using the Predator is a tactic, not a strategy."

Exum says that he's worried by the remote-control nature of Predator warfare. "As a military person, I put myself in the shoes of someone in FATA"—Pakistan's Federally Administered Tribal Areas—"and there's something about pilotless drones that doesn't strike me as an honorable way of warfare," he said. "As a classics major, I have a classical sense of what it means to be a warrior." An Iraq combat veteran who helped design much of the military's doctrine for using unmanned drones also has qualms. He said, "There's something important about putting your own sons and daughters at risk when you choose to wage war as a nation. We risk losing that flesh-and-blood investment if we go too far down this road."

Bruce Riedel, who has been deeply involved in these debates during the past few years, sees the choices facing Obama as exceedingly hard. "Is the drone program helping or hurting?" he asked. "It's a tough question. These are not cost-free operations." He likened the drone attacks to "going after a beehive, one bee at a time." The problem is that, inevitably, "the hive will always produce more bees." But, he said, "the only pressure currently being put on Pakistan and Afghanistan is the drones." He added, "It's really all we've got to disrupt al-Qaeda. The reason the Administration continues to use it is obvious: it doesn't really have anything else."

PART II
TARGETED KILLING AND "COLLATERAL DAMAGE"

5

A GLOBAL ASSASSINATION PROGRAM

Tom Reifer[1]

> "The lifeblood of empires is blood."
> Charles Maier, *Among Empires:*
> *American Ascendancy & its Predecessors.*

INTRODUCTION

Soon after the September 11, 2001, terrorist attacks, the United States embraced a policy of targeted assassinations via so-called unmanned aerial vehicles, known as drones. Today, the Pentagon hosts a "family" of 10,000 drones, with another 10,000 commissioned. They fly at 50,000 feet in the air, in an odd mixture of robot and human, piloted by both the Pentagon, with its Joint Special Operations Command (JSOC), and the Central Intelligence Agency (CIA). The latter is increasingly a paramilitary arm of the president, though the National Security Council has some involvement in these operations.[2]

JSOC, with a budget of over $10 billion, has grown threefold since the September 11th attacks. JSOC today includes some 4,000 civilians and soldiers and has over fifty operations in a dozen or more countries around the world. JSOC launches drone strikes in Pakistan and Yemen, while the CIA carries out drone strikes in Pakistan. The newly expanded Special Operations Command (SOCOM) has some 60,000 personnel, 20,000 of them in the Special Operations Forces of the JSOC (SOF), with broad authority to conduct military operations worldwide in more than a dozen countries, including recruiting foreign paramilitaries.

Regional combatant commands, from Central to Southern Command to United States Africa Command (Africom), along with theater commanders in Afghanistan, now have authority to use personnel from SOF, including those of JSOC, for regional task forces. In 2009, JSOC was formally granted broad authority to use all military resources as needed for counterterrorist operations anywhere in the world, a capability it had been developing since 2004.

By putting such covert power in JSOC and SOF in the Pentagon rather than the CIA, the Bush and Obama administrations have largely escaped Congressional oversight. Neither administration has felt the need for Congressional notifications or presidential findings of these operations, as mandated under the 1991 Intelligence Authorization Act,[3] passed in the wake of the Iran-Contra scandal. That act exempted traditional military activities, as well as routine maneuvers, for anticipated and ongoing military operations. The Bush administration broadly interpreted this authority to include events involving SOF years before actual military forces were deployed. This included campaigns of the highly secret "Special Access Programs" (SAP)—the code names for which alone come to over 300 pages. SAPs were created by an executive order, and some are considered waived SAPs that largely escape Congressional oversight. The result has been the blurring of the roles between the Pentagon and the CIA, with the former becoming increasingly covert and the latter moving more and more into covert paramilitary operations.[4]

Today, JSOC might be considered the most important government agency that most people have never heard of. JSOC's major mission, as described by a former high-level JSOC commander, is "to track and kill terrorists, to 'mow the lawn.'"[5] The rise of the drones has occurred with funding from the Pentagon's Defense Advanced Research Projects Agency (DARPA), which also finances projects on artificial intelligence. This being said, among national security experts and human rights activists, there is an important unresolved debate about which agency would allow for greater adherence to human rights norms and related international treaty obligations, with analysts like Laura Pitter of Human Rights Watch highlighting the danger of CIA control over such operations because of its legendary secrecy and lack of transparency.[6]

THE UNDECLARED WAR IN PAKISTAN

Ben Emmerson, the Special Rapporteur on the Promotion and Protection of Human Rights and Fundamental Freedoms While Countering Terrorism, of the United Nations (UN) Commission on Human Rights, publicly called US drone attacks in Pakistan a violation of the latter's sovereignty.[7]

Emmerson pointed out that on April 12, 2012, both houses of Pakistan's parliament declared all further drone strikes illegal and demanded that they cease immediately. Both houses passed laws overturning any existing oral consent for drone strikes on Pakistani territory and announced that any such oral consent would not be sufficient to authorize new strikes. New authorizations must be in writing, with the additional scrutiny of two parliamentary committees, and subject to authorization on the floor of the house. As the democratic representatives of the Pakistani majority, such action is thus binding on the government and the rest of the world as a matter of international law. According to a *Washington Post* article at the time, "Pakistan's sovereignty shall not be compromised."[8] In an astonishing display of contempt for the democracy it is supposedly supporting, two hours after the passage of these resolutions, the United States carried out yet another drone strike in Waziristan. The actions of the Pakistani parliament, while powerful, also appear to have enabled the Pakistani government to authorize once again the movement of NATO convoys, which had been halted for many months after the November 26, 2011, military strikes that killed twenty-seven Pakistani soldiers.[9]

Tensions over the drone program and ongoing covert and quasi-overt wars in both Afghanistan and Pakistan also continue to increase conflict between the United States and its two "allies," as well as between them. This included long-standing issues resulting from the colonial drawing of borders and related infringements on state sovereignty by outside powers, increasing both countries' suspicion of the other.[10] Pakistan has long been an important base of support for Afghanistan's Taliban.

US drone strikes and related policies of military intervention continue to help fuel interstate, intrastate, and regional tensions, with potentially deadly implications for the region and the world. Drone strikes are especially sensitive in Pakistan today, with the United States recently launching drone strikes outside the tribal areas, hitting a seminary. There have been mass protests in Pakistan against drones, replete with threats to block NATO supply routes until the attacks stop, at a time when Lieutenant General Raheed Sharif has just replaced long time army head General Kayani.[11]

Since JSOC's most famous raid, the May 2, 2011, killing of Osama bin Laden, few realize how dangerous tensions have become. President Obama had given the authorization to the SEAL team to fight off Pakistani military units if the latter moved to oppose them.[12] General David Petraeus, commander of US forces in Afghanistan, was ready to mobilize US warplanes if the Pakistanis scrambled their fighter jets.[13] Just before the SEALs left the compound, the Pakistani director of military operations, Major General Ishfaq Nadeem, called General Ashfaq Parvez Kayani, the head of Pakistan's army, saying he feared that the operation had been a possible Indian military strike being launched inside Pakistan.[14] Kayani called the chief of the Pakistani air force and ordered him to "confront any unidentified aircraft."[15] This created the apocalyptic potential for a nuclear armed Pakistan confronting what it considered to be its nuclear armed greatest adversary, India, or its superpower master. But US forces left before Pakistani forces arrived.[16] Today, the constant drone strikes and related border, regional, and global geopolitical tensions are converging to pose new threats to regional and global security.

In late April and early May of 2013, new clashes erupted between the Pakistani and Afghan militaries over disputed border outposts set up by Pakistan and destroyed by the Afghans. Both countries claimed the posts were within their borders. After the incident, thousands of Afghans carried the bodies of the slain policemen through Jalalabad while shouting "death to Pakistan," and calls for war with Pakistan began appearing on social media sites in Afghanistan. The border dispute is left over from the period of British colonial rule with its arbitrary drawing of borders, notably the Durand line, of uncertain demarcation. Neither Afghanistan nor the Pashtuns have ever recognized the border as it cuts through the Pashtun ethnic heartland. Cross-border and regional tensions have risen over the last decades for a host of reasons. These include Pakistani intelligence support for the Taliban, in part due to their desire for strategic depth against their Indian rival, as well as popular support for the Taliban by ethnic Pashtuns on both sides of the Afghan-Pakistani border.[17]

This violent incident is the worst clash between the two countries in a decade, despite high-level meetings between Afghan Prime Minister Hamid Karzai and Pakistan Army Chief of Staff General Ashfaq Parvez Kayani, hosted by US Secretary of State John Kerry just a week prior, on improving relations and bringing the Taliban into negotiations.[18] The most accurate analysis of this state of play has come from leading analyst Anatol Lieven, who noted:

> A very strange idea has spread in the Western media concerning Afghanistan: that the US military is withdrawing from the country next year, and that the present Afghan war has therefore entered into an "endgame." The use of these phrases reflects a degree of unconscious wishful thinking that amounts to collective self-delusion.
>
> In fact, according [to] a treaty signed by the United States and the Karzai administration, US military bases, aircraft, special forces, and advisers will remain in Afghanistan at least until the treaty expires in 2024. These US forces will be tasked with targeting remaining elements of al-Qaeda and other international terrorist groups operating from Afghanistan and Pakistan; but equally importantly, they will be there to prop up the existing Afghan state against overthrow by the Taliban. The advisers will continue to train the Afghan security forces. So whatever happens in Afghanistan after next year, the United States military will be in the middle of it—unless of course it is forced to evacuate in a hurry.[19]

THE HUMAN TOLL

In addition to the widespread death and destruction they cause, drone strikes can lead to post-traumatic stress disorder (PTSD). Its symptoms include depression, anxiety, phobia, permanent hyper-alert, and panic attacks. These symptoms are often exacerbated when the trauma affects children at the vulnerable developmental stages of early life when their basic personality and sense of trust and safety, or lack thereof, is being formed.[20]

Analysts visiting areas subject to drone attacks report "hollowed out shells of children," sullen looking, with no spark, whose dreams are of drones and dead persons, with the larger effect of pouring kerosene on insurgencies there.[21] In fact, there is a particular aspect of drone strikes that is tantamount to torture, which in classic definitions, includes being subjected to a fear of imminent death. While in general the context for torture is the physical captivity of the victim, with drone strikes, whole communities are subjected to an imminent fear of death, without being formally in the control of others.[22]

Drone strikes cause death and injury through blast waves that crush internal organs and shrapnel that causes hearing and vision loss, burns, and loss and incineration of body parts. Besides raining down death and destruction from the sky, America's ongoing drone program has undermined public safety to such an extent that people are prevented from attending or concentrating at school. In addition, drone strikes have discouraged community and social gatherings such as *jirgas*, an institution central to Pakistani society. They also deter humanitarian aid workers who are afraid to assist victims and survivors.

Strikes have devastated local infrastructure and dwellings. They cause great emotional and economic hardship by depriving families of the ability to work and provide income, while requiring the payment of medical costs associated with the strikes. *Reuters* reporter David Rohde describes living with drones continuously heard overhead by residents in the following way: "The drones were terrifying. . . . The buzz of a distant propeller is a constant reminder of imminent death." The experience is "hell on earth," producing waves of terror.[23]

Drone strikes have played a key role in turning the opinion of the Pakistani population against the United States. Large majorities now see the United States as an enemy.[24] In June 2012, more than two dozen members of Congress signed a letter to President Obama describing drones as "faceless ambassadors that cause civilian deaths, and are frequently the only direct contact with Americans that targeted communities have."[25] The use of drones against these communities is now leading other groups, reportedly including Hezbollah, Hamas, the Free Syrian Army, the Assad regime, Iran, China, Russia, India, and Pakistan, to get into the drone act.[26]

KILLING BY REMOTE CONTROL: DISTANCE, OBEDIENCE, PILOT TRAUMA, HUMAN RIGHTS, AND THE RIGHT TO LIFE

For some time, there has been a hushed silence from drone pilots themselves about this new mode of warfare. The Stanley Milgram obedience experiments demonstrate that the combination of higher authority and distance from the victims ensures obedient behavior, whether in administrating electroshocks or killing at a distance.[27] Currently, decisions to fire missiles are often made at CIA headquarters in Langley, Virginia. Yet CIA personnel are neither trained in the laws of war nor bound by the Uniform Code of Military Justice. Despite assurances that the program avoids civilian casualties, the cameras, sensors, and computers are problematic in terms of identifying persons, even under the best of conditions.[28]

For nearly a decade, silence and secrecy has enshrouded America's new drone warriors. Recently, then twenty-seven-year-old former drone pilot Brandon Bryant spoke out about killing by remote control. Bryant noted his experiences during training: "It's like playing Dungeons & Dragons . . . Roll a d20 to see if you hit your target. His training inspector, watching over his shoulder, would count down to impact and say, 'Splash! You killed everyone.'"[29] He describes operating drones at 10,000 feet in the air and scanning roads from a windowless bunker for years. He noted that heat signatures from IEDs were for him, a fan of *The Lord of the Rings*, akin to the glowing Eye of Sauron. Bryant recounts one incident in particular, among many:

> We get this word that we're gonna fire . . . . We're gonna shoot and collapse the building. They've gotten intel that the guy is inside. . . . This figure runs around the corner, the outside, toward the front of the building. And it looked like a little kid to me. Like a little human person. . . . There's this giant flash, and all of a sudden there's no person there. . . . [I then say to my fellow pilot] "Did that look like a child to you?"[30]

Years later, Bryant, like so many other drone operators, suffers from complex post-traumatic stress disorder.[31] There is now an extensive body of literature containing first-person testimony, of which Bryant's is just one example, on the effects of drones on PTSD, both on the pilots and the communities affected. New reports on drones and human rights were released in 2013, including Amnesty International's "Will I Be Next? US Drone Strikes In Pakistan, Human Rights Watch's Between a Drone and Al-Qaeda: The Civilian Cost of U.S. Targeted Killings in Yemen,"[32] Christof Heyns' "Report of the Special Rapporteur on extrajudicial, summary or arbitrary executions"; and Ben Emmerson's "Special Rapporteur on the promotion and protection of human rights and fundamental freedoms while countering terrorism."[33] These reports raise a host of new questions and concerns about human rights, most especially the right to life.

Drone operators report levels of stress similar to those in actual combat situations. They also experience high levels of tension with burnout rates of 30 percent or more. Seventeen percent are clinically distressed, though oftentimes they go with no counseling or psychological support.[34] Today, in the United States, some 1,100 pilots operate drones at distances far from the battlefield for long hours. This means pilots are surveying humans for hours or days, sometimes killing these very same people by remote control.[35]

In March 2013, the Armed Forces Health Surveillance Center published an article in its *Medical Surveillance Monthly Report*, comparing all active US Air Force (USAF) drone operators from October 1, 2003 to December 31, 2011 to active USAF pilots deploying in Iraq and Afghanistan during this same time period. According to the USAF report, drone operators reported higher levels of at least one mental health problem.[36]

CONCLUSION

US drones strikes will continue to fuel ongoing insurgencies, ethnic-religious nationalism, cross-border, and regional tensions. Future drone campaigns also threaten peace in other parts of the world. There are plans in place to utilize fully autonomous drones and killer drone robots with no human component at all. Analysts fear that these autonomous planes could set off a new arms race in East Asia, particularly between the United States and China, according to journalist Richard Parker.[37] Some argue that the advent of these new remotely piloted drones may make killing seem more akin to video games, less real and less lethal, while Christoph Heyns, the UN Special Rapportuer on extrajudicial, summary or arbitrary executions, recently released a report stating his concerns.[38]

The move toward drone warfare and targeted killings has allowed the United States to pursue a global air war and related policy of assassination from the air, with little transparency or accountability. Warfare at greater distances, as well as related moves toward fully autonomous armed robots and weaponry, have created additional risks to targeted communities and world society, arguably undermining US and global security due to blowback.[39]

Analysts have argued that robotic warfare makes war easier, by minimizing civilian casualties, at least for the state using these killer robots, and by minimizing human interaction and emotions such as empathy.[40]

Despite the claims of many proponents of state-sanctioned assassination via drones and targeted killings, the movement against the practice has begun to garner support, not only in the countries currently being targeted, but also in the United States. Whether the opposition is enough to stop this new mode of warfare remains to be seen. The implications for the future are incalculable.

NOTES

[1] In the preparation of this chapter, I benefitted from discussions with Noam Chomsky and Daniel Ellsberg. The responsibility for the piece, of course, is mine alone.

[2] "Rise of the Drones" (*Nova* broadcast Jan. 23, 2013), *available at* video.pbs.org/video/2326108547/.

[3] Intelligence Authorization Act, Pub. L. No. 102-88, 105 Stat. 429 § 402 (1991).

[4] Jennifer D. Kibbe, *Conducting Shadow Wars*, 5 J. NAT'L SEC. LAW & POL. 379-382 (2012); DANA PRIEST & WILLIAM M. ARKIN, TOP SECRET AMERICA: THE RISE OF THE NEW AMERICAN SECURITY STATE (Little, Brown and Company 2011); MARK MAZETTI, THE WAY OF THE KNIFE: THE CIA, A SECRET ARMY & A WAR AT THE ENDS OF THE EARTH (Penguin 2013). *See also "Way of the Knife" Explains Shift from Spying to Killing*, NPR (April 9, 2013), www.npr.org/2013/04/09/176172590/way-of-the-knife-explains-

cia-shift-from-spying-to-killing; Mark Mazetti & Terry Gross, *"The Way of the Knife": Soldiers, Spies & Shadow Wars*, NPR (April 10, 2013), www. npr.org/2013/04/10/176778712/the-way-of-the-knife-soldiers-spies-and-shadow-wars.

5   Kibbe, *supra* note 4, at 378; *See also* JEREMY SCAHILL, DIRTY WARS: THE WORLD IS A BATTLEFIELD (Nation Books 2013); MARK AMBINDER & D.B. GRADY, DEEP STATE: INSIDE THE GOVERNMENT SECRECY INDUSTRY (Wiley 2013); PRIEST & ARKIN, *supra* note 4.

6   *US: Move Drone Strike Program to Military: Transfer from CIA Could Improve Transparency, Accountability*, HUMAN RIGHTS WATCH (March 21, 2013), www.hrw.org/news/2013/03/21/us-move-drone-strike-program-military.

7   Reuters, *U.N. Official Says U.S. Drones Breach Pakistan's Sovereignty*, N.Y. TIMES (Mar. 15, 2013), www.nytimes.com/2013/03/16/world/asia/un-official-denounces-us-drone-use-in-pakistan.html?_r=0.

8   Richard Leiby, *Pakistan calls for end to U.S. drone attacks*, WASH. POST (Apr. 12, 2012), articles.washingtonpost.com/2012-04-12/world/35452351_1_drone-attacks-pakistani-army-pakistani-soldiers.

9   *Id.*; Ben Emmerson, *Drone Wars: Counterterrorism and Human Rights*, NEW AMERICA FOUNDATION (May 14, 2013), newamerica.net/events/2013/drone_wars_human_rights; *See also* AKBAR AHMED, THE THISTLE AND THE DRONE: HOW AMERICA'S WAR ON TERROR BECAME A WAR ON GLOBAL ISLAM (Brookings 2013).

10   *See* Rod Norland & Salman Masood, *Recent U.S. Drone Strikes Strain Ties With Afghanistan and Pakistan*, N.Y. TIMES (Nov. 29, 2013), www.nytimes. com/2013/11/30/world/asia/drone-strike-pakistan.html?_r=1&.

11   *Id.*.

12   Scahill, *supra* note 5, at 441–443.

13   *Id.*

14   *Id.* at 449-450.

15   *Id.* at 450.

16   *Id. See also* FEROZ HASSAN KHAN, EATING GRASS: THE MAKING OF THE PAKISTANI BOMB, (Stanford University Press 2012); GEORGE PERKOVICH, INDIA'S NUCLEAR BOMB: THE IMPACT ON GLOBAL PROLIFERATION UPDATED EDITION WITH A NEW AFTERWORD (University of California Press 2001).

17   Yaroslav Trofimov, *Afghan, Pakistani Forces Clash: Battle Over Disputed Border Outpost Complicates U.S. Plans to Wind Down War*, WALL ST. J. (May 2, 2013), online.wsj.com/article/SB10001424127887324266904578458101275857288.html; *See also* RIAZ MOHAMMAD KAHN, AFGHANISTAN & PAKISTAN: CONFLICT, EXTREMISM & RESISTANCE TO MODERNITY (Johns

Hopkins University Press 2011); *See also* TALIBANISTAN: NEGOTIATING THE BORDERS BETWEEN TERROR, POLITICS & RELIGION (Peter Bergen & Kathryn Tiedemann eds., Oxford University Press 2013).

18   Trofimov, *supra* note 17.

19   Anatol Lieven, *Afghanistan: The Way to Peace*, NEW YORK REVIEW OF BOOKS (April 4, 2013), www.nybooks.com/articles/archives/2013/apr/04/ afghanistan-way-peace/?pagination=false; *See also* VAHID BROWN & DON RASSLER, FOUNTAINHEAD OF JIHAD: THE HAQQANI NEXUS, 1973-2012 (Columbia University Press 2013).

20   M Khan Chishti, *Drone Strikes and Their Psychological Impact*, THE INTERNATIONAL NEWS (June 11, 2013), www.thenews.com.pk/Todays-News-6-183049-Drone-strikes-and-their-psychological-impact; Andrea Germanos, *Doctor: Children 'Traumatized and Re-Traumatized by Drones' in Yemen*, COMMON DREAMS (Mar. 6, 2013), www.commondreams.org/ headline/2013/03/06-8.

21   *Drones Attacks 'Traumatizing a Generation of Children'*, Channel 4 (Mar. 5, 2013), www.channel4.com/news/drone-attacks-traumatising-a-generation-of-children.

22   *See* STEVEN DEWULF, THE SIGNATURE OF EVIL—REDEFINING TORTURE IN INTERNATIONAL LAW (Intersentia, 2011).

23   Stanford Law Sch. & New York Univ. Sch. of Law, Living Under Drones: Death Injury, and Trauma to Civilians from US Drone Practices in Pakistan 80-81 (2012), available at www.livingunderdrones.org/wp-content/ uploads/2012/10/Stanford-NYU-LIVING-UNDER-DRONES.pdf.

24   *Id.* at 138.

25   *Id.* at 132.

26   *Id.* at 141.

27   Stanley Milgram, *Obedience to Authority: An Experimental View* (Harper Perrenial Modern Classics Reprt. Ed., 2009); first published 1975. *See also* HERBERT C. KELMAN & V. LEE HAMILTON, CRIMES OF OBEDIENCE: TOWARD A SOCIAL PSYCHOLOGY OF AUTHORITY AND RESPONSIBILITY (Yale University Press 1989); Gina Perry, *Beyond the Shock Machine: The Untold Story of the Notorious Milgram Psychology Experiments*, (New York: New Press, 2013); David Luban, *Legal Ethics & Human Dignity* (Cambridge University Press 2009); Martha Minow, *Living Up to the Rules: Holding Soldiers Responsible for Abusive Conduct & the Dilemma of the Superior Orders Defence*, 52 MCGILL L.J. 2-54 (2007)

28   Mary Ellen O'Connell, *Unlawful Killing with Combat Drones: A Case Study of Pakistan, 2004-2009, in* SHOOTING TO KILL: SOCIOLEGAL PERSPECTIVES ON THE USE OF FORCE 263-64 (Simon Bronitt, Miriam Gani & Saskia Hufnagel eds., Hart Publishing 2012).

29 Matthew Power, *Confessions of a Drone Warrior*, GQ (Oct. 23, 2013) (internal quotation marks omitted), www.gq.com/news-politics/big-issues/201311/drone-uav-pilot-assassination?printable=true.

30 *Id. See also* Interview with Brandon Bryant, Drone Operator (Oct. 25, 2013), *available at* www.cnn.com/2013/10/23/us/drone-operator-interview/; JUDITH HERMAN, TRAUMA & RECOVERY (Basic Books 1997); PAT BARKER, REGENERATION (Plume 2013); NPR Staff, *The Hidden Costs of the Drone Program*, NPR (May 5, 2013), www.npr.org/2013/05/05/181403067/the-hidden-cost-of-the-drone-program (internal quotation marks omitted); Helen Pow, *"Did we just kill a kid?": The moment drone operator who assassinated Afghans with the push of a button on a computer in the U.S. realized he had vaporized a child . . . and could not go on*, MAIL ONLINE (Dec. 16, 2012), www.dailymail.co.uk/news/article-2249252/Brandon-Bryant-Drone-operator-followed-orders-shoot-child--decided-quit.html.

31 NPR Staff, *The Hidden Cost of the Drone Program*, NPR (May 5, 2013), www.npr.org/2013/05/05/181403067/the-hidden-cost-of-the-drone-program.

32 *"Will I Be Next?" US Drone Strikes in Pakistan*, AMNESTY INT'L (Oct. 22, 2013), www.amnestyusa.org/research/reports/will-i-be-next-us-drone-strikes-in-pakistan; *Between a Drone and Al-Qaeda: The Civilian Cost of U.S. Targeted Killings In Yemen*, HUMAN RIGHTS WATCH (Oct. 22, 2013), www.hrw.org/reports/2013/10/22/between-drone-and-al-qaeda.

33 General Assembly, *Report of the Special Rapporteur on extrajudicial, summary or arbitrary executions*, Christof Heyns, UN Doc A/68/382, 68th sess. (2013), justsecurity.org/wp-content/uploads/2013/10/UN-Special-Rapporteur-Extrajudicial-Christof-Heyns-Report-Drones.pdf; General Assembly, *Special Rapporteur on the promotion and protection of human rights and fundamental freedoms while countering terrorism*, Ben Emmerson, UN Doc A/68/389, 68th sess. (2013), www.un.org/en/ga/search/view_doc.asp?symbol=A/68/389.

34 Rachel Martin, *High Levels Of 'Burnout' In U.S. Drone Pilots*, NPR (Dec. 18, 2011), www.npr.org/2011/12/19/143926857/report-high-levels-of-burnout-in-u-s-drone-pilots.

35 James Dao, *Drone Pilots Are Found to Get Stress Disorders Much as Those in Combat Do*, N.Y. TIMES (Feb. 22, 2013), *www.nytimes.com/2013/02/23/us/drone-pilots-found-to-get-stress-disorders-much-as-those-in-combat-do.html?_r=0Id.* Martin, *supra* note 22.

36 Jean L. Otto & Bryant J. Webber, *Mental Health Diagnoses and Counseling Among Pilots of Remotely Piloted Aircraft in the United States Air Force*, MED. SURVEILLANCE MONTHLY REP., March 2013, *available at* www.afhsc.mil/viewMSMR?file=2013/v20_n03.pdf.

37 Richard Parker, *Pilotless Planes, Pacific Tensions*, N.Y. TIMES, May 13, 2013, at A21; Julian E. Barnes & Adam Entous, *Navy Catches the Drone Bug: Test*

Flight Set for Plane that Admirals Says Will Extend an Aircraft Carrier's Range, WALL ST. J., May 14, 2013, at A6; P.W. SINGER, WIRED FOR WAR: THE ROBOTICS REVOLUTION & CONFLICT IN THE 21ST CENTURY (Penguin 2010): Peter W. Singer, *Do Drones Undermine Democracy?*, N.Y. TIMES, Jan. 22, 2012, at SR5; *See also* RICHARD PARKER, UNBLINKING: THE RISE OF THE MODERN SUPERDRONES (Clear Hot Media 2013); NORMAN FRIEDMAN, UNMANNED COMBAT AIR SYSTEMS: A NEW KIND OF CARRIER AVIATION (Naval Institute Press 2010).

38   *See* Laura Pitter, Senior National Security Researcher, Human Rights Watch, Cdr. Michael J. Dobbs, USN (Ret), Cdr. David Glazier, Professor of Law, Loyola Law School Los Angeles, Drones, International Law and the 'Forever War,' at Joan B. Kroc Institute for Peace & Justice (Dec. 10, 2013), www.sandiego.edu/peacestudies/academics/news/events/past_events/events_detail.php?_focus=46779; Human Rights Council, Special Rapporteur on extrajudicial, summary or arbitrary executions, Christof Heyns, UN Doc A/HRC/23/47, 23rd sess. (2013), www.ohchr.org/Documents/HRBodies/HRCouncil/RegularSession/Session23/A-HRC-23-47_en.pdf.

39   *See Quigley* chapter 12.

40   *See* David Luban, *What Would Augustine Do?*, BOS. REV. (June 6, 2012), www.bostonreview.net/BR37.3/david_luban_obama_drones_just_war_theory.php.

6

THE GRIM TOLL DRONES TAKE ON INNOCENT LIVES

Medea Benjamin[1]

From Pakistan to Yemen to Somalia, the ominous drones cast shadows over schools, homes, weddings, and funerals. Villagers never know when they will fire, whether at dawn before the households wake for morning prayers, at night when families are sleeping, or in the middle of the day when men are out at work, women are preparing meals, and children are playing in courtyards.

Hellfire missiles that come hurtling down from the sky can instantly incinerate their victims or kill them with flying shrapnel or powerful blast waves capable of crushing internal organs. Survivors often suffer painful wounds and disfiguring burns, limb amputations, vision loss, and hearing loss. With poor government services and extreme poverty, survivors can face a lifetime of misery and pain.

The US government sticks to the myth that drone strikes are only killing militants. According to the official story, the places where the drones are used—from Pakistan to Yemen to Somalia—are infested with militants planning acts of mass murder against Americans. These terrorists, the worst of the worst, are the only ones being killed.

The American government likes to highlight the militant ringleaders it executes, victories that help mask any concerns about due process and civilian deaths. In the Obama administration, there is little talk about capturing suspected militants instead of killing them. It is simply assumed that everywhere we are using the drones are places so remote or dangerous that capture is not an option. As for civilian casualties, we are told they are minimal. But it's important to peel back the mask of invisibility that hides the loss of so many innocent lives.

STORIES OF THE VICTIMS

One such loss occurred in Pakistan on September 7, 2009, when two drones were hovering over the skies of Mirali Tehsil in North Waziristan. It was the month of Ramadan, and people in the area were angry that the drones were interfering in their religious activities. They were also scared, but in Pashtun culture showing one's fear is cowardice and a matter of shame, so the fear remained unspoken.

Fifteen-year-old Sadaullah, a local student, was particularly happy that day as there was a feast for iftar (breaking of the fast) planned at his house that evening. His relatives were coming, and his mother was cooking his favorite meal. Sadaullah saw the unmanned machine in the air and joked with his friends about the "bangana," a local name given to drones in the area due to the constant noise they make.

After eating, all the men in the family proceeded to the courtyard for prayers. The lucky ones had already re-entered the house when the missile struck. Not Sadaullah. He fell unconscious under the debris of the fallen roof. When he awoke at a hospital in Peshawar, he was blind in one eye from the shrapnel and both of his legs had been amputated. He later learned that his elderly uncle, who had been in a wheelchair, was dead, as were two of his cousins, Kadaanullah Jan and Sabir-ud-Din.

"I had a dream to be a doctor," said Sadaullah, "But now I can't even walk to school." So he studies religion in the village madrassa and has little hope for the future.

Another man with little hope is Karim Khan, a resident of a village near Mir Ali in North Waziristan. On December 31, 2009, as most Americans were gearing up for an evening of festivities to welcome the new year, a drone was hovering over Khan's home.

Khan was not in the village that night—he was hundreds of miles away in Islamabad. His brother, Asif Iqbal, and his eighteen-year-old son, Zaeenullah Khan, were home, though. They were chatting in the courtyard when the drone let loose its Hellfire missile. When the chaos of the explosion dissipated, both men had been blown to bits.

Karim Khan rushed home to bury his beloved brother and son on New Year's Day, 2010. News reports alleged that the target of the drone had been Haji Omar, a Taliban commander. But the villagers insisted that Omar had been nowhere near the village that night. The tragedy that forever scarred the lives of Khan's family was the product of a mistake.

Khan's brother, Iqbal, was not a militant or even a militant sympathizer, but a schoolteacher. After receiving his master's degree in English literature from the National University of Modern Languages, Iqbal had returned to work as a teacher. For eight years, he bravely confronted the myriad challenges of educating a population riven by war, and threats from the Taliban, always arguing for the distant benefits of education against the instant power of firearms.

Iqbal left behind a young bride, a widow so distraught she could not speak for weeks after the attack, and a two-year-old boy who would never remember his father.

Zaeenullah was a recent high school graduate who went home to work with his uncle in the village school. He died close to his mentor that night, leaving behind hundreds of students with scant chance of resuming their education—young people now mired in hatred for the drone that had killed their teacher, aching for revenge.

Unlike many families of drone victims, Karim Khan was an educated man, a journalist, and he vowed that the deaths of his son and brother would never be forgotten. In November 2010, Khan won his first small victory. With the help of an Islamabad-based human rights lawyer named Shahzad Akbar, he accused the CIA Station Chief in Islamabad of murder, forcing the latter to flee the country. And in the ensuing days and months, Khan began to organize the families of other victims.

In October 2011, a group of elders and drone-victim families met in Islamabad with Pakistani and British lawyers to discuss how they could use the courts to seek redress, and how they could train local people to better document drone strikes.

Among those who volunteered to provide documentation was a shy sixteen-year-old boy named Tariq Aziz. Aziz had a personal motivation. Eighteen months earlier, his cousin, Anwar Ullah, had been killed by an unmanned drone as he drove his motorcycle through the village of Norak.

Aziz also had plenty of firsthand experience with drones. Neil Williams, a British investigator with Reprieve who was at the tribal meeting, recalled having asked Aziz if he had ever seen a drone. "I expected him to say, 'Yes, I see one a week.' But he said they saw ten or fifteen every day," said Williams. "And he was saying, at nighttime it was making him crazy, because he couldn't sleep."

When the meeting ended, Aziz returned to his village in Waziristan, encouraged in his documenting efforts by the activists and journalists who vowed to publicize the plight of the Waziris. But neither he nor the foreigners he met with could have imagined that the first documentation of drone deaths after their gathering in Islamabad would be that of Aziz himself.

Three days after the meeting, Aziz, together with his twelve-year-old cousin, Waheed Rehman, went to pick up his newlywed aunt. When the two boys were just 200 yards from her house, two missiles slammed into their car, killing them both instantly.

A US official acknowledged to ABC News that the attack was not a mistake—the CIA had chosen this target because the two people in the car were supposedly militants. Pratap Chatterje, a journalist at the Bureau of Investigative Journalism (BIJ) who met Aziz at the Islamabad meeting, was dumbfounded. "If this sixteen-year-old was indeed a suspected terrorist, he should have been arrested in Islamabad," said Chatterje. "It would have been very easy to find him at the hotel and arrest him." Instead, he was simply murdered.

In April 2013, for the first time ever in the US Congress, someone from Yemen—one of the countries where US drones are most frequently used—was asked to testify about how drone attacks were affecting his country. The twenty-two-year-old witness, Farea al-Muslimi, gave such a moving testimony in the Senate Judiciary Subcommittee on the Constitution, Civil Rights, and Human Rights that members of the public were crying. He described the case of Ali al-Amodi, a fisherman from the seaside town of Abyan, whose home was destroyed in a drone attack, and how al-Amodi was grief-stricken as his four-year-old son and six-year-old daughter died in his arms on the way to the hospital. Al-Muslimi insisted that the fisherman had no links to al-Qaeda in the Arabian Peninsula (AQAP), and that his house was targeted by mistake. Also killed in that strike were four other children and a woman.

In a tragic coincidence, just six days before al-Muslimi's testimony in Congress, his own tiny hometown of Wessab, a village so small it doesn't even register on Google maps, was hit by a drone in an attack that terrified thousands of simple, poor farmers. "The drone strike and its impact tore my heart," said al-Muslimi, "much as the tragic bombings in Boston [in April 2013] tore your hearts and also mine."[2]

"Why was the United States trying to kill a person with a missile when everyone knows where he is and he could have been easily arrested?"[3] the villagers wanted to know. In fact, earlier on the night he was killed, the target, Hameed al-Radmi, was meeting with the General Secretary of Local Councilors, the head of the local government, and he had met with security and government officials at the security headquarters just three days before the strike. So Yemeni officials could have easily found and arrested him.

The farmers in the village were angry because al-Radmi had a close relationship with government security chiefs and local government agencies. If there was a reason to suspect him of terrorist activities, he should have been arrested and questioned. The villagers were left terrorized, said al-Muslimi, with the fear that their home or a neighbor's home could be bombed at any time with a US drone.

What the villagers in this impoverished town of Wessab really need is schools to educate their children and clinics to help decrease the number of women and children dying every day.

> Had the United States built a school or hospital, it would have instantly changed the lives of my fellow villagers for the better and been the most effective counterterrorism tool. . . . Instead . . . , most people in Wessab first experienced America through the terror of a drone strike. What radicals had previously failed to achieve in my village, one drone strike accomplished in an instant: there is now an intense anger and growing hatred of America.[4]

LIVING IN FEAR

The terror that al-Muslimi described in Yemen is the same in northern Pakistan. A key study by Stanford and New York University law schools released in October 2012, called "Living Under Drones,"[5] exposed how the constant hovering of drones and the uncertainty about if and when they might strike terrorizes men, women, and children, and has a profound impact on community life. This was something I also found when I talked to residents of Waziristan during my 2012 visit to Pakistan.

There are some 800,000 people living in Waziristan, and many of them live in a state of constant fear. Whether they are working on their farms, performing their chores, going to the market, driving their cars, or just sitting at home, they are always worried a drone might strike. Their inability to protect themselves and their loved ones compounds the stress. So does their inability to hold anyone accountable.

Residents I met with said they had a hard time sleeping, that many people suffer from depression and post-traumatic stress disorder, and that there is widespread use of anti-depressants and anti-anxiety medications. They also reported a spate of suicides, something they said never existed before.

Some families are afraid to send their children to school, some children beg not to be sent to school, and teachers are often afraid to work in the drone-strike areas. "These fears are not without a legitimate basis, as drones have reportedly struck schools in the past, resulting in extensive damage to educational infrastructure, as well as the deaths of dozens of children," the "Living Under Drones" study reported.[6]

The people said their fear of drones keeps them away from social gatherings, and makes it difficult to carry out day-to-day activities and hold community functions. Even the solemn rituals related to death and funerals have been altered. Since drone victims are often incinerated, with body parts—if indeed there are any—left in pieces and unidentifiable, traditional burial processes are impossible. And with drone strikes having targeted funerals and spaces where families have gathered to offer condolences to the deceased, families are unable to hold their traditional, dignified burials.

One of the most troubling consequences is the erosion of the *jirga* system, a community-based conflict-resolution process that is fundamental to Pashtun society. People in the region have vivid memories of the *jirga* that was taking place on March 17, 2011, in the village of Datta Khel, North Waziristan, to resolve a dispute between two local tribes over the ownership of a chromite mine in the area. The Hellfire missiles the United States launched into the heart of the *jirga* killed forty-two people, including the most respected elders of the community.

"The tribal elders who had been killed could not be identified because there were body parts strewn about," said the son of one of those killed. "The smell was awful. I just collected the pieces of flesh that I believed belonged to my father and placed them in a small coffin." He added that the sudden loss of so many elders and leaders in the community had a tremendous impact. "Everyone is now afraid to gather together to hold *jirgas* and solve our problems. Even if we want to come together to protest the illegal drone strikes, we fear that meeting to discuss how to peacefully protest will put us at risk of being killed by drones."[7]

THE "DOUBLE TAP"

Also undermining community values is the US practice of striking one area multiple times. The United States has, on numerous occasions, targeted a site many times in quick succession, a practice known as "double tap." A February 2012 report by the BIJ found that from January 2009 until January 2012, at least fifty civilians were killed in follow-up strikes when they had gone to help victims.

Secondary strikes have discouraged people from helping the wounded, and even inhibited the provision of emergency medical assistance by humanitarian workers.

Hayatullah Ayoub Khan, interviewed by "Living Under Drones" researchers, recounted a particularly harrowing incident. While driving in Waziristan, a missile was fired at a car about 300 hundred meters in front of him. When he got out of his car and approached the wreckage, he saw an arm moving inside the crushed vehicle. The wounded man in the car yelled that he should leave immediately because another missile would likely strike. Khan started to return to his car when a second missile hit and killed the wounded person. He said that nearby villagers waited another twenty minutes before removing the bodies, which included the body of a teacher from his village.

The threat of the "double tap" also affects professional humanitarian workers. One humanitarian organization told researchers they had a policy to wait for six hours before going to the site of a reported drone strike.

Legal experts say that the "double tap" strikes on first responders violates international humanitarian law's basic rules of distinction, proportionality, and precaution.[8] It also violates specific legal protections for medical and humanitarian personnel, and for the wounded.

Christof Heyns, the UN Special Rapporteur on extrajudicial, summary or arbitrary executions, said, "If civilian 'rescuers' are indeed being intentionally targeted, there is no doubt about the law: those strikes are a war crime."[9]

NEGATIVE REPERCUSSIONS FROM DRONE STRIKES

US drone strikes have also sown mistrust inside communities. In Pakistan, many Waziris believe that paid informants help the CIA identify potential targets, including placing small tracking devices, often referred to as "chips," in vehicles or houses.

Whether true or not, these beliefs have bred an intense fear of outsiders, as well as widespread division within the community. Neighbors suspect neighbors of spying for US, Pakistani, or Taliban intelligence.

US drone attacks have also claimed innocent victims in Afghanistan, Iraq, Yemen, Somalia, and Libya. As in Pakistan, their stories are usually buried along with their bodies. Even the drone killing of an American teenager living in Yemen elicited little discussion.

Sixteen-year-old Abdurahman Anwar al-Aulaqi was born in Denver, but left for Yemen with his family in 2002. The teenager's Facebook page showed him as a typical, smiling teenager with glasses, who liked hip-hop and swimming. Not so typical, however, was his father, Anwar al-Aulaqi, one of al-Qaeda's prominent propagandists. His father was put on a hit list by President Obama and killed on September 30, 2011, along with another American who was not on the list but was in the same car. Two weeks later, al-Aulaqi's son was killed with a group of Yemeni teenagers.

If the killing of a sixteen-year-old American fails to spark any substantial debate in the US media regarding the blatantly extrajudicial nature of drone attacks, then certainly the killing of poor Yemenis or Somalis is not going to cause a stir.

The United States is not the only country killing by remote control. The Israeli military has been using drones to both spy on and kill people living in Gaza, a tiny sliver of land where 1.8 million Palestinians live in crowded quarters. In 2009, Human Rights Watch relayed numerous reports of drones hitting civilians during the 2009 Israeli invasion of Gaza. In one case, a mother was sitting on the roof while her small son Mu'mim rode a bicycle. Suddenly there was a powerful explosion. When Nahla Allaw managed to see through the dust and smoke, she looked at her son in horror. "His legs were crushed, his chest had tiny holes in it, and blood poured from them. I carried him, crying. He was breathing his last breath. I talked to him, saying, 'It's alright my dear.'"

From Pakistan to Yemen to Gaza, drone warfare snuffs out the lives of innocent civilians with impunity and renders thousands more maimed psychologically, left homeless and without livelihoods. In the name of the war on terror, drone warfare terrorizes entire populations and represents one of the greatest travesties of justice in our age.

NOTES

1   This chapter is based on personal interviews the author conducted with victims and families of drone-attack victims in Pakistan in October 2012.

2   *Location Change and Time Change: Drone Wars: The Constitutional and Counterterrorism Implications of Targeted Killing: Hearing Before the Subcomm. on the Constitution, Civil Rights, and Human Rights of the*

S. Comm. on the Judiciary, 113th Cong. 1 (2013) (statement of Farea Al-Muslini) (available at www.judiciary.senate.gov/pdf/04-23-13Al-MuslimiTestimony.pdf).

3   *Id.* at 3.

4   *Id.* at 4.

5   Stanford Law Sch.& New York Univ. Sch. of Law, Living Under Drones: Death Injury, and Trauma to Civilians from US Drone Practices in Pakistan (2012).

6   *Id.* at 90.

7   *Eye of the Drone*, HARPER'S MAGAZINE, June 2012, *available at* harpers.org/archive/2012/06/eye-of-the-drone/.

8   *See* Owen Bowcott, *UN to Investigate Civilian Deaths from US Drone Strikes*, THE GUARDIAN (Oct. 25, 2012), www.theguardian.com/world/2012/oct/25/un-inquiry-us-drone-strikes.

9   Jack Serle, *UN expert labels CIA tactic exposed by Bureau 'a war crime'*, THE BUREAU OF INVESTIGATIVE JOURNALISM (June 21, 2012), www.thebureauinvestigates.com/2012/06/21/un-expert-labels-cia-tactic-exposed-by-bureau-a-war-crime/.

7

DOCUMENTING CIVILIAN CASUALTIES

Alice K. Ross

On the evening of June 15, 2011, Akram Shah left Miranshah with four friends in his car, heading toward the village of Spalga, North Waziristan, in Pakistan's tribal regions. The vehicle was some miles from town when drones attacked, firing multiple missiles at the moving car, tribesmen told reporters.[1] The attack could be heard from over a mile away, and the car was "engulfed in flames." The car was left looking "like a sandwich bent in half," witnesses later said. Nobody inside survived.[2]

The strike had killed "four militants," an unnamed security official initially told reporters, suggesting the dead men were members of one of the many armed groups that hide out in this remote, rugged region on the border of Afghanistan; fugitive al-Qaeda members and other terrorists claim shelter here. So do other militant groups who are more focused on local aims such as factions of the Afghan and Pakistan Taliban.[3] But the families of five of the dead men furiously rejected any connection between their relatives and militancy, and hundreds of tribesmen gathered to protest the strike, blocking the road to Miranshah with the coffins of the deceased.[4]

Multiple investigations have now identified those killed that evening as Atiq-ur-Rehman, also known as Tariq, who ran a pharmacy in Miranshah Bazaar, and Umar Khan, who ran a car-parts store, along with two students, Sherzada and Irshad Khan. Irshad also worked in Atiq-ur-Rehman's pharmacy.[5] Akram Shah, the driver, was "a former taxi driver who worked for the Pakistani Water and Power Development Authority as a driver" and a father of three. Three of the dead belonged to the same tribe.[6]

The families insist the drone strike of June 15 killed civilians. Field investigations by the Bureau of Investigative Journalism (BIJ) and legal charity Reprieve corroborated this claim. Locals later traveled to Peshawar to confirm this to researchers from Stanford University and New York University.[7]

However, the US government later insisted no civilians were killed by its drones between May 2010 and August 2011.[8]

The US administration claims drones are an exceptionally accurate weapon, capable of hunting down al-Qaeda terrorists who hide in hard-to-reach parts of the world and plot attacks on the United States, which cause almost no collateral damage. The United States has embraced the weapon, launching over 380 drone strikes in Pakistan alone since 2004. During a particularly intense phase in 2010 and 2011, the CIA carried out an average of one drone strike every four days.[9] But Washington's narrative of exceptional accuracy is contradicted by the work of multiple independent casualty recorders, who have pieced together evidence from sources including field studies, press reports, court affidavits and witness testimonies, and social media. They have uncovered evidence of hundreds of civilian casualties, including over 160 children, killed in US covert actions in Pakistan, Yemen, and Somalia.

CASUALTY RECORDING

Attempting to track and understand who dies in conflicts matters. Where deaths go uncounted, vital information about the human cost of a conflict is lost. Where civilian deaths and injuries go unacknowledged, the families of the dead are denied recognition of their losses, the prospect of compensation, and the chance to hold anybody to account.

"Many violent deaths from conflict around the world are either poorly recorded or not recorded at all," writes Elizabeth Minor of the Oxford Research Group (ORG), a UK think tank.[10] The ORG has made a study of the emerging discipline of casualty recording—the process of systematically recording information about who is killed, where and how, and publishing the information for public consumption. ORG has examined the work of dozens of practitioners globally, from those tracking hostilities as they happen to those piecing together a picture of conflict years, or even decades, after the violence has ended.

Collecting information on deaths while a conflict is ongoing is challenging and often dangerous. Participants frequently have a vested interest in preventing details, particularly of civilian casualties, from emerging. Sources such as news reports, on-the-ground contacts, and research by non-governmental organizations (NGOs) may all yield partial and sometimes conflicting information, so results can often be uncertain or vague. But research by the ORG, working with over forty casualty-recording organizations worldwide, indicates that even limited or partial contemporaneous recording can be valuable.[11] It provides an important way of understanding trends in violence and how a conflict is developing, helping humanitarian organizations respond to victims' needs, and warning others of trouble hot spots.

For casualty recording to be effective, each incident of violence in a conflict and its casualties should be recorded separately, to provide the fullest record possible, and to enable others to scrutinize and corroborate the claimed deaths.[12] Simply providing overall figures of how many people are estimated is not precise enough. In the case of Shah and his passengers, for instance, incident-level recording would allow his family to know whether the United States believes it killed militants or terrorists when it fired on Shah's car, or whether their deaths have gone unrecorded.

An up-to-date understanding of who is being killed, where, and how this is happening can help shape strategy and policy. It is essential for assessing the effectiveness of particular tactics and weapons, and the proportionality and legality of military activities.

This same early information can be used as contextual material for legal actions brought by victims and in any possible criminal trials of perpetrators, and can feed into detailed investigations by the United Nations (UN) and others. It can also be used as the basis for more detailed post-conflict casualty recording, preserving the historical record of violence, aiding reconciliation and memorialization efforts and ensuring the dead are not forgotten.

Civilian deaths are vulnerable to being left unrecorded, particularly when violence happens in parts of the world that are largely out of reach to independent observers. Governments and armed forces often track and acknowledge combatant deaths, through announcements of how many enemy fighters have been killed in particular engagements and how many of their own soldiers have been lost. But they are far less likely to systematically acknowledge civilian deaths. "There are a number of reasons for this: it may be concern they might be unfairly blamed; or reports of civilian casualties may undermine militaries' own reporting of improving stabilization; or it may be they are simply 'none of our business,'" wrote two ORG experts and a British Army colonel in a military magazine.[13]

But a failure to recognize civilian casualties can create deep-seated resentment in affected populations: "[N]ot only does the endemic failure to record the civilian casualties of military actions provide them with impunity, the bitterness and indeed rage resulting from this failure can itself be a driver for future conflict," the ORG noted.[14]

The ORG maintains there is a legal obligation under international human rights law and international humanitarian law for nations and other actors in violence to systematically and publicly record casualties, particularly civilian deaths.[15] Every Casualty, a campaign of which the BIJ is a founding member, is calling for international recognition of the duty for states and other actors to carry out casualty recording. At present, the obligation is routinely ignored by parties to conflicts. Because of this, in most conflicts, any recording that takes place is the work of independent groups and organizations.

Three western organizations carry out casualty recording on drone strikes in Pakistan's tribal belt and on air attacks in Yemen and Somalia.[16] The BIJ, a London-based non-profit journalism organization, runs a database aggregating news reports, sworn affidavits, and field research, both by the BIJ and by other organizations—showing at least 416 civilians have died in Pakistan since 2004, out of a minimum of 2,296 killed. At least 168 of these were children.[17]

Meanwhile the New America Foundation (NAF), a Washington think tank that tracks drone strikes in Pakistan and Yemen, reported at least 258 civilians had died in Pakistan over the same time period, alongside at least 1,623 militants and at least 199 individuals whose status was unknown.[18] The organization classified 2 percent of the dead as militant leaders, NAF's Peter Bergen told a Senate hearing in April 2013. "Overwhelmingly the victims of the strikes are lower-level militants," he added.[19] The *Long War Journal*, a national security blog that reports on every strike and runs a tally of reported deaths in Pakistan and Yemen, estimated 156 civilians and 2,574 militants died between 2006 and 2013.[20]

The variations in civilian casualty counts reflect differing methodologies and the challenges of recording casualties in an ongoing conflict, where early reports are often vague or conflicting. The picture of a strike can change considerably as new information emerges weeks or even years later. But each count presents compelling evidence of extensive civilian casualties by US drones.[21]

Drones certainly offer unique opportunities for extremely rich, detailed casualty recording: their video feeds showing surveillance before a strike and the conversations between operators and intelligence analysts are all recorded and stored. A drone can loiter above the site of a strike, allowing analysts to count bodies and monitor the aftermath, while the CIA also monitors communications and uses human sources where possible to confirm deaths.[22] In Afghanistan, certain drone strikes have been intensively investigated, providing a detailed picture of the chain of events leading up to incidents with high civilian casualties.[23]

There is a vast, detailed repository of information on drone strikes that is unavailable to independent observers. But even this information does not necessarily paint a complete picture of drone strikes and their casualties. It's easy to see, for example, how operators might not know of the presence of a bed-bound child.[24] They might also be unaware of those who later die of wounds inflicted in a strike. Communications are poor in Waziristan, and militants are aware their conversations are vulnerable to being monitored, while human sources might provide an incomplete or biased picture. So it's important to be able to compare the accounts of strikes emerging from sources available to drone operators to those reported by locals, journalists, and human rights groups, in order to identify possible errors and omissions in each and arrive at the most complete and accurate picture possible in such confused and challenging circumstances.

THE POSITION OF THE OBAMA ADMINISTRATION

The United States has emphatically and repeatedly claimed drones are highly accurate and have caused very limited civilian casualties. In President Obama's first public comments on the covert drone campaign in January 2012, he told viewers of a Google Town Hall debate: "I want to make sure that people understand actually drones have not caused a huge number of civilian casualties, for the most part they have been very precise precision strikes against al-Qaeda and their affiliates."[25]

John Brennan, Obama's former counterterrorism director and currently director of the CIA, is credited with overseeing the expansion of covert drone usage. In an April 2012 speech, Brennan conceded that drones had accidentally wounded and killed civilians, but said such incidents were "exceedingly rare."[26] The very nature of the technique enabled the CIA to minimize collateral damage, he claimed. "With the unprecedented ability of remotely piloted aircraft to precisely target a military objective while minimizing collateral damage, one could argue that never before has there been a weapon that allows us to distinguish more effectively between an al-Qaeda terrorist and innocent civilians," Brennan added.[27]

In a previous strike, Brennan described the Obama administration's targeted killing policy as "delivering targeted, surgical pressure" to terrorist groups.[28] In April 2012, he extended the metaphor, claiming: "It's this surgical precision, the ability, with laser-like focus, to eliminate the cancerous tumor called an al-Qaeda terrorist while limiting damage to the tissue around it, that makes this counterterrorism tool so essential."

But in over a decade of carrying out lethal drone strikes, the US administration has consistently refused to provide a clear, detailed accounting of the human toll of its covert campaigns that can be compared to independent monitoring. It has consistently claimed that civilian casualties are exceptionally low, sometimes falling to none at all during extended periods of intensive bombing. It has released a handful of lump-sum estimates of casualties for Pakistan, and nothing at all about how many people it believes have died in its operations in Yemen or Somalia.

This lack of transparency makes it hard to objectively assess Washington's claims of near-perfect accuracy and to reconcile it with accounts of independent casualty recorders. "Preventing civilian harm isn't only saying that you do, but also showing and proving it, both with Congress and the public," Sarah Holewinski, the executive director of the Center for Civilians in Conflict, told Micah Zenko, an analyst at the Council for Foreign Relations who has written extensively on drones.[29]

It is particularly important to understand the accuracy of drones as an emerging weapons platform—and one whose use is rapidly expanding. There are suggestions that the accuracy of drone use may have "fallen short of intended goals." An analysis of classified military data relating to drones in Afghanistan carried out by the Center for Naval Analyses found that drones were "an order of magnitude more likely to result in civilian casualties per engagement."[30] Larry Lewis, the analyst behind the research—who also advises the military—told a reporter drones were ten times more deadly to civilians than manned airstrikes.[31]

"As the US government anticipates the continued and expanded use of lethal drone technology, it owes the public a genuine assessment of the impact of drone strikes, including the effects on local civilian populations," wrote researchers at Columbia Law School's Human Rights Clinic. "The US government should, to the extent practicable, provide its own estimate of the number of individuals killed and their identities."[32]

The strikes in Pakistan and Yemen are widely reported and analyzed by media, academics and activist organizations like the American Civil Liberties Union and Reprieve. They are even discussed selectively in detail by US officials, usually speaking anonymously. These campaigns are covert in name only. But the CIA has been able to use the classified nature of its operations to refuse to systematically publish any casualty recording of its own. "The problem with maintaining that drone strikes are covert is that both the American and international publics often misunderstand how drones are used," writes analyst Micah Zenko.[33]

The absence of published casualty records enables the CIA to present the strikes in a favorable light, acknowledging attacks that kill specific, named militants, almost always through officials speaking to reporters on condition of anonymity. This strategy allows the government to celebrate purported successes without accepting accountability for "collateral damage" or for the scores of further incidents where the victims are not publicly named or identified.

After a drone strike in June 2012, anonymous US officials confirmed to reporters that Libyan-born al-Qaeda commander Abu Yahya al-Libi had died in the attack, underlining the strategic effectiveness of the kill. "There is no one who even comes close in terms of replacing the expertise (al-Qaeda) has just lost," an official told CNN.[34] An unnamed US source told the Associated Press, "Abu Yahya was among al Qaeda's most experienced and versatile leaders—operational trainer and Central Shura head—and played a critical role in the group's planning against the West, providing oversight of the external operations efforts."[35]

Although President Obama's press spokesman, Jay Carney, later declined to comment on whether a drone had killed al-Libi, he described al-Libi's death as a "major blow to core al-Qaeda, removing the number-two leader for the second time in less than a year."[36] Tribesmen and local officials told reporters between four and seventeen other alleged militants died with al-Libi—a figure dismissed by a US official as "wildly" inaccurate.[37]

On other strikes, such as the one that killed Shah and his fellow passengers, the US administration is entirely silent.

This strategy of responding selectively and usually anonymously to specific incidents enables the administration to present the program as both accurate and highly effective. Following al-Libi's death, former CIA agent Paul Pillar pointed out that al-Libi's "prominent" name "bolsters the [CIA]'s push to continue the drone program despite the continued political resistance from Pakistan and collateral damage."[38]

The US administration has rejected the suggestion that drones cause extensive civilian casualties, sometimes in aggressive terms. This has included the CIA briefing reporters that a study by the BIJ showing high civilian casualties was "suspect," claiming one of its sources, lawyer Shahzad Akbar, worked for the Pakistani intelligence services—a charge Akbar denied.[39] After the BIJ published an investigation for the *Sunday Times* showing drones were returning to strike sites to deliberately target both civilians and militants carrying out rescue work, an anonymous official told the *New York Times*: "One must wonder why an effort that has so carefully gone after terrorists who plot to kill civilians has been subjected to so much misinformation. Let's be under no illusions—there are a number of elements who would like nothing more than to malign these efforts and help al-Qaeda succeed."[40]

In February 2013, Brennan used his confirmation hearing for the position of CIA director to say anti-drone protesters were misinformed by "falsehoods" about the numbers of civilians killed by drones. But even he conceded that more transparency was needed over civilian casualties. The public misunderstood "the care that we take and the agony that we go through to make sure that we do not have any collateral injuries or deaths," he said. "We need to be able to go out and say that publicly and openly."[41]

In his first formal speech on the United States' covert use of drones, in May 2013, President Obama adopted a more conciliatory tone about the disparity between his administration's estimates of casualties and those of other organizations. "There's a wide gap between US assessments of such [civilian] casualties and nongovernmental reports. Nevertheless, it is a hard fact that US strikes have resulted in civilian casualties, a risk that exists in every war. And for the families of those civilians, no words or legal construct can justify their loss. For me, and those in my chain of command, those deaths will haunt us as long as we live."[42]

Since early 2012, the Obama administration has shed some light on its covert use of drones, giving speeches on targeting policy and its legal justifications and, after congressional tussles, providing senators with legal memos justifying the use of lethal force. But many aspects of its targeted killing program remain shrouded in mystery. Zenko points out, "[I]t is unclear if there is a process in place to investigate accidental civilian casualties, hold willful perpetrators of those actions accountable, or provide compensation to the families of unintended victims—similar to the process for accidental civilian casualties as a result of US military operations in Afghanistan."[43]

There are indications from the upper echelons of the Obama administration that this move toward transparency may include greater openness around casualty recording. While Brennan served as Obama's counterterrorism adviser, before becoming CIA director in early 2013, he was instrumental in expanding the targeted killing program. Following his confirmation hearing, Brennan wrote to senators, "[T]o the extent that U.S. national security interests can be protected, the U.S. Government should make public the overall numbers of civilian deaths resulting from U.S. strikes targeting al-Qaida."[44]

At the time of writing, this pledge had yet to be fulfilled: the government has issued no formal estimate of civilian drone casualties. It is important that, if Washington chooses to take this commendable step toward transparency, it releases the data in enough detail so the administration's casualty recording can be compared with independent monitoring. That could reveal possible omissions and anomalies in each, and the fullest possible picture of casualties—both civilian and militant—can be pieced together.

WASHINGTON'S ESTIMATES

In a study on the impact of drone strikes on civilians, the Columbia Law Center identified five occasions on which the US administration had provided its casualty estimates for its campaign in Pakistan. The US government's estimate of civilians killed, leaked to the media by anonymous officials, remained consistently below 50 even as the number of dead alleged combatants spiraled.[45]

In August 2011, the CIA told the *New York Times* its drones had killed 2,000 militants and 50 civilians in the seven years since its first lethal drone strike in Pakistan. Between May 2010 and mid-August 2011, a period of heavy bombing when the BIJ has charted almost 150 strikes, drones had killed 600 "militants" and no civilians at all, the CIA claimed.[46] This echoed a previous claim, made by Brennan in late June 2011, that not a single civilian had been killed by a US drone strike for nearly a year.[47] Yet Shah and his friends died in June 2011, weeks before Brennan's comments. There has been no official explanation for this apparent omission.

The claim that no civilians died in such an extended period, in which over 100 drone strikes reportedly took place, has been questioned by some within the US military. Former Air Force legal adviser Jeffrey Addicott told *Reuters* there was "no way" civilian casualties could be as low as the United States claimed, "[K]illing from that high above, there's always the 'oops' factor."[48]

A further hint of the administration's estimate of how many non-combatants have been killed by drones emerged during Brennan's confirmation hearing in February 2013. Dianne Feinstein, Democratic chair of the Senate Select Committee on Intelligence, which has oversight of the CIA, used her opening remarks to say that civilian drone deaths were "typically in the single digits" for every year of the drone campaign.[49]

Even what little information has been released has differed sharply from independent estimates. But the United States refuses to provide more detailed information that can be effectively scrutinized—adopting what Micah Zenko describes as the "trust us" position on civilian casualties, making bold statements about casualties "without providing any supporting evidence to reinforce that trust."[50]

The claims of low civilian casualties have been contradicted by the Pakistani government, which told a visiting UN investigator in March 2013, "The [Pakistani] Government has been able to confirm that at least 400 civilians had been killed as a result of drone strikes, and that a further 200 individuals were regarded as probable non-combatants." At least 2,200 people had been killed in total, the Pakistani government added.[51]

It should be noted that the Pakistani government's own figures on civilian casualties have been somewhat inconsistent: the tribal administration, the FATA Secretariat, had previously submitted figures to the Peshawar High Court claiming that 1,449 civilians had been killed in drone strikes in the five years ending in December 2012, along with 47 "foreigners."[52] This figure appears to class all non-foreigners as civilians. And later, in October 2013, Pakistan's Ministry of Defense said in a statement to the Senate that 67 civilians had been killed in drone strikes in the previous five years, apparently contradicting the government's previous estimates.[53] However, within a week the ministry appeared to retract the estimate, with senior officials telling local newspapers that the figures were "wrong and fabricated." A Ministry of Defense spokeswoman added that new figures would be provided "in the next few days," but these did not appear.[54]

Strike-by-strike recording by the BIJ and the NAF also reveals significantly higher civilian casualties, with the BIJ's own present estimate of 407 civilian deaths close to that of the Pakistani government's statement to the UN.

It is vital that the public has trust in the administration's recording of casualties in Pakistan. This is data the CIA uses to decide whether strikes have been successful or not, to inform their planning, and to evaluate whether any collateral damage they caused was proportionate—and therefore legal—under international law. But when even the lump-sum figures present such a vastly different picture from all other estimates, important questions emerge about whether the administration's methodology for counting civilian casualties is effective.

In the unblemished fifteen-month period when the CIA claimed no civilians had been killed, the BIJ has identified eighty-nine civilians credibly reported to have died, including at least sixteen children, of a minimum of 990 people killed.[55] Along with the attack that killed Akram Shah, Atiq-ur-Rehman, Umar Khan, Sherzada Khan, and Irshad Khan, the period contained one of the bloodiest strikes on record in Pakistan. On the morning of March 17, 2011, drones attacked a large group of men gathered in the shade of the bus depot of the town of Dattakhel, North Waziristan. This infamous strike reportedly killed up to forty-two people, many of whom were civilians, including tribal elders and khassadars (tribal policemen). A handful of Taliban also died, but the strike had targeted what turned out to be a *jirga*—a tribal meeting—convened to resolve a dispute about chromite mining rights.

Following the *jirga* strike, the Pakistani government took the then-rare step of publicly protesting against the strike. The strike had killed "peaceful citizens including elders of the area," the head of Pakistan's military, General Ashfaq Kayani, said in a statement.[56] The United States took the unusual step of denying that account. "These guys were terrorists, not the local men's glee club," an unnamed US spokesman retorted to the *Wall Street Journal*.[57] In strikingly similar terms, an unidentified US official told the *New York Times*: "These people weren't gathering for a bake sale. . . . They were terrorists."[58]

A US source later suggested the strike was a "signature" strike, in which the decision to strike was based on patterns of behavior deemed to indicate militant activity—but did not concede any civilian casualties. "There's no question the Pakistani and US governments have different views on the outcome of this strike. The fact is that a large group of heavily armed men, some of whom were clearly connected to al Qaeda and all of whom acted in a manner consistent with AQ-linked militants, were killed."[59]

Repeated investigations by journalists, NGOs, and lawyers have all corroborated the claims of high civilian deaths in the *jirga* strike, including identifying at least twenty-five by name.[60] Relatives of those killed have lodged legal action, including a successful petition, to the high court at Peshawar and an attempt to launch proceedings against the British government for sharing intelligence that could lead to fatal drone strikes.[61]

Confronted by mounting evidence of heavy civilian casualties, Brennan later softened his earlier claim that no civilians had died, telling TV interviewer George Stephanopoulos, "[W]hat I said was that over a period of time before my public remarks that we had no information about a single civilian, a noncombatant being killed."[62] But it later emerged that the administration was informed almost immediately of the high civilian casualties. The Pakistani government had furiously summoned the then-US ambassador to protest the heavy toll, and he passed the message on to senior officials in Washington, the BIJ later reported.[63]

The absence of official, public casualty recording masks trends in a conflict and a weapon whose technology is evolving rapidly. It also obscures what appears to be a significant improvement in the CIA's efforts to avoid civilian harm.

According to the work of independent monitors, 2012 was the first year since 2007 to even come close to Dianne Feinstein's claim that the number of civilians killed had been in the "single digits." In 2012, the NAF reports that of 306 or more people killed by drones, a minimum of 5 were civilians—a huge decrease from 2009, when at least 70 civilians were among 549 to die.[64] The BIJ's initial recording found an even steeper estimated decline in civilian deaths, from at least 100 civilians reported killed in 2009 to 4 in 2012.[65] This later rose to 13 following an Amnesty International field investigation that corroborated several earlier accounts of civilian deaths, raising the BIJ's minimum estimate.[66] However, in 2013, for the first time since strikes began in Pakistan, BIJ recorded no confirmed civilian casualties. NAF recorded 4 civilian deaths.

Civilian casualties are the most fiercely contested and emotive issue of the debate on covert drone strikes. Yet the debate largely ignores this sharp decline in "collateral damage." If the administration agrees that the decline represents a success, its lack of systematic publishing prevents it from effectively capitalizing on it.

WHO IS A CIVILIAN?

The gulf between the United States' estimates of the civilian toll of its drone campaign and those of independent monitors and the Pakistani government lends weight to reports that the United States uses a controversial and highly problematic definition of who is a civilian and who is militant. In an asymmetric campaign against non-state actors on the territory of a purported ally, defining who is—and who is not—a legitimate target for drone strikes is far from clear-cut.

In Pakistan's tribal regions, where members of militant groups live alongside ordinary Pashtun tribesmen, the risk of civilians being mistaken for legitimate targets is high, tribal *maliks* (elders) told a UN special rapporteur when he visited Pakistan to investigate the impact of the drone campaign. "All Pashtun tribesmen tended to have similar appearance to members of the Pakistan Taliban, including similar (and often indistinguishable) tribal clothing, and since it had long been a tradition among the Pashtun tribes that all adult males would carry a gun at all times."[67]

The difficulty of distinguishing between Taliban members and non-combatants is highlighted in the reporting of strikes. Victims are routinely described to reporters by locals and Pakistani officials using vague terms such as "militants," "tribesmen," "locals," and "people." The reporting of which groups alleged militants belong to can be contradictory and inconsistent, making it hard to assess who the strikes are targeting, and who is being killed.

The vagueness of the reporting is illustrated by an attack in the village of Mizar Madakhel on March 10, 2010. Drones attacked what was variously described as a building or a vehicle, reportedly killing between eight and twelve people. A further twelve were injured, according to reports. People rushed to the scene to carry out rescue work, and drones struck again.

Those killed in this second attack were described simply as "people" by BBC and Al Jazeera. The Pakistani newspaper *Dawn* reported the missiles had hit "a group of men believed to be insurgents" who were attempting to rescue people from the wreckage, while news agency *Deutsche-Presse Agentur* reported "a crowd of villagers" who had died, and cited an unnamed Pakistani intelligence official as saying the dead had not yet been identified. The dead were "Taliban fighters," according to the *Long War Journal*, while an unnamed tribal elder told the Pakistani paper *News International* the strike had killed both militants and "some residents of the nearby Ziarat village."[68] Two years later, the BIJ investigated reports that drones had repeatedly attacked those carrying out rescue work—a tactic legal scholars suggested may breach international law—and found that two unnamed Taliban members had died alongside four civilians, named as Gulzar, Shamin, Majan, and Sarwar.[69] The ambiguous initial reporting did not adequately reflect the more complicated toll of the strike that emerged through later investigations.

The terms "militant" and "civilian" are also "muddled and controversial," noted researchers at Columbia Law School:

> They are not defined by the U.S. government, though U.S. officials use them; the terms sound vaguely legal, although they only loosely track legal and scholarly debates about who may be lawfully targeted. . . . Whether these primary sources are unnamed U.S. and Pakistani officials, or unnamed local villagers and witnesses, identification of those killed as "militants" or "civilians" is likely driven by political interests, and colored by the perspective and experiences of the source.[70]

To make things more complex, there may be a "slippage" between the commonly understood definitions of the words and the legal definitions the US government may be using, academics at Columbia Law School add. "As a legal matter, under some circumstances civilians may lawfully be targeted—perhaps leading US and Pakistani government sources to refer to such civilians as 'militants.'"[71]

In a spring 2012 speech in Chicago, US Attorney General Eric Holder outlined the administration's legal justification for targeted killings, stating that lawful targets included "civilians directly participating in hostilities."[72] An article published two months later contained claims about how the administration defined legitimate targets that appear to stretch the definition of "direct participation." Obama had "embraced a disputed method for counting civilian casualties that did little to box him in," a detailed *New York Times* piece on targeted killing policy under Obama claimed. "It in effect counts all military-age males in a strike zone as combatants, according to several administration officials, unless there is explicit intelligence posthumously proving them innocent."[73] Under this logic, all adult men in the tribal region are guilty until they are found innocent: "[P]eople in an area of known terrorist activity, or found with a top Qaeda operative, are probably up to no good," officials explained to *Times*.

The term "military-aged males" has cropped up before in a way that suggests that if this classification is not formal policy throughout the military, it is at least a well-known concept. In 2006, four soldiers charged with killing three men on a raid in Iraq claimed their orders had been to kill all "military-aged males," although this did not prevent them from being convicted for the killings.[74]After a disastrous February 2010 airstrike in Afghanistan killed between fifteen and twenty-three civilians traveling in a convoy, transcripts of the US military inquiry showed the drone crew tracking the vehicles describing their passengers as "military-aged males." Following the strike, General Stanley McChrystal, then commander of US forces in Afghanistan, reportedly banned the use of the term "military-aged male" as "it implied that every adult man was a combatant," the *Los Angeles Times* reported.[75]

The US government has not commented on the record about whether the *Times* report accurately reflects its definitions of who is a legitimate target for drone strikes. As Columbia Law School and others have pointed out, this could go some way toward explaining the discrepancy between the United States' own estimates and those of independent monitoring organizations. Under this categorization, for example, Akram Shah and his fellow passengers in the car that was destroyed in the strike of June 15, 2011, would be considered potential combatants and therefore legitimate targets, at least in advance of their deaths.

The suggestion that the United States had adopted the "military-aged male" definition drew protests from human rights groups. "It surely need not be explained that the government's obligation is to distinguish combatants from noncombatants *while they are still alive*, not after they have been killed. A 'shoot first, ask questions later' policy is entirely inconsistent with international law, not to mention morally grotesque," wrote Jameel Jaffer and Nathan Freed Wessler of the American Civil Liberties Union (ACLU).[76] Elisa Massimino, president of Human Rights First, wrote in a letter to President Obama, saying that the definition suggested by the *Times* article "permits both the targeting of innocent civilians in violation of international law, and allows the administration to undercount the number of civilian casualties resulting from such strikes."[77]

Even former presidential insiders have voiced concern over the administration's counting of civilian casualties. In May 2013, Harold Koh, a former legal adviser on drones to President Obama, used a speech at Oxford Union to call on the administration to be more transparent about its use of drones, and to "clarify its method of counting civilian casualties, and why that method is consistent with international humanitarian law standards."[78]

Even using this problematic definition, the number of collateral deaths recorded by monitoring organizations consistently outstrips the CIA's estimates. In December 2009, for example, a US official told Scott Shane of the *Times* that in "less than two years" of strikes "just over 20" civilians had died, "and those were people who were either at the side of major terrorists or were at facilities used by terrorists."[79] Yet according to data assembled by the BIJ, between January 1,

2008 and December 1, 2009—a period of less than two years—57 children and at least 28 women were among the 139 dead recorded as civilians using more conventional counting methods. During the fifteen months between May 2010 and August 2011, when the CIA repeatedly claimed a perfect record, the BIJ's data shows a minimum of eight children, while reporting explicitly refers to at least fourteen women reportedly killed in drone strikes.[80]

Using the lump-sum numbers provided, it is hard to tell whether individual incidents are acknowledged by the CIA as having caused civilian harm, even when they have been recognized as such by other official sources. Just before 9 PM on January 23, 2009, an explosion rocked the village of Ganghi Khel, South Waziristan. The house of Malik Gulistan Khan was partially destroyed. Inside, at least five people died, including Khan, three of his sons, and at least one nephew. Khan was not a combatant but a "pro-government tribal elder," local officials told the BBC.[81] "We did nothing, have no connection to militants at all," a relative later told researchers.[82]

A letter from the local political agent, dated January 24, 2009, provides official confirmation of the deaths: "[O]n the night of 23-01-09 at about 2035 hours, Spy Plan [sic] fired one Missile on the house of [redacted]. As a result [redacted], his two children, one cousin has been died [sic] and his nephew was injured, names of whom could not be ascertained at the moment."[83]

It appears that the United States' initial assessment was also that civilians had died. Daniel Klaidman reported that to those monitoring the video feeds, "[I]t soon became clear that something had gone horribly awry," and that children and other civilians had died.[84] President Obama, then just three days into his presidency, was told of the deaths. "You could tell from his body language that he was not a happy man," an aide recalled of a meeting the day after the strike.[85] But there is no way of telling whether Malik Gulistan Khan and his family are included in the CIA's lump-sum estimate of fifty civilians killed on August 2011.

LEAKED REPORTS

Although the United States and Pakistan have only released lump-sum estimates, a handful of more detailed official casualty records have also been leaked to the press, revealing some of both governments' internal assessments of strikes.

Thanks to these strike-by-strike reports, it is possible to compare small sections of the official accounts to independent estimates, and to compare the Pakistani internal estimate with that of the United States. This reveals worrying gaps, inconsistencies, and vagueness in the official recording of civilian casualties. Some level of discrepancy between the different accounts may be expected, given the considerable difficulties of reporting from the tribal regions and the differing sources used, each of which might yield only a partial picture. But if the administration's claims about the "surgical" accuracy of drone strikes is to be credible, it must demonstrate its mechanisms for collecting data are accurate and rigorous. Yet a strike-by-strike comparison reveals the possibility that the United States is significantly undercounting civilian drone deaths.

A US report showing strike-by-strike assessments has twice been partially leaked to reporters. A "US document, conveyed to Pakistan" was leaked to *Dawn* in 2009. It covered strikes that took place under President Bush in 2008.[86] In April 2013, US news agency *McClatchy* published reports based on a fuller version of the same document, covering "most—although not all" of 2006–08 and 2010–11.[87]

It is possible that, if this was a document intended for sharing, including with Pakistan's government, casualty estimates were deliberately obscured. But while the document names multiple alleged militants and identifies the allegiances of many more, it barely mentions civilian deaths that have been recorded by other observers. This indicates either a deliberate attempt to downplay civilian casualties or a failure in the process for gathering and reporting civilian casualties.

Separately, the BIJ's Chris Woods obtained a leaked report containing the Pakistani tribal government's own estimates of strike casualties between 2006 and October 2009, although 2007 is omitted.[88] The Pakistani report is precise for early strikes, but rapidly becomes less detailed, noting just "Civilians" killed for twelve strikes in the Bush era. Civilian casualties vanish almost entirely from the record following Obama's first strike, despite 2009 being the bloodiest year of the campaign for civilian deaths to date, according to both the BIJ's data and that of the NAF.

Comparing the reports reveals several strikes in which the Pakistanis believed civilians died, but the United States apparently did not. *Dawn* published details of fourteen strikes from the US report. Only one of these mentioned civilian casualties. The Pakistani analysis of the same strikes found that four attacks killed civilians; the BIJ's data shows at least six died, including at least six children.

The US report's only mention of civilian casualties is vague. In September 2008, a huge strike on the home and madrassa (religious school) belonging to Jalaluddin Haqqani, leader of the Haqqani Network, reportedly killed twenty-three. Eight children, all grandchildren of Haqqani, and three women, reportedly including one of his wives and his sister, were among the dead.[89] The US secret report says: "Members of the extended Haqqani family were killed." The Pakistani internal document is more precise, stating: "8 female 05 children 07 male all civilians."

For another strike, the US report omits civilian casualties even when its own officials have reportedly previously admitted such casualties. Of a strike on July 28, 2008, the US report notes only that Abu Khabab al-Misri and "other al Qaeda activists" died. Yet the *Washington Times* reported that the day after the strike, CIA director Michael Hayden personally apologized to Pakistani Prime Minister Yousaf Raza Gilani for "collateral damage."

In the leaked sections of the US report, the administration concedes only one further civilian casualty—and this directly contradicts Brennan's claim no civilians died in drone strikes in nearly a year leading up to August 2011.[90] The strike hit a house and guesthouse before dawn on April 22, 2011. "The entire compound was turned into rubble," local elder Mehboob Jan told reporters.[91] At least three women and four or five children were among the twenty-four or twenty-five killed, multiple sources reported in the strike's aftermath.[92] Field researchers working for the *Associated Press* later reported three children and two women had died, although researchers for the BIJ reported "some local dispute over whether women had died" and identified one of the dead as a twelve-year-old boy named Atif.[93]

The strike occurred at a highly sensitive moment: a month after the release of CIA contractor Raymond Davis and the bloody *jirga* strike, and just weeks before the raid that killed Osama bin Laden. The drone program was feeling the strain, too. The Pakistani government ordered the CIA and its drones out of the Shamsi air base. Shortly after the attack, the US administration took the unusual step of denying the reported civilian casualties: "There is no evidence to support that claim [of civilian casualties] whatsoever," a US official told CNN.[94] Yet the administration's assessment in the report is that one civilian did die—and there is no way to tell whether this was one of the individuals identified by the reporters and field researchers, or someone else entirely.

A comparison of the Pakistani document with independent monitoring demonstrates several incidents of civilian casualties recorded by the government that were not reported elsewhere; this was the case for four strikes in 2008. But it also omits many civilian deaths widely reported by independent sources, including almost no mention of collateral deaths after the first strike of Obama's presidency.

"[E]ach and every victim of drone attacks has the right to have their death recorded, investigated and, if appropriate, prosecuted," wrote ORG international law specialists in a paper on casualty recording in Pakistan and Yemen. They concluded the United States has a legal duty under international human rights law to carry out casualty recording. "These are basic human rights, granted by the various instruments of IHRL [international human rights law]."[95]

This apparent obligation is not being addressed by the United States. From the very limited insight into official estimates provided by these documents, recording of civilian casualties by the authorities appears to be patchy and vague. It is not clear whether this reflects the significant difficulties of gathering information, a tendency to assume that the dead are militants, or a reluctance to contradict the official narrative of "surgical" strikes.

At the very least, the discrepancy between the administration's claims of civilian casualties and the detailed evidence presented by independent casualty recorders indicates an urgent need for further investigation. It also highlights the value of presenting data on a strike-by-strike basis that can be effectively compared with other sources to ensure that civilian casualties are not being overlooked from either official or independent accounts.

OTHER COVERT CONFLICTS – SOMALIA AND YEMEN

Incomplete and conflicted as it is, the administration's record of civilian harm in Pakistan is detailed in comparison to that offered for its other covert campaigns in Somalia and Yemen. Although President Obama has acknowledged that the United States has launched non-battlefield operations—by drones and other means—the administration has never released casualty estimates for those countries. And in each country, the picture of conflict is far more complex, making casualty recording and the task of establishing who was behind specific incidents challenging.

Somalia

In Somalia, the fragile government and dominance of al Shabaab and other militant groups over large swaths of the country makes conditions extremely dangerous for civil society organizations, reporters, and NGOs. In 2012, eighteen media workers were killed in Somalia, according to journalism organization Reporters Without Borders.[96] This limits the amount of comprehensive, reliable reporting available on drone strikes and other violent incidents in the country. News agencies report on major attacks based on conversations with locals, but it is possible that further incidents go unreported, and the capacity for field investigations following up on specific strikes is almost non-existent.

US drones are just one operation among many in Somalia. That country has seen between five and eight drone strikes, along with at least seven further US operations, according to a study by the BIJ.[97] But these reports may reflect only a fragment of the total US activity in the country. A UN monitoring report identified more than fifteen unauthorized drone flights over Somalia in a fourteen-month period. The former head of the monitoring group noted the report might capture only half the picture: "There is a lot more going on," he told the BIJ.[98] Meanwhile, troops from several other nations are present as members of the African Union Mission in Somalia (AMISOM) force, and the Ethiopian army invaded in 2007.[99]

To complicate matters further, an Iranian news outlet, PressTV, reported fifty-six drone strikes in Somalia, reportedly killing over 1,370 civilians, which were all later exposed by the BIJ as likely to be false.[100]

No civilian deaths by drone have been confirmed in Somalia, although civilians have reportedly died in other airstrikes. But given the huge challenges faced by external organizations in comprehensively tracking casualties in the conflict, it is doubly important that Brennan's pledges to release casualty estimates are realized for Somalia, to bring a modicum of transparency and systematic recording of casualties to this most opaque of campaigns.

Yemen

In Yemen, too, the picture is complex. The country was the site of the first off-battlefield drone killing, in November 2002, but strikes began in earnest under President Obama in 2009 and escalated sharply in 2012 after militants took over swaths of Yemen's south. Both the CIA and Joint Special Operations Command (JSOC) carry out drone strikes, manned air strikes, and even cruise missile launches on alleged members of al-Qaeda in the Arabian Peninsula (AQAP), with the consent of the government. And while "air strikes" are now routinely described as "drone strikes" in news reporting, it is often far from clear whether they were launched by manned or unmanned aircraft. The Yemeni air force carries out strikes, although it is hampered by its outdated fleet.[101] Even Yemen's president, Abdu Rabbou Mansour al-Hadi, has admitted Yemen's air force is incapable of carrying out strikes at night—and "[e]ven if they did, it's highly unlikely they will be successful," he told an audience in Washington.[102] And in January 2013, the *Times* reported that the Saudi Arabian air force had bombed targets in the country too, although the Saudi foreign minister denied this.[103]

Establishing what and who carried out a particular strike is made still more challenging by the fact that the Yemeni government routinely claims credit for attacks, even when they are far beyond the apparent capabilities of its air force. It is considered more palatable to successive Yemeni governments to accept responsibility for attacks—even ones that go wrong—than to admit that it allows US operations on its soil. "We'll keep saying the bombs are ours, not yours," then-President Saleh reassured General Petraeus, then in command of operations in Yemen, weeks after a bloody cruise missile strike killed over forty civilians in al-Majala, according to a diplomatic cable.[104]

Saleh's successor, Hadi, is similarly supportive of US operations, acknowledging the United States has "helped us in using drones" and praising their accuracy: "[T]hey have zero margin of error, if you know exactly what target you're aiming at."[105]

Because of this, it is far from certain even how many strikes the United States has launched, let alone the number of people killed. Neither the CIA nor JSOC has ever released any casualty estimates for their operations in the country. Perversely, more is known of the administration's casualty estimates for the CIA-run covert campaign in Pakistan than the United States' operations in Yemen, which are partially under military control, and which intuitively might be expected to be more transparent. As Zenko points out, "It is unclear if JSOC maintains a similar or a different method of comparing civilian casualties." Zenko cites a Pentagon official saying, "We're very confident that the number is very low."[106]

Unlike in Pakistan, the administration has never attempted to deny it has killed non-combatants in Yemen. In December 2012, a US official told the *Washington Post*, "We don't go after people in dwellings where we don't know who everyone is. We work very hard to minimize the collateral damage. 'Having said all that, like any programs managed and operated by human beings, mistakes happen. We are not perfect.'"[107]

However, the administration has never published the results of any investigations into US operations in which civilians have been reportedly killed.

The NAF's monitoring has found that the United States has carried out ninety-three drone strikes and fifteen other airstrikes since 2002. At least 775 people were killed, of whom at least 663 were militants, according to NAF's counts.[108] The BIJ differentiates between "confirmed" drone strikes, described as such by US sources or by multiple credible local sources, and additional "possible" drone strikes. It reports at least sixty-three confirmed drone strikes killing at least 330. At least 34 were civilians. A further ninety-three or more air strikes that may have been carried out by drones killed at least 315 additional people, including 24 civilians, while other recorded US operations in the country killed at least 150, including at least 59 civilians.[109] The Bureau's estimates found that while reports of civilian casualties have fallen since 2011 in Pakistan, they have risen in Yemen.

In Yemen, air strikes and their victims are often well-documented. They are reported by both English-language and local media, and have been known to be documented in near real time by eyewitnesses and locals on Twitter.[110] The Yemeni government often names alleged militant leaders as being killed in strikes, on a website run by the Ministry of Defense.[111]

The support for US actions by successive Yemeni presidents has meant Yemen's government has frequently taken responsibility for US strikes. More recently, Yemen has tended to announce strikes, and name some of the dead, without saying who launched them. The multiple overlapping forces operating in the country mean there is inadequate accountability or redress when civilians are harmed in air strikes, whether carried out by drones or other means.

This was the case when a vehicle traveling near the city of Rada'a in al Bayda province was attacked from the air on September 2, 2012. Missiles hit a minibus, killing everyone inside. Local officials initially said it was a Yemeni air force attack, but reporters noted the possibility it had been a drone or manned US attack.[112] The target was reportedly an alleged al-Qaeda commander named Abdelraouf al-Dahab. But within hours, tribal sources and unnamed military officials were telling reporters up to fourteen civilians had died, including women, with military sources blaming "faulty intelligence" leading to the wrong vehicle being attacked.[113]

Multiple later reports of the strike are in agreement that a dozen civilians died that day. Researchers working for a trio of human rights NGOs visited the hospital in Sana'a where the dead and injured had been taken, to speak to wounded survivors and see the bodies of the dead. They found eleven civilians had died in the strike, including three children ages twelve and thirteen, and named two of the children. Another man died later of his wounds, they reported. "The plane came very close to us, which enabled them with all certainty to see us and confirm to them that we were civilians and that we had children and women with us," one of the survivors said, in testimony that was later submitted to the US Senate.[114] Eyewitnesses and relatives traveled to Sana'a to describe the strike to Human Rights Watch. "The bodies were charred like coal. I could not recognize the faces . . . . Then I recognized my mother because she was still holding my sister in her lap. That is when I cried," farmer Ahmed al-Sabooli, 22, told Human Rights Watch. His parents and sister were also killed, he said.[115]

The attack provoked local outrage. The families of the victims threatened to take the bodies of the dead to President Hadi's residence but were turned back by security forces, eyewitnesses told *CNN*. The protest flared as families blocked off the main roads, joined by "hundreds of angry armed gunmen" demanding answers, CNN added.[116] Within days, parliamentarians summoned the interior ministry to demand a response to the claim of high civilian deaths, and President Hadi dispatched emissaries to calm the tribes with offers of money and promises to investigate the events.[117] Initial reports claimed the strike was carried out by a US drone, but an unnamed Department of Defense official refused to comment, telling Bloomberg, "[A]s a general rule, we don't comment on reports of specific counterterrorism operations in Yemen."[118]

The United States did not accept its role in the strike for another three months. When the admission did come, it was made through unnamed administration officials acknowledging to the *Post* that US military aircraft had carried out the strike, although they did not specify whether the attacks were launched by manned aircraft or drones. Still there was no formal acknowledgement of the strike, and no mention of any US investigation into the claims of civilian deaths. At the time of this writing, the Yemeni parliamentary investigation had not published any report. The three survivors were each given $5,000 for their medical treatment, they told researchers. One later died of his wounds.[119] It is not known whether the families of the dead received reparations for their losses.

The Rada'a strike is by no means the first time the Yemeni government attempted to cover up for a US strike that killed large numbers of civilians. In December 2009, the United States launched its first strike in seven years, a catastrophic cruise missile attack on a tented camp in al-Majala that reportedly killed fifty-eight people, including over forty civilians. They died alongside their livestock. "[T]heir bodies were so decimated it was impossible to differentiate between those of children, women, and their animals," a Yemeni journalist and activist later told the US Senate.[120]

Following the strike, the US Ambassador to Yemen cabled Washington, remarking that then-President Saleh's vice president was "not overly concerned" about claims of heavy civilian casualties, and his government would continue to assume responsibility.[121] At a meeting weeks after the strike, Saleh attempted to raise reports of high civilian deaths at al-Majala with General Petraeus, but the general insisted, "[T]he only civilians killed were the wife and two children of an AQAP operative at the site." Saleh agreed Yemen would continue claiming credit for US strikes. A diplomatic cable concluded Saleh's claim over civilian casualties showed he had "not been well briefed by his advisors."[122]

A Yemeni government investigation later named forty-one civilians, including twelve women, five of whom were pregnant, and twenty-two children.[123] (Further civilians later died after treading on cluster munitions.) The government report insisted the United States "had not been involved in any way." But diplomatic cables published by WikiLeaks revealed missile fragments found at the site, and later leaks from within the US government all indicated the United States had in fact carried out the strike.[124] Requests by the ACLU for information on any investigations carried out by the US government have gone unanswered. The families of the victims received just a few hundred dollars' compensation from the Yemeni government.[125] This is vastly different from the amount the United States pays when it acknowledges civilian harm. For a 2012 strike in Afghanistan, the United States paid $46,000 for each person killed.[126]

A LACK OF ACCOUNTABILITY

The in-depth investigation the al-Majala and Rada'a strikes received is a rarity in Yemen. As in Pakistan, the vast majority of attacks receive little in-depth investigation. With no official estimates with which to cross-reference field investigations, reporting, and other documentation, there is a significant chance that some civilian casualties have been overlooked in initial reporting and remain unrecorded.

Survivors and the families of the dead are denied the ability to hold anyone to account for their losses, due to the lack of transparency about who is carrying out strikes. And the toxic perception of the United States, as an unaccountable force that inflicts heavy civilian casualties without explanation or redress, reportedly fuels anti-American sentiment in the country.[127] Describing a strike on his own village, Yemeni activist Farea al-Muslimi told senators the United States' enemies were able to exploit this to win support:

> AQAP paid the owner of the house in Ja'ar 38,000 Saudi riyals [£6,500] as compensation for causing damage to her house after the air strike. As far as I know, the US government has never paid any sort of compensation to civilian victims in my country and the Yemeni government has paid next to nothing. Here, again, AQAP scores points in the propaganda war while the United States and Yemen do not.[128]

In its work documenting casualties, the ORG advocates for an obligation of states to systematically record casualties in their own conflicts and to share this information "at the level of incidents and individuals" with other organizations "as long as it is safe to do so."[129] The CIA director himself, John Brennan, indicated he would be in favor of releasing casualty figures, although for the Yemen and Somalia conflicts, the secretive JSOC command would also have to release its own data to provide a full account of US casualties.

During a prior era, the United States was able to carpet-bomb Laos in a virtual news blackout. But in an increasingly networked world, its actions are widely reported and tracked. More openness about strikes and who they kill would allow the United States to take advantage of important changes such as the apparent near-disappearance of civilian deaths in Pakistan. It would also enable those affected—who live in some of the world's poorest regions—to claim redress.

There is a further reason for the administration to be more forthcoming on the impact of its activities. "Over the next decade, the US near-monopoly on drone strikes will erode as more countries develop and hone this capability," writes Zenko. "In this uncharted territory, US policy provides a powerful precedent for other states and nonstate actors that will increasingly deploy drones with potentially dangerous ramifications." "Without reform from within, drones risk becoming an unregulated, unaccountable vehicle for states to deploy lethal force with impunity."[130]

Drones are uniquely well-suited for conducting attacks on hard-to-reach places, which by their nature are also hard to monitor comprehensively. It is crucial that the United States set a responsible precedent for recording the impact of its operations. Should other countries or even non-state actors adopt the US model of refusing to account publicly for the human cost of sustained bombing campaigns, the consequence may be that deaths—both combatant and civilian—go unrecorded and forgotten.

NOTES

1   Dawn, *Tribesmen Protest Drone Attacks*, DAWN (June 17, 2011), dawn. com/2011/06/17/tribesmen-protest-drone-attacks/.

2   Hasbanullah Khan, *US Drones Kill Eight Militants in Pakistan*, AFP (June 15, 2011) www.google.com/hostednews/afp/article/ALeqM5jJGoBfRYzea AzuAc88gIioBa3Ysg?docId=CNG.921d971040a618e5fd16673c1ea984a7.5 01&hl=en&lr=all; Stanford Law Sch. & New York Univ. Sch. of Law, Living Under Drones: Death Injury, and Trauma to Civilians from US Drone Practices in Pakistan 64 (2012), *available at* www.livingunderdrones.org/wp-content/uploads/2012/10/Stanford-NYU-LIVING-UNDER-DRONES.pdf [hereinafter Stanford Law Sch.].

3   House of Commons Foreign Affairs Committee, Global Security: Afghanistan and Pakistan, 2008-09, H.C. HC 302, at 58-60 (U.K.).

[4]   Dawn, *Tribesmen Protest Drone Attacks*, DAWN (June 17, 2011), dawn.
       com/2011/06/17/tribesmen-protest-drone-attacks/; Chris Woods &
       Rahimullah Yusufzai, *Get the data: Twenty-five deadly strikes*, BUREAU OF
       INVESTIGATIVE JOURNALISM (July 18 2011), www.thebureauinvestigates.
       com/2011/07/18/get-the-data-twenty-five-deadly-strikes/; The News
       International Correspondent, *NWA tribesmen protest drone attack casualties*,
       THE NEWS INT'L (June 17 2011), www.thenews.com.pk/Todays-News-13-
       6797-NWA-tribesmen-protest-casualties-in-drone-attacks.
       www.thenews.com.pk/TodaysPrintDetail.aspx?ID=52979&Cat=7&
       dt=6/17/2011.

[5]   Stanford Law Sch., *supra* note 2, at 63-64.

[6]   The News International Correspondent, *supra* note 4; Stanford Law Sch.,
       supra note 2, at 63.

[7]   Stanford Law Sch., *supra* note 2.

[8]   Woods & Yusufzai, *supra* note 4.

[9]   Chris Woods, *Drone strikes rise to one every four days*, BUREAU OF
       INVESTIGATIVE JOURNALISM (July 18, 2011), www.thebureauinvestigates.
       com/2011/07/18/us-drone-strikes-rise-from-one-a-year-to-one-every-four-
       days/.

[10]   Elizabeth Minor, *Towards the Recording of Every Casualty: Analysis and
       policy recommendations from a study of 40 casualty recorders*, OXFORD
       RESEARCH GROUP 3 (Oct. 22, 2012), www.oxfordresearchgroup.org.uk/sites/
       default/files/TowardsTheRecordingOfEveryCasualty_0.pdf.

[11]   *Id.* at 10.

[12]   *Id.* at 20.

[13]   Hamit Dardagan, John Sloboda & Richard Iron, *In Everyone's Interest:
       Recording all the dead, not just our own*, THE BRITISH ARMY REV., Summer
       2010, at 24, *available at* www.oxfordresearchgroup.org.uk/sites/default/files/
       In%20everyones%20interest.pdf.

[14]   Susan Breau & Rachel Joyce, *Discussion Paper: The legal obligation to record
       civilian casualties of armed conflict*, OXFORD RESEARCH GROUP 2 (June
       2011), www.oxfordresearchgroup.org.uk/sites/default/files/1st%20legal%20
       report%20formatted%20FINAL.pdf.

[15]   *Id.* at 1.; Minor, *supra* note 10, at 4.

[16]   Pakistani organizations tracking drone casualties in the country include the
       Pakistan Institute for Peace Studies and Pakistan Body Count.

[17]   *Covert Drone War – The Datasets*, BUREAU OF INVESTIGATIVE JOURNALISM,
       (last visited Apr. 24, 2014), www.thebureauinvestigates.com/category/
       projects/drones/drones-graphs/.

[18]   *The Drone War in Pakistan statistics*, New America Foundation (last visited Apr. 24, 2014), natsec.newamerica.net/drones/pakistan/analysis.

[19]   *Drone Wars: The Constitutional and Counterterrorism Implications of Targeted Killing: Hearing Before the Subcomm. on the Constitution, Civil Rights, and Human Rights of the S. Comm. on the Judiciary*, 113th Cong. 4 (2013) (statement of Peter Bergen), *available at* www.judiciary.senate.gov/pdf/04-23-13BergenTestimony.pdf.

[20]   Bill Roggio & Alexander Mayer, *Charting the data for US airstrikes in Pakistan*, Long War Journal (last visited Apr. 24, 2014) (charting the data for US airstrikes in Pakistan, 2004-2013), www.longwarjournal.org/pakistan-strikes.php.

[21]   Chantal Grut & Naureen Shah, *Counting Drone Strike Deaths*, Columbia Law School Human Rights Clinic 6, 19 (Oct. 2012), web.law.columbia.edu/sites/default/files/microsites/human-rights-institute/files/COLUMBIACountingDronesFinal.pdf.

[22]   Naureen Shah, *The Civilian Impact of Drones: Unexamined costs, unanswered questions*, Columbia Law School and Center for Civilians in Conflict 36 (Oct. 2012), web.law.columbia.edu/sites/default/files/microsites/human-rights-institute/files/The%20Civilian%20Impact%20of%20Drones.pdf.

[23]   *See Id.* at 31-32; *See* David S Cloud, *Anatomy of an Afghan war tragedy*, L.A. Times (Apr. 10, 2011), articles.latimes.com/2011/apr/10/world/la-fg-afghanistan-drone-20110410.

[24]   Shah, *supra* note 22, at 15.

[25]   *Your Interview with the President* January 30, 2012, YouTube (last visited Aug. 16, 2013: 9:16 PM), www.youtube.com/watch?v=eeTj5qMGTAI.

[26]   John Brennan, Assistant to the President for Homeland Security and Counter Terrorism, The Ethics and Efficacy of the President's Counterterrorism Strategy (Apr. 30, 2012), *available at* www.cfr.org/counterterrorism/brennans-speech-counterterrorism-april-2012/p28100.

[27]   John Brennan, Assistant to the President for Homeland Security and Counter Terrorism, Ensuring al-Qa'ida's Demise (June 29, 2011), *available at* www.whitehouse.gov/the-press-office/2011/06/29/remarks-john-o-brennan-assistant-president-homeland-security-and-counter.

[28]   John Brennan, United States Homeland Security Advisor, Obama Administration Counterterrorism Strategy (June 29, 2011), www.c-spanvideo.org/program/AdministrationCo.

[29]   Micah Zenko, *Talking in circles*, Foreign Policy (May 9, 2013), www.foreignpolicy.com/articles/2013/05/09/targeted_killings_koh_policy_obama?page=full.

30 *Drone Strikes: Civilian Casualty Considerations (Unclassified Executive Summary)*, CNA (June 18, 2013), www.cna.org/sites/default/files/research/Drone_Strikes.pdf.

31 Spencer Ackerman, *US drone strikes more deadly to Afghan civilians than manned aircraft – adviser*, GUARDIAN (July 2, 2013), www.theguardian.com/world/2013/jul/02/us-drone-strikes-afghan-civilians.

32 Grut & Shah, *supra* note 21, at 6.

33 Micah Zenko, *Reforming US Drone Strike Policies*, COUNCIL ON FOREIGN RELATIONS 15 (Jan. 2013), i.cfr.org/content/publications/attachments/Drones_CSR65.pdf.

34 CNN Wire Staff, *White House: Al Qaida no 2 leader is dead*, CNN (June 6, 2012), edition.cnn.com/2012/06/05/world/asia/pakistan-drone-libi/index.html?hpt=hp_t1.

35 *Abu Yahya al-Libi, Al Qaeda deputy leader, killed in US drone strike*, ASSOCIATED PRESS (June 5, 2011), www.cbsnews.com/8301-202_162-57447601/abu-yahya-al-libi-al-qaeda-deputy-leader-killed-in-u.s-drone-strike/.

36 Jay Carney, White House Press Secretary, Remarks at the daily White House press briefing concerning the death of al-Libi (June 5, 2012), www.whitehouse.gov/the-press-office/2012/06/05/press-briefing-press-secretary-jay-carney-secretary-education-arne-dunca.

37 Joby Warrick & Greg Miller, *Al Qaeda's No 2 leader killed in US airstrike*, WASH. POST (June 5, 2012), articles.washingtonpost.com/2012-06-05/world/35462533_1_cia-drone-abu-yahya-drone-strikes; *Abu Yahya al-Libi, al Qaeda deputy leader, killed in US drone strike*, CBSNews (June 5, 2012), www.cbsnews.com/8301-202_162-57447601/abu-yahya-al-libi-al-qaeda-deputy-leader-killed-in-u.s-drone-strike/; Jon Boone & Jason Burke, *Al-Qaida number two Libi killed in Pakistan drone strike*, GUARDIAN (June 5, 2012), www.theguardian.com/world/2012/jun/05/al-qaida-abu-yahya-libi-pakistan.

38 *Al-Libi, supra* note 35.

39 Chris Woods, *Attacking the messenger: how the CIA tried to undermine drone study*, BUREAU OF INVESTIGATIVE JOURNALISM (Aug. 12, 2011), www.thebureauinvestigates.com/2011/08/12/attacking-the-messenger-how-the-cia-tried-to-undermine-drone-study/.

40 Rachel Oldroyd, *Senior US official accuses Bureau of 'helping al Qaeda'*, BUREAU OF INVESTIGATIVE JOURNALISM (Feb. 6, 2012), www.thebureauinvestigates.com/2012/02/06/senior-us-official-accuses-bureau-of-helping-al-qaeda/; Chris Woods & Christina Lamb, *CIA tactics in Pakistan include targeting rescuers and funerals*, BUREAU OF INVESTIGATIVE JOURNALISM/SUNDAY TIMES (Feb. 4, 2012), www.thebureauinvestigates.

com/2012/02/04/obama-terror-drones-cia-tactics-in-pakistan-include-targeting-rescuers-and-funerals/.

41   *Senate Select Committee on Intelligence nomination hearing for CIA. director nominee*, C SPAN (Feb. 7, 2013), www.c-span.org/Events/Senate-Committee-Hears-from-CIA-Director-Nominee/10737437877/; Dan De Luce, *Obama's choice to run CIA defends US drone war*, AFP (Feb. 7, 2013), www.google.com/hostednews/afp/article/ALeqM5h3bdxMU_cozoz2Iw8mw k95j9qCig?docId=CNG.3d9adb69b7d42275b0679a99252bff61.261.

42   Barack Obama, President of the United States, Remarks by the President at the National Defense University (May 23, 2013), www.whitehouse.gov/the-press-office/2013/05/23/remarks-president-national-defense-university.

43   Zenko, *supra* note 33, at 14.

44   *Questions for the record, Mr. John Brennan: Hearing Before the S. Select Committee on Intelligence*, 113th Cong. (Feb. 2013), *available at* www. intelligence.senate.gov/130207/posthearing.pdf.

45   Shah, *supra* note 22, at 29-30.

46   Scott Shane, *CIA is disputed on civilian toll in drone strikes*, N.Y. Times (Aug. 11, 2011), www.nytimes.com/2011/08/12/world/asia/12drones. html?pagewanted=all.

47   Obama Administration Counterterrorism Strategy, *supra* note 28.

48   Adam Entous, *How the White House learned to love the drone*, Reuters (May 18, 2010), uk.reuters.com/article/2010/05/18/us-pakistan-drones-idUSTRE64H5SL20100518; Shah, *supra* note 22, at 31.

49   Senate Intelligence Committee nomination hearing for C.I.A. director nominee, Feb. 7, 2013, www.c-span.org/Events/Senate-Committee-Hears-from-CIA-Director-Nominee/10737437877/.

50   Micah Zenko, *How many civilians are killed US by drones?*, Council on Foreign Relations (June 4, 2012), blogs.cfr.org/zenko/2012/06/04/how-many-civilians-are-killed-by-u-s-drones/.

51   United Nations Office of the High Commissioner for Human Rights, *Statement of the Special Rapporteur following meetings in Pakistan* (March 14, 2013), *available at* www.ohchr.org/EN/NewsEvents/Pages/DisplayNews. aspx?NewsID=13146&LangID=E.

52   *See In the Peshawar High Court, Peshawar Judicial Department*, Writ Petition No. 1551-P/2012, at *4 (2013), *available at* http://www.peshawarhighcourt. gov.pk/images/wp%201551-p%2020212.pdf; *see also* Alice K. Ross, *Pakistani Court Rules CIA Drone Strikes are Illegal*, Bureau of Investigative Journalism (May 9, 2013), www.thebureauinvestigates.com/2013/05/09/pakistani-court-rules-cia-drone-strikes-are-illegal-and-war-crimes/.

[53] Mubashir Zaidi, *Drones killed 67 civilians in five years: Pakistan* Dawn (Oct. 30, 2013) www.dawn.com/news/1052933/drones-killed-67-civilians-in-five-years-pakistan.

[54] Ahmad Noorani, *Defence ministry admits sending wrong drone figures to PM,* The News International (Nov. 6, 2013) www.thenews.com.pk/Todays-News-13-26495-Defence-ministry-admits-sending-wrong-drone-figures-to-PM.

[55] *Covert Drone War – The Datasets, supra* note 17. (from May 1, 2010 to Aug. 10, 2011).

[56] Associated Press in Islamabad, *Pakistan army chief condemns drone attack that killed 38 people,* Guardian (Mar. 17, 2011), www.theguardian.com/world/2011/mar/17/pakistan-army-chief-drone-attack.

[57] Tom Wright & Rehmad Mehsud, *Pakistan slams US drone strike,* Wall St. J. (Mar. 18, 2011), online.wsj.com/article/SB10001424052748703818204576206873567985708.html.

[58] Salman Masood & Pir Zubair Shah, *C.I.A. drones kill civilians in Pakistan,* N.Y. Times (Mar. 17, 2011), www.nytimes.com/2011/03/18/world/asia/18pakistan.html.

[59] Scott Shane, *Contrasting reports of drone strikes,* N.Y. Times (Aug. 11, 2011), www.nytimes.com/2011/08/12/world/asia/12droneside.html?_r=0.

[60] *See, E.g., Complaint Against the United States of America for the Killing of Innocent Citizens of the Islamic Republic Of Pakistan,* UN Human Rights Council 9-10 (Feb. 22, 2012), *available at* www.reprieve.org.uk/media/downloads/2012_02_22_PUB_drones_UN_HRC_complaint.pdf?utm_source=Press+mailing+list&utm_campaign=89f3db0a75-2012_02_23_drones_UN_complaint&utm_medium=email; Stanford Law Sch., *supra* note 2, at 57-62; Woods & Yusufzai, *supra* note 4; *High court challenge to Hague over UK complicity in CIA drone attacks,* Leigh Day (Mary 12, 2012), www.leighday.co.uk/News/2012/March-2012/High-Court-Challenge-To-Hague-over-UK-complicity-i; Associated Press in Islamabad, *Report sheds new light on drone war's death toll,* Associated Press (Feb. 26, 2012), english.alarabiya.net/articles/2012/02/26/197138.html.

[61] Alice K. Ross, *Pakistani court rules CIA drone strikes are illegal,* Bureau of Investigative Journalism (May 9, 2013), www.thebureauinvestigates.com/2013/05/09/pakistani-court-rules-cia-drone-strikes-are-illegal-and-war-crimes/; Alice K. Ross, *High court rejects first challenge to CIA's drone campaign,* Bureau of Investigative Journalism (Dec. 22, 2012), www.thebureauinvestigates.com/2012/12/22/court-of-appeal-rejects-first-uk-challenge-to-cias-drone-campaign/.

[62] Interview with John Brennan, President's Chief Counterterrorism Adviser, on *This Week,* ABC News (Apr. 29, 2012), *available at* abcnews.go.com/Politics/week-transcript-john-brennan/story?id=16228333.

[63] Chris Woods, *New questions over CIA nominee Brennan's denial of civilian drone deaths*, BUREAU OF INVESTIGATIVE JOURNALISM (Jan. 9, 2013), www.thebureauinvestigates.com/2013/01/09/new-questions-over-cia-nominee-john-brennans-denial-of-civilian-drone-deaths/.

[64] New America Foundation, *The Drone War in Pakistan* (last visited Apr. 24, 2014), natsec.newamerica.net/drones/pakistan/analysis.

[65] The Bureau, *Pakistan drone statistics visualised*, BUREAU OF INVESTIGATIVE JOURNALISM (last visited Apr. 22, 2014), www.thebureauinvestigates.com/2012/07/02/resources-and-graphs/.

[66] *See Will I be Next?* AMNESTY INTERNATIONAL (Oct. 2013), www.amnestyusa.org/sites/default/files/asa330132013en.pdf.

[67] United Nations Office of the High Commissioner for Human Rights, *supra* note 51.

[68] Deutsche-Presse Agentur, *12 killed in US drone strikes in Pakistan*, HINDUSTAN TIMES (Mar. 11, 2010), www.hindustantimes.com/world-news/SouthAsia/12-killed-in-US-drone-strikes-in-Pakistan/Article1-517638.aspx; *Drone raid 'kills 12' in north-west Pakistan*, BBC NEWS (Mar. 11, 2010) news.bbc.co.uk/1/hi/world/south_asia/8561357.stm; *Lethal US drone raid in Pakistan*, AL JAZEERA (Mar. 10, 2011), www.aljazeera.com/news/asia/2010/03/201031018114779678.html; Pazir Gul, *Drone attack kills 14 in N. Waziristan*, DAWN (Mar. 11, 2010), archives.dawn.com/archives/41256; Bill Roggio, *US airstrike kills 15 in North Waziristan*, THE LONG WAR JOURNAL (Mar. 10, 2010), www.longwarjournal.org/archives/2010/03/us_airstrike_kills_1.php; Malik Mumtaz Khan & Mushtaq Yusufzai, *US drones kill 14 in NWA*, THE NEWS INTERNATIONAL (Mar. 11, 2010), www.thenews.com.pk/TodaysPrintDetail.aspx?ID=27723&Cat=13&dt=3/11/2010.

[69] Chris Woods, *Get the data: Obama's terror drones*, BUREAU OF INVESTIGATIVE JOURNALISM (Feb. 4, 2012), www.thebureauinvestigates.com/2012/02/04/get-the-data-obamas-terror-drones/; Chris Woods, *A question of legality*, BUREAU OF INVESTIGATIVE JOURNALISM (Feb. 4, 2012), www.thebureauinvestigates.com/2012/02/04/a-question-of-legality/.

[70] Grut & Shah, *supra* note 21 at 15.

[71] *Id.* at 16.

[71] Eric Holder, United States Attorney General, Speech at Northwestern University School of Law (Mar. 5, 2012), www.justice.gov/iso/opa/ag/speeches/2012/ag-speech-1203051.html.

[73] Jo Becker & Scott Shane, *Secret 'kill list' proves a test of Obama's principles and will*, N.Y. TIMES (May 29, 2012), www.nytimes.com/2012/05/29/world/obamas-leadership-in-war-on-al-qaeda.html?pagewanted=all.

74 *Accused troops: We were under orders to kill*, Associated Press (July 21, 2006), www.nbcnews.com/id/13974639/ns/world_news-mideast_n_africa/t/accused-troops-we-were-under-orders-kill/#.UX0z26XhDC4.

75 David S Cloud, *Anatomy of an Afghan war tragedy*, L.A. Times (Apr. 10 2011), articles.latimes.com/2011/apr/10/world/la-fg-afghanistan-drone-20110410.

76 Jameel Jaffer & Nathan Freed Wessler, *First the 'targeted killing' program, then the targeted propaganda campaign*, American Civil Liberties Union (June 7, 2012), www.aclu.org/blog/national-security/first-targeted-killing-campaign-then-targeted-propaganda-campaign (emphasis in original).

77 Letter from Elisa Massimino, President and CEO, Human Rights First, to Barack Obama, President, United States, (May 29, 2012), *available at* www.humanrightsfirst.org/wp-content/uploads/Letter-to-President-Obama-on-Targeted-Killing.pdf.

78 Harold Koh, Law Professor, Yale Law School, How to End the Forever War *15 (May 7, 2013), www.lawfareblog.com/wp-content/uploads/2013/05/2013-5-7-corrected-koh-oxford-union-speech-as-delivered.pdf.

79 Scott Shane, *C.I.A. to expand use of drones in Pakistan*, N.Y. Times (Dec. 3, 2009) www.nytimes.com/2009/12/04/world/asia/04drones.html?pagewanted=all&_r=0.

80 *See* The Bureau, *Obama 2010 Pakistan strikes*, Bureau of Investigative Journalism (Aug. 10, 2011), www.thebureauinvestigates.com/2011/08/10/obama-2010-strikes/; *see* The Bureau, *Obama 2011 Pakistan strikes*, Bureau of Investigative Journalism (Aug. 10, 2011), www.thebureauinvestigates.com/2011/08/10/obama-2011-strikes/.

81 *Deadly missiles strike Pakistan*, BBC (Jan. 23, 2009), news.bbc.co.uk/1/hi/7847423.stm; *US drone attacks kill 14 in Waziristan: First Obama-era strikes in tribal areas*, Dawn (Jan. 24, 2009), archives.dawn.com/archives/33530; Shah, *supra* note 22, at 21 ("I lost my father, three brothers, and my cousin in this attack.").

82 Shah, *supra* note 22, at 21.

83 Letter from Asstt. Political Agent, South Waziristan Agency Wana (Jan. 24, 2009), *available at* www.thebureauinvestigates.com/wp-content/uploads/2011/08/Sth-Wana-letter-Jan-20091.jpg.

84 Daniel Klaidman, *Drones: How Obama learned to kill*, The Daily Beast (May 28, 2012), www.thedailybeast.com/newsweek/2012/05/27/drones-the-silent-killers.html.

85 *Id.*

86 Dawn Correspondent, *High-value targets hit by drones*, Dawn (June 2, 2009), archives.dawn.com/archives/39900.

[87] Jonathan S. Landay, *Obama's drone war kills 'others,' not just al Qaida leaders*, McClatchy (Apr. 9, 201), www.mcclatchydc.com/2013/04/09/188062/obamas-drone-war-kills-others.html.

[88] Chris Woods, *Leaked Pakistani report confirms high civilian death toll in CIA drone strikes*, Bureau of Investigative Journalism (July 22, 2013), www.thebureauinvestigates.com/2013/07/22/exclusive-leaked-pakistani-report-confirms-high-civilian-death-toll-in-cia-drone-strikes/; Chris Woods, *Get the Data: The Pakistan government's secret document*, Bureau of Investigative Journalism (July 22, 2013), www.thebureauinvestigates.com/2013/07/22/get-the-data-the-pakistan-governments-secret-document/.

[89] Haji Mujtaba, *US drones kill 23 in missile attack in Pakistan*, Reuters (Sept. 8, 2008), www.reuters.com/article/2008/09/08/us-pakistan-violence-idUSISL24250220080908?feedType=nl&feedName=usmorningdigest; Jane Perlez & Pir Zubair Khan, *U.S. attack on Taliban kills 23 in Pakistan*, N.Y. Times (Sept. 8, 2008), www.nytimes.com/2008/09/09/world/asia/09pstan.html?_r=0.

[90] Jack Serle & Chris Woods, *Secret US documents show Brennan's 'no civilian drone deaths' claim was false*, Bureau of Investigative Journalism (Apr. 11, 2013) www.thebureauinvestigates.com/2013/04/11/secret-us-documents-show-brennans-no-civilian-drone-deaths-claim-was-false/.

[91] Zahid Hussain, *CIA drone kills 26 in Pakistan, raising tensions*, Wall St. J. (Apr. 23, 2011), online.wsj.com/article/SB10001424052748703387904576278122411803628.html.

[92] *US drone raid 'kills 25' in N Waziristan*, BBC (Apr. 22, 2011), www.bbc.co.uk/news/world-south-asia-13167425; *US drone strike kills 25 in North Waziristan*, Dawn (Apr. 22, 2011), dawn.com/2011/04/22/us-drone-strike-kills-five-in-north-waziristan/; Malik Mumtaz Khan & Mushtaq Yusufzai, *Drone attack in North Waziristan kills 25*, The News International (Apr. 22, 2011), www.thenews.com.pk/TodaysPrintDetail.aspx?ID=5477&Cat=13&dt=4/23/2011.

[93] Sebastian Abbot, *AP Impact: New light on drone war's death toll*, Associated Press (Feb. 25, 2012), www.guardian.co.uk/world/feedarticle/10112681; Chris Woods & Rahimullah Yusufzai, *Get the data: 25 deadly strikes*, Bureau of Investigative Journalism (July 18, 2011), www.thebureauinvestigates.com/2011/07/18/get-the-data-twenty-five-deadly-strikes/.

[94] Nick Paton Walsh & Nasir Habib, *Source: US departs Pakistan base*, CNN (Apr. 22, 2011), edition.cnn.com/2011/WORLD/asiapcf/04/22/pakistan.drone.strike/?hpt=T2; The Bureau, *Obama 2011 Pakistan strikes*, Bureau of Investigative Journalism (Aug. 10, 2011), www.thebureauinvestigates.com/2011/08/10/obama-2011-strikes/.

[95] Susean Breau, Marie Aronsson & Rachel Joyce, *Discussion Paper: Drone Attacks, International Law, and the Recording of Civilians in Armed Conflict*, Oxford Research Group 19-20 (June 2011), www.oxfordresearchgroup.

org.uk/sites/default/files/ORG%20Drone%20Attacks%20and%20
International%20Law%20Report.pdf.

96 *Radio Kulmiye humourist becomes 18th media worker to be killed this year*,
    REPORTERS WITHOUT BOARDERS (Oct. 30, 2012), en.rsf.org/somalia-radio-
    kulmiye-humourist-becomes-30-10-2012,43613.html.

97 *See* Drones Team, *Somalia: reported US covert actions 2001-2013*, BUREAU
    OF INVESTIGATIVE JOURNALISM (Feb. 22, 2012), www.thebureauinvestigates.
    com/2012/02/22/get-the-data-somalias-hidden-war/.

98 Jack Serle, *US and others have 'licence to ignore international law' in
    Somalia*, BUREAU OF INVESTIGATIVE JOURNALISM (Sept. 24, 2012), www.
    thebureauinvestigates.com/2012/09/24/us-and-others-given-licence-to-
    ignore-international-law-in-somalia/.

99 *Id.*

100 Emma Slater & Chris Woods, *Iranian TV station accused of faking reports of
    Somalia drone strikes*, THE GUARDIAN (Dec. 2, 2011),
    www.guardian.co.uk/world/2011/dec/02/iranian-tv-fake-drone-somalia.

101 Jack Serle, *Yeme''s 'barely functional' air force points to US involvement in
    strikes*, BUREAU OF INVESTIGATIVE JOURNALISM (Mar. 29, 2013), www.
    thebureauinvestigates.com/2012/03/29/barely-functional-why-us-is-likely-
    to-be-behind-yemens-precision-airstrikes/.

102 Abdu Rabbou Mansour al-Hadi President, Yemen, Speech at the Woodrow
    Wilson Center *11 (Sept. 28, 2012), *available at* www.wilsoncenter.org/sites/
    default/files/yementranscript.pdf.

103 Iona Craig & Nico Hines, *Saudi jets join America's secret war in Yemen*,
    THE TIMES (Jan. 4, 2013), www.thetimes.co.uk/tto/news/world/americas/
    article3647656.ece; Reuters, *'Saudi air force did not strike Yemen targets'*,
    GULFNEWS.COM (Jan. 6, 2013), gulfnews.com/news/gulf/yemen/saudi-air-
    force-did-not-strike-yemen-targets-1.1128340.

104 Diplomatic cable from Stephen A. Seche, Ambassador to Yemen,
    United States, on General Petraeus' Meeting With Saleh On Security
    Assistance, Aqap Strikes, 10SANAA4 ¶5 (Jan. 4, 2010), *available at* www.
    cablegatesearch.net/cable.php?id=10SANAA4&q=petraeus%20saleh.

105 Al-Hadi, *supra* note 102.

106 Zenko, *supra* note 33, at 12.

107 Sudarsan Raghavan, *When US drones kill civilians, Yemen's government tries
    to conceal it*, WASH. POST (Dec. 25, 2012), www.washingtonpost.com/world/
    middle_east/when-us-drones-kill-civilians-yemens-government-tries-to-
    conceal-it/2012/12/24/bd4d7ac2-486d-11e2-8af9-9b50cb4605a7_print.html.

108 *US Covert War in Yemen*, NEW AMERICA FOUNDATION (last visited Apr. 24,
    2014), yemendrones.newamerica.net.

109 *Drone Strikes in Yemen*, BUREAU OF INVESTIGATIVE JOURNALISM (last visited Apr. 29, 2014), www.thebureauinvestigates.com/category/projects/drones/drones-yemen/.

110 Chris Woods and Jack Serle, *How Twitter mapped a 'covert' US drone strike in Yemen*, BUREAU OF INVESTIGATIVE JOURNALISM (May 18, 2012), www.thebureauinvestigates.com/2012/05/18/how-twitter-mapped-a-covert-us-drone-operation-in-yemen/.

111 *See generally* www.26sep.net (Arabic).

112 Ahmed al Haj, *Yemen: drone kills suspected tanker attacker*, ASSOCIATED PRESS (Sept. 2, 2012), www.guardian.co.uk/world/feedarticle/10420172.

113 *See Deaths in US drone strike in Yemen*, AL JAZEERA (Sept. 2, 2012), www.aljazeera.com/news/middleeast/2012/09/201292165153495957.html; Xinhua, *US drone kills 13 civilians in central Yemen: official*, ENGLISH NEWS CN (Sept. 2, 2012), news.xinhuanet.com/english/world/2012-09/02/c_131823003.htm.

114 *Submission by the National Organization for Defending Rights and Freedoms: Hearing Before the Subcomm. on the Constitution, Civil Rights, and Human Rights of the S. Comm. On the Judiicary*, 113th Cong. 9 (2013), *available at* www.ccrjustice.org/files/HOOD,_Alkarama,_CCR_SJC_Submission.pdf.

115 Letta Tayler, *Anatomy of an air attack gone wrong*, FOREIGN POLICY (Dec. 26, 201), www.foreignpolicy.com/articles/2012/12/26/yemen_air_attack_civilians_dead?page=full.

116 Hakim Almasmari, *Suspected US drone strike kills civilians in Yemen, officials say*, CNN (Sept. 4, 2012), edition.cnn.com/2012/09/03/world/meast/yemen-drone-strike/?hpt=hp_t3.

117 Xinhua, *Yemeni president orders investigation into botched U.S. drone strikes*, CHINA.ORG.CN (Sept. 5, 2012), www.shanghaidaily.com/article/article_xinhua.asp?id=93255; AFP, *Yemen probes civilian deaths in apparent US drone strike* (Sept. 4, 2012), www.google.com/hostednews/afp/article/ALeqM5g-lcy97e1q00-ocw0WVO2B1-J2AQ?docId=CNG.addf2dcbfe9b931f f7fc97a6c01cf101.6d1.

118 Mohammed Hatem, *Yemen strike on vehicle kills 11 civilians, website says*, BLOOMBERG (Sept. 2, 2012), www.bloomberg.com/news/2012-09-02/yemen-strike-on-vehicle-kills-11-civilians-website-says.html.

119 *The United States' War on Yemen: Drone Attacks*, Alkarama (June 3, 2013), *available at* en.alkarama.org/documents/ALK_USA-Yemen_Drones_SRCTwHR_4June2013_Final_EN.pdf.

120 *Location Change and Time Change: Drone Wars: The Constitutional and Counterterrorism Implications of Targeted Killing: Hearing Before the Subcomm. on the Constitution, Civil Rights, and Human Rights of the S. Comm. on the Judiciary*, 113th Cong. 1 (2013) (statement of Farea

Al-Muslimi), *available at* www.judiciary.senate.gov/pdf/04-23-13Al-MuslimiTestimony.pdf [hereinafter Muslimi].

[121] *US embassy cables: Yemen trumpets strikes on al-Qaida that were Americans' work*, THE GUARDIAN (Dec. 4, 2010), www.guardian.co.uk/world/us-embassy-cables-documents/240955.

[122] Diplomatic cable from Stephen A. Seche, *supra* note 104, at ¶4.

[123] Drones Team, *Yemen: reported US covert actions 2001-2011*, BUREAU OF INVESTIGATIVE JOURNALISM (Dec. 17, 2009), www.thebureauinvestigates.com/2012/03/29/yemen-reported-us-covert-actions-since-2001/.

[124] *Images of missile and cluster munitions point to US role in fatal attack in Yemen*, AMNESTY INTERNATIONAL (June 7, 2010), www.amnesty.org/en/news-and-updates/yemen-images-missile-and-cluster-munitions-point-us-role-fatal-attack-2010-06-04; Jeremy Scahill, *The dangerous US game in Yemen*, THE NATION (Mar. 30, 2011), www.thenation.com/article/159578/dangerous-us-game-yemen?page=0,2.

[125] *Yemen: reported US covert actions 2001-2011*, *supra* note 123; Klaidman, *supra* note 84; *Royg Looks Ahead Following Ct Operations, But Perhaps Not Far Enough*, 09SANAA2251, WIKILEAKS (last visited Sept. 17, 2013), cablegatesearch.wikileaks.org/cable.php?id=09SANAA2251&q=saleh%20yemen.

[126] Chris Woods, *Who is held to account for civilian deaths by drone in Yemen?*, THE GUARDIAN (Sept. 6, 2012), www.guardian.co.uk/commentisfree/2012/sep/06/drone-deaths-yemen.

[127] Sudarsan Raghavan, *In Yemen, U.S. airstrikes breed anger, and sympathy for al-Qaeda*, WASH. POST (May 29, 2012), articles.washingtonpost.com/2012-05-29/world/35456187_1_aqap-drone-strikes-qaeda.

[128] Al-Muslimi, *supra* note 120, at 7.

[129] Minor, *supra* note 10, at 20.

[130] Zenko, *supra* note 33, at 4.

PART III
ILLEGAL AND IMMORAL

8

US POLICY OF TARGETED KILLING WITH DRONES: ILLEGAL AT ANY SPEED

Jeanne Mirer

Come you masters of war
You that build all the guns
You that build the death planes
You that build the big bombs
Let me ask you one question
Is your money that good
Will it buy you forgiveness
Do you think that it could
I think you will find
When your death takes its toll
All the money you made
Will never buy back your soul
Selected verses, "Masters Of War," Bob Dylan, 1963

INTRODUCTION

On May 29, 2012, the *New York Times* printed an extensive report revealing that killer drones were being used in Yemen, Pakistan, and Somalia.[1] Since that article appeared, a controversy has raged in the United States over the use of these remotely operated armed drones in the so-called war on terror. At times, the controversy appears to die down, only to surface again when, for example, a drone strike is alleged to have mistakenly killed members of a wedding party in Yemen, such as occurred in December 2013.[2]

Nonetheless, it is now officially known that President Obama has worked from "kill lists,"[3] which, at least in Pakistan, included both individual "personality" and "signature" strikes.[4] There are claims that the president's actions are legal.[5] No official legal opinion justifying these strikes has been made public, even though several members of the Obama administration have tried to explain the rationale in general terms.[6] Nonetheless, the revelations of the "kill lists" spawned arguments for and against the policy and practice of using drones for targeted killing. The most common argument in favor of remotely operated armed drone use is based on cost—both economic and military.[7] That is, targeting the "enemy" remotely is less expensive to than deploying "boots on the ground" and exposing US troops to danger. The United States further claims this type of targeted killing is a form of self-defense against those planning to harm the United States on a worldwide battlefield in the "war on terror."[8]

The most common arguments against targeted killing using drones are loosely based on International Humanitarian Law (IHL), the laws of war, which primarily addresses the protection of civilians during armed conflict. Critics of drones maintain that too many civilians, or "innocents," have been killed, and targeted communities are suffering psychological trauma, not knowing if they will be singled out next.[9] Other opponents argue the "blowback" from targeted killing with drones will inevitably be the growth of anti-American terrorists.[10] Others are concerned about the legal justification for the policy and how the decisions have been made about whom to target. They cite the lack of transparency and the refusal of the Bush and Obama administrations to reveal how targets have been selected and the legal basis for their selection.[11]

These arguments, however, do not address the core legal issue of whether it is ever lawful to kill designated people who have not been accused or convicted of any crime, where there is no valid argument that self-defense, including on a battlefield in war, justifies such killing. Everyone has the right to life and the right not to have their life taken arbitrarily.[12] This chapter addresses these legal issues.

In this chapter, it is argued that using armed drones to target people for death outside armed conflict amounts to illegal extrajudicial targeted killing. The chapter makes a distinction, however, between the use of drones on active battlefields like Afghanistan and Iraq, and in countries where there is no active battlefield, such as Pakistan, Yemen, and Somalia. In the cases of Afghanistan and Iraq, drones have been used in the context of illegal wars, which makes their use illegal. If drones have been used in ways that violate the laws of war, their use is also illegal. In the cases of Pakistan, Yemen, and Somalia, the United States is not involved in an armed conflict. Therefore, the only law that applies is International Human Rights Law (IHRL), which protects the right to life from arbitrary deprivation. The use of drones in this context is governed by a law enforcement approach, in which the right to use lethal force may constitute an act of self-defense to prevent the taking of another's life. Thus, the United States can be held accountable for its illegal use of force in Afghanistan and Iraq, and its illegal use of drones for targeted extrajudicial killing outside of Afghanistan and Iraq.

WHAT IS TARGETED KILLING?

"[T]argeted killing is the intentional, premeditated and deliberate use of lethal force, by States or their agents acting under colour of law, . . . against a specific individual who is not in the physical custody of the perpetrator."[13] If the person against whom lethal force is directed has not been convicted of a crime for which a death sentence is permissible in the state where the killing occurs, the targeted killing is also an "extrajudicial" killing, outside of any legal process. Targeted extrajudicial killing is, by its very nature, illegal.

USE OF DRONES FOR TARGETED/EXTRAJUDICIAL KILLING

Remotely operated armed drones are weapons of war particularly suited to targeted killing. Although sometimes smaller, they are used in the same manner as helicopters and bombers. What makes drones different is the technology that allows an operator thousands of miles away to have a view of a particular person or persons, and to pull the trigger, discharging the drone's weapon.

LEGALITY OF TARGETED/EXTRAJUDICIAL KILLING

The practice of extrajudicial targeted killing is illegal. Indeed, governments that engage in it do not readily admit to having a policy allowing such killing. For example, Israel denied its policy of targeted killing until classified documents were exposed by an Israeli Defense Force soldier.[14] The Israeli Supreme Court ruled on the policy in 2006,[15] but no court before or since has dealt with this issue. The ruling in Israel is thus an isolated, anomalous decision. Nonetheless, the Israeli Supreme Court rejected the government's contention that terrorists were unlawful combatants who could be killed at any time. The court described the conflict between the Israelis and the Palestinians as an international armed conflict and applied IHL to those conflicts. The court did not address IHL of non-international armed conflict, or the duties of an occupying power under IHRL. It held that targeted killing could be legal if those targeted were proven to be directly participating in hostilities and if less harmful means were not available.[16] The court ruled that the targets had to be "directly participating in hostilities" under strict conditions of verification and post-killing independent investigation, and further required proof that means of capture were not available, and that the killing was carried out so as to prevent harm to civilians.[17]

In the US context, no matter how carefully vetted a name may be before it is placed on a "kill list," those targeted for death by armed drones are suspects. They have not been formally accused of or convicted of any crimes. Therefore, all targeted killings by armed drones also constitute extrajudicial killings. This makes them no different than killings carried out by death squads, except that death by drone is delivered from a remotely controlled hovering unmanned craft rather than by means of a night raid with guns.[18]

QUESTIONS TO BE ANSWERED

To address more broadly the legality of the United States' use of armed drones for targeted/extrajudicial killings as they have been employed in combat operations in Afghanistan and Iraq, and counterterrorism operations in Pakistan, Yemen, and Somalia, the following questions need to be addressed:

1. The use of drones constitutes a use of force. If the United States were to illegally use force in another country, international criminal law may apply to punish those responsible for prosecuting an illegal war of aggression or acts of aggression.[19] When is it legal to employ force against people in another country?

2. The adage "All's fair in love and war" is not true. There are laws that govern the conduct of war and the use of force. What law covers the use of force with drones for targeted extrajudicial killing in other countries?

These questions are distinct because there are different bodies of law that address when it is permissible to use force (*jus ad bellum*) and, once force is initiated, how force may be used (*jus in bello*). However, even when it is not permissible to use force, any use of force must be conducted lawfully in accordance with the laws of war (*jus in bello*). The United Nations (UN) Charter governs when force can be used. IHL prescribes rules for the conduct of war. IHRL also governs conduct during war and is to be upheld unless it conflicts with IHL. These concepts will be explained more fully below.

For war crimes, crimes against humanity, genocide, and the crime of waging a war of aggression, International Criminal Law (ICL) applies.[20] Thus, if a war is illegal, even if soldiers cannot be prosecuted for war crimes because they acted in conformity with IHL, the heads of state responsible for planning, preparing, or initiating the war are not exempt from international criminal responsibility.

WHEN IS IT LAWFUL TO USE ARMED FORCE AGAINST ANOTHER COUNTRY?

The answer to this question is based on *jus ad bellum*. The UN Charter limits the right of any country to mount a military attack against another county. Article 2(3) of the charter requires states to use peaceful means to settle their international disputes. Article 2(4) requires states to refrain from threatening to use or using force against the territorial integrity of another state. The only two exceptions to the charter's prohibition on the use of force are narrow. One is the inherent right of self-defense contained in Article 51. The other is the authorization of force by the UN Security Council in Article 42. However, the right to self-defense is limited to instances in which the state has been subjected to an armed attack by another state,[21] and is further limited by the requirement to bring the matter to the Security Council and discontinue the use of force once the council has taken measures to maintain or restore international peace and security.[22]

The charter represents a break from prior law with respect to both use of force and the right of self-defense. Before the adoption of the charter, many states used force preemptively. However, in the wake of the devastation wrought by the two World Wars, the charter, determined "to save succeeding generations from the scourge of war,"[23] by severely limiting the circumstances in which force may be used. The charter also prohibits "reprisals," which are defined as attacks against a state after cessation of a prior attack.[24] Reprisals have been held unlawful under international law, as evidenced by numerous General Assembly and Security Council Resolutions, as well as judgments of the International Court of Justice.[25] The prohibition on reprisals is consistent with the Customary International Law (CIL)[26] of self-defense under which a state cannot use force in self-defense when there is no immediacy or imminence requiring such force.[27]

Since September 11, 2001, the United States invaded both Afghanistan and Iraq, where drones have been used for targeted killing as part of combat operations. The United States also employs drones for targeted/extrajudicial killing in Pakistan, Yemen, and Somalia. The difference between Afghanistan and Iraq on the one hand, and Pakistan, Yemen, and Somalia on the other, is that in Afghanistan and Iraq the United States is and was involved in an "armed conflict" with forces on the ground where drones have been used as part of "combat operations." In Pakistan, Yemen, and Somalia, the United States is not involved in armed conflict with these States. The United States is using force against countries that have not launched armed attacks. This targeting is based on the US assertion of a broad right of self-defense, as a counterterrorism strategy to kill "suspected militants" wherever they are located.[28] There is no basis in law for this claimed right of self-defense. It illegally stretches the meaning of self-defense to claim the right to kill someone who is merely suspected of being a terrorist or a member of a terrorist group.

Was the US invasion of Afghanistan lawful?

Shortly after the September 11, 2001, terrorist attacks, the United States invaded Afghanistan. There have been active hostilities in Afghanistan ever since, and the United States has used armed drones to attack targets in that country.

The US Congress gave then-President George W. Bush an Authorization for the Use of Military Force (AUMF) "to use all necessary and appropriate force" against those responsible for the terrorist attacks on September 11, 2001.[29] The AUMF does not trump US obligations under the UN Charter. It cannot authorize actions that conflict with the charter's prohibition of the use of force.[30] Since the United States ratified the charter, it is part of our domestic law by virtue of Article VI section 2 of the US Constitution, which makes ratified treaties part of US law.[31]

However, instead of taking actions consistent with the charter, such as complying with Security Council resolutions 1368[32] and 1373,[33] which listed non-military actions to be taken,[34] the United States invaded Afghanistan. The United States engaged in regime change, ousting the existing government, which was still involved in a civil war. In the process, although many people were rounded up and imprisoned in both Afghanistan and at Guantánamo Bay, the invasion of Afghanistan did not result in a finding that those imprisoned were responsible for planning the September 11 attacks.[35]

Although most of the world's nations were sympathetic to the United States after the 9/11 attacks, the actions taken by the United States against Afghanistan have never been declared legitimate self-defense by the UN. In fact, the Security Council later passed a series of resolutions for the creation of an International Stabilization Assistance Force[36] to assist the Afghan people to promote self-rule. But no UN body, either before or after the United States' invasion of Afghanistan, passed a resolution stating that the US invasion of Afghanistan was legal. While active hostilities have continued in Afghanistan, giving rise to consideration of the strictures of *jus in bello,* the actual invasion of Afghanistan was in fact, illegal.[37] Indeed, the heads of state responsible for planning, preparing or initiating, and waging the war of aggression in Afghanistan should be held to account.

Was the invasion of Iraq lawful?

There is widespread international consensus that the US invasion of Iraq was illegal.[38] Many of the same arguments supporting the illegality of the invasion of Afghanistan apply with even more force to the invasion of Iraq, as no one operating on Iraqi soil ever attacked anything or anyone in the United States; therefore, any argument that the United States was acting in self-defense to repel an armed attack from Iraq, as allowed under Article 51 of the charter, is not available. With Iraq, however, the allegation that Saddam Hussein had weapons of mass destruction was the Bush administration's rationale for invoking the right of preemption, also known as anticipatory self-defense.[39]

There is no consensus in the international community that "anticipatory" self-defense is ever permissible. However, where the concept has been recognized, it is limited to a narrow and strict set of guidelines set forth in the exchange of diplomatic notes between US Secretary of State Daniel Webster and Lord Ashburton in the 1837 Caroline incident.[40] These letters established that anticipatory self-defense is justified only in cases where the "necessity of that self-defense is instant, overwhelming, and leaving no choice of means, and no moment for deliberation."[41] The possible possession of weapons of mass destruction by Saddam Hussein did not come close to meeting the Caroline standard. Furthermore, the Security Council refused to give the United States authorization to invade Iraq.[42] The active hostilities in Iraq, which existed from March of 2003 until the United States withdrew its troops in December 2011, constituted an unlawful use of force (crime of aggression) by the United States.[43] The war in Iraq was, however, governed by *jus ad bellum.*

The discussion of the *jus in bello* applicable to the invasions and wars in Afghanistan and Iraq follows, but, since the invasions of Afghanistan and Iraq were illegal, such illegality should not be granted impunity. As noted above, the United States is subject to International Criminal Law for crimes of aggression and crimes against peace as required under the Nuremberg principles[44] and should also be responsible for all damages resulting from those illegal wars, including compensation to the victims for the loss of life from the use of armed drones for targeted/extrajudicial killing.[45]

WHAT IS INTERNATIONAL HUMANITARIAN LAW?

IHL, or *jus in bello*, is the body of law that began to be codified before the charter prohibited the use of force in settling international disputes. The law grew out of an attempt by countries that, though not renouncing war, sought to make war less devastating to both combatants and non-combatants. The first codification of these laws appeared in the Hague Conventions of 1899 and 1907,[46] and outlawed various weapons of war, such as poisoned weapons, and weapons that cause unnecessary suffering. The Hague Conventions were the first to articulate the principle of *distinction* between civilian and military objects, stating that civilian objects should not be attacked.[47] The Hague Conventions were supplemented by the Geneva Conventions of 1949 and their Additional Protocols.[48] IHL requires countries to make a distinction between combatants, armies, tanks, and other military equipment, on the one hand, and civilians and civilian objects, such as schools, hospitals, and civilian residences, on the other. Civilians and civilian objects are not to be targeted. Weapons that do not discriminate between civilians and combatants are generally prohibited, and notice of planned attacks must be given to civilian populations to allow them to leave the area before an attack. IHL also requires *proportionality*[49] in the use of military strikes, allowing only that amount of force necessary to achieve the military objective.

WHAT ASPECTS OF INTERNATIONAL HUMANITARIAN LAW APPLY TO TARGETED KILLING WITH ARMED DRONES?

IHL applies in every international armed conflict, whether the conflict itself is lawful or not.[50] IHL is violated when armed drones are used to target persons who do not qualify as combatants and who are not directly participating in hostilities. IHL is also violated if there was no military necessity to target those who are subject to strikes. Generally, IHL is not violated in the context of active armed conflict in which combatants are targeted.

WHAT IS INTERNATIONAL HUMAN RIGHTS LAW?

IHRL has developed, largely since World War II, to protect the basic human rights of all people. One of the purposes of the UN is "[t]o achieve international co-operation in solving international problems of an economic, social, cultural, or humanitarian character, and in promoting and encouraging respect for human rights and fundamental freedoms for all without distinction as to race, sex, language, or religion."[51] To this end, the Universal Declaration of Human Rights (UDHR)[52] was signed and endorsed by the UN in 1948. Since then, the UN has created two key human rights treaties that more specifically set forth the rights contained in the UDHR. The International Covenant on Civil and Political Rights (ICCPR)[53] and the International Covenant on Economic, Social, and Cultural Rights (ICESCR)[54] codify the rights elaborated in the UDHR. Almost all countries have ratified both treaties.[55] The UDHR, ICCPR, and ICESCR together comprise the International Bill of Human Rights.[56]

WHAT ASPECTS OF INTERNATIONAL HUMAN RIGHTS LAW ARE APPLICABLE TO TARGETED/EXTRAJUDICIAL KILLING WITH ARMED DRONES?

Article 6 of ICCPR states: "Every human being has the inherent right to life. This right shall be protected by law. No one shall be arbitrarily deprived of his life." A person suspected of committing a crime should be charged and afforded due process. The ICCPR, in Article 14, guarantees the accused the right to be presumed innocent and to a fair trial by an impartial tribunal. When a suspect is deprived of his or her life in the absence of justified self-defense[57] or judicial process, it constitutes an extrajudicial killing. Extrajudicial killing by its very nature is unlawful. Therefore, when a remotely operated armed drone is used to target a person who has not been charged with or convicted of any crime, or whose death is not required by justified self-defense, it is an extrajudicial targeted killing and illegal under IHRL.[58]

The ways in which IHRL and IHL apply to the use of armed drones for targeted/extrajudicial killings is related to whether they occur in the context of an armed conflict. This issue is discussed below, first as it relates to Afghanistan and Iraq, where active hostilities have taken place over a period of years, and then to countries like Pakistan, Yemen, and Somalia, where targeted/extrajudicial killing is part of the US counterterrorism strategy and not related to an armed conflict.

WHICH LAWS OF WAR APPLY TO THE CONDUCT OF THE WARS IN AFGHANISTAN AND IRAQ?

As noted by Philip Alston, former UN Special Rapporteur on extrajudicial, summary or arbitrary executions,[59] in his May 2010 "Study on Targeted Killing," presented to the Human Rights Council, "Whether or not a specific targeted killing is legal depends on the context in which it is conducted: whether in armed conflict, outside armed conflict, or in relation to the interstate use of force." Alston does not address the illegality of the US invasions of Afghanistan and Iraq, but he does say they raise "sovereignty concerns." Alston states that generally in the context of an armed conflict, both IHL as well as IHRL apply simultaneously and coextensively unless there is a conflict between them. That is, under IHL:

> Targeted killing is only lawful when the target is a "combatant" or "fighter" or, in the case of a civilian, only for such time as the person "directly participates in hostilities." In addition, the killing must be militarily necessary, the use of force must be proportionate so that any anticipated military advantage is considered

in light of the expected harm to civilians in the vicinity, and everything feasible must be done to prevent mistakes and minimize harm to civilians. These standards apply regardless of whether the armed conflict is between States (an international armed conflict) or between a State and a non-state armed group (non-international armed conflict), including alleged terrorists. Reprisal or punitive attacks on civilians are prohibited.[60]

If a target is killed in conformity with the above strictures of IHL, IHRL to protect the right to life would not apply.

HAS IHL OR IHRL BEEN FOLLOWED IN AFGHANISTAN OR IRAQ?

Because the information regarding the actual target selection and use has not been made public, it is not possible to evaluate the actual targets under IHL in Iraq or Afghanistan. Alston's study on targeted killing leads to the conclusion that neither body of law was followed. Alston cites the target, or kill list, for Afghanistan. A Senate Foreign Relations Committee Report (Committee Report), released on August 10, 2009, disclosed that the military's list included drug lords suspected of helping to finance the Taliban.[61]

According to the Committee Report, "[t]he military places no restrictions on the use of force with these selected targets, which means they can be killed or captured on the battlefield . . . standards for getting on the list require two verifiable human sources and substantial additional evidence."[62] However, Alston notes:

> It was clear during my mission to Afghanistan how hard it is even for forces on the ground to obtain accurate information. Testimony from witnesses and victims' family members showed that international forces were often too uninformed of local practices, or too credulous in interpreting information, to be able to arrive at a reliable understanding of a situation. International forces all too often based manned airstrikes and raids that resulted in killings on faulty intelligence. Multiple other examples show that the legality of a targeted killing operation is heavily dependent upon the reliability of the intelligence on which it is based.[63]

Sikander Ahmed Shah addresses the mistaken practice of the United States in lumping together al-Qaeda and the Taliban for purposes of targeted killing. Although Shah admits there has been an alliance of sorts between them:

> their modes of operation [and agendas] are actually quite distinct from one another. Whereas al-Qaeda's aim is to inflict maximum harm upon the United States . . . Taliban insurgents are principally engaged with U.S. forces in an armed conflict involving guerilla warfare and recently, even conventional warfare, in an effort to regain control over Afghanistan . . . . It does not seem, however, that the Afghan Taliban are systematically involved in carrying out, or even have the capacity to carry out, terrorist, or for that matter, any attacks on U.S. soil, against U.S. civilians not present in Afghanistan, or against U.S. assets abroad.[64]

The United States engaged in targeted killing in Iraq. The Bush administration drew up a list of targets on a deck of cards with the faces of those the US government wanted to kill. Armed drones were also used in Iraq.[65]

The use of armed drones in combat operations in Afghanistan and Iraq was part of broader illegal military operations. In the video known as "collateral murder,"[66] made available by Bradley (Chelsea) Manning, through Wikileaks, a manned helicopter in visual contact with targets on the ground secured permission to kill two Reuters reporters, believing them to be combatants; they were in fact unarmed civilians.[67] If such errors are sometimes made even after there is visual contact with the targets and discussion between the pilots and the command center to obtain permission for the "kill order," it is highly likely that similar errors are made in the case of targets selected for death by unmanned drones.

Thus, it is evident that in Iraq and Afghanistan the United States targeted persons not directly involved in hostilities. The United States also impermissibly expanded the list of those directly participating in hostilities to include people such as drug lords suspected of helping the Taliban. Where a targeting decision violates International Humanitarian Law, it also violates International Human Rights Law, which protects the right to life.[68]

WHICH LAW APPLIES TO THE USE OF DRONES FOR TARGETED KILLING IN PAKISTAN, YEMEN, AND SOMALIA?

There is no state of armed conflict between the United States and the states of Pakistan, Yemen, or Somalia. Yet as part of the United States' counterterrorism strategy, armed drones for targeted/extrajudicial killing have been used in all three countries. As Alston states:

> The legality of a [targeted] killing outside the context of armed conflict is governed by human rights standards, especially those concerning the use of lethal force. Although these standards are sometimes referred to as the "law enforcement" model, they do not in fact apply only to police forces or in times of peace. The "law enforcement officials" who may use lethal force include all government officials who exercise police powers, including a State's military and security forces, operating in contexts where violence exists, but falls short of the threshold for armed conflict. Under human rights law: a [targeted] killing is legal only if it is required to protect life (making lethal force *proportionate*) and there is no other means, such as capture or nonlethal incapacitation, of preventing that threat to life (making lethal force *necessary*). The proportionality requirement limits the permissible level of force based on the threat posed by the suspect to others. The necessity requirement imposes an obligation to minimize the level of force used, regardless of the amount that would be proportionate through, for example, the use of warnings, restraint, and capture. This means that under human rights law, a targeted killing in the sense of an intentional, premeditated and deliberate killing by law enforcement officials cannot be legal . . . .[69]

In his extensive article on the legality of US drone attacks in Pakistan, Shah makes many important points that are similarly applicable to the actions by the United States in Yemen and Somalia. With respect to drone strikes in Pakistan, Shah correctly states that the only legal basis for the United States to utilize force against the territorial integrity of Pakistan is if the United States suffered an armed attack by non-state actors residing in Pakistan and Pakistan exercised sufficient control over the non-state actors to make the attack an attack by the Pakistani state.[70] As there have been no attacks by persons residing in Pakistan against the United States, self-defense is not available to justify the drone attacks.

The United States characterizes its drone attacks in Pakistan against al-Qaeda members, both Afghan and Pakistan Taliban, and militia leadership, as preemptive self-defense against terrorism as part of its "war on terror," incorrectly characterizing it as a "non-international armed conflict."[71] But the Caroline case prevents this paradigm from constituting a lawful use of force.[72] In addition, if these attacks are acts of reprisal for actions of September 11, 2001, they are unlawful under international law.[73] Alston clarifies that:

> [a] targeted killing conducted by one State in the territory of a second State does not violate the second State's sovereignty if either (a) the second State consents, or (b) the first, targeting State has a right under international law to use force in self-defence under Article 51 of the UN Charter.[74]

However, the right to consent is not unlimited. Consent, as stated by Alston, does not absolve either of the concerned states from their obligations to abide by IHL and IHRL with respect to the use of lethal force against a specific person.[75]

Christof Heyns, Alston's successor as UN Special Rapporteur on extrajudicial, summary or arbitrary executions, made a similar point in his September 13, 2013, report to the UN[76] as follows:

> States cannot consent to the violation of their obligations under international humanitarian law or international human rights law. A State that consents to the activities of another State on its territory remains bound by its own human rights obligations, including to ensure respect for human rights and thus to prevent violations of the right to life, to the extent that it is able to do so.[77]

Pakistan, Yemen, and Somalia have all ratified the ICCPR, which protects their citizens' right to life; this right may not be taken arbitrarily. The consenting state's responsibility to protect those on its territory from arbitrary deprivation of the right to life applies at all times. A consenting state may only lawfully authorize a killing by the targeting state to the extent the killing is carried out in accordance with applicable IHL or IHRL. To meet its legal obligations, therefore, the consenting state should, at a minimum, require the targeting State to demonstrate verifiably that the person against whom lethal force is to be used can be lawfully targeted and that the targeting state will comply with the applicable domestic law.

US JUSTIFICATIONS FOR ITS USE OF DRONES
FOR TARGETED/EXTRAJUDCIAL KILLING

As noted above, the United States has not made public an official legal opinion that supports either the policy of targeted killing or any particular targeted killing.[78] The only suggested rationales for using drones for extrajudicial killing have been provided in speeches given by members of the Obama administration, including President Obama himself. Administration speeches have been delivered by Legal Advisor to the State Department Harold Koh, National Security Advisor John Brennan, and Attorney General Eric Holder. Most of the speeches were given before the revelations in the May 29, 2012, *New York Times* articles. They responded to reports of drone use outside of Afghanistan and Iraq as well as the killing of Osama bin Laden and US citizen Anwar al-Aulaqi. While these speeches proclaim that the policy of targeted killing is legal, as Professor Christine Gray writes, these speeches raise more questions than they answer.[79] Professor Gray diplomatically states that the rationales for the United States' actions stated in the speeches "leave many gaps in the legal justification being put forward."[80] A review of the salient points in these speeches is set forth below.

Legal Adviser to the State Department Harold Koh:

Koh delivered his first speech on the subject to the American Society of International Law in 2010.[81] In it, he stated: "Thus, in the ongoing armed conflict, the US has authority under international law, and the responsibility to its citizens to use force, including lethal force, to defend itself, including by targeting such persons as high level [a]l-Qaeda leaders who are planning attacks . . . ." He characterized the US relationship with al-Qaeda as "a conflict with an organized terrorist enemy that does not have conventional forces but that plans and executes attacks against us and our allies while hiding among civilian populations." Koh described the criteria for determining whether a particular individual will be targeted to be: the imminence of the threat, the sovereignty of the other states involved, and the willingness or ability of those states to suppress the threat the target poses. Koh further claimed that the United States was complying with the laws of war regarding *distinction* and *proportionality*. He attempted to assure his audience that the procedures and practices for identifying targets were extremely robust. Koh further justified the killing of Osama bin Laden in a blog posting,[82] claiming that since bin Laden was in the leadership of al-Qaeda, that made him an imminent threat to the United States and therefore a legitimate lethal target. Koh claimed the materials allegedly found during the raid underscored the imminence of the threats. However, contrary to this assertion, declassified documents showed bin Laden was having major problems with control over the groups alleged to be affiliated with al-Qaeda.[83]

Former National Security Advisor (now CIA Director) John Brennan:

Brennan gave a speech at Harvard Law School on September 16, 2011.[84] In light of the killing of bin Laden, Brennan addressed whether there remained an "imminent threat" from al-Qaeda sufficient to justify ongoing attacks on al-Qaeda leaders outside the battlefields of Afghanistan and Iraq. He said, "Because we are engaged in an armed conflict with [al-Qaeda], the United States takes the legal position that—in accordance with international law—we have the authority to take action against [al-Qaeda] and its associated forces without doing a separate self-defense analysis each time. . . . We reserve the right to take unilateral action if or when other governments are unwilling or unable to take the necessary actions themselves." Thus, Brennan asserted there was no need for the United States to justify each targeted killing by showing it was a necessary or proportionate response to a particular threat. He argued that the targeted killings cumulatively are a response to the 9/11 attacks, in order to deter and prevent future attacks by those linked to the original attack.[85]

In April 2012, Brennan delivered a second speech, entitled "The Ethics and Efficacy of the President's Counter-Terrorism Strategy,"[86] in which he attempted to justify the ongoing use of targeted killing, despite the killing of Osama bin Laden and the release of letters detailing the difficulties facing al-Qaeda.[87] Brennan claimed nonetheless that the threat had not passed, as affiliated groups had arisen in Yemen, Somalia, and elsewhere. He then stated, "[T]he United States is in an armed conflict with [al-Qaeda], the Taliban, and associated forces, in response to the 9/11 attacks, and we may also use force consistent with our inherent right of self-defense." He claimed, "There is nothing in international law that bans the use of remotely piloted aircraft for this purpose or that prohibits us from using lethal force against our enemies outside of an active battlefield, at least when the country involved is unable or unwilling to take action against the threat." Regarding the choice of targets, Brennan stated, "[W]e conduct targeted strikes because they are necessary to mitigate an actual ongoing threat—to stop plots, prevent future attacks, and save American lives." While this speech was delivered before the revelation of "signature strikes" in the 2012 *Times* article, Brennan claimed that civilian casualties were "exceedingly rare."[88]

Attorney General Eric Holder:

Holder delivered a speech to the Northwestern University School of Law in March 2012, in which he attempted to address the legal rationale for the targeted killing of US citizen Anwar al-Aulaqi.[89] Holder also claimed, "[W]e are a nation at war" in an armed conflict with [al-Qaeda]. He asserted that Congress had authorized the president to use all necessary and appropriate force against al-Qaeda, the Taliban, and associated forces, and this authority is not limited to the battlefields of Afghanistan. Although recognizing that international legal principles, including respect for other nations' sovereignty, constrain our ability to act unilaterally, he maintained the use of force would be consistent with these principles if, for example, it was carried out with the consent of the nation involved or after a determination that the nation is unable or unwilling to deal effectively with the threat to the United States. He said it was lawful to target specific senior operational leaders of al-Qaeda and associated forces who present an imminent threat of violent attack. While American citizens, such as al-Aulaqi, who become leaders of al-Qaeda had constitutional rights under the Due Process Clause and Fifth Amendment, Holder noted, they do not have the right to a "judicial process." Regarding the definition of "imminent," Holder elaborated that "[t]he evaluation of whether an individual presents an "imminent threat" incorporates considerations of the relevant window of opportunity to act, the possible harm that missing the window would cause to civilians, and the likelihood of heading off future disastrous attacks against the United States"[90]

Holder does admit the United States must adhere to the principle of *distinction* and not target civilians, and to the principle of *humanity* to avoid unnecessary suffering. But his speech, unlike the others, references *necessity*. Military necessity is a limitation on the use of force, that is, a target must have military value to be targeted. Holder uses the term necessity, not as a limitation on what may be targeted, but as a justification of the use of force by targeted killing in the first instance.[91]

On June 15, 2012, after the publication of the May 2012 *Times* article, President Obama sent a letter to Congress under the War Powers Resolution, in which it was publicly acknowledged that the United States had engaged in targeted killing with drones in Yemen and Somalia against militants allegedly connected to al-Qaeda in the Arabian Peninsula (AQAP) and al-Shabab. He claimed this direct action was aimed at a limited number of al-Qaeda in the Arabian Peninsula who posed a terrorist threat to the United States and our interests.[92]

President Obama has not provided any further legal opinion even though in his May 23, 2013, speech at the National Defense University, he appeared to respond to some of the criticisms of the drone program. He commented most particularly on the choice of targets and the issue of their imminent threats. He stated, "America does not take strikes to punish individuals; we act against terrorists who pose a continuing and imminent threat to the American people, and when there are no other governments capable of effectively addressing the threat. And before any strike is taken, there must be near-certainty that no civilians will be killed or injured—the highest standard we can set."[94]

In May 2013, the White House issued a fact sheet regarding policies and procedures for counterterrorism operations, but did not publicly release a policy guidance. The fact sheet says, "The policy of the United States is not to use lethal force when it is feasible to capture a terrorist suspect." It states that "lethal force will be used outside areas of active hostilities" only when certain preconditions are met. It does not define "areas of active hostilities."[95]

Preconditions for using lethal force in the fact sheet include:

1. The requirement of a "legal basis" for the use of lethal force, although it does not define whether "legal basis" means complying with ratified treaties, including the UN Charter, which prohibits the use of military force except in self-defense or when approved by the Security Council.[96]

2. The target must pose a "continuing, imminent threat to U.S. persons," but the fact sheet does not define "continuing" or "imminent."[97] The recently leaked Department of Justice White Paper[98] says that a US citizen can be killed even when there is no "clear evidence that a specific attack on US persons and interests will take place in the immediate future."

3. There must be "near certainty" that the terrorist target is present. The fact sheet does not address whether the administration will continue "signature strikes" (known as crowd killings), which don't target individuals but rather areas of suspicious activity.[99]

4. There must be "near certainty" that noncombatants will not be injured or killed, apparently a departure from present practice, as many noncombatants have been killed in US drone strikes.[100]

5. There must be an assessment that "capture is not feasible" at the time of the operation, but feasibility is not defined. The white paper appears to indicate that "infeasible" means inconvenient.[101]

6. There must be an assessment that relevant governmental authorities in the country where the attack is contemplated cannot or will not effectively address the "threat to US persons," also left undefined.[102]

7. There must be an assessment that no other reasonable alternatives exist to address the "threat to US persons," also left undefined.[103]

The fact sheet would excuse these conditions when the president takes action "in extraordinary circumstances" that are "both lawful and necessary to protect the United States or its allies." "Extraordinary circumstances" is left undefined.[104]

ARE US JUSTIFICATIONS FOR TARGETED/EXTRAJUDICIAL KILLING SUPPORTED IN LAW?

All the justifications for the use of targeted killing are based on a claim that the United States is in an armed conflict with al-Qaeda and its associated groups.

While the Bush administration described this armed conflict as "a war on terror," the Obama administration now describes this armed conflict as being in the nature of a non-international armed conflict between the United States and these groups.[105] The law governing Armed Conflicts of a Non-International Nature is set forth in Common Article 3 of the Geneva Conventions, and Protocol II.[106] Although non-international armed conflicts are subject to a different and more limited legal regime than international armed conflicts, the law of international armed conflicts can still be applied. Nonetheless, in order to qualify as an armed conflict of either sort under international law, the conflict must meet two minimum criteria: 1) the existence of organized armed groups, 2) which are engaging in fighting of some intensity.[107]

As noted by Professor Gray, "The 'war against [a]l-Qaeda' does not meet the threshold of intensity of a non-international armed conflict, and [a]l-Qaeda does not meet the threshold of an organized armed group."[108] Factors relevant to assessing the existence of an organized armed group include "command structure; exercise of leadership control; governing by rules; providing military training; organized acquisition and provision of weapons and supplies; recruitment of new members; existence of communications infrastructure; and space to rest."[109] In order for a group to be organized enough to engage in an armed conflict of a non-international nature, there must be a command structure in place in order for the basic requirements of Common Article 3 to the 1949 Geneva Conventions to be implemented.[110]

Professor Gray cites seventeen letters declassified from the raid on bin Laden's compound that show "that Osama bin Laden had little control over groups affiliated with [a]l-Qaeda, and that senior leaders disagreed about the proper relationship with these groups. Al-Qaeda had collaborated with jihadi groups around the world, but had not formalized these relations into a unified command."[111] Thus, al-Qaeda and its associated groups do not meet the definition of an armed conflict, as the groups involved do not meet the definition of an organized armed group.

As to intensity of fighting, factors to consider in determining whether fighting is of sufficient intensity to qualify as an armed conflict include: "number of fighters involved; the type and quantity of weapons used; the duration and territorial extent of fighting; the number of casualties; the extent of destruction of property; the displacement of the population; and the involvement of the Security Council or other actors to broker cease-fire efforts. Isolated acts of violence do not constitute armed conflict."[112] It is thus erroneous to categorize persons in "terrorist" groups as combatants.[113]

The European Commission for Democracy Through Law (Venice Commission) concurs:[114]

[T]he organised hostilities in Afghanistan before and after 2001 have been an "armed conflict" which was at first a non-international armed conflict, and later became an international armed conflict after the involvement of US troops. On the other hand, sporadic bombings and other violent acts which terrorist networks perpetrate in different places around the globe and the ensuing counter-terrorism measures, even if they are occasionally undertaken by military units, cannot be said to amount to an "armed conflict" in the sense that they trigger the applicability of International Humanitarian Law.

The Venice Commission considers that counter-terrorist measures which are part of what has sometimes been called "war on terror" are not part of an "armed conflict" in the sense of making the regime of International Humanitarian Law applicable to them.[115]

Sir Christopher Greenwood, a British judge on the International Court of Justice, likewise states:

> In the language of international law there is no basis for speaking of a war on al-Qaeda or any other terrorist group, for such a group cannot be a belligerent, it is merely a band of criminals, and to treat it as anything else risks distorting the law while giving that group a status which to some implies a degree of legitimacy.[116]

Therefore, there is no basis in law for the United States to claim that it is engaged in a non-international armed conflict with al-Qaeda and its associated groups. Al-Qaeda and what are called "associated groups" should thus be treated like people engaged in other criminal behavior. They must be monitored, and may be subject to arrest and detention.

It is irrelevant that the United States claims to be targeting individuals for death consistent with IHL, because IHL does not apply to drone strikes targeting individuals in Yemen, Pakistan, and Somalia.[117] Because the United States is not in a state of armed conflict with terrorist groups in Yemen, Pakistan, and Somalia, or the States themselves, the only law that applies to the drone strikes is IHRL to prevent arbitrary deprivation of the right to life.

As noted by Special Rapporteur Christof Heyns:

> The right against the arbitrary deprivation of life has been described as a rule of customary international law, in addition to a general principle of international law and a rule of *jus cogens*. It is included in the Universal Declaration of Human Rights (art. 3), which is widely regarded as setting out rules of general international law. The right to life is recognized in the constitutional and other legal provisions of States and through a wide range of national and international actions and practices, and unlawful killing is universally criminalized. Some violations of the right to life are considered to be war crimes or crimes against humanity.[118]

Heyns also notes, "The view that mere past involvement in planning attacks is sufficient to render an individual targetable even where there is no evidence of a specific and immediate attack distorts the requirements established in international human rights law."[119]

The legal justifications for killing people in Pakistan, Yemen, and Somalia are still associated with a "war on terror," even though there is no legal justification under international law for targeted extrajudicial killing of specific people labeled as "terrorists."[120] In countries in which the United States is not engaged in armed hostilities, the law enforcement approach must be utilized. This approach is stated in the outcome document of the1990 United Nations Congress on the Prevention of Crime and the Treatment of Offenders. It provides the basic principles for the use of force in law-enforcement operations and elaborates on what is meant by Article 6 of the ICCPR's protection of the right to life as follows:

> Law enforcement officials shall not use firearms against persons except in self-defence or defence of others against the imminent threat of death or serious injury, to prevent the perpetration of a particularly serious crime involving grave threat to life, to arrest a person presenting such a danger and resisting their authority, or to prevent his or her escape, and only when less extreme means are insufficient to achieve these objectives. In any event, intentional lethal use of firearms may only be made when strictly unavoidable in order to protect life.[121]

Furthermore, nowhere in the United States' arguments in support of its targeted killings has there been any reference to or acknowledgement of the limited right of self-defense under Article 51 of the UN Charter, which allows use of force only in response to an armed attack against a member state. As noted above, the charter does not allow for anticipatory self-defense except under the strictures of the Caroline case where the threat is "is instant, overwhelming, and leaving no choice of means, and no moment for deliberation."[122] To the extent Koh, Brennan, or Holder refer to imminence of harm (or to mitigate ongoing plots and prevent future attacks) to justify a targeted killing, they are arguing for a definition of imminence that is so broad as to render the term imminence meaningless. In fact, their claim of imminence would amount to a preemptive strike, and/or an illegal reprisal rather than a use of force that is taken because the threat is so instant, overwhelming, and leaving no choice of means and no moment for deliberation (as recognized in the law enforcement model as well).

INTERNATIONAL EFFORTS TO ADDRESS THE VIOLATIONS OF INTERNATIONAL LAW RESULTING FROM USE OF DRONES FOR TARGETED/EXTRAJUDICIAL KILLING

There is a mounting chorus of voices condemning the use of drones for targeted extrajudicial killing. In addition to authoritative reports concerning their impact on people's lives, there is a growing concern that the United States' use of drones for counterterrorism is setting a dangerous precedent that we may not be able to stop. As noted by Heyns, "The expansive use of armed drones by the first states to acquire them, if not challenged, can do structural damage to the cornerstones of international security and set precedents that undermine the protection of life across the globe in the longer term."[123] He adds:

Given that drones greatly reduce or eliminate the number of casualties on the side using them, the domestic constraints—political and otherwise—may be less restrictive than with the deployment of other types of armed force. This effect is enhanced by the relative ease with which the details about drone targeting can be withheld from the public eye and the potentially restraining influence of public concern. Such dynamics call for a heightened level of vigilance by the international community concerning the use of use.[124]

Also, Ben Emmerson, the UN Special Rapporteur on the promotion and protection of human rights and fundamental freedoms while countering terrorism, has been investigating many of the drone strikes that have killed people who cannot be said to have anything to do with terrorism. His work, as well as that of Heyns, was instrumental in the unanimous passage in October 2013 of a UN General Assembly (GA) resolution calling for regulation on the use of remotely piloted aircraft against suspected terrorists.[125] Pakistan strongly supported that resolution. This was the first time that the GA had spoken out on the use of armed drones, especially inside Pakistan. The resolution urges states "to ensure that any measures taken or means employed to counter terrorism, including the use of remotely piloted aircraft, comply with their obligations under international law, including the Charter of the United Nations, human rights law and international humanitarian law, in particular the principles of distinction and proportionality."[126]

In early March 2014, European politicians voted by a landslide (534 to 49 members of European Parliament) to propose a ban on US drone strikes that have killed thousands of people in Yemen and Pakistan, calling the killings "unlawful." The European Parliament voted to support a resolution demanding that European Union member states "not perpetrate unlawful targeted killings or facilitate such killings by other states, and calling on them to oppose and ban practices of extra judicial targeted killings."[127]

CONCLUSION

Since September 11, 2001, the United States has launched wars in Afghanistan and Iraq. These wars are illegal. But as admittedly armed conflicts, IHL applies to them. The United States is accountable to the people who suffered in these illegal wars for damages inflicted as a result of violations of IHL that may have occurred either using drones or other weapons.

With respect to the use of drones for targeting people for killing in Yemen, Somalia, and Pakistan, IHRL applies with the law enforcement principles for the use of lethal force. The 1990 law enforcement principles cited above were written more than a decade before the use of drones for targeted/extrajudicial killing. They have not changed. The United States is identifying persons or profiles of persons suspected of planning terrorist attacks.[128] But it appears these persons are being killed because they are suspected of engaging in plots against the United States. The persons targeted are not charged with any crime, nor has any evidence against them been brought in a proper tribunal before they are placed on the "kill list." There is no or little attempt to capture or arrest them. The administration issuing the kill orders plays the role of judge, jury, and executioner. This is the type of action the laws of war and human rights law were designed to prevent.

Special Rapporteur Heyns, like his predecessor, Alston, is seriously concerned that the practice of targeted killing as justified by the United States could set a dangerous precedent, in that any government could, under the cover of counterterrorism imperatives, decide to target and kill an individual on the territory of any state if it considers that individual to constitute a threat.[129] A decade ago, the use of armed drones was relatively novel and untested. Their human impact and further technological development were hard to predict, and a full discussion of the proper application of the international legal framework had yet to emerge. A vast body of academic and advocacy literature has now developed, and civil society watchdogs are tracking the issue and pursuing transparency.[130]

The actions taken by the United States expose the leaders of this country to potential criminal liability. Under the Nuremberg Principles, planning and executing wars of aggression are the ultimate crime for which Nazi leaders were tried, convicted, and put to death.[131] Violations of the laws of war under Nuremberg are also war crimes.[132] US leaders, in the name of fighting "terrorism," are acting criminally, and are subject to prosecution in the International Criminal Court.

Will any American president or official who approved the policy of targeted/extrajudicial killing ever pay a price for implementing this policy? In the short run, it is not likely. Perhaps someday they will be held to account by another country under the doctrine of *universal jurisdiction*.[133] Proclaiming that these policies will make us safe does not render the actions they condone legal. They distort the notion of self-defense. With new weapons of war, the United States purports to get away with illegal actions consistent with military might. That makes the United States a government of lawbreakers, without respect for treaties and international obligations. The "masters of war" who provide the technology to kill remotely will never be able to buy back the souls of those who have made it a policy to use them.

NOTES

[1] Jo Becker & Scott Shaw, *Secret 'Kill List' Proves a Test of Obama's Principles and Will*, N.Y. TIMES (May 29, 2012), www.nytimes.com/2012/05/29/world/obamas-leadership-in-war-on-al-qaeda.html?pagewanted=all&_r=0.

[2] Robert F. Worth, *Drone Strike in Yemen Hits Wedding Convoy, Killing 11*, N.Y. TIMES (Dec. 12, 2013), www.nytimes.com/2013/12/13/world/middleeast/drone-strike-in-yemen-hits-wedding-convoy-killing-11.html?_r=0.

[3] Becker & Shaw, *supra* note 1. Although the reaction to the revelations of "kill lists" as a major part of the US's counterterrorism strategy in Yemen, Pakistan, and Somalia was significant because of the lists' secrecy, the United States used armed drones for targeted killing in combat operations in Iraq and Afghanistan. *See* Jonathan Masters, *Targeted Killing*, COUNCIL ON FOREIGN RELATIONS (May 23, 2013), www.cfr.org/counterterrorism/targeted-killings/p9627#.

[4] Becker & Shaw, *supra* note 1 ("In Pakistan, Mr. Obama had approved not only "personality" strikes aimed at named, high-value terrorists, but "signature" strikes that targeted training camps and suspicious compounds in areas controlled by militants.").

[5] Council of Foreign Relations *Update on Targeted Killing* by Jonathan Masters reports claims that drone strikes for targeted killing can be legal have been made by "Harold Koh, legal adviser of the U.S. Department of State, in 2010; White House Chief Counterterrorism Adviser John Brennan in 2011, Defense Department General Counsel Jeh Johnson in 2012, as well as Attorney General Eric Holder in 2012, and Brennan again in 2012," although the actual legal opinions have never been released. Masters, *supra* note 3.

[6] *See infra* sections: Legal Adviser to the State Department, Harold Koh, Former National Security Adviser (Now CIA Director) John Brennan, Attorney General Eric Holder.

[7] *See* Benjamin Forley, *Drones and Democracy: Missing out on Accountability*, 54 S. TEX. L. REV. 365, 389-90 (2012).

[8] *See* Stanford Law Sch. & New York Univ. Sch. of Law, Living Under Drones: Death Injury, and Trauma to Civilians from US Drone Practices in Pakistan 106-07 (2012), *available at* www.livingunderdrones.org/wp-content/uploads/2013/10/Stanford-NYU-Living-Under-Drones.pdf [hereinafter Stanford Report]; The Center for Civilian Conflict, The Civilian Impact of Drones: Unexamined Costs, Unanswered Questions (Columbia Law School 2012), *available at* web.law.columbia.edu/sites/default/files/microsites/human-rights-institute/files/The%20Civilian%20Impact%20of%20Drones.pdf [hereinafter Columbia Report].

[9] *See, e.g.*, Columbia Report, *supra* note 8, at 24.

[10] *See, e.g.*, Leila Hudson, Colin S. Owens & Matt Flannes, *Drone Warfare: Blowback from the New American Way of War*, MIDDLE EAST POLICY COUNCIL (last visited Sept. 15, 2013), www.mepc.org/journal/middle-east-policy-archives/drone-warfare-blowback-new-american-way-war; *see Quigley* chapter 12.

11   While transparency is important, as is holding persons accountable for targeted or extrajudicial killing (as required by international law), these arguments tend to be made by civil libertarians who generally support President Obama and want to give him the benefit of the doubt, in the hope that there actually is legal justification for the policy. The reluctance of the administration to be fully transparent may also reveal that target selection does not comply with the law. But the United Nations has enacted a set of principles on the Effective Prevention and Investigation of Extra-Legal, Arbitrary and Summary Executions. UN Economic and Social Counsel, *Effective Prevention and Investigation of Extra-Legal, Arbitrary and Summary Executions* 52, UN Doc. E/1989/89, 1st sess. (1989). These principles require countries to criminalize extrajudicial killings and to investigate all such instances of these killings in order to ensure transparency.

12   International Covenant on Civil and Political Rights, art. 6, Mar. 23, 1976, 999 U.N.T.S. 171.

13   Human Rights Council, *Report of the Special Rapporteur on extrajudicial, summary or arbitrary executions, Philip Alston,* ¶ 1, UN Doc A/HRC/14/24/ Add.6, 14th sess. (2010) [hereinafter Alston].

14   *Id.*

15   HCJ 769/02 The Public Committee Against Torture in Israel v. Government of Israel [2006] (Isr.); *see Menuchin* chapter 11.

16   HCJ 769/02 The Public Committee Against Torture in Israel v. Government of Israel [2006] (Isr.); Alston, *supra* note 13, at ¶ 15.

17   Alston, *supra* note 13, at ¶ 15.

18   The issue of civilians killed by drone strikes is not specifically addressed by this chapter. Civilians are killed and wounded, and in the case of documented "double tap" strikes (where a second strike follows shortly after the first target strike) family members and first responders are also killed by drone attacks. Killing civilians in the context of a drone strike is just as illegal as the targeted extrajudicial killing of the person targeted. *See* Stanford Report, *supra* note 8, at 115; *see Ross* chapter 7.

19   *See Responsibility of States for Internationally Wrongful Acts,* GA Res. 56/83, UN GAOR , 53rd sess., (Vol. II), UN Doc. A/RES/56/83 (Jan. 28, 2002).

20   Rome Statute of the International Criminal Court, July 17, 1998, 2187 U.N.T.S. 3.

21   In the case of an attack by nonstate actors such as what occurred on September 11, 2001, in order to have attributed the attack to the Taliban government in Afghanistan, it must have been demonstrated that Afghanistan had effective control over the al-Qaeda forces operating in Afghanistan. *See* Military and Paramilitary Activities in and Against Nicaragua (Nicar. v. U.S.), 1986 I.C.J. 14 (June 27), at ¶¶ 105–115.

[22] UN Charter, art. 51.

[23] UN Charter, Preamble.

[24] Sikander Ahmed Shah, *War On Terrorism: Self Defense, Operation Enduring Freedom, and the Legality of U.S. Drone Attacks in Pakistan*, 9 WASH. U. GLOBAL STUD. L. REV 77, 91-92 (2010).

[25] *See, e.g.*, Vienna Convention on the Law of Treaties, art. 60(5), May 23, 1969, 1155 U.N.T.S. 331; *see generally Practices Relating to Rule 145. Reprisals*, ICRC, (last visited September 20, 2013), www.icrc.org/customary-ihl/eng/docs/v2_rul_rule145. For examples of reprisals, see: *Declaration on Principles of International Law Concerning Friendly Relations and Co-operation Among States in Accordance with the Charter of the United Nations*, GA Res. 2625 (XXV), UN GAOR, 25th sess., UN Doc. A/8082 (Oct. 24, 1970); *Complaint by Yemen*, SC Res. 188, SCOR, 1111th meeting, UN Doc. S/RES/188 (Apr. 9, 1964); *Case Concerning Military and Paramilitary Activities in and Against Nicaragua (Nicaragua v. United States)*, 1986 I.C.J. 14.

[26] CIL is typically defined as a "customary practice of states followed from a sense of legal [as opposed to moral] obligation." RESTATEMENT (THIRD) OF THE FOREIGN RELATIONS LAW OF THE UNITED STATES § 102(2) (1987).

[27] *See* discussion *infra*, "Was the invasion of Iraq lawful?"

[28] Jeremy Scahill, *Dirty Wars, Continued: How Does the 'Global War on Terror' Ever End?*, NATION (Oct. 29, 2013), www.thenation.com/article/176869/dirty-wars-continued-how-does-global-war-terror-ever-end#; *see* Barack Obama, President, United States, Remarks by the President at the National Defense University (May 23, 2013), *available at* www.whitehouse.gov/the-press-office/2013/05/23/remarks-president-national-defense-university.

[29] Authorization for Use of Military Force, 115 Stat 224 (2001) ("The President is authorized to use all necessary and appropriate force against those nations, organizations, or persons he determines planned, authorized, committed, or aided the terrorist attacks that occurred on September 11, 2001, or harbored such organizations or persons, in order to prevent any future acts of international terrorism against the United States by such nations, organizations or persons.").

[30] This is because any use of force to invade another country not authorized under the Charter, or not in self-defense, is a war of aggression. Wars of aggression are not only violations of the Nuremberg Charter (*See* MARJORIE COHN, COWBOY REPUBLIC: SIX WAYS THE BUSH GANG HAS DEFIED THE LAW 27-28 (Polipoint Press 2007)), but wars of aggression violate the *jus cogens* norm, from which there is no derogation. It is generally accepted that *jus cogens* includes the prohibition of genocide, piracy, slaving and slavery, torture, and wars of aggression. *E.g.*, M. Cherif Bassiouni, *International Crimes: Jus Cogens and Obligatio Erga Omnes' Law and Contemporary Problems*, Vol. 59, No. 4, LAW & CONTEMP. PROBS. 68 (1996).

[31] US Const. art. VI, cl. 2 ("This Constitution, and the Laws of the United States which shall be made in Pursuance thereof; and all Treaties made, or which shall be made, under the Authority of the United States, shall be the supreme Law of the Land; and the Judges in every State shall be bound thereby, any Thing in the Constitution or Laws of any State to the Contrary notwithstanding."). Sikander Ahmed Shah argues that non-state terrorist organizations, even while residing in one state, cannot undertake armed attacks, for purposes of article 51 and the customary international law of self- defense, against another state without the presence of state sponsorship. Therefore, absent state sponsorship, any resulting use of force on the basis of self -defense on the territory of another State to neutralize terrorists without the consent of the attacked state is a violation of article 2, section 4 of the Charter. Shah, *supra* note 24, at 94.

[32] *Threats to International Peace and Security Caused by Terrorist Acts*, S.C. Res. 1368, UN Doc. S/RES/1368 (Sept. 12, 2001).

[33] *Threats to International Peace and Security Caused by Terrorist Acts*, S.C. Res. 1373, UN Doc. S/RES/1373 (Sept. 28, 2001).

[34] Resolutions 1368 and 1373 condemn the September 11 attacks and order the freezing of assets; the criminalizing of terrorist activity; the prevention of the commission of and support for terrorist attacks; the taking of necessary steps to prevent the commission of terrorist activity, including the sharing of information; and urging the ratification and enforcement of the international conventions against terrorism.

[35] The argument against regime change in Afghanistan does not imply support of the regime. The Taliban regime was very unpopular and few countries had recognized it. Moreover, forcible regime change violates article 1(1) of the ICCPR. International Covenant on Civil and Political Rights, art. 1, cl. 1., Mar. 23, 1976, 999 U.N.T.S. 171 ("All peoples have the right of self-determination. By virtue of that right they freely determine their political status and freely pursue their economic, social and cultural development.").

[36] *Afghanistan*, S.C. Res. 1386, 2, U.N. Doc. S/RES/1386 (Dec. 20, 2001).

[37] *See* Marjorie Cohn, *Obama's Af-Pak War Should Be Considered Illegal*, Huffington Post (Dec. 21, 2009), www.huffingtonpost.com/marjorie-cohn/obamas-af-pak-war-should_b_398728.html.

[38] Kofi Annan, UN secretary general, stated, "[f]rom our point of view and the UN Charter point of view [the war] was illegal." *E.g.*, Ewen MacAskill & Julian Borger, *Iraq war was illegal and breached UN charter, says Annan*, The Guardian (Sept. 15, 2004), www.theguardian.com/world/2004/sep/16/iraq.iraq. Chief Prosecutor for the Nuremburg tribunals Benjamin Ferencz stated, "a prima facie case can be made that the United States is guilty of the supreme crime against humanity, that being an illegal war of aggression against a sovereign nation." Benjamin Ferencz, *Forward to* Michael

HAAS, GEORGE W. BUSH, WAR CRIMINAL?: THE BUSH ADMINISTRATION'S LIABILITY FOR 269 WAR CRIMES (Praeger 2008). *See also* Nikolaus Schultz, *Was the War on Iraq Illegal?*, 7 GERMAN L. J. 25 (2006).

[39] Shah, *supra* note 24, at 90 n.83. Shah uses the terms of preemptive self-defense and anticipatory self-defense interchangeably. *Id.* at 91.

[40] The incident arose after the British attacked the *SS Caroline*, in US waters, dispatched the crew, and set the *Caroline* on fire, sending it over Niagara Falls. In the process one American was killed. The *Caroline* had been used by Americans (non-state actors) to bring arms, money, and other supplies to a group of Canadians who were trying to establish a republic of Canada. Having failed, they retreated to a Canadian island between the United States and Canada. *See* Letter from Daniel Webster to Lord Ashburton (6 Aug. 1842), *in* 2 J.B. Moore, *A Digest of International Law* 412 (Washington 1906).

[41] *Id.*

[42] *See* Cohn, *supra* note 30, at 21–25.

[43] The "crime of aggression" is the planning, preparation, initiation, or execution, by a person in a position effectively to exercise control over or to direct the political or military action of a state, of an act of aggression, which, by its character, gravity, and scale, constitutes a manifest violation of the UN Charter. *Amendments on the Crime of Aggression to the Rome Statute of the International Criminal Court*, CR Res. 6 , UN Doc. RC/11 (June 11, 2010), *available at* www.icc-cpi.int/iccdocs/asp_docs/Resolutions/RC-Res.6-ENG.pdf. An "act of aggression" means the use of armed force by a state against the sovereignty, territorial integrity, or political independence of another state, or in any other manner inconsistent with the charter. The amendments adopt the definition of act of aggression in General Assembly Resolution 3314 (XXIX) of 14 December 1974. *Id.; Definition of Aggression*, GA Res. 3314, GAOR 29th sess., UN Doc. A/RES/3314 (Dec. 14, 1974).

[44] Principles of International Law Recognized in the Charter of the Nurnberg Tribunal and in the Judgment of the Tribunal (II Y.B.I.L.C. 374 (1950)), adopted by the United Nations International Law Commission. Formulation of the Nurnberg Principles, GAOR 5th sess., UN Doc. A/RES/488(V) (Aug. 2, 1950). The principles are binding international law and are supplementary to, and not replaced by, the Rome Statute (*supra* note 20) creating the International Criminal Court. The Rome Statute applies only to those countries that have ratified it. The Rome Statute covers the crime of genocide, which was not specifically outlawed before Nuremberg. Although the Rome Statute initially did not define a war of aggression, the UN General Assembly has. See *supra* text accompanying note 43. Thus, US leaders would have to be held accountable under the Nuremberg Principles:

> Principle I: Any person who commits an act which constitutes a crime under international law is responsible therefor and liable to punishment.

... Principle III: The fact that a person who committed an act which constitutes a crime under international law acted as Head of State or responsible Government official does not relieve him from responsibility under international law. Principle IV: The fact that a person acted pursuant to order of his Government or of a superior does not relieve him from responsibility under international law, provided a moral choice was in fact possible to him. . . . Principle VI: The crimes hereinafter set out are punishable as crimes under; international law: (a) Crimes against peace: (i) Planning, preparation, initiation or waging of a war of aggression or a war in violation of international treaties, agreements or assurances . . . . (b) War crimes: Violations of the laws or customs of war which include, but are not limited to, murder, . . . wanton destruction of cities, towns, or villages, or devastation not justified by military necessity. (c) Crimes against humanity: Murder, . . . and other inhuman acts done against any civilian population . . . when such acts are done . . . in execution of or in connection with any crime against peace or any war crime. Principle VII: Complicity in the commission of a crime against peace, a war crime, or a crime against humanity as set forth in Principles VI is a crime under international law.

Principles of International Law Recognized in the Charter of the Nurnberg Tribunal and in the Judgment of the Tribunal, *supra* note 44.

[45] *See* Responsibility of States for Internationally Wrongful Acts, GA Res. 56/83, GAOR 56th sess., UN Doc. A/RES/56/83 art. 31 (Jan. 28, 2002).

[46] See the complete versions of the Conferences at, *Laws of War*, YALE LAW SCHOOL (last visited September 10, 2013), avalon.law.yale.edu/subject_menus/lawwar.asp.

[47] *See* UN Economic and Social Council, *Second Protocol to the Hague Convention of 1954 for the Protection of Cultural Property in the Event of Armed Conflict The Hague*, art. 6(a), UN Doc. HC/1999/7, (1999).

[48] Convention for the Amelioration of the Condition of the Wounded and Sick in Armed Forces in the Field, Aug. 12, 1949, 75 U.N.T.S. 31; Convention for the Amelioration of the Condition of Wounded, Sick and Shipwrecked Members of Armed Forces at Sea, Aug. 12, 1949, 75 U.N.T.S. 85; Convention Relative to the Treatment of Prisoners of War; Aug. 12, 1949, 75 U.N.T.S. 135; Convention Relative to the Protection of Civilian Persons in Time of War, Aug. 12, 1949, 75 U.N.T.S. 287; Protocol Additional to the Geneva Conventions of 12 August 1949, and relating to the Protection of Victims of International Armed Conflicts, June 8, 1977, 1125 U.N.T.S. 3; Protocol Additional to the Geneva Conventions of 12 August 1949, and relating to the Protection of Victims of Non-International Armed Conflicts; June 8, 1977, 1125 U.N.T.S. 609; Protocol Additional to the Geneva Conventions of 12 August, 1949, and relating to the adoption of an Additional Distinctive Emblem, Aug. 12, 2005, 2404 U.N.T.S 261. For a general discussion on the principle of distinction, *see* *The Principle of Distinction between Civilian Objects and Military Objectives*, ICRC (last visted Sept. 20, 2013), www.icrc.org/customary-ihl/eng/docs/v1_cha_chapter2_rule7#Fn_28_17.

49 *Rule 14. Proportionality in Attack*, ICRC (last visited Sept. 22, 2013), *available at* www.icrc.org/customary-ihl/eng/docs/v1_cha_chapter4_rule14.

50 UN Office of the High Commissioner on Human Rights, *International Legal Protection of Human Rights in Armed Conflict* 5 (2011), *available at* www. google.com/url?sa=t&rct=j&q=&esrc=s&frm=1&source=web&cd=1&ca d=rja&ved=0CCwQFjAA&url=http%3A%2F%2Fwww.ohchr.org%2FDoc uments%2FPublications%2FHR_in_armed_conflict.pdf&ei=_3s-UrHOM OHgiAKNy4HgAQ&usg=AFQjCNGr3H1I9KLrS1sL1jsn1ewahyxy5g&s ig2=-9nCg6WlG1qqfsfMrIQxrQ ("international humanitarian law has to be applied equally by all sides to every armed conflict, regardless of whether their cause is justified.").

51 UN Charter art 1, ¶ 3.

52 UN General Assembly, *Universal Declaration of Human Rights*, 71-77, UN Doc. A/810, 3rd sess. (1948).

53 International Covenant on Civil and Political Rights (ICCPR), Mar. 23, 1976, 999 U.N.T.S. 171.

54 International Covenant on Economic, Social and Cultural Rights (ICESCR), Jan. 3, 1976, 993 U.N.T.S. 3.

55 The United States has ratified the ICCPR (United Nations Treaty Collection, treaties.un.org/pages/ShowMTDSGDetails.aspx?src=UNTSO NLINE&tabid=1&mtdsg_no=IV-4&chapter=4&lang=en#Participants (last visited Apr. 10, 2014), and signed but has not ratified the ICESCR (United Nations Treaty Collection, treaties.un.org/pages/ShowMTDSGDetails. aspx?src=UNTSONLINE&tabid=1&mtdsg_no=IV-3&chapter=4&lang=en# Participants (last visited Apr. 10, 2014).

56 For a general discussion on each of these instruments, *see Fact Sheet No.2 (Rev.1), The International Bill of Human Rights*, Office of the High Commissioner on Human Rights, www.ohchr.org/Documents/ Publications/FactSheet2Rev.1en.pdf (last visited Apr. 10, 2014).

57 Justifiable self-defense requires an immediate or imminent danger. *See* discussion *infra*, "U.S. JUSTIFICATIONS FOR ITS USE OF DRONES FOR TARGETED/EXTRAJUDCIAL KILLING."

58 There may also be instances, especially in relation to "signature strikes," in which issues of freedom of association under Article 22 of the ICCPR are implicated. Drone strikes may also violate ICCPR Article 17 (prohibition on cruel, inhuman, or and degrading treatment or punishment); article 9.1 (right to freedom from arbitrary interference with privacy, family, and home); and Article 21 (freedom of assembly).

59 Alston, *supra* note 13, at ¶ 28.

60 *Id.* at ¶ 30.

61 S. Rep. No. 111-29, at 16 (2009); Alston, *supra* note 13, at ¶ 21; *see also,* Nicolas Rostow, *The Laws of War And the Killing of Suspected Terrorists: False Starts, Rabbit Holes, and Dead Ends,* 63 RUTGERS L. REV. 1215, 1225 (2011) ("More attenuated acts, such as providing financial support, advocacy, or other non-combat aid, does [sic] not constitute direct participation.").

62 Afghanistan's Narco War: Breaking the Link Between Drug Traffickers and Insurgents, S. Rep. No. 111-29, at 15-16 (2010); Alston, *supra* note 13, at ¶ 21.

63 Alston, *supra* note 13, at ¶ 83.

64 Shah, *supra* note 24, at 118.

65 Masters, *supra* note 3.

66 COLLATERAL MURDER (Sept. 21, 2013, 11:24 PM), www.collateralmurder.com/.

67 *See* Marjorie Cohn, *Bradley Manning's Legal Duty to Expose War Crimes,* TRUTHOUT (June 3, 2013), www.truth-out.org/news/item/16731-bradley-mannings-legal-duty-to-expose-war-crimes.

68 International Covenant on Civil and Political Rights (ICCPR), Mar. 23, 1976, 999 U.N.T.S. 171, art. 2.

69 Alston, *supra* note 13, at ¶ 31–33.

70 *See* Shah, *supra* note 24, at 120; ICJ, *See also* Military and Paramilitary Activities in and Against Nicaragua (Nicar. v. U.S.), 1986 I.C.J. 14 (June 27), at ¶¶ 105–115.

71 *See* Gray, *infra* note 79, at 90–91.

72 *See supra* text accompanying note 40.

73 *See* Vienna Convention on the Law of Treaties, *supra* 25.

74 Alston, *supra* note 13, at ¶ 35.

75 *Id.*

76 *See* Report of the Special Rapporteur on Extrajudicial, Summary or Arbitrary Executions, G.A. Res 382, GAOR 68th sess., UN Doc A/68/382 (September 13, 2013).

77 *Id.* at ¶ 38.

78 The leaked white paper on targeted killing primarily addressed the right of due process and other constitutional rights of US citizens. Department of Justice White Paper: Lawfulness of a Lethal Operation Directed Against a U.S. Citizen Who Is a Senior Operational Leader of Al-Qa'ida or An Associated Force (Nov. 8, 2011); *See* Appenix A.

79 Christine Gray, *Targeted Killings: Recent US Attempts to Create a Legal Framework,* 66 CURRENT LEGAL PROBLEMS 75 (2013).

80 *Id.,* at 81.

81 Harold Hongiu Koh, Legal Advisor, U.S. Department of State, The Obama Administration and International Law (Mar. 25, 2010), *available at* www. lawfareblog.com/wp-content/uploads/2013/01/Speech-by-Harold-Hongju-Koh-State-Department-Legal-Adviser-at-the-Annual-Meeting-of-the-American-Society-of-International-Law-Mar-25-2010.pdf.

82 Harold Hongiu Koh, *The Lawfulness of the U.S. Operation Against Osama bin Laden*, Opinio Juris (May 19, 2011), opiniojuris.org/2011/05/19/the-lawfulness-of-the-us-operation-against-osama-bin-laden/.

83 *Id.* at 88.

84 John Brennan, Assistant to the President, Homeland Security, Strengthening Our Security by Adhering to Our Values and Laws (Sept. 16, 2011), www.whitehouse.gov/the-press-office/2011/09/16/remarks-john-o-brennan-strengthening-our-security-adhering-our-values-an.

85 *Id.*

86 John Brennan, Assistant to the President, Homeland Security, The Ethics and Efficacy of the President's Counterterrorism Strategy (Apr. 30, 2012), *available at* http://www.lawfareblog.com/2012/04/brennanspeech/.

87 Gray, *supra* note 79, at 88.

88 *Id.*

89 Eric Holder, Attorney General, United States, Remarks at Northwestern University School of Law (Mar. 5, 2012), *available at* www.justice.gov/iso/opa/ag/speeches/2012/ag-speech-1203051.html.

90 *Id.*

91 *Id.*

92 Letter from Barack Obama, President, United States, to Congress (June 15, 2012), *available at* www.whitehouse.gov/the-press-office/2012/06/15/presidential-letter-2012-war-powers-resolution-6-month-report.

93 Barack Obama, President, United States, Remarks by the President at the National Defense University (May 23, 2013), *available at* www.whitehouse.gov/the-press-office/2013/05/23/remarks-president-national-defense-university.

94 Press Release, Fact Sheet: U.S. Policy Standards and Procedures for the Use of Force in Counterterrorism Operations Outside the United States and Areas of Active Hostilities (May 23, 2013), *available at* www.whitehouse.gov/the-press-office/2013/05/23/fact-sheet-us-policy-standards-and-procedures-use-force-counterterrorism [hereinafter Fact Sheet]; *see* Appendix B.

95 *Id.*

96 *Id.*

97 *Id.*

[98] White Paper, *supra* note 78.

[99] Fact Sheet, *Supra* note 94.

[100] *Id; See also Ross* chapter 7.

[101] White Paper, *supra* note 78.

[102] Fact Sheet, *Supra* note 94.

[103] *Id.*

[104] *Id.*

[105] Gray, *supra* note 79, at 83, n. 26.

[106] Geneva Convention Relative to the Treatment of Prisoners of War, 75 U.N.T.S. 135 (Aug. 12, 1949). Common Article 3 states:

> In the case of armed conflict not of an international character occurring in the territory of one of the High Contracting Parties, each Party to the conflict shall be bound to apply as a minimum, the following provisions: (1) Persons taking no active part in the hostilities, including members of armed forces who have laid down their arms and those placed *hors de combat* by sickness, wounds, detention, or any other cause, shall in all circumstances be treated humanely, without any adverse distinction founded on race, colour, religion or faith, sex, birth or wealth, or any other similar criteria. To this end the following acts are and shall remain prohibited at any time and in any place whatsoever with respect to the above-mentioned persons: (a) violence to life and person, in particular murder of all kinds, mutilation, cruel treatment and torture; (b) taking of hostages; (c) outrages upon personal dignity, in particular humiliating and degrading treatment; (d) the passing of sentences and the carrying out of executions without previous judgment pronounced by a regularly constituted court affording all the judicial guarantees which are recognized as indispensable by civilized peoples. (2) The wounded and sick shall be collected and cared for.

[107] The Hague Conference, Final Report on the Meaning of Armed Conflict in International Law, Use of Force Committee 2 (2010), *available at* www.google.com/url?sa=t&rct=j&q=&esrc=s&source=web&cd=1&cad=rja&uact=8&ved=0CCkQFjAA&url=http%3A%2F%2Fwww.ila-hq.org%2Fdownload.cfm%2Fdocid%2F2176DC63-D268-4133-8989A664754F9F87&ei=8GlHU_uCN8ry8QXRioKQBQ&usg=AFQjCNHjr0685NkfCRIjs50cZZres9Us nQ&sig2=EqXDnv23Adwyw3otJJsn7w [hereinafter Armed Conflict in International Law].

[108] Gray, *supra* note 79, at 84–84.

[109] Mary Ellen O'Connell, What is War?: An Investigation in the Wake of 9/11 361 (Martinus Nijhoff 2012).

[110] Armed Conflict in International Law, *supra* note 107, at 29.

[111] Gray, *supra* note 79, at 88.

[112] Armed Conflict in International Law, *supra* note 107, at 30.

[113] According to the Armed Conflict in International Law, *supra* note 107, at 26:

> Other terrorist attacks since 11 September 2001 have not been treated as armed conflict, but rather have been characterized as crimes. Police methods, not military force, have been used in response. For example, in 2008, terrorists based in Pakistan carried out coordinated attacks at a number of sites in Mumbai, India, that left 174 persons dead. Within a year of the attacks, civil trials were underway in India and Pakistan of persons suspected of involvement. The indications are that most states recognized that these attacks belonged in the same category as those that have occurred subsequent to 11 September in London, Madrid, and Bali, all of which have been characterized as crimes, not armed conflict. Police methods, not military force, have been used in response.

[114] Eur. Consult. Ass., *European Commission for Democracy Through Law (Venice Commission): Opinion on the International Legal Obligations of Council of Europe Member States in Respect of Secret Detention Facilities and Inter-State Transport of Prisoners*, 66th Sess., Doc. No. CDL-AD(2006)009, *available at* http://www.venice.coe.int/webforms/documents/default. aspx?pdffile=CDL-AD(2006)009-e.

[115] *Id.* at ¶¶ 78-79.

[116] Mary Ellen O'Connell, *Enhancing the Status of Non-State Actors Through a Global War on Terror?*, 43 COLUM. J. TRANSNAT'L L. 435 (2005); *See also Lawful Use of Combat Drones: Hearing Before the Subcomm. on National Security and Foreign Affairs of the H. Comm. on Oversight and Government Reform*, 111th Cong. 1 (2010) (statement of Mary Ellen O'Connell). ("Drones are not lawful for use outside combat zones. Outside such zones, police are the proper law enforcement agents.").

[117] Also troubling are recent revelations about the role of the National Security Agency (NSA) in targeting individuals for death, as reported by Jeremy Scahill and Glenn Greenwald. They demonstrate that there is not a "robust" vetting of targets and protection of civilians. Instead, targets are being selected for death by metadata secured through suspects' cell phone SIM cards. Jeremy Scahill & Glenn Greenwald, *The NSA's Secret Role in the U.S. Assassination Program*, THE INTERCEPT (Feb. 10, 2014), firstlook.org/ theintercept/article/2014/02/10/the-nsas-secret-role/

[118] Report of the Special Rapporteur on Extrajudicial, Summary or Arbitrary Executions, UN GAOR 68th sess., UN Doc. A/68/382 ¶ 30 (Sept. 13, 2013). Heyns also says:

> A further layer of protection is added to the right to life by various human rights treaties and the monitoring mechanisms that they have created to tackle violations by States parties. The International Covenant on Civil and Political Rights calls it an inherent right (art. 6 (1)), which suggests that it exists independently from its recognition in the Covenant . . . .

> The Convention for the Protection of Human Rights and Fundamental
> Freedoms (European Convention on Human Rights) (art. 2) and the
> American Convention on Human Rights (art. 4), in addition to the African
> Charter on Human and Peoples' Rights (art. 4), similarly recognize the
> importance of the right to life.

Id. at ¶ 31. Premeditated killing of an individual is generally unlawful.
"Where intentional killing is the only way to protect against an imminent
threat to life, it may be used. This could be the case, for example, during
some hostage situations or in response to a truly imminent threat. *Id.* at ¶ 35.
While the standards of human rights law remain the same even in situations
approaching armed conflict, they have to be applied in ways that are realistic
in the context." *Id.*

[119] *Id.* at ¶ 37.

[120] In many instances, the people killed are not even called "terrorists," but
are referred to as "militants." The reference to someone being a militant is
even more problematic, as there is no definition of a "militant." It means
that people are being killed in Pakistan, Yemen, and Somalia based on what
they feel passionately about and with whom they may politically agree or
associate. This is one of the problems of the "signature strikes," in which it is
assumed that military-age males in the vicinity of those targeted are either
"militants" or "terrorists" despite no evidence of their identity. *See* Columbia
Report, *supra* note 8, at 8-10; *see* Stanford Report, *supra* note 8, at 30-31;
The Bureau, *Obama 2012 Pakistan Strikes*, THE BUREAU OF INVESTIGATIVE
JOURNALISM (January 11, 2012), http://www.thebureauinvestigates.com/
blog/2012/01/11/obama-2012-strikes/.

[121] *Basic Principles on the Use of Force and Firearms by Law Enforcement
Officials*, UNITED NATIONS HUMAN RIGHTS OFFICE OF THE HIGH
COMMISSIONER FOR HUMAN RIGHTS 2 (Sept. 7, 1990), http://www.ohchr.
org/EN/ProfessionalInterest/Pages/UseOfForceAndFirearms.aspx.

[122] Letter from Daniel Webster to Lord Ashburton, *supra* note 40, at 412.

[123] Report of the Special Rapporteur on Extrajudicial, Summary or Arbitrary
Executions, *Supra* note 118, at ¶ 16.

[124] *Id.* at ¶18.

[125] Protection of Human Rights and Fundamental Freedoms While Countering
Terrorism, GA Res. 178, GAOR 68th sess., UN Doc. A/RES/68/178 ¶ 17
(2013). Masood Haider, *Drones Should Comply with International Law: UN*,
DAWN (Dec. 20, 2013), http://www.dawn.com/news/1075207/drone-use-
should-comply-with-international-law-un.

[126] *Id.* at ¶ 6(s).

[127] Jessica Elgot, *'Illegal' Drone Strikes Condemned In Landslide Vote By
European Politicians*, HUFFINGTON POST (Feb. 27, 2014) (internal quotation

marks omitted), www.huffingtonpost.co.uk/2014/02/27/europe-meps-vote-against-drone-strikes_n_4866217.html.

[128] *See* Columbia Report, *supra* note 8, at 8-10; *see* Stanford Report, *supra* note 8, at 30-31.

[129] Report of the Special Rapporteur on Extrajudicial, Summary or Arbitrary Executions, Christof Heyns, HRC 23rd sess., UN Doc. A/HRC/20/22/Add.3 ¶ 84 (2012).

[130] Heyns has also warned about the next level of automated weapons known as LETHAL AUTOMATED ROBOTS, or LARs, which can be programed to kill with no human intervention. Audiotape: Use of Lethal Autonomous Robots May Violate International Law, United Nations Radio (May 30, 2013), *available at* www.unmultimedia.org/radio/english/2013/05/use-of-lethal-autonomous-robots-may-violate-international-law/. Article 36 of the Additional Protocol of the Geneva Conventions requires a review of any new weaponry for compliance with standards under International Humanitarian Law. Protocol Additional to the Geneva Conventions of 12 August 1949, and relating to the Protection of Victims of International Armed Conflicts, art. 36, June 8, 1977, 1125 U.N.T.S. 3.

> Official statements from governments with the ability to produce LARs indicate that their use during armed conflict or elsewhere is not currently envisioned. While this may be so, it should be recalled that aeroplanes and drones were first used in armed conflict for surveillance purposes only, and offensive use was ruled out because of the anticipated adverse consequences. Subsequent experience shows that when technology that provides a perceived advantage over an adversary is available, initial intentions are often cast aside.

> Report of the Special Rapporteur on extrajudicial, summary or arbitrary executions, Christof Heyns, HRC 23rd sess., UN Doc. A/HRC/23/47 ¶¶ 28-30 (2013).

[131] *Report of the International Law Commission to the General Assembly, Principles of International Law Recognized in the Charter of the Nürnberg Tribunal and in the Judgment of the Tribunal,* (1950), *reprinted in* 2 Y.B. Int'l L. Comm'n 97, UN Doc. A/1316.

[132] Principles of International Law Recognized in the Charter of the Nurnberg Tribunal and in the Judgment of the Tribunal, *supra* note 44, at Principle VI (b).

[133] "The principle of universal jurisdiction is based on the notion that certain crimes are so harmful to international interests that states are entitled—and even obliged—to bring proceedings against the perpetrator, regardless of the location of the crime or the nationality of the perpetrator or the victim. Human rights abuses widely considered to be subject to universal jurisdiction include genocide, crimes against humanity, war crimes and torture." Hon.

Mary Robinson, *Foreword to* Princeton Univ., The Princeton Principles on Universal Jurisdiction 16 (2001), *available at* lapa.princeton.edu/hosteddocs/ unive_jur.pdf. *See also* Marjorie Cohn, *Spain Investigates What America Should*, S.F. CHRONICLE (Apr. 6, 2009), www.sfgate.com/opinion/article/ Spain-investigates-what-America-should-3245679.php.

9
DRONE WARFARE AND JUST WAR THEORY

Harry van der Linden

INTRODUCTION

Unmanned aerial vehicles (UAVs), better known as drones, have been used by the United States in conventional war situations in Afghanistan, Iraq, and Libya. Their most controversial purpose has been their use, especially by the Obama administration, in the targeted killing of suspected terrorists in non-battlefield settings, notably in the Federally Administered Tribal Areas (FATA) in Pakistan and Yemen.[1] Targeted killing of civilian "militants" can also take place through cruise missile strikes, manned aircrafts, and "boots on the ground" (as is illustrated by the killing of Osama bin Laden), but targeted killing by drones has several distinct advantages for the United States.

Unlike targeted killing executed by counterinsurgency troops, drone targeted killing poses few risks to the lives of US soldiers because the teams that launch and recover drones are typically hundreds of miles away from the search and strike area, while the teams that fly the plane (consisting of a pilot and a sensor operator controlling the cameras), together with their supporting teams of data analysts, etc., are thousands of miles away in the United States, watching or searching for their target until the optimal moment has arrived to unleash the missiles. Moreover, drones are considerably cheaper strike platforms than manned aircrafts and can stay in the air much longer (over twenty hours). And, like cruise missiles, drones do not turn the target area into a battlefield where humans face one another as enemies, but they are superior to cruise missiles in terms of a much shorter strike time so that the killing can be executed on the basis of a last-moment assessment of the intended target.[2] Accordingly, it not surprising that most US targeted killings have been executed by remote-controlled aircraft.

The targeted killings by the Obama administration show that drones enable war to be fought in a fundamentally new way. My main aim here is to argue that drone warfare poses moral problems and risks of such nature and magnitude that we should support an international ban on weaponized drones and, certainly, that we should seek an international treaty against drone systems that operate without the remote-control link; namely, autonomous, lethal UAVs (and killer robots in general). My argument will develop in two steps.

First, I will articulate some moral objections to drone warfare on the basis of a just war theory analysis of the Obama administration's targeted killings. To make my analysis manageable, I will focus on the drone targeted killings executed mostly under Central Intelligence Agency (CIA) supervision in the FATA, but, on the whole, the analysis also applies to the drone killings in Yemen.

The CIA drone campaign in Pakistan peaked in 2010 with 128 strikes and 751 to 1,109 "militant" and civilian casualties, and ceased as of January 2014, at the request of the Pakistani government in order to facilitate its peace talks with the Pakistan Taliban, one of the main armed groups operating in the FATA.[3] The respite in drone strikes might become permanent, but this would not signal a change in US policy because the drone targeted killing is ongoing in Yemen with several strikes a month in early 2014.

Second, I will explore some additional moral objections to combat drones on the basis of principles of "just military preparedness" or *jus ante bellum* (justice before war), a new category of just war thinking. Let me begin by introducing traditional just war theory and its normative principles.

JUST WAR THEORY

Just war theory consists of a historically evolved set of normative principles for determining when resort to military force is just (*jus ad bellum* principles) and how war can be justly executed (*jus in bello* principles). The most important *jus ad bellum* principle is that war must have a just cause, i.e., a goal of a kind and weight that seems to make resort to military force appropriate. Further, war must be declared by a legitimate or right authority, and must be pursued with right intention or the just cause as its primary motive. The three final *jus ad bellum* principles are that war must be a last-resort measure (diplomacy and other nonviolent measures should generally be pursued first); that it must have a reasonable chance of success in realizing its intended goal; and that it must be proportional in the sense that the anticipated goods of militarily pursuing the just cause must be commensurate with the expected harms.

The most essential *jus in bello* principle is the principle of discrimination, or noncombatant immunity, which requires that combatants distinguish between civilians and enemy combatants, and only directly attack the latter. Unintended civilian deaths are permitted, but due care must be taken to minimize their number, and the value of the military target must make it worth the civilian cost of life. There is also a separate *jus in bello* principle of micro-proportionality, stipulating that military force should be used economically in that the anticipated harms of a military action should not be excessive in proportion to its military value. Traditionally, the *jus ad bellum* decision was seen as chiefly the responsibility of political leaders, while using force in accordance with the *jus in bello* principles fell on the shoulders of soldiers. But in a modern democracy this seems no longer tenable: war in all its aspects has also become the responsibility of the citizens, and, arguably, a volunteer army entails that soldiers also have *jus ad bellum* responsibility and should refuse to fight unjust wars or, at least, not re-enlist for them.

The just war principles are quite broad and general, and contemporary just war theorists offer slightly different sets of principles, interpret the individual principles in dissimilar ways, and give different weight to the various principles. Thus just war theorists end up defending views that range from being rather bellicose and generally supportive of US interventionist policies, to views that are in practice close to pacifism and oppose most, if not all, recent US wars. Still, just war theory provides a widely shared moral framework for addressing new moral concerns raised by the ever-changing nature of warfare. This seems particularly important when the United Nations (UN) Charter and International Humanitarian Law (IHL) (which embody many just war principles) may not cover new military developments and threats, such as targeted killing by drones in response to the dangers posed by "global terrorism." Thus the moral analysis offered by just war theory may lead to a desire to revise the UN Charter and IHL, or may lead one to argue against misguided efforts in that direction.

DRONE WARFARE AND *JUS AD BELLUM*

In a speech at the National Defense University on May 23, 2013, President Barack Obama defended the targeted killings under his administration as morally and legally justified acts of war, as a part of a war of self-defense against al-Qaeda and its "associated forces" authorized by Congress in response to 9/11 in the 2001 Authorization for Use of Military Force (AUMF).[4] No doubt, in light of the scope and nature of the targeted killings executed under his authority, Obama rightly viewed them as acts of war rather than, say, as last-resort acts of law enforcement. But were they *justified* acts of war? Did they have a just cause? More specifically, the question is whether the "militants" targeted by the Obama administration's drone killings constituted a clear threat against the United States of a magnitude and type such that war acts against them were warranted. Jeff McMahan argues that the targeted killing of terrorists as an act of self-defensive war is morally quite similar to the killing of aggressor combatants who are asleep.[5] Aggressor combatants (who are in uniform), unlike civilian aggressors ("terrorists"), have a legal right to kill on the battlefield. But like civilian aggressors, they do not have a moral right to kill, and they intend to be instrumental in killing persons who have done nothing to warrant this fate. We may therefore kill both types of aggressors in order to prevent wrongful harm from being inflicted.

This analysis provides moral support for targeted killing as an act of war only in terms of the *type* of threat that is posed. What is also required for "just cause" is that the threat has a *magnitude* large enough so that war becomes a reasonable option. After all, a limited threat does not justify the initiation of war with all its inevitable, and often unexpected, harms. (The proportionality principle further assesses in particular cases whether the threat outweighs the harms involved in eliminating the threat; the just cause principle only requires the existence of a threat that meets the threshold of a serious threat.)

Moreover, it is only when the threat to a political community is very substantive that we may adopt the morally deeply-disconcerting war standard of killing on the basis of hostile status (as happens in drone strikes) in addition to the commonly accepted standard of killing in strict self-defense. Similarly, the threat must be great to warrant the adoption of a less strict standard in war than in law enforcement for avoiding the unintentional killing of non-hostile civilians. Typically, terrorists lack the weaponry, the organization, and the number of participants for meeting the threat threshold of just cause, and in that case civilian aggressors should be approached as very dangerous criminals who should be arrested, extradited if needed, and who may only be killed or incapacitated when they use lethal force or seek to escape. The horrific events of 9/11, however, gave credibility to the idea that al-Qaeda posed a danger that went above the threshold necessary for war. To be sure, the virtually unanimous support for war at the time might have been rooted more in retributive feelings than in the conviction that war was necessary to prevent large-scale future harms. But this only shows that the understanding of war as punishment, rejected by most modern just war theorists, is still prevalent.[6]

Credible just war thinking must see war as not only in need of justification at the point of its initiation, but should also assess its continuation and its various stages on the basis of *jus ad bellum* principles (i.e., we should temporalize the principles).[7] The Bush administration initiated a conflict in Pakistan (beyond the conflict in Afghanistan) with the targeted killing of civilian "militants" in the FATA. Obama hugely stepped up these killings immediately after his inauguration in 2009: about 85 percent of around 380 strikes in Pakistan were performed under Obama's orders.[8] Did this new campaign have a just cause? By 2009, the case that al-Qaeda constituted a threat serious enough to qualify as a just cause had greatly weakened. Surely, no major attacks had been launched or plotted against the United States after 9/11 that gave credibility to the view that law-enforcement measures would be largely inadequate to meet future al-Qaeda threats. Moreover, the war in Afghanistan had weakened al-Qaeda in this region and led to its dispersal to other countries. It may also be noted that other countries that suffered from horrendous terrorist attacks in the years after 2001, such as Indonesia (Bali bombing in 2002) and Spain (Madrid bombing in 2004), had not moved away from the law-enforcement model.

The Obama administration has never really tried to make the case that its drone killings in Pakistan were justified in terms of self-defense, since it executed these killings largely in secrecy. The only data we have about the number of strikes and people killed have been tabulated by civilian groups, based on reports by local individuals, government officials, and journalists in a region with rather limited access. This lack of transparency violates the requirements of the principle of legitimate authority. Congress failed in its responsibility as legitimate authority when it authorized the president, in the AUMF, to use US armed forces against any state, organization, or person linked to 9/11. Obama exploited this extremely open-ended authorization in his approval of greatly expanding US targeted killing in Pakistan, sidestepping the fact that the CIA is not part of the "armed forces." It should also be noted that the AUMF only authorized the president to take action against people connected to 9/11, not those suspected of other terrorist actions. The principle of legitimate authority demands full transparency (rather than limited reporting to some members of Congress) because it is only on the basis of debate and access to all facts that a body representing the people can declare war, as a communal enterprise, in the name of the people. The same can be said of new stages of development in a continuing war. Remarkably, it was not until early 2012 that Obama for the first time publicly discussed his drone program, and Congress has still not demanded a tally of the number of civilian and militant casualties in US targeted killings.[9]

Secrecy has also enabled the Obama administration to violate the principle of right intention in its targeted killing campaign in Pakistan. Even though the killings were justified as self-defense, they must have served other goals. Notably, in drone strikes on Pakistan during the Obama administration, fewer than 10 percent of the identified targets were directed against al-Qaeda, and less than 2 percent of all "militants" killed were named leaders of al-Qaeda or other targeted organizations.[10] In short, it seems that the militants killed were mostly low-level insurgents with local aims (such as members of the Pakistan Taliban), and most strikes were not aimed at named individuals (so-called personality strikes) but rather at individuals who fit the profile of a militant (so-called signature strikes). The US goals (other than self-defense) seem to have been to weaken the FATA as a basis of support for the Afghanistan Taliban and to assist the Pakistani government in its struggle with various armed opposition groups, such as the Pakistan Taliban, in the FATA. More broadly, the United States seems to have been guided by the motive of maintaining, and even extending, its role as global military hegemon. I will later suggest that the United States morally erred in pursuing these goals; what matters now is to note that the goals show a lack of "right intention" behind the Obama administration's drone killings.

The various violations of the first three *jus ad bellum* principles by the targeted killings in Pakistan point to several moral dangers of drone warfare. It is easy to use drones for preventing threats or harms that remain under the threshold of just cause, since drone warfare poses few risks for those who execute it, at least in asymmetric conflicts. And what greatly adds to this danger is that active public support is not needed to execute drone warfare, and that this type of war, accordingly, can easily be undertaken largely in secret without proper authorization and public debate, even in an "open" society.

Moreover, drone warfare makes it easy to pursue goals that are different from the stated goal of security that generally appeals to the public. Thus drone warfare seems to be thus far the best enabler of war as "alienated war," that is, war as a collective activity that no longer requires public sacrifice and moral commitment.[11] The volunteer army, the use of private military contractors, the technology of precision bombs, and, now, drone warfare, are all steps toward normalizing war for US citizens: war no longer feels like war, it no longer disrupts everyday life, and, so, war becomes acceptable. Long-term "boots on the ground," even if they are the boots of volunteers, threatens this normalization, as the wars in Afghanistan and Iraq have illustrated, but there is no such time-limit problem in drone warfare. Combat drones also have been proven to be very effective in conventional wars, as illustrated by the war in Libya. No troops on the ground were necessary for "success" in that war, and this played a role in President Obama simply announcing this war, rather than seeking public approval and congressional authorization. Drone warfare, then, as almost risk-free war for US soldiers, minimizes the number of occasions that the public is left wondering whether war and the United States playing "global cop" is worth the sacrifices of its soldiers. With drone warfare, the public is left free to admire the military in a cultural sort of way only (video games, technological awe, "support the troops," parades, etc.), while the government is left free to pursue its political and military interests.

Drone warfare shields the US public from the reality of war, but war is still very real at the receiving end. The buzz of the combat drones is heard overhead for hours on end in Pakistan, leaving the local people in enduring states of deep fear since the missiles could strike at any moment. And the strikes wreak human devastation: the total casualties (from 2004–2013) are between 2,296 and 3,719; the non-hostile civilian casualties are between 416 and 957, including as many as 202 children. Another 1,089 to 1,639 people have been injured.[12]

Other costs of the drone strikes were that Pakistan's sovereignty has been violated and that the strikes have led to growing resentment among the Pakistani people against the United States. Moreover, the strikes created fertile recruiting grounds in the FATA for new civilian aggressors and set a bad precedent for future targeted killing campaigns by other countries. It seems that all these costs could reasonably have been foreseen when the drone campaign in Pakistan was expanded in 2009, and so it should have been clear to the Obama administration that the campaign, with its uncertain and limited threat prevention impact, would violate the proportionality principle. And, surely, the more these costs have become impossible to ignore in subsequent years, the stronger the case has become in terms of proportionality considerations that the campaign has to stop.

The Obama administration, however, claimed that its drone strikes did not violate Pakistan's sovereignty because that government permitted the strikes. This defense has merit but is ultimately not convincing. A visible sign of Pakistan's permission, at least in the early years of the Obama drone attacks, is that the CIA launched drones not only from Afghanistan but also from Shamsi air base in Pakistan (the United States was evicted from the base in December 2011).[13] Similarly, we may see the fact that the Pakistani government claimed responsibility for some drone strikes prior to 2008 as reflective of its permission.[14] We should ask, though, how did Pakistan's permission came about? Was it the result of undue political pressure and conditional financial and military aid promised by the United States, or was it significantly the outcome of the Pakistani government's desire to combat (with US assistance) the growing oppositional violence and flagrant human rights violations by the Pakistan Taliban and other militant groups in the FATA? Similarly, it is unclear what we should make of the Pakistani government's frequent public protests against the US drone strikes. Did the protests reflect genuine concerns about violations of Pakistan's sovereignty, or were they mostly attempts to pacify the growing strong public opposition among the Pakistani people to the strikes? So, at least, the claim that the United States did not violate the sovereignty of the Pakistani government (state) is questionable.

But the real issue at stake is sovereignty in a broader sense, the sovereignty of the people of Pakistan, and here the picture is much clearer: the majority of the Pakistani people have consistently opposed drone strikes, even if the strikes were presented (in polls) as necessary to reduce militant violence against Pakistani citizens.[15] The obvious lesson is that most Pakistanis thought (and still think) that oppositional violence in their country is their battle to fight, and for good reason. US intervention has served as a destabilizing force and even might have fueled the flames of the violent opposition, exploiting anger at the "untouchability" of US military force and its arrogance of engaging in widespread killing in "secret." Likewise, the United States had no right to extend its war in Afghanistan to Pakistan in order to address its failure to prevent al-Qaeda and many Afghanistan Taliban fighters from making the FATA their new staging ground after the war was "won" in Afghanistan.

The Obama administration's drone killings violate the last resort principle. Alternatives, whether in the form of negotiations or law-enforcement measures, do not seem to have been considered. In fact, a remarkable feature of the Obama administration's counterterrorism strategy is that no prisoners are taken, and thus the problem so central to the Bush administration of how to treat captured suspected terrorists is largely avoided. It is certainly ironic that in the same year Obama reached out to the Islamic world and received the Nobel Peace Prize, he also greatly stepped up the drone strikes in the FATA. The brief hope for a more multilateral and cooperative American foreign policy was betrayed in secret by a continuation of the usual militarized foreign policy, clouding the prospect of finding enduring solutions for terrorism. Thus the principle of reasonable chance of success was also violated, because military force in accordance with this principle must lead to long-term threat reduction. The drone strikes in the FATA might have reduced some threats posed by al-Qaeda for the United States, but at the cost of worsening the economic and political conditions in the area and so inducing new threats in the long run, especially for the Pakistani people. Generally, militarized foreign policy errs in thinking that war is the answer; it fails to recognize that military force, at best, can bring people to the point of renewing cooperative efforts and finding nonviolent, enduring solutions for what gave rise to violent conflict in the first place.

These violations of the final three *jus ad bellum* principles further underline how drone warfare enables "alienated" war. Since targeted killing by drones does not place US soldiers in the areas under attack, it seems that sovereignty is not violated and that no war has been waged against the Pakistani people. Drone strikes, in other words, appear to eliminate only "terrorists" from afar, and drones, touted as very precise weapons,[16] can carefully excise this evil. With this mode of thought, the very fact that drones have been harming the Pakistani people has remained largely outside the US national discourse, and there were no US soldiers on the ground to report otherwise and bring stories home of great human suffering. Our news about drones at war is not the news of a country at war; at most, drone strikes are reported in the sidelines with the number of estimated terrorists killed and the occasional mention of civilians who also may have died. "Alienated" war is war for which people do not take full responsibility, and combat drones facilitate this denial of responsibility.

DRONE WARFARE AND *JUS IN BELLO*

Granted that the Obama drone campaign in the FATA was unjust in *jus ad bellum* terms, it follows that all US drone killings during this campaign were wrongful killings, and that the just course of action would have been to request Pakistan to arrest all those civilian militants against whom US courts would have a legal case. No doubt, this would have been a tall order and success might have been limited, even if the Pakistani government would have accepted US assistance. But justice comes with a price, and the moral costs of drone killings as the alternative were much greater. Still, it remains important to address the wrongful drone killings in *jus in bello* terms, both in order to rebut the Obama administration's view that the drone strikes were justly executed and to point out *jus in bello* moral dangers of drone warfare in general. Limited data and the scope of this chapter make it impossible to assess individual drone attacks, but the aggregate data allow for *just in bello* assessment of the Pakistani drone campaign over the years.

The United States has frequently executed several missile strikes in short succession on the same target in the FATA with the result that responders to the first strike, such as rescue workers and family members, were killed.[17] This policy violates the principle of discrimination or noncombatant immunity because it reflects lack of due care in seeking to minimize civilian casualties; worse even, it suggests the intentional killing of civilians, a war crime. Besides requiring due care, the principle of discrimination also demands that the civilian costs of individual strikes are not excessive in light of the military value of the strikes. The percentage of civilians killed was approximately 22 percent in 2009, 11 percent in 2010, 14 percent in 2011, 7 percent in 2012, and as low as 0 percent in 2013.[18] Is this range of killing civilians proportionate?

How do you decide this question? A recent defender of the drone strikes suggests that "we can compare the number of civilians that targets are killing and the number of civilians killed in the targeting to see which number is bigger."[19] Noting that al-Qaeda (and its affiliates) had been responsible for over 4,400 civilian deaths throughout the years and that at most 700 civilians had been killed in Pakistan (through 2011), this supporter of drone strikes concludes that the civilian deaths in Pakistan were clearly not excessive. I have already pointed out the flaw in this reasoning: the total number of civilians killed by al-Qaeda is as such not an adequate reflection of the threat level posed by this group in 2009, when Obama stepped up the drone warfare in Pakistan. Certainly, there is no evidence to support the notion that the drone campaign against al-Qaeda has saved the lives of even remotely as many US civilians as the number of Pakistani civilians killed during this campaign. Proportionality seems to demand that the estimated number of saved lives should be much higher.[20]

Another argument to the effect that the civilian-killing percentage of the drone warfare in Pakistan was acceptable is that alternative military strategies, such as putting boots on the ground, would have led to greater numbers of civilians killed.[21] Generally, it might be true that non-drone counterterrorism operations may result in more civilian deaths—soldiers, for example, may be more discriminate than drones (they know who shoots at them), but more civilians might be caught in crossfire in a ground battle. But one cannot conclude that since one operational strategy brings fewer civilian deaths than another that, therefore, this strategy has an acceptable rate of civilian deaths. After all, the other strategy might be grossly disproportionate. At best, the comparative proportionality advantage of drone warfare helps to explain why drone warfare is a preferred US option. It also might be a factor in the United States opting for drone warfare in regions where it would not use traditional conventional military force.

Officials of the Obama administration have regularly emphasized that combat drones are very accurate weapons and so lead to very minimal civilian deaths. Former defense secretary Leon Panetta, for example, claimed in 2011 that drones "are probably the most precise weapons in the history of warfare."[22] However, the very fact that drone technology has accurate capabilities in terms of identifying its target and then striking the target with a limited blast area does not mean that due care is taken to avoid civilian casualties. The fact that the number of civilian casualties decreased greatly the more drone warfare in Pakistan was protested and subjected to public scrutiny suggests that the capability of technological accuracy in the early years of the Obama drone campaign in Pakistan went hand in hand with a lack of "moral accuracy." Relatedly, precision in finding and hitting the target does not imply that there is precision in the *selection* of the target.[23]

The Obama administration's process of naming the militants it puts on its killing lists is shrouded in secrecy and might not be very reliable. Flawed intelligence may lead to misidentification of civilians as hostile militants. It also should be noted that there is no general agreement on the criteria for determining the hostile status of civilians in the first place. The bomb maker of al-Qaeda is a threat, but what about the propaganda maker, the paid armed chauffeur, or a seemingly inactive member? The little we know about the identities of "militants" killed by the Obama administration suggests that it adheres to a rather broad understanding of what counts as being militant. Signature strikes, with their vague killing standard of "fitting the profile of hostile militants," add greatly to the problem that many people killed might have been misidentified or mischaracterized. Accordingly, the Obama administration's claim of limited unintended civilian deaths, even if taken at face value, is misleading in that drone strikes may have killed many people conceived of as militants who were actually civilians. Even the data gathered by various civilian groups might over-report the number of genuine militants, since often the only evidence for claiming that the casualties were militants is the reporting by "anonymous Pakistani officials," presumably army officials with an interest in having broad standards of militancy and pleasing the US military.[24] Thus the unintended civilian deaths of the drone campaign in Pakistan might be considerably greater than the mere numbers or percentages of "civilians killed" suggest, so that the campaign, even in its later years, might have been to some degree disproportionate.

The principle of macro-proportionality prohibits excessive use of force, taking into consideration both civilian and militant casualties. Based on the assumption that the goal of the drone campaign in Pakistan was to eliminate threats posed by al-Qaeda, signature strikes violate this principle because, surely, there was no way of telling whether an individual who fit the profile of "militant" belonged to al-Qaeda or some other militant group. Moreover, since, as previously noted, less than 10 percent of all drone strikes in Pakistan (during the Obama administration) were specifically directed against al-Qaeda, military force was used excessively in terms of the stated goal of combatting "global terrorism" because no attempt was made to avoid the killing of militants with local aims only, and their deaths had only marginal value with respect to the goal of weakening al-Qaeda.

In sum, all the praise of combat drones as very precise killing machines obscures difficult moral problems of setting (and executing) morally convincing standards for determining the hostile status of civilians and of deciding what counts as disproportionate civilian deaths. Similar problems also emerge with regard to defining military targets in civilian settings. Technological accuracy lulls people into thinking that "moral accuracy" has been reached, making drone warfare a more acceptable form of warfare. What further enables the comfort of drone warfare as "alienated war" is that US military superiority leaves people unconcerned that drone warfare brings war home in a manner that raises significant *jus in bello* concerns: military drone pilots are combatants during their working hours on their base and they "hide" their combatant status after work when they mix into the civilian population and return home. Moreover, the CIA agents who assist in drone strikes are civilians who help to kill civilian militants who are blamed for hiding their hostile intentions.[25]

TARGETED KILLING: BETWEEN WAR AND LAW ENFORCEMENT

In his speech at the National Defense University, Obama not only defended his drone warfare record, but he also looked at the future of the war against global terrorism.[26] He said: "America is at a crossroads. We must define the nature and scope of this struggle, or else it will define us. We have to be mindful of James Madison's warning that 'No nation could preserve its freedom in the midst of continual warfare.'" More specifically, Obama reiterated his commitment to bring the troops home from Afghanistan and proposed that we no longer define US counterterrorism as a "global war on terror," but rather "as a series of persistent, targeted efforts to dismantle specific networks of violent extremists that threaten America." These "targeted efforts" foremost refer to drone strikes, and, apparently, Obama seems to think that the continuation of targeted killing strikes, at a reduced rate thanks to "the progress we've made against core al-Qaeda," is no longer really war. Correspondingly, he said that he would like Congress and the American people to engage "in efforts to refine, and ultimately repeal, the AUMF's mandate."

Concomitant with the speech at National Defense University, the White House released a fact sheet,[27] outlining standards (taken from a classified Presidential Policy Guidance on targeted killing) for how to use lethal force against terrorists in countries where the United States is not at war. In short, the standards permit a drone attack against a terrorist only if capture is not feasible, local authorities will not or cannot take effective measures to deal with the "imminent threat to U.S. persons," and there is "near certainty that the terrorist target is present" and "near certainty that non-combatants will not be injured or killed." The "fact sheet" maintains that the standards "are either already in place or will be transitioned into place."

What are we to make of these standards and the proclaimed "end" of the war on terror? It is clear that the standards have not been fully implemented in the ongoing drone war in Yemen, but then an Obama administration spokesperson said in April 2014, almost a year after the first announcement of the new standards, that "I'm not going to speculate on how long the transition [toward the new standards] will take, but we're going to ensure that it's done right and not rushed."[28] The "end" of the war on terror and the new standards are attempts to normalize war and so ensure that war remains "alienated war." By emphasizing that the continuation of drone killings of civilian militants is not a continuation of the "war on terror" and can be done with a refinement or even repeal of the AUMF, Obama seems to want the American public to accept a permanent war that is no longer called war. And, of course, the legal restrictions of the homeland security state, so typical of being at war, will largely remain in effect. What the Obama administration also seems to be doing is to push targeted killings by drones in the direction of a hybrid model of the war and law-enforcement legal models of the use of force, following the example of the Bush administration's hybrid treatment of captured terrorists. Targeted killing by drones might not meet the level of intensity of conflict to be legally counted as war (it is "force away from hot battlefields"), but it still uses force in a manner typical of war, that is, hostile status killing (with some fine-tuning perhaps in terms of the scope of acceptable civilian deaths). And so a hybrid model might give greater respectability to US targeted killing by drones, avoiding censure that might come from either the war model or law-enforcement model of the use of force. Further, combat drones, it is widely admitted, do not meet legal obstacles as such when used in conventional war theaters. Thus, we would be led toward a world in which drone warfare would be the new legal "normal," both in international conflicts and armed conflicts with non-state actors. Would a just military and society want such a world?

COMBAT DRONES, KILLER ROBOTS, AND *JUS ANTE BELLUM*

Just war theorists tend to look at each war as a separate moral event, paying little attention to the fact that how we prepare for war has a great impact on how likely it is that war will be justly initiated and executed. To address this shortcoming I have articulated in some prior essays a new category of just war thinking, "just military preparedness," with principles that set forth requirements for the military as a just institution.[29] In line with the commonly used naming of the other just war theory categories, the new category may be called *jus potentia ad bellum* or, more briefly (but less accurately), *jus ante bellum*. Just military preparedness addresses two justice concerns. First, it raises questions about whether the military preparation of a country is just toward its military personnel, places a fair burden on the civilian population, and the like. Second, it raises questions about whether the military preparation of a country is such that it is conducive to the country resorting to force only when justice is on its side and to executing war justly. The ultimate concern of *jus ante bellum* as part of just war theory is military preparedness that is just in the second sense, but justice in the first sense must also be addressed since it impacts the possibility of justice in the second sense. In what follows, I will discuss five *jus ante bellum* principles, emphasizing the first two principles since they have the greatest bearing on the question of whether a just military would want to include drones in its preparation for the possibility of war.

The first principle says that the basic defense structure of a country should accord with its general purpose of using military force only for the sake of protecting people against extensive basic human rights violations caused by large-scale armed violence. This principle of "just purpose" requires that a country is able to meet acts of aggression and has the capacity to contribute to the collective tasks of assisting other countries in their self-defense and preventing humanitarian catastrophes caused by armed force (humanitarian intervention). The United States, with its relentless pursuit of military superiority, its professional army of around 1.4 million active duty personnel, its "empire of bases,"[30] and its military expenditures close to 50 percent of global military spending and five times the size of the second-largest spender (China), is in clear violation of this principle. The US military does not seek capability of self-defense and global security through collective efforts, but rather aims at military hegemony and global "power" projection to serve its political and economic needs.

The first principle requires that new military technology is introduced only if it is necessary for, or conducive to, the global protection of basic human rights. In the past, new military technology has often been developed by a party in order to gain advantage in a conflict that otherwise could not have been won or only won at very great human costs. But this does not describe how during the past few decades the United States has introduced new military technology. The main motivations behind its continuous military technological innovations seem to be the desire to maintain military superiority and dominance and to satisfy huge financial interests at stake in the research, development, production, and sale of new weapons. The introduction of combat drones illustrates this point. Drone warfare extends the global reach of US military power, and major weapon industries are increasingly investing in further developing and producing combat drones. A recent report for Congress, for example, projects that the Department of Defense will spend around $13 billion on the Reaper, the current combat drone of choice in targeted killing, between 2011 and 2020.[31] Now the problem with new military technologies is that they tend to spread to other countries, and this is certainly happening with combat drones. Thus we may fairly soon live in a world in which a significant number of countries (e.g., China, Russia, India, and Iran) will use combat drones in war zones as well as nonwar zones and engage in the targeted killing of their "terrorists," their militants seeking secession, etc. This danger of a highly destabilized world with military violence exercised by many countries outside their borders and off the battlefield is a clearly foreseeable risk. So, had the US military been just in terms of military preparedness, it would not have introduced combat drones.

Some recent defenders of combat drones have argued that they might actually be used in the service of protecting human rights. The basic argument is that countries such as the United States with a low tolerance for casualties among its troops might use drones to execute humanitarian interventions it would otherwise not have executed for being too risky to the troops.[32] Here the argument that combat drones make war too easy is turned around: it is a good thing that it becomes easier to intervene in unfolding humanitarian crises. And the punch line is that "humanitarian drones" were already very effective in the "humanitarian intervention" in Libya, and that future "ground drones" (remote-controlled mobile strike platforms) would be of even greater assistance in meeting humanitarian goals.[33]

One problem with this argument is that most of what happened in Libya was not a humanitarian intervention in accordance with U.N. Security Council Resolution 1973,[34] but rather NATO choosing a side in a civil war and actively supporting the overthrow of Qaddafi. Another problem is that it is unclear how combat drones could effectively protect populations under threat and actually stop génocidaires in their tracks. What seems more plausible is that killing from above would fan the flames on the killing fields. Similarly, drones on the ground would not seem particularly effective in defusing human hatred in action. A much better alternative is to create a permanent rapid intervention force under UN authority, specially trained for peacekeeping and dealing with violent humanitarian conflicts and composed of soldiers from across the globe. This would avoid reinforcing the role of the United States as military hegemon and it would make addressing humanitarian crises a collective responsibility, not requiring US soldiers alone to risk their lives.

Combat drones are quite vulnerable to attack from modern air-defense systems, and so the United States is developing stealth drones and drones with air-to-air attack abilities. Especially noteworthy is the stealth X-47B with its ability to land and take off from aircraft carriers.[35] It has a much larger flying range than current weaponized UAVs and it can fly itself. So the future seems to be that US combat drones will be used in more conflicts, will begin to replace even the most advanced manned aircrafts, and can reach all the corners of the world. Also, the X-47B points to a future where the human role is limited to overriding the decisions of unmanned killing systems, as a step toward fully autonomous systems where humans are taken out of the loop altogether, and the killer robots "select" their own targets and "decide" on their own when to pull the trigger. Generally, drone pilots and sensors have limitations of concentration, duration, and processing data, and so there is a push toward taking them out of the loop or at least limiting their role. Other developments in the US military pipeline include the miniaturization of UAVs (micro killer drones), drones operating in swarms, and weaponized underwater unmanned vehicles (UUVs).

The move toward autonomous lethal systems, or "killer robots," in the air, on the ground, or undersea will further increase some of the moral dangers noted with regard to remote-control killing. The threshold for resorting to force will be further lowered because the risks to soldiers will be further minimized. The illusion that borders can be crossed without violation of sovereignty will become even more compelling, and political leaders will be even less inclined to seek public authorization for war. Robotic warfare is also likely to strengthen war as alienated war for those who have the robots on their side. Robots seem to promise security without human costs; no tears need be shed over fallen robots. But, here again, we must wonder what would happen if other countries catch up with the United States, or even surpass it in killer robot innovations. Robotic killers have neither loyalty nor mercy and will kill for all who can afford them, the just and unjust alike, including non-state actors. Their presence will be a great threat to human rights unless one assumes that in the future all centers of political and economic power somehow miraculously coalesce with all the centers of justice, leaving robots only to fight unjust militants at the periphery. More likely, it will be a world of extreme asymmetric warfare, in which robots fight civilian militants who in some cases rightfully and other cases wrongfully refuse to obey the policies of the controllers of the killer robots. Ironically, in a world in which there is a diminishing number of human soldiers to fight, militant civilians might increasingly turn in desperation to attacking civilians under the protection of killer robots.

The second *jus ante bellum* principle—the moral competency and autonomy principle—demands that military personnel be educated and trained with the just purpose of resort to force (articulated in the first principle) in mind, and be treated as morally competent and autonomous agents. Part of the rationale of this principle is that it is deeply immoral to turn soldiers into mere instruments of the state, deny them the opportunity to exercise their *jus ad bellum* responsibility, and let them pay the moral and psychological costs of coming to reject a war through the experience of fighting the war. All too often soldiers come to regret their participation in war. Yet, it does not seem to be the case that the US military is encouraging any independent *jus ad bellum* thinking among its troops or even officers.[36] The second principle further requires that combatants are trained to become experts in protecting human rights, and this includes, but is not limited to, taking on *jus in bello* responsibility. The US military is somewhat more successful in training its soldiers in *jus in bello* responsibility, partly because the changed nature of warfare, notably counterinsurgency by US ground troops in Iraq and especially Afghanistan, has necessitated better training in this regard: military success requires winning the hearts and minds of local civilian populations. Nevertheless, there are many documented instances of the commission of war crimes by US forces.[37]

Drone warfare is likely to have some eroding impact on soldiers taking on *jus ad bellum* responsibility and strictly adhering to *jus in bello* norms. The justice of their war should be of equal concern to remote-control soldiers and soldiers on the physical battlefield. But remote-control soldiers have a reduced incentive to ponder the issue since they are not risking their lives as are the traditional soldiers. Moreover, since drone operators are not directly experiencing the consequences of their actions, they are less likely to come to question whether justice is indeed on their side. Also, unlike traditional soldiers, drone soldiers cannot get feedback from enemy soldiers or local civilians that might lead them to address *jus ad bellum* issues.

With regard to *jus in bello* norms, killing in a remote-controlled way seems to invite less due care in trying to avoid violating these norms because one can experience the harm that one has caused only in a mediated way. To be sure, remote-control killers, like killers on the physical battlefield, see the harm they have caused—and PTSD has been reported among drone operators.[38] But it is also the case that the drone killers are only watching a monitor, that they watch without being seen, that they do not hear the sounds of suffering, and that they watch with others, and all these features seem to create emotional distance and with it moral distance and greater risk of moral indifference.[39] What seems to add to the unreality of the harm and the risk of moral sliding is that the mediated battlefield experience is an interruption of everyday life with family, driving to and from work, and so on.

Even if one were to conclude that drone warfare as such is not likely to have some erosive moral impact on a military that seeks to adhere to moral standards, there is still the problem that effective drone operators may simply be skilled gamers who think flying a drone is a cool video game. The drone soldiers do not need courage; they do not need to feel a loyalty to fellow soldiers or country that requires them to be prepared to risk their lives; they do not have to face their victims and confront the fact that the video game is not really a game; and they do not even have to be paid very well (say, as compared to mercenaries, who risk their lives but fight without political allegiance). In short, drone warfare enables war to be partly executed by human agents who are the very opposite of the human agents who may justifiably use force according to the second *jus ante bellum* principle: agents committed to protecting human rights and using force only for the sake of this purpose. For a just military, the fact that flying drones might be outsourced to skilled gamers with no concern for protecting human rights would be an additional reason not to embrace drone warfare.

Combat drones operative in war zones do not seem to pose direct moral problems for soldiers on the ground as long as a clear command structure is in place. However, once drones morph into autonomous lethal systems, this will change. When human soldiers and killer robots fight side by side, the robots will place significant limits on the scope of decision making of human soldiers, and the human soldiers may be helpless to prevent situations when robots malfunction, misjudge a threat, use excessive force, or violate the laws of war. And, these *jus in bello* violations may also emerge when robots fight on their own in both war and non-war zones. Proponents of fully autonomous killing systems have argued that such problems can be circumvented by designing killer robots so that *jus in bello* constraints are integrated into their artificial intelligence. Even better, they argue, killer robots lack emotions of anger and hatred that may lead human soldiers to commit *jus in bello* crimes. In response, it should be noted that it is doubtful that machines will any time soon, if ever, have the capacity to act in accordance with the laws of war, and so there is the definite danger that killer robots will be developed and used that fall significantly short in this regard. Moreover, why should we assume that all militaries would even want to build these constraints into their killer robots? To be sure, unjust militaries may also use and train rogue soldiers, but unlike rogue killer robots, most human killers have some emotive resistance to killing that may at least offer some protection for non-hostile civilians, surrendering combatants, and the like.[40]

The third principle of just military preparedness—the principle of priority to nonviolence—demands that preference be given to nonmilitary means of preventing extensive basic human rights violations caused by armed force. In theory, the Obama administration seems to agree with this principle and the criticism it implies with regard to US military preparation. In his speech at the National Defense University, Obama said: "[F]oreign assistance cannot be viewed as charity. It is fundamental to our national security. And it's fundamental to any sensible long-term strategy to battle extremism. Moreover, foreign assistance is a tiny fraction of what we spend fighting wars that our assistance might ultimately prevent."[41] Similarly, Obama's first defense secretary, Robert M. Gates, argued for a "balanced strategy," noting that there is a definite misbalance in US spending on the "war on terror" because "over the long term, the United States cannot kill or capture its way to victory." He continued, "Where possible, what the military calls kinetic operations should be subordinated to measures aimed at promoting better governance, economic programs that spur development, and efforts to address the grievances among the discontented, from whom the terrorists recruit."[42]

In practice, however, the Obama administration has done little to bring US military preparation closer to satisfying the third *jus ante bellum* principle. The State Department/USAID budget, which also includes billions of dollars in military assistance, has been flat under the Obama administration after significant increases during the Bush administration, and has been consistently less than 10 percent of the Department of Defense budget (which in itself is considerably less than total US military spending). In short, the Obama administration's foreign policy is thoroughly militarized, and this supports my earlier argument that it is implausible to see the drone warfare in Pakistan as satisfying the *jus ad bellum* principle of last resort. More broadly, as long as the United States spends so little on foreign aid, diplomacy, peace education, arms control, refugee assistance, and the numerous nonmilitary programs of the United Nations as compared to its military spending, we have good reason to doubt that any future US war will satisfy the principle of last resort.

The fourth *jus ante bellum* principle—the principle of proper balance of values and resource allocation—requires that the value of security (against the threat of widespread basic human rights violations by armed force) and the resources committed to this value are carefully balanced against other values that good government should promote (e.g., education and health) and the resources set aside for their realization. US governments after World War II have consistently violated this principle by disproportionate military spending, and one enabling factor has been to stoke the flames of fear, from exaggerating the threat of communism to exaggerating the threat of terrorism. Surely, if, say, 50 percent of the money spent on the war on terrorism would have been spent on improving traffic safety, preventive health care, cancer research, and a cleaner environment, many more human life years in the United States would have been saved than this war, even on the most fantastic threat assumptions, ever could have prevented.[43] Moreover, the money so spent would have enhanced the quality of life for millions of Americans. But the politics of fear sells. Politicians, the military brass, weapons producers, and many research scientists profit from the "military-industrial complex." And the "empire of bases" guarantees access to essential material resources. All these interests are extraneous to the concern of having a military for protecting human rights, and they cast into doubt the *jus ad bellum* required "right intention" behind any (future) US interventions.

Military research and development (R&D) may have significant civilian payoffs. For example, the civilian drone industry is expected to boom in the coming years, and the current R&D in robotic warfare systems may sooner or later also bring considerable civilian benefits. This very fact, however, does not mean that the typically more than 50 percent of the government-supported R&D spent on defense is not a violation of the fourth *jus ante bellum* principle. For one thing, the road through military R&D to various civilian applications is an indirect one, and so it is a road that costs much more in terms of human resources and talent than it would had the civilian products been pursued directly. For another thing, we cannot assume that the civilian payoffs of military R&D always match with items high on our civilian R&D lists. Relatedly, the argument that military spending is good for the economy fails. Military production comparatively creates few jobs, and so we would create many more employment opportunities by, say, investing in mass transit or installing solar panels than by manufacturing combat drones.[44]

The fifth and final *jus ante bellum* principle—the principle of competent and right authority—demands that matters of military preparedness be settled by a recognized authority competent to make such decisions, with the right intention, aiming for just military preparedness rather than extraneous interests. In a democratic society, the representatives of the people should be this competent and right authority, requiring them to communicate openly and honestly with the citizens about the costs and benefits of alternative "just military preparedness" proposals. The defense budget should be transparent to the representatives. Guided by broad public input, they should allocate resources on the basis of careful balancing of the value of security against other governmental goals. Clearly, US military preparedness fails to satisfy these guidelines in several respects. Congressional representatives relentlessly push for military investments to keep jobs in their districts and please their campaign contributors, even beyond what the Pentagon might want (as illustrated by the budget fight over the F-22 Raptor aircraft).[45] Significant parts of the Pentagon budget are secret, including allocations for special operation forces. Weapons industries routinely have huge overruns and are a revolving door for politicians and military brass. And, the corporate media seldom question global US military presence.

The introduction of drone warfare illustrates how the United States fails in terms of the competent and right authority principle. The first combat drone, the Predator, was developed as a surveillance system and used as such in the Balkan wars in the mid-1990s. After 9/11, the Bush administration authorized the CIA to retrofit the Predator with Hellfire missiles and kill "high-value targets" of its own choosing, and in early 2002 this form of warfare was first executed. In short, drone warfare became deeply embedded in US counterinsurgency strategy before it came to public awareness. Similarly, it is not clear how far the Pentagon has traveled down to the road to robotic warfare and where it actually wants to go, but at least public concerns are being raised now. Perhaps in response, the Department of Defense issued a directive on "Autonomy in Weapon Systems" on November 21, 2012.[46] A somewhat positive point is that the directive approves only the development of fully autonomous weapon systems with nonlethal capabilities, but the restriction is in effect for only five years and can be waived by top officials.[47] A clear negative point is that "semi-autonomous weapon systems" with lethal capabilities are fully embraced. The dividing line between semi- and full autonomy is that humans in semi-autonomous systems must select the target that the systems pursue and destroy, and this line can be easily crossed once the R&D for semi-autonomous weapons systems has been completed.[48]

WHAT IS TO BE DONE?

In 2009, the International Committee for Robot Arms Control (ICRAC) called for a discussion to consider an international ban on autonomous weapon systems, and in 2012, Human Rights Watch actually called for a ban. In April 2013, Christof Heyns, UN Special Rapporteur on extrajudicial, summary or arbitrary executions, wrote a comprehensive report on lethal autonomous robotics (LARs). He noted, "there is widespread concern that allowing LARs to kill people may denigrate the value of life itself." Heyns called on all countries "to declare and implement national moratoria on at least the testing, production, assembly, transfer, acquisition, deployment and use of LARs until such time as an internationally agreed upon framework on the future of LARs has been established."[49] And also in April 2013, a broad international coalition of nongovernmental organizations (NGOs) launched the Campaign to Stop Killer Robots. The proposal for a global ban on fully autonomous weapons is morally convincing and politically tenable. The moral risks involved in the use of these weapons are easy to recognize. Since the weapons are still in a state of development, we are not faced with the hard task of trying to turn back the clock, as a proposal to ban remote-controlled weaponized UAVs would imply. Indeed, the political tenability of "stop killer robots" is underlined by the fact that during the 2013 meeting of states party to the Convention on Conventional Weapons (CCW), it was decided to organize a four-day meeting of experts in May 2014 on "lethal autonomous weapons systems."[50] So should we forget about trying to ban our current combat drones?

One major concern with our current combat drones is that they are a stepping stone to fully autonomous weapons. A ban of killer robots would take care of this concern. Another major worry is that our current combat drones enable targeted killing campaigns in nonwar zones. These campaigns violate international law,[51] and so we may wish to call for a stricter enforcement of international law rather than a campaign to stop remote- control killing by drones. Still, for three reasons, we should continue to work toward banning our present combat drones. First, it is the case that killing by remote control makes it too easy to resort to war, enables alienated war, and places too few demands on its executioners. Second, it is not at all clear that calling for stricter international law enforcement will be successful. International law is fluid and the US drone campaigns seem to gradually create their own legal norms. Third, killing by drones is an affront to humanity, a form of killing that we should ban on this ground alone.[52]

Robert Sparrow recently noted that "there is something inherently dishonorable about killing people one is observing on a video screen from thousands of kilometers away and who have no opportunity to return fire." He adds, "[t]his is, I think, a widespread and powerful intuition but it turns out to be remarkably hard to unpack."[53] I agree on both scores, but let me nonetheless try to say a few words about what might be behind the intuition. There are several features of drone killing that raise moral concerns, but these features are shared with other weapons that don't raise the same moral recoiling. Drone killing is risk-free killing, but in current modern warfare this is hardly a distinctive feature of drone killing. Due to US military superiority, pilots of manned planes run very few risks (other than mechanical failings and pilot errors), and unleashing cruise missiles from a ship is also virtually risk-free. Fighters killed by drones have no opportunity to return fire, but this is also true for cruise missiles. Similarly, militants killed by drones are not given an opportunity to surrender, but again, this is also true for cruise missiles. Drones have been criticized as fundamentally asymmetric weapons, giving no fighting chance to the enemy, but again this is not unique to drones: witness the utter destruction wrought by US aerial bombing campaigns. What is, however, distinctive about drones is that they are deadly *surveillance* platforms. The target is watched, sometimes for days on end, and then killed. Is it the power of being able to extinguish life at the moment of one's choosing that is deeply morally disturbing here? That surely seems important, but the most morally disturbing feature is that in watching the militant to be killed, one is gradually watching a person to be killed. In other words, during the time of watching, the target turns from a threat into a human being, and then the kill becomes the kill of this human being. So, to come back to McMahan's claim that the targeted killing of a militant is similar to killing a sleeping aggressor soldier, it should be noted that an attack at night when enemy soldiers are asleep might not be wrong, but to watch a soldier asleep for some time and experience his humanity rather than his hostile status, and then pull the trigger, is deeply wrong. To go after humanity instead of the threat is an affront to humanity, and this is what remote killing by drones often involves.[54]

NOTES

[1] A limited number of targeted killings have also taken place in Somalia. The conflict between Yemen and al-Qaeda in the Arabian Peninsula is a traditional armed conflict, but the United States is not an official party to this conflict and views its direct military role as limited to the targeted killing of civilian "militants" who are a threat to the United States. *See Between a Drone and Al-Qaeda: The Civilian Cost of US Targeted Killings in Yemen*, HUMAN RIGHTS WATCH (Oct. 22, 2013), www.hrw.org/reports/2013/10/22/between-drone-and-al-qaeda.

[2] *Cf.* Micah Zenko, Reforming U.S. Drone Strike Policies 6 (2013).

[3] For these figures, *see* The Bureau, *Get the Data: Drone Wars - Obama 2010 Pakistan Strikes*, Bureau of Investigative Journalism (Aug. 10, 2011), www.thebureauinvestigates.com/2011/08/10/obama-2010-strikes/; *see Ross* chapter 7.

[4] Authorization for Use of Military Force, 115 Stat 224 (2001); Barack Obama, President, United States, Remarks by the President at the National Defense University (May 23, 2013), *available at* www.whitehouse.gov/the-press-office/2013/05/23/remarks-president-national-defense-university.

[5] Jeff McMahan, *Targeted Killing: Murder, Combat or Law Enforcement?, in* Targeted Killing: Law and Morality in an Asymmetrical World 137-41(Claire Finkelstein, Jens David Ohlin, & Andrew Altman eds. 2012). McMahan speaks of unjust combatants, but aggression is the main reason that wars are unjust.

[6] McMahan notes the same with regard to the public response to the killing of Osama bin Laden. The typical response was vindictive satisfaction rather than relief that a great danger had passed. McMahan, *id.* at 135-36.

[7] *See* John W. Lango, The Ethics of Armed Conflict: A Cosmopolitan War Theory 37 (2014).

[8] *See Get the Data: Drone Wars – Pakistan Drone Statistics Visualized*, Bureau of Investigative Journalism (last visited May 15, 2014), http://www.thebureauinvestigates.com/2012/07/02/resources-and-graphs/. It may also be noted that all but one of the ninety-three drone strikes in Yemen (as of mid-April 2014) were executed under Obama's orders. *See Drone Wars Yemen: Analysis*, New American Foundation (last visited May 14, 2014), natsec.newamerica.net/drones/yemen/analysis.

[9] *See* Jeremy Scahill, Dirty Wars: The World is a Battlefield 515-16 (Nation Books 2013). The occasion was a Google+ video forum on January 30, 2012. In a response to a question from the audience, Obama said that "drones have not caused a huge number of civilian casualties" and they are aimed at "active terrorists" who are trying to "harm Americans . . .." David Jackson, *Obama Defends Drone Strikes*, USA Today (Jan. 31, 2012), *available at* content.usatoday.com/communities/theoval/post/2012/01/obama-defends-drone-strikes/1#.U3QIr8uYaFk. A few members of Congress have introduced a bill (without success) that would require the Obama administration to provide casualty figures. Zoë Carpenter, *Lawmakers Ask Obama for a Tally of People Killed by Drones*, The Nation (April 2, 2014), www.thenation.com/blog/179165/lawmakers-ask-obama-tally-people-killed-drones#.

[10] The figures were considerably higher during the Bush administration. *See Drone Wars Pakistan: Analysis*, New American Foundation (last visited May 14, 2014), natsec.newamerica.net/drones/pakistan/analysis; *see Drone*

Wars Pakistan: Leaders Killed, NEW AMERICAN FOUNDATION (last visited May 15, 2014), natsec.newamerica.net/drones/pakistan/leaders-killed.

11   See CHEYNEY RYAN, THE CHICKENHAWK SYNDROME: WAR, SACRIFICE, AND RESPONSIBILITY 5 (2009). Medea Benjamin raises similar concerns in DRONE WARFARE: KILLING BY REMOTE CONTROL 145–60 (2013). My understanding of drone warfare has profited from this excellent work.

12   *Monthly Updates on the Covert War*, BUREAU OF INVESTIGATIVE JOURNALISM (last visited May 14, 2014), www.thebureauinvestigates.com/category/projects/drones/monthly-updates/. The New American Foundation provides a much lower number of civilian casualties, listing many casualties as "unknown." A recent report of the Human Rights Clinic at Columbia Law School claims that the figures of the Bureau of Investigative Journalism are more reliable. Chantal Grut & Naureen Shah, *Counting Drone Strike Deaths*, COLUMBIA LAW SCHOOL HUMAN RIGHTS CLINIC 29 (Oct. 2012), web.law.columbia.edu/sites/default/files/microsites/human-rights-institute/files/COLUMBIACountingDronesFinal.pdf.

13   For more details, *see* BRIAN GLYN WILLIAMS, PREDATORS: THE CIA'S DRONE WAR ON AL QAEDA 121-23 (2013).

14   Stanford Law Sch. & New York Univ. Sch. of Law, "Living Under Drones: Death Injury, and Trauma to Civilians from US Drone Practices in Pakistan" 15 (2012), *available at* www.livingunderdrones.org/wp-content/uploads/2013/10/Stanford-NYU-Living-Under-Drones.pdf [hereinafter "Living Under Drones"].

15   *Id.* at 16-17. Widespread demonstrations against drone attacks point in the same direction. The current Pakistani government seems more unambiguously opposed to the drone strikes than prior governments.

16   *See infra* section Drone Warfare and *Jus in Bello.*

17   "Living Under Drones," *supra* note 14, at 74-76.

18   These figures are derived from comparing the minimum estimated number of civilian deaths each year to the minimum estimated number of total deaths. Obviously, the percentage of civilian deaths for each year would be much lower if one compares the minimum number of civilian deaths to the maximum of total deaths and much higher if one compares the maximum number of civilian deaths to the minimum of total deaths. Thus the range of percentages is 14–45% for 2009, 8–26% for 2010, 8–42% for 2011, 3–32% for 2012, and 0–4% for 2013. The numbers for each year can be found at the Bureau of Investigative Journalism, *Get the Data: Drone wars. Obama 2009 Pakistan strikes*, BUREAU OF INVESTIGATIVE JOURNALISM (last visited May 23, 2014), www.thebureauinvestigates.com/2011/08/10/obama-2009-strikes/. This page provides access to the data for 2010-13.

19 See Avery Plaw, *Counting the Dead: The Proportionality of Predation in Pakistan, in* KILLING BY REMOTE CONTROL: THE ETHICS OF AN UNMANNED MILITARY 144 (Bradley Jay Strawser ed. 2013).

20 Why much higher? One reason is that it is a matter of conservative risk-taking: the deaths one seeks to prevent are not certain, unlike the civilian deaths that result from the use of force, and so one must err on the side of the number of deaths prevented. Another reason is that it is better for a community to suffer wrongful harm than to inflict it, unless indeed the harm suffered becomes a very high and intolerable price to pay. Still, people have different moral intuitions about this issue and it is an unresolved matter among just war theorists.

21 Plaw develops this argument by comparing the Pakistani drone campaign to several traditional counterterrorism campaigns. Plaw, *supra* note 19, at 147-50. Obama made a similar argument in his National Defense University speech.

22 Interview by Charlie Rose with Leon Panetta, Secretary of Defense, PBS (Sept. 6, 2011), *available at* www.defense.gov/transcripts/transcript. aspx?transcriptid=4872.

23 My comments here have profited from Sarah E. Kreps & John Kaag, *The Use of Unmanned Aerial Vehicles in Contemporary Conflict: A Legal and Ethical Analysis*, 44 POLITY 260, 260-285 (2012).

24 See Grut & Shaw, *supra* note 12, at 17–18, 26.

25 *Cf.* Claire Finkelstein, *Targeted Killing as Preemptive Action, in* TARGETED KILLING: LAW AND MORALITY IN AN ASYMMETRICAL WORLD 164 (Claire Finkelstein, Jens David Ohlin, & Andrew Altman eds. 2012).

26 Obama, *supra* note 4.

27 Press Release, Fact Sheet: U.S. Policy Standards and Procedures for the Use of Force in Counterterrorism Operations Outside the United States and Areas of Active Hostilities (May 23, 2013), *available at* www.whitehouse.gov/the-press-office/2013/05/23/fact-sheet-us-policy-standards-and-procedures-use-force-counterterrorism; *see* Appendix B.

28 Mark Marzetti, *Delays in Effort to Refocus C.I.A. From Drone War*, N.Y. TIMES (April 5, 2014), www.nytimes.com/2014/04/06/world/delays-in-effort-to-refocus-cia-from-drone-war.html?_r=0 (quoting Caitlin Hayden, spokeswoman of the National Security Counil).

29 The essays are available at SELECTED WORKS OF HARRY VAN DER LINDEN, works.bepress.com/harry_vanderlinden/ (last visited May 14, 2014). The number of principles and their wording varies slightly between the essays. The most detailed discussion can be found in *From Hiroshima to Baghdad: Military Hegemony versus Just Military Preparedness, in* PHILOSOPHY AFTER HIROSHIMA (Edward Demenchonok ed. 2010). Another new category of just

war thinking is *jus post bellum*, first articulated in the work of Brian Orend. "Justice after war" has received much attention in recent years, but is less relevant than the other categories for the assessment of drone warfare.

30   *See* CHALMERS JOHNSON, THE SORROWS OF EMPIRE: MILITARISM, SECRECY, AND THE END OF THE REPUBLIC 151-185 (2004).

31   JEREMIAH GERTLER, CONG. RESEARCH SERV., R42136, U.S. UNMANNED AERIAL SYSTEMS 33 (January 3, 2012).

32   Zack Beauchamp & Julian Savulescu, *Robot Guardians: Teleoperated Combat Vehicles in Humanitarian Military Intervention, in* KILLING BY REMOTE CONTROL: THE ETHICS OF AN UNMANNED MILITARY (Bradley Jay Strawser ed. 2013).

33   *Id.* at 119-20.

34   *See* Harry van der Linden, *Barack Obama as Just War Theorist: The Libyan Intervention,* works.bepress.com/harry_vanderlinden/49/; *See also* Marjorie Cohn, *The Responsibility to Protect – The Cases of Libya and Ivory Coast,* MARJORIE COHN (May 15, 2011), www.marjoriecohn.com/2011/05/responsibility-to-protect-cases-of.html.

35   Sharon Weinberger, *X-47B Stealth Drone Targets New Frontiers,* BBC (Dec. 19, 2012), www.bbc.com/future/story/20121218-stealth-drone-targets-life-at-sea.

36   *See generally* Roger Wertheimer, *The Morality of Military Ethics Education, in* EMPOWERING OUR MILITARY CONSCIENCE (Roger Wertheimer ed. 2010).

37   Even after the adoption of the Counterinsurgency Field Manual 3-24 (2006), which emphasizes the importance of protecting the civilian population in counterinsurgency operations, U.S. soldiers still regularly commit war crimes. *See, e.g.,* CHRIS HEDGES & LAILA AL-ARIAN, COLLATERAL DAMAGE: AMERICA'S WAR AGAINST IRAQI CIVILIANS (2009), *see also* Mark Boal, *The Kill Team: How U.S. Soldiers in Afghanistan Murdered Innocent Civilians,* ROLLING STONE (Mar. 27, 2011), www.rollingstone.com/politics/news/the-kill-team-20110327.

38   *See Reifer* chapter 5.

39   *Cf.* Derek Gregory, *Drone geographies,* RADICAL PHILOSOPHY 183 (Jan/Feb 2014), 7-19, 9-10.

40   My discussion here has benefited from International Human Rights Clinic at Harvard Law School & Human Rights Watch, "Losing Humanity: The Case Against Killer Robots" (Nov. 12, 2012), www.hrw.org/reports/2012/11/19/losing-humanity-0 [hereinafter "Losing Humanity"].

41   Obama, *supra* note 4.

42   Robert M. Gates, *A Balanced Strategy: Reprogramming the Pentagon for a New Age,* 88 FOREIGN AFFAIRS 28, 28-40 (Jan. 2009).

43 The same basic point is forcefully made by Thomas W. Pogge in POLITICS AS USUAL: WHAT LIES BEHIND THE PRO-POOR RHETORIC ch. 7 (2010).

44 *Cf.* Robert Pollin & Heidi Garrett-Peltier, *The Employment Effects of Downsizing the U.S. Military*, POLITICAL ECONOMY RESEARCH INSTITUTE 3 (2007), www.peri.umass.edu/fileadmin/pdf/working_papers/working_papers_151-200/WP152.pdf. They conclude that $1 billion in new spending would create around 50 percent more jobs if spent on construction targeted at home weatherization and infrastructure repair rather than on military, and investment in mass transit would create more than twice the number of jobs.

45 *See generally* WILLIAM D. HARTUNG, PROPHETS OF WAR: LOCKHEED MARTIN AND THE MAKING OF THE MILITARY-INDUSTRIAL COMPLEX 1-30 (2011).

46 Department of Defense, Directive No. 3000.09, Autonomy in Weapon Systems (2012).

47 *Id.*

48 *Cf.* Mark Gubrud, *US Killer Robot Policy: Full Speed Ahead*, BULLETIN OF THE ATOMIC SCIENTISTS (Sept. 20, 2013), thebulletin.org/us-killer-robot-policy-full-speed-ahead.

49 Human Rights Council, Special Rapporteur on extrajudicial, summary or arbitrary executions, Christof Heyns, UN Doc A/HRC/23/47, 23rd sess. (2013), www.ohchr.org/Documents/HRBodies/HRCouncil/RegularSession/Session23/A-HRC-23-47_en.pdf.

50 *Disarmament: Lethal Autonomous Weapons*, UNOG, www.unog.ch/80256EE600585943/(httpPages)/6CE049BE22EC75A2C1257C8D00513E26?OpenDocument (last visited May 14, 2014).

51 *See Mirer* chapter 8.

52 In "Losing Humanity," Human Rights Watch argues that the Martens Clause provides a legal ground for prohibiting killer robots. "Losing Humanity," *supra* note 40, at 25–26, 35–36. This clause, first stated in the 1899 Hague Conventions, requires that the means of warfare are evaluated in terms of the "principles of humanity" and the "dictates of public conscience." Drone killings, in my view, should be banned on basis of this clause.

53 Robert Sparrow, *War without Virtue?*, in KILLING BY REMOTE CONTROL: THE ETHICS OF AN UNMANNED MILITARY 98-99 (Bradley Jay Strawser ed. 2013) .

54 *Cf.* Thomas Nagel, *War and Massacre*, vol. 1 no. 2 PHILOSOPHY & PUBLIC AFFAIRS 123-138 (Winter 1972). Of course, drone killings do not always take the form of drone operators recognizing humanity only to extinguish it, but we prohibit weapons (e.g., chemical weapons) on the basis of the kind of moral wrongs that they enable, fully recognizing that in some situations they can be used so that the wrong will not occur.

10

AL-AULAQI V. OBAMA: TARGETED KILLING GOES TO COURT

Pardiss Kebriaei

Since 2001, the United States has killed as many as 4,500 people in "targeted killing" operations pursuant to its "war on terror" or "armed conflict with al-Qaeda and associated forces."[1] While thousands have been left dead and injured in the wars in Afghanistan and Iraq,[2] these thousands of other killings occurred outside of those battlefields,[3] and, until relatively recently, under a cloak of official—if implausible—secrecy. Even today, despite open public acknowledgement of these operations,[4] the Obama administration continues to withhold basic data, including how many have been killed and where, and legal memos explaining its rationale for the power to use lethal military force worldwide.[5]

THE KILLING OF US CITIZEN AL-AULAQI

The first legal challenge to the targeted killing program came in 2010 after the reported authorization for the killing of a US citizen in Yemen.[6] Early that year, media sources quoting anonymous officials reported that Anwar al-Aulaqi had been added to government "kill lists" maintained by the CIA and the military's Joint Special Operations Command (JSOC), and that he was being actively pursued.[7] The reports emerged in the context of an escalation in the targeted killing program more broadly. By the end of 2009, the Obama administration had conducted as many strikes in Pakistan as the Bush administration had conducted over two terms.[8]

Al-Aulaqi was ultimately killed in US drone strikes in Yemen on September 30, 2011, along with another US citizen, Samir Khan, and others. Two weeks later, another drone strike killed al-Aulaqi's sixeen-year-old son, Abdulrahman al-Aulaqi, also an American citizen, as he was eating dinner outside with his teenage cousin.[9]

The lawsuit challenging the authorization for al-Aulaqi's killing before it was carried out, brought by al-Aulaqi's father acting as his next friend, raised arguments that addressed several continuing concerns with the program: the global scope of the battlefield, the standards for targeting, and the lack of adequate transparency. At its core, the suit sought to exercise a still much-needed check on a dangerous claim of executive power.

THE LEGAL ARGUMENTS

The Obama administration rationalizes its targeted killing program on the premise that, since 9/11, the United States has been in a continuous, global armed conflict with the Taliban, al-Qaeda, and associated forces, and that the United States may therefore use lethal force under the 2001 Authorization for the Use of Military Force (AUMF) and the laws of war against suspected enemies potentially wherever they may be found.[10] The administration also asserts a national self-defense rationale for its targeted killing operations, which goes only to the question of whether the United States' use of armed force violates the sovereignty of states in which targeting operations are taking place, and is distinct from the question of whether such use of armed force violates the rights of targeted individuals and bystanders.[11]

The lawsuit challenging the authorization for al-Aulaqi's killing argued that armed conflict has a geographic dimension and exists only where there is intense and protracted fighting between organized armed groups[12]—conditions that were absent in Yemen at the time al-Aulaqi was being targeted.[13] Even assuming arguendo the existence of an armed conflict between the United States and al-Qaeda that extends beyond Afghanistan, the lawsuit further argued that the particular group al-Aulaqi was said to be part of—al-Qaeda in the Arabian Peninsula (AQAP)—was not an "associated force" that could be brought within the fold of the AUMF.[14]

Even among experts who dispute a geographic limitation on armed conflict, there are questions about whether all the purported al-Qaeda "affiliates" and "adherents" the administration has identified as current or potential targets legitimately fall within the AUMF's ambit.[15] Administration officials have claimed or suggested AUMF authority to target so-called associated groups in at least half a dozen countries so far.[16] Answers to those questions are critical, because it is the targeting of associated forces—not "core" al-Qaeda—that has driven the dramatic expansion and escalation of the targeted killing program since 2009.[17]

Given the argument that targeting al-Aulaqi was outside the context of armed conflict, the lawsuit argued that the appropriate legal framework for any use of lethal force against him was not the more permissible laws of war, but the narrower standards that govern law enforcement.[18] Under the Constitution and International Human Rights Law, lethal force is prohibited in the absence of charge and trial, except as a last resort against a specific and imminent threat.[19] The lawsuit argued that the placement of al-Aulaqi on the government's kill lists amounted to a standing authorization to use lethal force against him, and was fundamentally inconsistent with those requirements.[20]

In February 2013, a Justice Department white paper discussing the authority to kill American citizens, which summarizes a still classified legal memorandum justifying the killing of al-Aulaqi, was leaked to the press.[21] While the white paper identifies *imminence* as a criterion for targeting, it ultimately negates the requirement by stating that *imminence* does not require "clear evidence . . . [of] a specific attack . . . in the immediate future."[22] Moreover, the white paper makes clear that it applies only to a situation where the government believes that an individual is a "senior operational leader of an associated force;" it does not describe the outer edges of the administration's claimed authority to use lethal force against Americans,[23] and it does not at all describe the government's claimed authority against foreign citizens, who have accounted for almost all of those killed in targeting operations.[24]

Even under the laws of war, there are constraints on the use of lethal force. In the context of armed conflict involving non-state armed groups—non-international armed conflict—the law-of-war requirement of *distinction* permits killing only if the target is "directly participating in hostilities."[25] Yet the administration, analogizing to situations of international armed conflict between nation states, has claimed the legal authority to kill anyone who is "part of" al-Qaeda or associated groups,[26] suggesting a far broader net than the laws of war permit.[27]

The secrecy about the legal criteria that govern the administration's targeting decisions was itself another issue in the lawsuit. Al-Aulaqi's father claimed that his son's Fifth Amendment right to due process entitled him to notice of the conduct that could subject a US citizen to killing by his government.[28] Freedom of Information Act lawsuits have also been brought, seeking information about the legal standards for targeting, among other information, which the administration has continued to fight.[29]

The administration responded to the lawsuit by moving to dismiss it, claiming in part that judicial review would violate the separation of powers.[30] In public statements, it has similarly taken the position that judicial review of its targeting decisions is inappropriate, reassuring the public that its decisions are nonetheless subject to rigorous internal review.[31]

The Supreme Court rejected a similar argument by the Bush administration in the case of another US citizen nearly a decade ago, in the case of *Hamdi v. Rumsfeld*. Yasser Hamdi was an American citizen captured in Afghanistan in 2001 and deemed by the executive to be an "enemy combatant." When Hamdi brought a habeas corpus petition challenging the legality of his detention, the government initially argued that any judicial review of the executive's war-time determination would be inappropriate. The Fourth Circuit rejected the government's argument, finding that it would require the court to "embrac[e] a sweeping proposition—namely that, with no meaningful judicial review, any American citizen alleged to be an enemy combatant could be detained indefinitely without charges or counsel on the government's say-so."[32] The Obama administration's claim in *Al-Aulaqi v. Obama* was essentially no different—that its targeting decision, made pursuant to a closed unilateral process and secret standards and evidence, was entirely unreviewable. While the district court ultimately dismissed the *Al-Aulaqi* case on jurisdictional grounds,[33] the decision was not appealed, leaving open the question of the availability of judicial review.[34]

THE FUTURE OF TARGETED KILLING

Since the lawsuit, the administration has made some steps in the right direction, but the same fundamental concerns with the program remain. On May 23, 2013, President Obama gave a major national security speech in which he outlined a new policy guidance for targeting operations.[35] The guidance outlines ostensibly narrower criteria for the use of lethal force "outside of areas of active hostilities"—requiring a "continuing, imminent threat," infeasibility of capture, and a "near-certainty" that civilians will not be killed or injured.[36] Exactly how these criteria are being interpreted is unknown; however, drone strikes in the weeks and months following the president's speech make clear that the standards are, at bottom, discretionary, and that the administration's claimed legal authority remains broader.[37]

In his speech, the president also made promises of greater transparency and accountability. He discussed a decision to declassify the targeting operations that killed al-Aulaqi, Samir Khan, Abdulrahman al-Aulaqi, and another American citizen, Jude Kenan Mohammed, as an effort to "facilitate transparency and debate on this issue"[38] and stated that the administration would be "review[ing] proposals to extend oversight of lethal actions outside of warzones that go beyond our reporting to Congress."[39] Yet still today, the administration continues to withhold basic information about the program—not only its legal memos, but any and all data about those killed that would allow the public to evaluate its claims about the efficacy and wisdom of its actions. To date, the only available data is from non-governmental sources, and the administration has openly acknowledged only four of the thousands killed and injured.[40] As for judicial review, two months after Obama's speech, administration lawyers continued to argue that the courts should have no role at all in reviewing constitutional claims brought after the killings of al-Aulaqi, Samir Khan, and sixteen-year-old Abdulrahman al-Aulaqi.[41]

In his May 23 speech, the president foreshadowed a future where the United States would finally shift away from the "war on terror" paradigm of the past eleven years,[42] and announced that he would ultimately seek to repeal the AUMF.[43] For the present, however, he reasserted and defended the same dangerous premise of a killing program that still continues.[44]

NOTES

1   Alice K. Ross, *Covert Drone War – The Complete Datasets*, Bureau
    of Investigative Journalism (last visited Sept. 24, 2013), www.
    thebureauinvestigates.com/2012/09/06/covert-drone-war-the-complete-
    datasets/ (estimating as many as 4,545 deaths from confirmed drone strikes
    and other covert operations in Pakistan, Yemen and Somalia); George W.
    Bush, President, United States, Address to a Joint Session of Congress and
    the American People (Sept. 20, 2001), *available at* georgewbush-whitehouse.
    archives.gov/news/releases/2001/09/20010920-8.html ("Our war on terror
    begins with al Qaeda, but it does not end there."); Harold Hongju Koh, "The
    Obama Administration and International Law," Annual Meeting of the
    American Society of International Law, Washington, D.C. (Mar. 25, 2010),
    www.state.gov/s/l/releases/remarks/139119.htm ("[T]he United States is in
    an armed conflict with al-Qaeda, as well as the Taliban and associated forces,
    in response to the horrific 9/11 attacks . . . .").

2   Watson Institute for International Studies, *Over 300,000 Killed by Violence,
    $4 Trillion Spent and Obligated*, Costs of War (last visited Sept. 24, 2013),
    costsofwar.org/ (finding that as many as 134,000 Iraqi civilians, 19,013
    Afghan civilians, and 6,656 US troops have died in the wars in Iraq and
    Afghanistan).

3   *See* John O. Brennan, Assistant to the President for Homeland Sec.
    & Counterterrorism, The Ethics and Efficacy of the President's
    Counterterrorism Strategy (Apr. 30, 2012), www.wilsoncenter.org/event/the-
    efficacy-and-ethics-us-counterterrorism-strategy (discussing targeted killing
    operations by the United States "beyond hot battlefields like Afghanistan");
    Letter from Eric Holder, Attorney General, to the Honorable Patrick J. Leahy,
    Chairman of the Committee on the Judiciary (May 22, 2013), *available at*
    www.justice.gov/slideshow/AG-letter-5-22-13.pdf (acknowledging that four
    American citizens were killed by US drone strikes "outside of areas of active
    hostilities" in Yemen and Pakistan in 2011).

4   *See, e.g.*, Brennan, *supra* note 3. ("Yes, in full accordance with the law, and in
    order to prevent terrorist attacks on the United States and to save American
    lives, the United States Government conducts targeted strikes against
    specific al-Qaida terrorists, sometimes using remotely piloted aircraft, often
    referred to publicly as drones.").

5   *See* Brief for Defendants-Appellees, *New York Times Co. et al., v. Dep't of
    Justice et al.*, (2nd Cir. pending) (Nos. 13-442 & 13-445), 2013 WL 3171502
    [hereinafter Defendants Brief].

6   *See* Complaint, *Al-Aulaqi v. Obama*, 727 F.Supp.2d 1 (D.D.C. 2010) (No. 10-
    1469) 2010 WL 3478666 ¶ 1.

7   Dana Priest, *U.S. military teams, intelligence deeply involved in aiding Yemen
    on strikes*, Wash. Post (Jan. 27, 2010), www.washingtonpost.com/wp-dyn/

content/article/2010/01/26/AR2010012604239_pf.html (reporting that Anwar Al-Aulaqi had been added to "a shortlist of U.S. citizens" that the Joint Special Operation Command was specifically authorized to kill); Greg Miller, *Muslim cleric Aulaqi is 1st U.S. citizen on list of those CIA is allowed to kill*, WASH. POST (Apr. 7, 2010), www.washingtonpost.com/wp-dyn/content/article/2010/04/06/AR2010040604121.html?hpid=moreheadlines.

8   Ross, *supra* note 1 (estimating 51 total drone strikes in Pakistan between 2004–2009 under President Bush, and 52 total drone strikes in Pakistan in 2009 under President Obama). Of 371 total reported U.S. drone strikes in Pakistan from 2004–2013, 320 were under President Obama. *Id.*

9   A second lawsuit was brought in 2012 after the killings of Anwar Al-Aulaqi, Samir Khan, and Abdulrahman Al-Aulaqi, which is pending at the time of writing. *Al-Aulaqi v. Panetta*, No. 12-cv-1192 (D.D.C. 2012) (unreported).

10 *See, e.g.*, Brennan, *supra* note 3.

11 *See* Human Rights Council, *Report of the Special Rapporteur on extrajudicial, summary or arbitrary executions, Philip Alston*, ¶ 44, UN Doc A/HRC/14/24/Add.6, 14th sess. (2010) ("[E]ven if the use of inter-state force is offered as justification for a targeted killing, it does not dispose of the further question of whether the killing of the particular targeted individual or individuals is lawful.").

12 Reply Memorandum in Support of Plaintiff's Motion for a Preliminary Injunction and in Opposition to Defendants' Motion to Dismiss, *Al-Aulaqi v. Obama*, 727 F.Supp. 1 (D.D.C. 2010) (No. 10-1469) 2010 WL 4974323 (discussing the criteria for armed conflict under *Prosecutor v. Tadic*, Case No. IT-94-1-T) [hereinafter Plaintiff's Reply Memorandum]; Declaration of Mary Ellen O'Connell, *Al-Aulaqi v. Obama*, 727 F.Supp. 1 (D.D.C. 2010) (No. 10-1469), ccrjustice.org/files/Declaration%20of%20Mary%20Ellen%20O%27Connell%2010-08-2010.pdf ¶¶ 11, 13 (discussing the criteria for armed conflict and the territorial limits of armed conflict).

13 *See* Declaration of Bernard Haykel, *Al-Aulaqi v. Obama*, 727 F.Supp. 1 (D.D.C. 2010) (No. 10-1469), www.google.com/url?sa=t&rct=j&q=&esrc=s&frm=1&source=web&cd=1&cad=rja&ved=0CCwQFjAA&url=http%3A%2F%2Fccrjustice.org%2Ffiles%2FDeclaration%2520of%2520Bernard%2520Haykel%252010-08-2010.pdf&ei=PgFCUoKZEuTAigKpgoHoBQ&usg=AFQjCNGnXsFPwMItcmvuAwbUamcPtQ4Dxw&sig2=n_i5qjp5qssCkja-eakzuQ (discussing al-Qaeda in the Arabian Peninsula); *see* Declaration of Mary Ellen O'Connell, *supra* note 12, at ¶ 15 (concluding that the United States was not engaged in armed conflict in Yemen during the relevant period).

14 Plaintiff's Reply Memorandum, *supra* note 12.

15 *See* Brennan, *supra* note 3 (identifying al-Shabaab in Somalia, AQAP in Yemen, al-Qaeda in the Islamic Maghreb (AQIM) in North and West Africa, and Boko Haram in Nigeria as "affiliates" and "adherents" of al-Qaeda

that threaten the United States). At a Senate Armed Services Committee hearing on the AUMF in May 2013, the DOD Acting General Counsel acknowledged that the AUMF could also be read to authorize lethal force against "associated forces" in Mali, Libya, and Syria. *Oversight: The Law of Armed Conflict, the Use of Military Force, and the 2001 Authorization for the Use of Military Force: Hearing Before the S. Comm. on Armed Services,* 113th Cong. 15 (2013) (statement of Robert Taylor) *available at* armed-services.senate.gov/Transcripts/2013/05%20May/13-43%20-%205-16-13.pdf [hereinafter Oversight: The Law of Armed Conflict]; *see id.* at 9 (Assistant Secretary of Defense for Special Operations and Low-Intensity Conflict stating that it would be "difficult for the Congress to get involved in trying to track the designation of which are the affiliate forces.").

16 *See* Brennan, *supra* note 3; Oversight: The Law of Armed Conflict, *supra* note 15.

17 *See* Brennan, *supra* note 3 (discussing the diminishing capacity of "al-Qaida core," but the active threat from its "affiliates" and "adherents"); Media Conference Call, Office of the Director of National Intelligence, Background briefing on the state of Al-Qaida (Apr. 27, 2012) (*available at* www.dni.gov/index.php/newsroom/speeches-and-interviews/99-speeches-interviews-2012/563-background-briefing-on-the-state-of-al-qaida-media-conference-call 2 (Deputy Director Robert Cardillo discussing "a movement that will be more decentralized" due to the weakening of al-Qaeda, where "regional al-Qaida affiliates [will conduct] the bulk of the terrorist attacks.").

18 Plaintiff's Reply Memorandum, *supra* note 12.

19 *See id.*

20 *See id.*

21 Michael Isikoff, Justice Department memo reveals legal case for drone strikes on Americans, NBC NEWS (Feb. 4, 2013), investigations.nbcnews.com/_news/2013/02/04/16843014-justice-department-memo-reveals-legal-case-for-drone-strikes-on-americans?lite.

22 Lawfulness of a Lethal Operation Directed Against a US Citizen Who Is a Senior Operational Leader of Al-Qa'ida or An Associated Force, at 7-8 (Nov. 8, 2011); *see* Appendix A. The white paper also identifies "infeasibility" of capture as another loosely defined criterion. *Id.*

23 *Id.* at 1 ("The paper does not attempt to determine the minimum requirements necessary to render such an operation lawful; nor does it assess what might be required to render a lethal operation against a U.S. citizen lawful in other circumstances, including an operation against . . . a U.S. citizen who is not a senior operational leader of such forces.").

24 *See* Letter from Eric Holder, *supra* note 3 (openly acknowledging the deaths of four U.S. citizens in targeted killing operations "outside of areas of hostilities").

[25] *See* Convention for the Amelioration of the Condition of the Wounded and Sick in Armed Forces in the Field, art. 3, Aug. 12, 1949, 75 U.N.T.S. 31; *see* Convention for the Amelioration of the Condition of Wounded, Sick and Shipwrecked Members of Armed Forces at Sea, art. 3, Aug. 12, 1949, 75 U.N.T.S. 85; *see* Convention Relative to the Treatment of Prisoners of War, art. 3, Aug. 12, 1949, 75 U.N.T.S. 135; *see* Convention Relative to the Protection of Civilian Persons in Time of War, art. 3, Aug. 12, 1949, 75 U.N.T.S. 287; *see* Protocol Additional to the Geneva Conventions of 12 August 1949, and relating to the Protection of Victims of International Armed Conflicts, art. 13, June 8, 1977, 1125 U.N.T.S. 3; *see* Nils Melzer, *Interpretive Guidance on the Notion of Direct Participation in Hostilities under International Humanitarian Law*, ICRC 27 (2009), www.icrc.org/eng/assets/files/other/icrc-002-0990.pdf ("In non-international armed conflict, organized armed groups . . . consist only of individuals whose continuous function it is to take a direct part in hostilities.").

[26] *See* Brennan, *supra* note 3 ("[I]ndividuals who are part of al-Qaida or its associated forces are legitimate military targets. We have the authority to target them with lethal force just as we target [sic] enemy leaders in past conflicts, such as Germans and Japanese commanders during World War II.").

[27] *See* Gabor Rona, *Thoughts on Brennan's Speech*, OPINIO JURIS, May 2, 2012, opiniojuris.org/2012/05/02/thoughts-on-brennans-speech/ (objecting to Brennan's claim as a "sweeping and incorrect claim of who is targetable under international law . . . .").

[28] Plaintiff's Reply Memorandum, *supra* note 12.

[29] *See* Defendants Brief, *supra* note 5.

[30] Opposition to Plaintiff's Motion for Preliminary Injunction and Memorandum in Support of Defendants' Motion to Dismiss, *Al-Aulaqi v. Obama*, 727 F.Supp. 1 (D.D.C. 2010) (No. 10-1469) 2010 WL 3863135 (arguing that the plaintiff's constitutional claims should be dismissed under the political question doctrine, in part because the court does not have constitutional authority to review the claims).

[31] *See* Jeh Johnson, General Counsel, Department of Defense, National Security Law, Lawyers, and Lawyering in the Obama Administration (Feb. 22, 2012), *available at* www.cfr.org/defense-and-security/jeh-johnsons-speech-national-security-law-lawyers-lawyering-obama-administration/p27448 ("[C]ontrary to the view of some, targeting decisions are not appropriate for submission to a court."); Eric Holder, Attorney General, Attorney General Eric Holder Speaks at Northwestern University School of Law (Mar. 5, 2012), *available at* www.justice.gov/iso/opa/ag/speeches/2012/ag-speech-1203051.html (asserting that "'[d]ue process' and 'judicial process' are not one and the same, particularly when it comes to national security.").

[32] *Hamdi v. Rumsfeld*, 296 F.3d 278, 283 (4th Cir. 2002), *vacated*, 542 U.S. 507 (2004). The Supreme Court went even further, affirming that the Judiciary retained a role in reviewing Hamdi's detention, but holding that such review should be fuller than the limited review prescribed by the Fourth Circuit in order to be meaningful. *Hamdi v. Rumsfeld*, 542 U.S. 507, 535 (2004).

[33] *Al-Aulaqi v. Obama*, 727 F.Supp. 2d 1, 35, 52 (D.D.C. 2010) (granting the government's motion to dismiss on the basis of standing and the political question doctrine).

[34] The question of judicial review is at issue in the pending case of *Al-Aulaqi v. Panetta*, which challenges the constitutionality of the killings of Anwar Al-Aulaqi, Samir Khan and Abdulrahman Al-Aulaqi. *See Al-Aulaqi v. Panetta*, No. 12-cv-1192 (D.D.C. 2012) (unreported).

[35] Barack Obama, President, United States, Remarks by the President at the National Defense University (May 23, 2013), *available at* www.whitehouse. gov/the-press-office/2013/05/23/remarks-president-national-defense-university.

[36] Office of the Press Secretary, U.S. Policy Standards and Procedures for the Use of Force in Counterterrorism Operations Outside the United States and Areas of Active Hostilities (May 23, 2013); *see* Appendix A.

[37] *See* Greg Miller, *Obama administration authorized recent drone strikes in Yemen*, WASH. POST (Aug. 6, 2013) articles.washingtonpost.com/2013-08-06/world/41107162_1_u-s-embassy-u-s-drone-activity-yemeni-government-officials (reporting that the "new rules . . . allow for strikes to resume in response to an elevated threat."); Mark Mazetti and Mark Landler, *Despite Administration Promises, Few Signs of Change in Drone Wars*, N.Y. TIMES (Aug. 2, 2013), www.nytimes.com/2013/08/03/us/politics/drone-war-rages-on-even-as-administration-talks-about-ending-it.html?pagewanted=all (reporting that "there is little public evidence of change" in the administration's strategy) .

[38] *See* Letter from Eric Holder, *supra* note 3 (openly acknowledging that American citizens Anwar Al-Aulaqi, Samir Khan, Abdulrahman Al-Aulaqi, and Jude Kenan Mohammed were killed by the United States "outside of areas of active hostilities").

[39] Obama, *supra* note 35.

[40] *See* Letter from Eric Holder, *supra* note 3.

[41] *See* Transcript of Oral Argument, *Al-Aulaqi v. Panetta*, (No. 12-1192) (D.D.C. 2013) (unreported) (D.D.C. 2013), *available at* www.ccrjustice.org/files/Transcript%20of%20July%2019,%202013,%20Oral%20Argument%20on%20Defendants%E2%80%99%20Motion%20to%20Dismiss.pdf (argument on the defendants' motion to dismiss Fourth and Fifth Amendment claims on behalf of Anwar Al-Aulaqi, Samir Khan, and Abdulrahman Al-Aulaqi for their deaths by U.S. drone strikes on September 30, 2013, and October 14, 2013).

42   Obama, *supra* note 35 (stating that "this war [against al Qaeda], like all wars, must end," and that the current threat of terrorism "closely resembles the types of attacks we faced before 9/11.").

43   *Id.* (stating that he would "engag[e] Congress and the American people in efforts to refine, and ultimately repeal, the AUMF's mandate.").

44   *Id.* (stating that we are at war with al-Qaeda and its affiliates).

11

THE CASE OF ISRAEL: A COVERT POLICY OF POLITICAL CAPITAL PUNISHMENT

Ishai Menuchin[1]

Assassinations have plagued us long before documented history. Contrary to its common image in the public sphere, assassination is sometimes a political tool and not only an instrument of prevention or justice. Currently, although it is alleged to prevent the explosion of a "ticking bomb"—the common supporting argument in the Israeli public sphere—assassination usually serves as a day-to-day execution weapon in the "war on terror" as an "easy" solution for military difficulties, as a means for promoting deterrence, or as a method for delivering political messages.[2] In Israeli discourse, most of the time, the political agenda is concealed. The discourse speaks of the elimination of terrorists and of preemptive action against "ticking bombs." Not surprising is the contrary theme in the Palestinian discourse of day-to-day acts of Israeli state terror and repression. Both discourses have opposite narratives; both sides of this ongoing conflict are invested in the language of violence and revenge, and they hide their political agendas.

Sometimes assassinations are sanitized with euphemisms such as "targeted preemption," "preemptive prevention," "extrajudicial punishment," or with the legal-official "clean" term "targeted killing," suggesting that the assassination hindered a bad event, that it was a just surgical punishment or a legitimate military operation. All these terms refer to the definition by the Special Rapporteur on extrajudicial, summary or arbitrary executions: "A targeted killing is the intentional, premeditated and deliberate use of lethal force, by States or their agents acting under colour of law, or by an organized armed group in armed conflict, against a specific individual who is not in the physical custody of the perpetrator."[3] Yael Stein noticed that "'Assassination' is also the term by which international human rights organizations, such as Amnesty International and Human Rights Watch, refer to this [targeted killing] policy."[4] In spite of the "clean" language used in the political and judicial spheres, clear-cut terms, such as extermination or liquidation, are also used in the Israeli public sphere discourse.

Capital punishment is only authorized by the Israeli criminal code in cases of severe treason or for Nazi crimes.[5] It has been implemented only twice since the establishment of the State of Israel—once in 1949 in an illegal military court, which consequently led to the trial of some of the participants,[6] and once in 1962 when Nazi war criminal Adolf Eichmann was executed.[7] Even the military court system, which has authority to order death sentences, resists public calls to execute perpetrators of abhorrent acts of terrorism. Despite the reticence of the courts to apply capital punishment, assassination has been a covert military practice for many years. There has been no formal public approval of assassination, the government has been very vague about it, and the army has denied the practice for a long time.

On November 9, 2000, forty-two days after the outbreak of the second Intifada, Hussein Abayat, a local Palestinian Fatah activist, was assassinated. Renata Capella and Michael Sfard stated, "This event marked the beginning of the state of Israel's official assassination policy. From that day, this policy becomes official, approved, and openly admitted by the political and military establishment. On [July 3,] 2001, the 'kitchen cabinet' gave the Israeli army 'a broader license to liquidate Palestinian terrorists' and allowed the army 'to act against known terrorists even if they are not on the verge of committing a major attack.' In February 2002, the Judge Advocate General of the Israeli army issued further guidelines for assassinations."[8]

The Israeli army used that "broader license." According to the Israeli Information Center for Human Rights in the Occupied Territories (B'Tselem), between September 2000 and October 2012, 437 Palestinians were assassinated in "target killing methods"—261 were actually targeted and the rest were collateral killings.[9] The Special Rapporteur on the promotion and protection of human rights and fundamental freedoms while countering terrorism estimated, "As far as targeted killings are concerned, according to the information at my disposal a total of 254 Palestinians have been the object of targeted killings by Israeli security forces since September 2000, 21 of whom were killed since 'Operation Cast Lead.'"[10]

These extrajudicial executions became the official policy of the Israeli government with little public or legal criticism. This raises three troubling policy issues:

- How is it that despite the fact that the death penalty in Israel is largely moot, the legal system does not challenge this governmental policy of extrajudicial executions?

- How is it possible that a covert cohort of security officials and politicians has the power to devise lists of potential targets for execution with no oversight, no due process, no transparency, and no accountability?

- How is it that in a "democratic society" such a list exists, no one is responsible or accountable for it, and there is no public critique?

A LEGAL COVER-UP UNDER THE GUISE OF SECURITY

The first question regarding this official policy is how the legal system shields extra-judicial executions, allowing them to continue unchallenged. Although the international legal consensus that a continuous policy of assassination crosses legitimate boundaries has become looser, such policy is still prohibited by international law.[11] A policy that does not differentiate between Palestinian civilians and combatants is illegal, contravening international humanitarian law and international human rights law, and thus could be defined as a war crime.[12] Yael Stein claims:

> [G]iven that the assassinations are carried out against civilians, Israel has to provide evidence that they were 'participating in the hostilities' . . . Since Israel has never provided such evidence, these killings must be considered illegal, and according to Article 147 of the Fourth Geneva Convention, a grave breach of the law of war.[13]

On the few occasions the assassinations policy was discussed by the Israeli High Court of Justice (HCJ), the court found a way to avoid challenging the policy while granting immunity to the executioners.

In *Siham Thabit vs. Attorney General*,[14] Thabit petitioned the state because her husband, Dr. Thabit Thabit, was assassinated in December 2000 by the Israeli Defense Force (IDF) while he was driving in his car in Tulkarm, a Palestinian town in the West Bank. In January 2002, she requested that the HCJ order a criminal investigation against then Prime Minister Ehud Barak and General Shaul Mofaz, the former IDF chief of staff. Four years later, the court rejected the petition and refused to order a criminal investigation.[15]

Ido Rosenzweig and Yuval Shany examined the *Thabit* decision and wrote that:

> [F]ollowing the HCJ's 2006 decision in the "Targeted Killing" case, which did not exclude the use of such measures, the legality of targeted killing operations was to be determined on a case by case basis. . . Such an examination should be made by an independent committee of inquiry. The HCJ should only consider cases after they have been reviewed by the committee of inquiry (since the HCJ does not have the professional tools to make an independent professional evaluation *de novo*). . . The Court's decision to reject the petition, in part because of the failure of the petitioner to make use of the existing inquiry committee, strikes us as problematic. It is less than clear that the existing inquiry committee is even authorized to handle such a complaint.[16]

The next HCJ petition that we will examine is *The Public Committee Against Torture in Israel (PCATI) v. government of Israel*.[17] The court published its decision in December 2006 and declared that "targeted killings" are not illegal as such, but can be used only for prevention and not as a tool for punishment, revenge, or deterrence. Although this decision maintains the status quo, it put a theoretical restriction on assassinations. First, targeted killings cannot be used against civilians, even when they take part in hostilities, if less severe measures are available. Second, the judges were concerned with the issue of *proportionality*— the proportions between the collateral damage and the legitimate military advantage of the operation. In paragraph 46, Chief Justice Aharon Barak explains and gives an example:

> The rule is that combatants and terrorists are not to be harmed if the damage expected to be caused to nearby innocent civilians is not proportionate to the military advantage in harming the combatants and terrorists. . . . Performing that balance is difficult. . . . Take the usual case of a combatant, or of a terrorist sniper shooting at soldiers or civilians from his porch. Shooting at him is proportionate even if as a result, an innocent civilian neighbor or passerby is harmed. That is not the case if the building is bombed from the air and scores of its residents and passersby are harmed . . . . Indeed, in international law, as in internal law, the ends do not justify the means.[18]

Finally, the court decided that each case must be examined post facto by an independent and professional committee of inquiry rather than by the court itself because the court cannot make an independent evaluation of such security issues. Since then, and contrary to the HCJ ruling, we know of only one so-called independent professional committee discussion—the Strasberg-Cohen Commission, dealing with the assassination of Mr. Salah Shehada, the victim discussed in the next petition.

On July 22, 2002, an Israeli bomber dropped a one-ton bomb on a civilian neighborhood in the Gaza strip. The target was Salah Shehada, the military leader of Hamas in Gaza. As a result of the bombing, 14 people were killed along with Mr. Shehada. His wife and fourteen-year-old daughter, 7 other children, and about 150 people were injured. After recurring failed attempts to convince the military and the state attorneys general to initiate a criminal investigation, Yesh Gvul—the soldiers' refusal movement—approached the HCJ.

In *Yoav Hass v. the Military Advocate General*,[19] Yesh Gvul demanded that the attorney general and the military advocate general order a criminal investigation of all parties involved, whether by order or execution, in the assassination of Mr. Salah Shehada by a one-ton bomb in a civilian district in the middle the of night. As a result of the HCJ's former decision, the government appointed an "independent and objective" commission of inquiry consisting of two ex-generals and one former General Security Service official to investigate the case. The commission operated according to the procedures of a military debriefing—which is to say that its proceedings and conclusions were secret, and the testimony given was inadmissible in a court of law. No civilians took part in the commission, neither as members nor as witnesses.[20] The commission found that the assassination was justified and legitimate and that it was carried out according to Israeli and the international legal standards. On December 23, 2008, the HCJ rejected the petition on the grounds that the Strasberg-Cohen Commission rendered a criminal investigation superfluous.[21]

Even when an arrest was a possible "less severe measure" and it is clear that the assassination was used as revenge or as a way for promoting deterrence or delivering a rough political message, the HCJ does not give a remedy to the victims. It does not stand behind its ruling that assassinations cannot be used against civilians if less severe measures are available. A powerful example is the assassination of Issa Debabseh, a shepherd from South Hebron hills, who was suspected of the 1998 killing of Dov Driban, an Israeli settler. The evidence indicated that Debabseh was assassinated even though it was possible to arrest him. In November 2001, four members of the border police "mista'arvim" unit[22] went to the home of Debabseh, who was overseeing the digging of a water cistern in his yard. Two of the undercover officers separated him from his neighbor who was standing close by. A third officer shot Debabseh to death. After the first shot to Debabseh's heart, the officer proceeded to "confirm the kill" by firing the remaining rounds of ammunition in his weapon's magazine into Debabseh's body. The Border Police officers loaded his corpse onto a vehicle and drove away. A uniformed soldier positioned a few dozen meters from the Debabseh home stood guard while the assassination was executed. A few hours later, the family was informed that Debabseh's body was in the District Coordinating Office in Hebron.[23]

When PCATI petitioned the HCJ to force the Military Advocate General to order a criminal investigation in this case,[24] the HCJ found a way not to intervene because of the delay in delivering the petition. In addition, the judges decreed the operation a legitimate arrest operation—"a military operation to catch a wanted man, done in rough security period"—and not an assassination.[25]

The results of these four petitions, and many other petitions on related security issues, were not surprising. The Israeli legal system in general, and the HCJ in particular, do not treat extrajudicial executions differently from other security issues. This policy was clearly defined in one of the first petitions against assassinations—*Mohammad Barakeh v. The Prime Minister and the Minister of Defense*:[26] "This Court will not intervene in the choice of military weapons, which the respondents use in order to prevent vicious terrorist attacks."

The HCJ has dismissed most of the assassinations petitions on the ground that it doesn't render rulings on security issues. In *PCATI v. government of Israel*,[27] the court set forth a list of parameters for "legal" executions. It is part of the Israeli legal system's ongoing policy of minimizing confrontation with the security systems and their unwillingness to challenge Israeli public opinion. The court effectively legalizes almost every act committed by Israel's security forces. One can only conclude that Israel's HCJ is one of the primary enablers of the ongoing Israeli occupation of the Occupied Palestinian Territories.

THE ART OF "TARGET BANKING"

The second troubling issue is the power of a covert cohort of security and political officials who have the authority to devise lists of potential targets for execution with no oversight, no due process, no transparency, and no accountability.

Armies prepare target lists for their forthcoming military operations.[28] The main problem is not with "regular" wars or combat operation plans, but with lists of individuals meant to be eliminated without any due process, such as the US list mentioned in the *New York Times* headline, "Secret 'Kill List' Proves a Test of Obama's Principles and Will."[29] The need for moral oversight has been blunted to such a degree that it has become routine to mention offhandedly a "bank" of potential targets for execution. How is it that in what we have been accustomed to define as a democratic society such a list exists and is accepted with no public critique?

Two of the foundational assumptions of democratic procedural activities are the state monopoly on the use of coercive force and the rule of law. These pillars are protected by the traditional democratic separation of powers, ensuring that each authority—the legislative, executive, and judiciary—has its own role. Even in soft parliamentary separation of powers, in times of terror, it is the role of the judiciary, and not the role of the executive authority, to adjudicate and punish. This is more than a principle of procedural checks and balances; it is a way to avoid politically motivated punishment or "legal" action.

Furthermore, when punishment takes place as a result of executive activity rather than legal authority, it is the first and foremost obligation of the legal system to investigate its legality, its chain of command, and protect the rule of law. When the legal authority neglects its obligation to adjudicate assassinations, it is easy for the executive authority to act without accountability and beyond its mandate.

The political agenda is more transparent when the security forces use their "broader license to liquidate Palestinian terrorists" even when "they are not on the verge of committing a major attack."[30] The political agenda is evident when the news reports that "IDF opts for targeted killing over large-scale W. Bank operation—targeted killings of Islamic Jihad military leaders in Tulkarm area are expected in the coming days."[31] Or when the government's official policy is "to continue with targeted prevention policy against the leaders of Hamas."[32] Or when Ma'an, a Palestinian news agency, publishes a "new extermination target list that was leaked with the names of sixteen Palestinians.[33]

Uri Blau wrote:

> [T]he IDF approved assassinations in the West Bank even when it could have been possible to arrest the targets instead, and that top-ranking army officers authorized the killings in advance, in writing, even if innocent bystanders would be killed as well . . . contrary to what the state told the High Court.[34]

But the response centered around the leak of information rather than on the contradiction between the state's answer to the court and its actual conduct. Blau then reported:

> On March 28, 2007, a meeting was called by then-GOC Central Command Yair Naveh to discuss Operation Two Towers. "The mission" said Naveh, "is arrest," but "in case identification is made of one of the leaders of Palestinian Islamic Jihad—Walid Obeidi, Ziad Malaisha, Adham Yunis—the force has permission to kill them, according to the situation assessment while carrying out the mission." On April 12, Naveh convened another meeting on the subject. This time, he approved killing Malaisha and "another two people at most."[35]

This was a clear-cut violation of the HCJ ruling of December 2006, that assassinations are allowed only if the target cannot be arrested, and that "the rule is that combatants and terrorists are not to be harmed if the damage expected to be caused to nearby innocent civilians is not proportionate to the military advantage in harming the combatants and terrorists."[36]

Nothing happened when PCATI demanded:

> the attorney general order a criminal investigation to determine whether any crimes were committed in the planning and execution of past targeted assassinations. . . . asking him to clearly and unconditionally prohibit assassinations when detention is an alternative, and to prohibit giving advance approval to harming innocent bystanders. They also demanded Mazuz establish a committee to examine the constitutionality of past assassinations, as the High Court of Justice called for in a 2006 ruling.[37]

No one paid a price for this clear-cut violation of the HCJ decision. The military attorney's office found that the security forces involved were police and Israel Security Agency (ISA) forces. The deputy attorney general decided there was no need to investigate them. No response from the HCJ was publicized. GOC Central Command Yair Naveh was promoted and became the IDF deputy chief of staff.

Even when sections of the chain of command are known and fragments of the assassination target-list production process are recognized, there is still no oversight, no due process, no transparency, and no accountability. Assassinations continue to happen and no one is held to account.

ABSENCE OF PUBLIC ACCOUNTABILITY

It is well established in different societies that each member of society is responsible for his or her own judgments and actions. Public responsibility, in particular, can be regarded as the responsibility of the public at large, or the responsibility of public figures—political representatives or officials—toward the public. Former attorney general and retired Supreme Court justice Yitzhak Zamir characterized this responsibility as transparency, accountability, and personal responsibility.[38]

There are basically two types of responsibility. The first is prospective, the second retrospective. In the case of retrospective responsibility, one assumes responsibility for something done in the past. In the case of prospective responsibility, one takes responsibility for something happening now or that will be done in the future. In the case of producing target-killing lists, prospective responsibility means that agents who participated in the decision processes and production of the target lists should be held accountable for their decisions.

Individuals who took part in listing candidates for assassination should be held responsible for the outcome of the production of such lists—namely, they should be responsible for the assassinations themselves. But the whole process is not transparent; there is no accountability and no demand for personal responsibility. David Miller discusses responsibility and particularly the agent's (or agents') responsibility. He identifies four different types of responsibility—causal, moral, remedial, and communitarian. Without analyzing the relevance of each type of responsibility, when a policy of assassination is under discussion, each member of the target-killing-banking committee or process carries causal, moral, remedial, and communitarian responsibilities for the assassinations, according to Miller.[39]

He argues:

> [T]he biggest problem with the moral responsibility principle . . . is that it looks too exclusively to the past in assigning remedial responsibilities. The question it asks is always "Who is responsible for bringing this bad situation about?" And never, for instance, "Who is best placed to put it right?"[40]

It is evident that the target-banking-list committee carries most of the responsibility for the assassinations, but the HCJ also has important remedial responsibility, which it denies. That denial carries heavy moral implications.

Public responsibility must be expected of an authority involved with target-killing lists. An agent authorized to do something is held responsible for its outcome. That is, if one is responsible for the outcome, there was probably either no need for authorization, or one was authorized to do it. Authority without responsibility is incomplete, and the same goes for responsibility without authority. Regretfully, public deliberation on authority and responsibility usually takes place after catastrophes—when the public finds out the nature of the misconduct and discovers that all of the wrongdoers are "covered" by the protective blanket of "authority." Unfortunately, the most common responses are: "they were authorized to do it" or "it was an approved act"—therefore they are "not responsible" for the appalling results.

One of the aims of the struggle against assassination in Israel is to challenge the notion of "authorized and approved", to challenge the "kill lists" producers and their unlawful, covert and unchallenged authorization to assassinate Palestinian civilians. Today, assassins appear "blameless" because they act under governmental authorization that is illegal under Israeli and international law. Cutting this Gordian knot of "authorized and approved" can crack the silence which protects the Israeli policy of assassinations.

CONCLUSION

The relationship between the institutions of a state and its laws is complex. "The law is a supreme concern of any society and a condition for its existence," asserted Zamir,[41] reflecting a common declarative position stated by the government. The public is inundated by similar remarks and affirmations emphasizing the need to live under the "rule of law" and the "duty to respect the law," without which, so it is stated, anarchy will surely take hold. Yet the government, including all its security agencies, is the primary violator of this principle. Public authorities all too often seem indifferent to their own observance of the law when it interferes with a course of action they wish to take.

Similarly, the courts show remarkable tolerance toward civil servants and elected officials who often find "good reasons" for failing to observe the law when it suits them. This phenomenon is particularly evident in the case of security issues and the violation of the human rights of "others," which are either concealed or publicly justified under the sacred rationalization of "national security." Over the years, the Israeli public has become accustomed to this contradiction, and even finds it acceptable.

Assassination list-production group members enjoy a systemic legal immunity that is granted in advance, without any reference to their decisions. They are protected by layers of concealment, withholding of information, and immunity, shielding them like the layers of an onion. This systemic shield protects them and the Gordian knot of "authorized and approved" without transparency, accountability, and personal responsibility.

The first layer of protection to be granted to the list's authors on a daily basis is non-identification. The list producers remain nameless—no one outside of the political-security elite knows who prepared those lists.

The second layer of protection is the policy of no investigations into complaints of assassinations. Complaints submitted to the military or the state attorneys general have led to *no* criminal investigation into assassinations.[42] The example of the Strasberg-Cohen Commission proves that the HCJ ruling on target killings is an empty promise.

The third layer of protection, institutionalized with the help of the Israeli parliament (Knesset), is the ISA Law of 2002. It is well-known that ISA agents take part in targeted killings. This law ensures, on the one hand, that an ISA agent "will not bear criminal or civil liability for any act or omission committed in good faith and in a reasonable manner in the framework of his function and for the purpose of filling the said function."[43] On the other hand, and commensurate with this complete immunity, the law also ensures that all the operating methods and names of ISA personnel will remain confidential. This confidentiality prevents any exposure of who took part in the production of the list, who authorized it, and whether the actions taken against the target were authorized.

The fourth layer of protection is the unwillingness of the courts to challenge the political and security echelons in particular cases. As described earlier, the court at large, and the HCJ in particular, might sometimes be willing to rule on principle about issues such as assassinations and torture, but they are not willing to challenge the government on particular assassination cases.

In sum, Israel makes it impossible to identify the list producers. No one will bear accountability for it. There is no way to ensure that the court will have access to a full and precise memorandum describing the preparation of the list. All this is compounded by the full immunity granted to the ISA, IDF, and the political leadership by the law. Cutting the Gordian knot of "authorized and approved," and the opening of criminal investigations of suspected assassinations, could break the silence enshrouding the policies of target banking in Israel. It would end the total impunity of those suspected of authorizing and approving assassinations. All target-list producers would lose their systemic and complete immunity, and subsequent impunity inside Israel and outside the Israeli borders.

NOTES

[1] Executive Director, The Public Committee Against Torture in Israel and Lecturer, Ben-Gurion University of the Negev. I would like to thank my colleagues Carmi Lecker, Bana Shoughry-Badarne, and Michael Sfard for reading and improving this chapter.

[2] Renata Capella & Michael Sfard quoted the Israeli Prime Minister Ariel Sharon after the assassination of Iyyad Hardon on April 5, 2001, saying, "Sometimes we will announce what we did, sometimes we will not announce what we did. We don't have always to announce it." RENATA CAPELLA & MICHAEL SFARD, THE ASSASSINATION POLICY OF THE STATE OF ISRAEL (The Public Committee Against Torture in Israel 2002).

[3] U.N. Human Rights Counsel, *Special Rapporteur on extrajudicial, summary or arbitrary executions*, ¶ 1, U.N. Doc. A/HRC/14/24/Add.6, 14th sess. (May 28, 2010) (Philip Alston).

[4] Yael Stein, *By Any Name Illegal and Immoral: Response to "Israel's Policy of Targeted Killing"*, 17.1 ETHICS & INTERNATIONAL AFFAIRS: 127, 128 (2003).

[5] Some capital punishment verdicts handed down prior to the parliament legislation in 1954 were not implemented and the verdicts were changed to long-term imprisonments.

[6] Captain Meir Tobianski was executed on 30 June 1948 as a traitor after an illegal military trial.

[7]   An interesting description and analysis of the trial was published by Hannah Arendt. HANNAH ARENDT, EICHMANN IN JERUSALEM: A REPORT ON THE BANALITY OF EVIL (Penguin Books 1963).

[8]   Capella & Sfard, *supra* note 2.

[9]   B'TSELEM, www.btselem.org/hebrew/statistics (last accessed Aug. 16, 2013).

[10] U.N. Human Rights Counsel, *Special Rapporteur on the promotion and protection of human rights and fundamental freedoms while countering terrorism, Addendum - Follow-up report to country missions*, ¶ 45, N.N. Doc. A/HRC/20/14/Add.2, twentieth sess. (June 15, 2012) (Ben Emmerson).

[11] Philip Alston wrote, "In modern times, targeted killings by States have been very restricted or, to the extent that they are not, any de facto policy has been unofficial and usually denied, and both the justification and the killings themselves have been cloaked in secrecy. When responsibility for illegal targeted killings could be credibly assigned, such killings have been condemned by the international community – including by other States alleged to practice them." U.N. Human Rights UN Human Rights Counsel, *supra* note 3, at ¶ 11; *see Mirer* chapter 8

[12] Philip Alston explained, "Although in most circumstances targeted killings violate the right to life, in the exceptional circumstance of armed conflict, they may be legal. This is in contrast to other terms with which 'targeted killing' has sometimes been interchangeably used, such as 'extrajudicial execution', 'summary execution', and 'assassination', all of which are, by definition, illegal." U.N. Human Rights Counsel, *supra* note 3, at ¶ 10.

[13] Stein, *supra* note 4, at 130.

[14] HCJ 474/02 Siham Thabit v. Attorney General (Isr.).

[15] *Id.*

[16] Ido Rosenzweig & Yuval Shany, *HCJ Rejects Petition against Targeted Killing Incident from December 2000*, TERRORISM AND DEMOCRACY (Feb. 2011) (emphasis added), *available at* en.idi.org.il/analysis/terrorism-and-democracy/issue-no-26/hcj-rejects-petition-against-targeted-killing-incident-from-december-2000.

[17] HCJ 769/02 The Public Committee Against Torture in Israel v. Government of Israel [2006] (Isr.).

[18] *Id.* at 31-32.

[19] HCJ 8794/03 Yoav Hass v. the Military Advocate General [2008] (Isr.). *Yoav Hass* represented Yesh Gvul.

[20] The victim families' representatives were invited by the commission, but they refused to testify because of the committee's mandate and its members.

[21] Yoav Hass et al., *supra* note 19.

22 Army or police units operating without uniforms, the soldiers dress like civilian Palestinians in covert operations.

23 For additional details, *see* Public Committee Against Torture in Israel, www.stoptorture.org.il/en/node/992 (last visited Aug. 14, 2013).

24 HCJ 1901/08 Hana Debabseh, Mahmud Debabseh and Public Committee Against Torture v. Military Advocate General (Isr.).

25 *Id.*

26 HCJ 5872/01 Mohammad Barakeh v. The Prime Minister and the Minister of Defense (Isr.)

27 HCJ 769/02, *supra* note 17.

28 *See generally* Glenn Greenwald & Ewen MacAskill, *Obama orders US to draw up overseas target list for cyber-attacks*, The Guardian (June 7, 2013), www.theguardian.com/world/2013/jun/07/obama-china-targets-cyber-overseas; Amos Harel, *IDF preparing for next Lebanon war based on 'bank' of possible targets*, Haaretz (Oct. 13, 2012), www.haaretz.com/weekend/week-s-end/idf-preparing-for-next-lebanon-war-based-on-bank-of-possible-targets.premium-1.469660 (describes how the target bank for the next war in Lebanon was built).

29 Jo Becker & Scott Shane, *Secret 'Kill List' Proves a Test of Obama's Principles and Will*, N.Y. Times, May 29, 2012, A1.

30 Capella & Sfard, *supra* note 2.

31 Yoav Stern, *IDF Opts for Targeted Killing over Large-Scale W. Bank Operation*, Haaretz (Dec. 7, 2005), www.haaretz.com/news/idf-opts-for-targeted-killing-over-large-scale-w-bank-operation-1.176084.

32 Amir Buhbut & Dan Glikman, *We will shred everything connected to Hamas*, NRGMariv (Sept. 25, 2005), www.nrg.co.il/online/1/ART/988/335.html (translated).

33 Omar Shickler, The Palestinians: Israel has a New Extermination list, News1 (Feb. 10, 2006), www.news1.co.il/Archive/001-D-93634-00.html (translated).

34 Uri Blau, *IDF Ignoring High Court on West Bank Assassinations*, Haaretz (Nov. 26, 2008), www.haaretz.com/print-edition/news/idf-ignoring-high-court-on-west-bank-assassinations-1.258296.

35 *Id.* Blau based his article on classified documents taken by Anat Kam, an IDF soldier, during her military service in GOC Central Command Yair Naveh's office. She was charged with espionage and imprisoned for 3.5 years.

36 HCJ 769/02, *supra* note 17.

37 Tomer Zarchin, *Anti-torture group calls on AG to probe IDF assassinations in W. Bank*, Haaretz (Dec. 10, 2008), www.haaretz.com/print-edition/

news/anti-torture-group-calls-on-ag-to-probe-idf-assassinations-in-w-bank-1.259192.

38 Yitzhak Zamir, *Introduction: Public Responsibility, in* PUBLIC RESPONSIBILITY IN ISRAEL, 7-18 (Raphael Cohen-Almagor, Ori Arbel-Ganz, Asa Kasher Eds., Hakibbutz Hameuchad 2012).

39 Miller David, *Distributing Responsibilities*, 9 THE JOURNAL OF POLITICAL PHILOSOPHY 453 (2001).

40 *Id.*

41 Yitzhak Zamir & Avigdor Feldman, *The Boundary of Obedience in the Territories, in* DEMOCRACY AND OBEDIENCE 111-133 (Menuchin Ishai ed., Siman Kriah 1990).

42 *See also* PUBLIC COMMITTEE AGAINST TORTURE IN ISRAEL, ACCOUNTABILITY DENIED: THE ABSENCE OF INVESTIGATION AND PUNISHMENT OF TORTURE IN ISRAEL (2009); PUBLIC COMMITTEE AGAINST TORTURE IN ISRAEL, ACCOUNTABILITY STILL DENIED (2012).

43 Article 11 of the ISA Law, 2002.

PART IV
THE FUTURE OF TARGETED KILLING

12
DRONE STRIKE BLOWBACK
John Quigley

Faisal Shahzad was arrested in New York City in 2010 after explosives were found in an SUV he had apparently parked in Times Square. The explosives were set to ignite. Shahzad was prosecuted federally, and the case went to the US District Court for the Southern District of New York. At a pretrial hearing, Judge Miriam Goldman Cedarbaum asked Shahzad whether he was aware that the explosives could have killed dozens of civilians. Shahzad replied that he picked Times Square as the location precisely to injure and kill as many people as possible. Challenged on this statement by Judge Cederbaum, Shahzad retorted: "Well, the drone-hits in Afghanistan and Iraq don't see children; they don't see anybody. They kill women, they kill children. They kill everybody. It's a war," Shahzad said, describing himself as "part of the answer" for Muslims fighting that war.[1] Shahzad, a Pakistani-American, had recently been in the Waziristan region of Pakistan at the time of a missile strike from a US drone aircraft.

By 2010, the CIA and the military's Joint Special Operations Command (JSOC) were using missile-firing pilotless aircraft liberally over Pakistan, specifically in the Waziristan region. Their use was seen as an alternative to piloted aircraft for killing persons suspected of crossing the Waziristan border into Afghanistan for action there against NATO or Afghan government forces. The use of pilotless aircraft based at nearby friendly locations allowed for precision-targeted air strikes without putting US pilots at risk.

It is unclear from information available whether consideration was given to the possible broader impact of the use of missile-firing pilotless aircraft. In a speech to the American Society of International Law in 2010, Department of State Legal Adviser Harold Koh addressed the legality of the use of these aircraft under the rules for the conduct of warfare, the so-called *jus in bello*. Koh said such use was lawful if the aircraft "are employed in conformity with applicable laws of war." He did not provide detail on whether the US use is in conformity with applicable laws of war. In any event, he acknowledged that such use must conform.[2]

The Department of Justice (DoJ) did go into detail on US use of pilotless aircraft in light of the rules for the conduct of warfare. A white paper made public in 2013 stated that if care is taken as to targeting, no violation occurs.[3] But both Koh and the DoJ white paper confined themselves to the strictly legal aspect. Neither went one step further to address what one might call "blowback" from such use. The question they did not address was whether the use of lethal pilotless aircraft might bring the United States harm that one should weigh against the perceived benefits. Might it be, in other words, that these attacks would cause the United States more harm than good? Even if the use did not violate the rules on the conduct of warfare, could it nonetheless cause enough concern among affected populations that the United States would lose credibility? Might it even result in increased acts of violence against the United States and its citizens?

It is this issue that the Shahzad statement brings into focus. The experience in Pakistan and in the other countries in which the United States uses drones suggests that these concerns may be well taken. The drone attacks have been viewed negatively by the affected populations, engendering significant resentment against the United States.

International concern over drone strikes, in particular the accompanying civilian deaths, led a United Nations Human Rights Council official to initiate an inquiry into the use of lethal drones. A special office to focus on human rights violated in the name of fighting terrorism has been established. It is headed by an official with the title of Special Rapporteur on human rights and terrorism. Ben Emmerson, the office holder in 2013, organized a task force of experts to carry out the inquiry. A particular subject of investigation is a reported practice that a second missile is frequently shot a few minutes after a first missile, killing first responders.

As far back as 2003, drone strikes have been the subject of international inquiry. The United States began using drones to kill persons on the ground in the first years of the new century. In 2003, the UN Special Rapporteur on extrajudicial, summary or arbitrary executions investigated a US drone strike in Yemen that killed men riding in a vehicle and found the strike to be "a clear case of extrajudicial killing" in violation of international norms.[4]

IMPACT OF DRONE STRIKES

Pakistani cricketer and political activist Imran Khan has said that the strikes carried out in his country "are turning young men into angry Jihadis."[5] There is reason to believe that the Obama administration understands the social impact of drone strikes in Pakistan. In two instances, the administration temporarily halted them following an event that caused particular ill will against the United States. The first was a January 2011 incident in which a CIA contract worker, Raymond Davis, shot and killed two Pakistanis at a traffic intersection in the city of Lahore. Davis was driving his car, and the two Pakistanis were nearby on a motorcycle. Davis initially explained that the pair had tried to rob him. It later appeared that they may have been Pakistani intelligence agents tracking Davis on suspicion of his activities in Pakistan. In any event, the killing caused outrage in Pakistan, particularly after Davis was able to avoid prosecution. Pakistani officials released him after the United States claimed he enjoyed immunity from prosecution.[6]

Outrage in Pakistan over Davis's act and his subsequent release was so strong that the United States temporarily suspended drone attacks, fearing exacerbation of the anti-US sentiment. The fact that the United States suspended these attacks appeared to show that it understood the impact of the drone strikes. The United States hoped to minimize reasons for anti-US sentiment until the outrage over the Davis incident could blow over.

A second hiatus came after a November 26, 2011, incident in which NATO forces carried out a missile strike on two Pakistani posts on the Pakistan-Afghanistan border. Twenty-eight Pakistani military personnel were killed in the night raid; most of the Pakistanis were sleeping. US officials apologized and said that the targeting was inadvertent. But the government of Pakistan expressed outrage and took retaliatory measures by closing border traffic to US supply trucks. Drone attacks were suspended for several weeks.

While the United States has said as little as possible about drone strikes in Pakistan since they began, it has maintained that civilian casualties are slight. The matter came to public light in some measure when President Barack Obama nominated John Brennan in 2013 to become director of the CIA, Brennan, as a counterterrorism advisor to President Obama, had been a major architect of the drone program. His close identification with that program led to questioning of him on the issue when he appeared before the US Senate's Intelligence Committee. Senate confirmation was required for his nomination as CIA director.

Brennan was questioned about the drone program, and in particular about the Obama administration's silence on its rationale and impact. This demand for information prompted the administration to release the aforementioned DoJ white paper.

Brennan claimed that drone strikes are ordered only in the event of what he termed imminent threats, in order to save lives that might be lost as a result of attacks initiated by those being targeted by the drones. The white paper explained, however, that by "imminent threat" the United States did not limit itself to situations in which it was thought that the persons being targeted were about to undertake an act of violence. Imminence was understood in the sense that if the persons were thought to be planning acts of violence in the future they could be targeted.[7] That understanding of imminence means that strikes are ordered on an assessment about future activity. When one assesses future activity not related to a specific future attack, there is perforce a substantial chance of inaccuracy.

The impact on the local population, hence the strength of negative local reaction, is only partially measured by the numbers of individuals killed or injured. In the locales of intensive use, in particular the Waziristan region of Pakistan, the drones have radically altered life patterns for the population. Drones are capable of hovering for long periods. They are kept aloft over certain areas on a regular basis. They make a whirring sound heard on the ground. Anyone on the ground knows they are in the crosshairs. As a result, many local inhabitants alter their daily activities in an attempt to avoid sites where they think a drone-fired missile might land and explode. They do not attend funerals, which on occasion have been targeted. They keep their children home from school. They avoid large gatherings of any kind, out of fear that someone in the group might be targeted.[8]

Drone strikes are difficult to predict because some are undertaken to kill a particular known individual, others are undertaken, in particular in Pakistan, on the rationale that a group of individuals has been identified and located who fit the profile of the kind of person the United States seeks to kill.[9]

In one instance in 2011, a local meeting, called a *jirga*, was being held to resolve local issues in the North Waziristan sector of Pakistan. A drone-fired missile struck, killing several dozen persons. The United States claimed that all were "insurgents," calling them "terrorists."[10] There were apparently a handful of Taliban adherents among the dead, but the bulk were elders and others involved in sorting out the local issues under discussion.[11]

In some instances, a second drone attack is ordered within a short while after a first strike. These attacks are particularly likely to kill persons against whom there was no information, since bystanders often go to aid those they see in need of medical attention.

REPERCUSSIONS OF DRONE STRIKES

Drone strikes have been conducted in Pakistan by the United States since 2004. They had been conducted in Iraq from the time of the US invasion of 2003. Strikes have also been carried out in Yemen, Afghanistan, and Somalia.[12] Curiously, two separate agencies operate drone strikes for the United States. The CIA has one drone operation, while the military has another, conducted by the US Special Operations Command, which in turn is made up of special operations commands of the Army, Air Force, Navy, and Marine Corps.

Of the countries in which the United States has conducted drone strikes, Pakistan has seen the strongest opposition, but drone strikes have been received badly wherever they take place. Presently drones are in substantial use in Yemen, where they have generated ill will. A Yemeni defense official was quoted in 2011 as saying that the United States was "turning Yemen into another Pakistan." By that, he meant that the relatives of drone-strike victims might resort to terror tactics to avenge the deaths.[13]

In 2012, mass demonstrations were held in Yemen to protest the strikes.[14] In 2013, armed tribesmen in Yemen, angry over a drone strike on an area of concentrated civilian habitation, blocked the main road linking the capital city Sana'a with the provincial capital Maarib in Yemen's interior. In southern Yemen, armed tribesmen took to the streets to protest drone strikes there that they said had killed innocent civilians.[15]

A 2010 drone strike in Yemen demonstrated that strikes can have negative repercussions even in the short term. A drone that apparently targeted a group of al-Qaeda operatives killed the Maarib province's deputy governor along with the operatives. The deputy governor, a respected local figure, had been in talks with al-Qaeda to try to convince them to give up their fight. Yemen's president, Ali Saleh, was reportedly furious over the error, fearing an anti-American backlash. In evident reprisal for the killing of the deputy governor, an oil pipeline was attacked. According to the *New York Times*, the incident "produced a propaganda bonanza for al-Qaeda in the Arabian Peninsula."[16] The United States was forced to suspend drone strikes in Yemen for a time.[17]

Stanley A. McChrystal, the retired general who led JSOC, which has responsibility for the military's drone strikes, and former CIA director Michael V. Hayden, have expressed concern that the drone wars in Pakistan and Yemen are "targeting low-level militants who do not pose a direct threat to the United States."[18] "What scares me about drone strikes is how they are perceived around the world," said McChrystal. "The resentment created by American use of unmanned strikes is much greater than the average American appreciates. They are hated on a visceral level, even by people who've never seen one or seen the effects of one." McChrystal said the use of drones exacerbates a "perception of American arrogance."[19]

Drone strikes were conducted in Afghanistan over the years of combat there, but as the United States began reducing the number of its military personnel in Afghanistan in preparation for an end to a combat role, it employed drone strikes more liberally. Joshua Foust, a former adviser to the US military in Afghanistan, explained that drones allow for air strikes in Afghanistan, "without importing a bunch of pilots and the support infrastructure they'd need to remain based there."[20]

In 2012, US drone strikes in Afghanistan outnumbered those in Pakistan.[21] The accompanying civilian casualties caused further strain in the already delicate relationship between the United States and the government of Afghanistan.[22] In 2008, the British military began using lethal drones in Afghanistan. Like the United States, Britain increased their use as it drew down its troop levels.[23]

The impact of drone strikes in Somalia was also problematic. Strikes were conducted in 2006, against the forces of the Union of Islamic Courts, when that organization was consolidating power in Somalia. David Kilcullen, an Australian counterinsurgency expert who advised US General David Petraeus in planning the 2007 troop surge in Iraq, and Andrew Exum, of the Center for a New American Security, found the drone strikes in Somalia counterproductive because of the negative reaction to them. "Public anger over the American show of force," write Kilcullen and Exum, "solidified the power of extremists," by which they mean the Union of Islamic Courts. "The Islamists' popularity rose and the group became more extreme, leading eventually to a messy Ethiopian military intervention, the rise of a new regional insurgency and an increase in offshore piracy."[24]

In each country of use, drone strikes have produced unintended consequences that were negative for the United States, even in the short term. But the United States has continued to conduct strikes, viewing the benefits as compelling. Kilcullen "has warned that drone attacks create more extremists than they eliminate." Sir Sherard Cowper-Coles, formerly Britain's special representative to Afghanistan and Pakistan, finds drone attacks counterproductive because of the hatred they generate.[25] Kilcullen and Exum say that drone strikes in Pakistan have "created a siege mentality among Pakistani civilians." Kilcullen and Exum acknowledge that Pakistanis may not appreciate the elements being targeted. "While violent extremists may be unpopular, for a frightened population they seem less ominous than a faceless enemy that wages war from afar and often kills more civilians than militants." They write, "[E]very one of these dead noncombatants represents an alienated family, a new desire for revenge, and more recruits for a militant movement that has grown exponentially even as drone strikes have increased."

The drone strikes in Pakistan are confined to the regions along the border with Afghanistan. Nevertheless, the outrage is felt throughout the country. According to Kilcullen and Exum, the strikes have brought "visceral opposition across a broad spectrum of Pakistani opinion in Punjab and Sindh, the nation's two most populous provinces."[26]

A HISTORY OF RESENTMENT AGAINST US INTERVENTIONS

If drone strikes were the only instance of acts by the United States perceived negatively, the resentment might fade. However, they come against a background of activity regarded by many in the Middle East as promoting US interests without regard for negative impacts on local populations. Throughout the time in which the United States has been the major outside power in the Middle East, it has focused on short-term objectives. A failure to foresee consequences of measures taken has been a hallmark of its policy.

The United States helped other NATO countries remove Colonel Muammar Qaddafi from power in Libya in 2011, not realizing that the consequence would be the destabilization of North Africa as a whole. Elements of the Tuareg ethnic group who had served Colonel Qaddafi returned to their home areas in northern Mali to fight for independence for their region. Fundamentalist Islamist elements took control in northern Mali from the Tuareg nationalists, leading to a French-led military intervention. Elements from the Islamist group infiltrated into Algeria, where they took over a major oil facility, killing workers there, including three Americans.

The resulting situation in Mali has led the United States into yet another intervention. As a result of concern over the situation in Mali, the United States in 2013 beefed up the military's Europe-based Africa command. Then the United States set up a military operational base in Niger, which neighbors Mali, to provide support for the French in Mali. A key element of this move is the introduction of drone aircraft in Niger, to be used over Mali. The idea is that the drones may provide intelligence information through surveillance flights. For the moment they are not to be used to fire missiles, though they have that capability.

So a new front in the drone wars may be opening in North Africa. A contingent of one hundred US troops was sent to Niger in 2013 to staff the base from which drone aircraft would conduct surveillance in the region. The troops were largely air force logistics specialists, intelligence analysts, and security officers.[27]

The elements against which the United States is now acting in North Africa are a product of an earlier US action in the Middle East. Al-Qaeda in the Islamic Maghreb, the group that carried out the Algeria attack, which is active in Mali, and is the descendant by just a few generations of the mujahideen that operated in Afghanistan. The mujahideen was financed by the United States, starting in 1979, to oppose an Afghan government that maintained close ties to the USSR. That government was no particular threat to the West, but President Jimmy Carter started the operation to counter the USSR and potentially to destabilize it. The United States supplied surface-to-air missiles to use against Soviet helicopters. The United States focused on creating difficulty for the USSR without regard to the fact that those we financed opposed not only the USSR and its support for the then-government of Afghanistan, but opposed us as well. When they successfully evicted the pro-Soviet government, the mujahideen turned their guns on the United States.

Concern in the Middle East about US actions dates from the time the United States took over from Britain as the dominant outside power in the region. The United States is widely faulted for its role in the 1953 coup against the elected government of Iran.[28] The Iranian government had nationalized a British oil company, leading to fears that Western interests would lose access to Iran's oil. The coup led to a quarter-century rule by the tyrannical Shah Mohammad Reza Pahlavi, who protected Western oil interests in Iran.[29] Islamic rhetoric was used in Iran to denounce the United States for its support for the shah. The United States' support of the shah eventually led, for the first time, to the ascent to political power of a movement that looked to an Islamic religious philosophy for its rallying point. That event led to the first major instance of anti-US violence, when the embassy of the United States was invaded in 1979 and its personnel taken hostage.

In the 1990s, Osama bin Laden mirrored the approach of couching criticism of the United States in religious terms. Bin Laden, it was said, "Islamized the traditional discourse of Western anti-imperialism. So a lot of Muslims support him, not because they see him as a true warrior for Islam, but because they hate America."[30]

That hatred was based not on theological concerns but on our role in the region. Efforts to mold the politics of the region did not end with the 1953 coup in Iran. Rather, that action set a pattern that would only bring the United States into greater disrepute. In 1956, the United States paid Syrian military officers to overthrow a Syrian government that, like the pre-1953 government of Iran, sought to protect oil resources from unfair exploitation by Western companies. In 1957, the plotters turned themselves in and identified two US diplomats in Syria as CIA officers who had funded them.[31] Syria expelled the diplomats.[32]

In neighboring Lebanon, CIA funds were directed in 1957 to candidates in an upcoming parliamentary election in order to secure the election of candidates who would in turn elect a pro-US politician, Camille Chamoun, as president.[33] Our political intervention led elements previously identified as "nationalist" to move against the resulting government.

President Dwight Eisenhower dispatched US Marines the following year to Lebanon ostensibly as peacekeepers, but actually as protectors of the government that the United States had effectively purchased.[34]

President Eisenhower's intervention in Lebanon, like his efforts at regime change in Iran and Syria, was not a last-minute matter. They were part of a plan of activity aimed at ensuring US dominance in the region. Eisenhower had gained from Congress a statement of support for this aim. In 1957, a Joint Resolution of Congress announced what came to be known as the Eisenhower Doctrine. The critical language read:

> The United States regards as vital to the national interest and world peace the preservation of the independence and integrity of the nations of the Middle East. To this end, if the President determines the necessity thereof, the United States is prepared to use armed forces to assist any such nation . . . requesting assistance against armed aggression from any country controlled by international communism.[35]

BLOWBACK FROM US FOREIGN POLICY

Interventions of this type can engender so much ill will as to lead to violence. While the connection is rarely made in mass media, it did appear in a news interview conducted in the United States on the day after the September 11, 2001, attacks. Alon Pinkas, Consul General of Israel, was being interviewed by Dan Rather for CBS News. Rather asked a question that suggested US policy toward Israel may have been a factor in the September 11 attacks:

> RATHER: Mr. Consul General, to those Americans who may be thinking or may be even saying to one another, 'You know, we wouldn't be having this trouble if we hadn't supported Israel for more than half a century,' you say what?

> Amb. PINKAS: I say something very simple. This—this is not about Israel. Let's—let's delink. This is ridiculous to even link this.[36]

Rather did not press Pinkas on the issue, and other news media failed to pick up on it. But Rather had touched on a matter vital to US foreign policy. If the United States pursues policies that lead to anger, repercussions may follow. Rather might have expanded his question to other examples of US policy in the Middle East, but US policy on Israel would figure high on any such list.

President George W. Bush seemed oblivious, at least in public statements, to this phenomenon. President Bush addressed a joint session of Congress a few days after the September 11 attacks. He asked rhetorically, "Why do they hate us?" Answering his own question, Bush declared, "They hate what they see right here in this chamber: a democratically elected government. . . . They hate our freedoms: our freedom of religion, our freedom of speech, our freedom to vote and assemble and disagree with each other."[37]

But the issue surfaced again when a Saudi prince, Alwaleed bin Talal bin Abdul Aziz Alsaud, publicly presented a check for ten million dollars to New York City Mayor Rudolph Giuliani. Prince bin Talal said the check was to go to efforts at recovery from the September 11 attack. Giuliani publicly accepted the check and expressed thanks.

In a press statement that followed, Prince bin Talal opined on the cause of the September 11 attacks. He said, "[A]t times like this one, we must address some of the issues that led to such a criminal attack. I believe the government of the United States of America should reexamine its policies in the Middle East and adopt a more balanced stance towards the Palestinian cause."[38]

Prince bin Talal's statement was reminiscent of Rather's question to Pinkas. Prince bin Talal was suggesting that the attacks were related to US policy. Mayor Giuliani reacted angrily. "There is no moral equivalent for this act," he said. "The people who did it lost any right to ask for justification for it when they slaughtered 4,000 or 5,000 innocent people. And to suggest that there's a justification for it only invites this happening in the future." Giuliani announced that New York would not cash Prince bin Talal's check.[39]

In 2010, General Petraeus, testifying before the US Senate Armed Services Committee, made nearly the same point as Prince bin Talal. As head of the US Central Command, General Petraeus had responsibility for the US wars in Iraq and Afghanistan. His testimony related to those conflicts. But, probably surprising to the assembled senators, Petraeus raised the Israel-Palestine issue. He found US policy there an impediment to US goals in Iraq and Afghanistan. "The enduring hostilities between Israel and some of its neighbors," Petraeus said:

> [P]resent distinct challenges to our ability to advance our interests in the AOR [Centcom's Area Of Responsibility]. Israeli-Palestinian tensions often flare into violence and large-scale armed confrontations. The conflict foments anti-American sentiment, due to a perception of U.S. favoritism for Israel. Arab anger over the Palestinian question limits the strength and depth of U.S. partnerships with governments and peoples in the AOR and weakens the legitimacy of

moderate regimes in the Arab world. Meanwhile, al-Qaida and other militant groups exploit that anger to mobilize support. The conflict also gives Iran influence in the Arab world through its clients, Lebanese Hezbollah and Hamas.[40]

Petraeus spoke from considerable familiarity with the region. What he said was for many around the world a truism, but in the United States his statement caused shockwaves.

Just at the time Shahzad was arrested, an inquiry was ongoing in Britain over the legality of Britain's role in assisting the United States in its 2003 invasion of Iraq. The Chilcot Commission was taking testimony on the issue. One of the witnesses was Baroness Manningham-Buller, who headed the British equivalent of the FBI from 2002 to 2007. The baroness testified on the impact of the Iraq war on anti-Western terrorism. She said that the invasion of Iraq was counterproductive in that regard:

> Our involvement in Iraq, for want of a better word, radicalized a whole generation of young people—not a whole generation, a few among a generation—who saw our involvement in Iraq, on top of our involvement in Afghanistan, as being an attack on Islam.[41]

According to Manningham-Buller, who possessed considerable access to information as a result of her post in the British government, the invasion of Iraq brought an uptick in terrorism.

The possibility that US military action resulting in civilian deaths might be a cause of anti-US violence was taken seriously in US government circles. General McChrystal reported that he had warned his troops about killing civilians. He said what he called the "insurgent math" in Afghanistan is that "for each innocent person you kill, you make 10 enemies. Yet we keep killing and making more enemies."[42]

In 2010, a policy issue that surfaced in New York City brought the same matter to public attention. An Islamic community center was to be built not far from the site of the destroyed World Trade Center. On the CBS television program *60 Minutes*, newscaster Ed Bradley interviewed Imam Feisal Abdul Rauf, a principal backer of the project. Bradley raised the question of the September 11 attacks on the World Trade Center. Imam Rauf suggested that the attacks were related to US policy in the Middle East. Bradley posed a pointed question:

> BRADLEY: Are you in any way suggesting we in the United States deserved what happened?
>
> RAUF: I wouldn't say that the United States deserved what happened. But the United States' policies were an accessory to the crime that happened.
>
> BRADLEY: You say we're an accessory?
>
> RAUF: Yes.
>
> BRADLEY: How?

RAUF: Because we have been an accessory to a lot of innocent lives dying in the world. In fact, in the most direct sense, Osama bin Laden is made in the USA.[43]

Bin Laden often cited three issues that he held against the West: the presence of US troops at the Muslim holy sites of Mecca and Medina in Saudi Arabia, the deaths of more than 600,000 children caused by Western-imposed economic sanctions in Iraq during the 1990s, and Israel's treatment of the Palestinian Arabs.[44]

Another episode around the same time put the issue into the public arena. In Florida, Pastor Terry Jones of the Dove World Outreach Center announced that he would publicly burn the Koran on the 2010 anniversary of the September 11 attacks. Jones' plan was widely publicized both in the United States and in the Middle East. His announcement was generally interpreted abroad as reflecting US government policy, since the Obama administration said that the preacher enjoyed freedom of speech. In many countries, so-called hate speech directed at racial or religious groups is punishable by criminal penalties. General Petraeus commented on the situation, expressing concern that the publicity surrounding Jones' plan "puts our soldiers at jeopardy." Petraeus, who, as we saw, well understood that US actions have effects in the Middle East, said that, "images from such an activity could very well be used by extremists here and around the world.[45] Jones eventually backed down from his plan of Koran-burning.

CHANGE IN US POLICY?

President Obama caught the attention of the Arab and Muslim worlds with a speech he delivered in Cairo shortly after being elected. President Obama spoke as if he wanted to move US policy toward better understanding of that part of the world. He spoke about the Palestinians in a way that reflected an appreciation for their predicament and seemed to promise a new approach from the United States. He said that it was "undeniable that the Palestinian people—Muslims and Christians—have suffered in pursuit of a homeland." Referring to the displacement of Palestinian Arabs that accompanied the creation of Israel in 1948, he said, "For more than sixty years they have endured the pain of dislocation. Many wait in refugee camps in the West Bank, Gaza, and neighboring lands for a life of peace and security that they have never been able to lead."

President Obama touched on Israel's practices in the West Bank, which Israel occupies, saying that the Arabs living under Israel's occupation "endure the daily humiliations—large and small—that come with occupation. So let there be no doubt: the situation for the Palestinian people is intolerable. America will not turn our backs on the legitimate Palestinian aspiration for dignity, opportunity, and a state of their own."

In words that suggested the United States might use its influence with Israel to change Israeli policies, he said:

Israelis must acknowledge that just as Israel's right to exist cannot be denied, neither can Palestine's. . . . Israel must also live up to its obligation to ensure that Palestinians can live and work and develop their society. Just as it devastates Palestinian families, the continuing humanitarian crisis in Gaza does not serve Israel's security; neither does the continuing lack of opportunity in the West Bank. Progress in the daily lives of the Palestinian people must be a critical part of a road to peace, and Israel must take concrete steps to enable such progress.[46]

So the situation of the Palestinians was intolerable, and Israel was responsible. Obama's words were well received in the Arab and Muslim worlds.[47]

The United States did not follow up on the Cairo speech, however, with concrete action. It pursued the policies of prior administrations of placing only mild pressure on Israel to comply with international norms in its administration of occupied Palestine territory. The glow of Cairo quickly faded. Only one year after the Cairo speech, a Pew Research survey of opinion about the United States found the earlier negative view of the United States reasserting itself. "You get a sense of Muslim disappointment with Barack Obama," reported Andy Kohut, Pew Research's president. Kohut attributed the disappointment to discontent with US policy on the Israeli-Palestinian conflict and to expectations raised by Obama's Cairo speech.[48] Pew Research thus confirmed General Petraeus's observation that US policy on the Israel-Palestine issue is a key source of hostility against the United States.

In 2012, the United States stood practically alone in the UN General Assembly in opposing a resolution to acknowledge Palestine's statehood. The resolution, adopted November 29, 2012, recites that the observer mission of Palestine at the United Nations is the observer mission of a state.[49] The United States took this stance out of deference to Israel, but the negative ramifications are enormous. The United States places itself in opposition to a movement for Palestine independence that enjoys overwhelming support around the world, and in particular in the countries of the Middle East.

In 2011, the United States had opposed UN admission for Palestine. The effort exerted by the Obama administration to keep Palestine's admission from coming to a vote in the UN Security Council demonstrated that the administration understood its general backing of Israel over and against Palestine brings harm to the United States. When the admission application reached the Security Council, the United States lobbied other council members to oppose the application in order to avoid the matter coming to a vote. Had there been a vote with a majority of council members in favor of Palestine's admission, the United States would have cast a veto. But the administration understood that a veto would further increase the anger against the United States in the Middle East. Administration officials did not admit as much, but French President Nicolas Sarkozy said it for them. Sarkozy declared of a possible US veto on Palestine's admission, "Who could doubt that a veto at the Security Council risks engendering a cycle of violence in the Middle East?"[50]

France decided to save the United States from having to veto. While the matter was under discussion in a closed-door session in the Security Council, France announced it would abstain if the matter came to a vote. A French abstention would leave Palestine one vote short of the nine required for adoption of a Security Council resolution.[51] Hence the United States would not need to cast a veto to block Palestine membership.[52] The Security Council announced it would not bring the matter to a vote.[53]

The United States is seen as supporting Israel at a time when Israel stalls in peace talks, giving itself time to take over more Palestine territory by building settlements. The Obama administration, the Cairo speech notwithstanding, maintained a position held by other recent US administrations that places the United States out of the international consensus on this issue, and squarely on the side of Israel. The consensus position is that the settlements are unlawful in violation of the obligation of a belligerent occupant to refrain from facilitating the transfer of persons under its auspices into the occupied territory.[54] Early on in Israel's occupation of Palestinian territory the United States was part of the international consensus. In 1978, State Department Legal Adviser Herbert Hansell wrote an official opinion on the legality of Israel's settlements. Hansell found the settlements to be "inconsistent with international law."[55]

But a change of administration in Washington saw retrenchment on the issue. In 1981, President Ronald Reagan declared with regard to the settlements: "I disagreed when the previous administration referred to them as illegal— they're not illegal."[56] No subsequent US administration has disavowed Reagan's statement. Presidents who followed Reagan did not say that they considered the settlements unlawful.

President Obama went so far as to say that new settlements would lack "legitimacy." But he did not make the clear statement of Legal Adviser Hansell that they are illegal. Obama had said in his Cairo speech, "The United States does not accept the legitimacy of continued Israeli settlements. This construction violates previous agreements and undermines efforts to achieve peace. It is time for these settlements to stop."[57]

Obama's statement that "continued" settlements lack "legitimacy" implied that prior-built settlements do enjoy legitimacy. This policy line was taken up by Secretary of State Hillary Clinton, who said, "We do not accept the legitimacy of continued settlement activity."[58]

When the issue of Israel's settlements has come up in the Security Council, where the United States enjoys veto power, the United States has refused to condemn them. From the start of the Israel-Palestine negotiation process in 1993, the United States has taken the position that it will veto draft Security

Council resolutions that criticize Israel on any issue. When resolutions were put before the council in the mid-1990s to criticize Israel for settlement construction in east Jerusalem, the United States vetoed, announcing that the veto was cast not on the merits of settlement construction but on the rationale that the parties were working matters out through negotiations, and that any criticism by the council would constitute interference.[59] The United States is the only one of the five permanent members of the Security Council to take this view.

A major source of hostility toward the United States is the liberal monetary aid the United States gives Israel. That aid is seen as allowing Israel to invest in settlements. The United States also stands apart from the international consensus on the right of Palestinians displaced from their home areas in 1948, and out of the territory Israel captured in that year, to be repatriated. Since the early 1990s, the United States has removed itself from the consensus position held in the international community that these Palestinian Arabs and their descendants have a right under international law to be repatriated. Beginning in the 1990s, the United States stopped voting in favor of the resolution that the General Assembly would adopt annually, asking Israel to implement General Assembly Resolution 194 of 1948, which calls on Israel to repatriate the displaced Palestine Arabs.

CONCLUSION

The reaction in the Middle East to drone strikes comes against the long history of US actions regarded as adverse to local interests. Understanding this history and the reaction to drone strikes, the United States nonetheless continues to employ them. From the United States' standpoint, it is hardly surprising that drone strikes occupy a central position in US military strategy. A commander in chief wants to protect subordinates, and drones offer an opportunity to kill enemies without putting subordinates at risk. It is this logic that makes drone use so difficult to challenge. A commander in chief may also rationalize that using long-range missiles or piloted aircraft to kill enemies likewise involves hazards of harm to unintended victims. Even though drone strikes carry risk of harm to unintended victims, other methods of killing do as well.

That logic, of course, begs the question of whether any of these possible methods of killing is appropriate either as a matter of law or as a matter of sound policy. The case for the legality of drone strikes in the theaters in which the United States uses them is far from ironclad. The Iraq war was undertaken on the strength of Security Council resolutions that required strained interpretation to reach a conclusion of legality.[60] The underlying rationale of countering weapons of mass destruction turned out to be fantasy.

The Afghanistan invasion in 2001 was executed on the strength of a self-defense argument that stretched the meaning of the self-defense concept. The argument for legality in the Afghanistan case required a finding that the United

States had been subjected to an "armed attack" within the meaning of the UN Charter, as opposed to an act of violence appropriately handled by criminal prosecution. Further required was a finding that even if an "armed attack" had occurred, a full-scale invasion was the only manner in which it could be repelled. The result was the longest war in the history of the United States, with loss of life and harm to individuals far exceeding anything contemplated at the time of the invasion.

The legality of drone strikes in Pakistan rests in the first instance on the legality of military action in Afghanistan, since the rationale is to quiet military elements who base themselves in Pakistan to attack US or Afghan forces in Afghanistan. Beyond that hurdle, the expansion of the battlefield to a neighboring country raises serious questions of legality, in particular in light of less than avid acceptance of drone strikes by the government of Pakistan. And the final hurdle is the laws governing methods of warfare, which require protection of civilians. The rate of civilian casualties, though disputed, appears sufficiently high to cast doubt on compliance with this body of law.[61]

But even if legality was solid on all counts for all the countries where drones are used, the question remains whether the United States has improved its situation by their use, or whether, to the contrary, it has harmed itself. One side of that equation is the claimed military benefit. The Obama administration claims to have disabled the leadership of al-Qaeda, hence, to have achieved a military advantage. The claim is difficult to assess because of the silence of the administration on the details of strikes. The administration frequently claims that a particular victim of a drone strike holds a high position in al-Qaeda. The status of victims is difficult to gauge. A further source of uncertainty in this assessment is the difficulty of knowing the extent to which al-Qaeda leadership can be replaced.

Even if military advantage is indeed gained, the other side of the equation remains to be assessed. To what extent does the negative fallout weigh against the gain? Does the harm outweigh the benefit? This chapter has focused on the harm. It too is hard to quantify.

Attempts have been made to quantify the harm from anti-terrorism measures, but such projects present technical challenges.[62] The harm could turn out to be greater than anyone, this writer included, presently imagines. On the other hand, it could turn out to be manageable from the US point of view. Only time will answer the question. The evidence to date suggests, at the very least, that the United States is running a great risk that the harm will, in the long run, outweigh the gain.

This may be the kind of question that future historians will debate. Was our arming of the mujaheddin in Afghanistan with surface-to-air missiles to bring down Soviet helicopters beneficial to the United States in the long run? Was causing difficulty for the USSR in Afghanistan an appropriate objective? If it was, how much difficulty was in fact caused? To what extent did our arming of the mujahideen contribute to bringing down the Soviet government? And did the United States, by initiating the arming of guerrilla-type forces in Afghanistan, start a process of which the United States today is reaping the negative consequences?

It is hardly a surprise that al-Qaeda is able to recruit persons willing to give their lives to fight the United States. Our history, as briefly recounted above, of interfering in domestic matters in the Middle East has created a situation in which the bulk of the population in most countries there harbors resentment against the United States. In that context, al-Qaeda can appeal to patriotism to convince the youth that putting one's life on the line is a noble act.

It may well be that for the United States, the path to protection from acts of violence lies less in military action, whether using drone strikes or otherwise, than in a revised focus on national objectives. President Obama's 2009 Cairo speech, and the favorable reaction it engendered, demonstrated that the cause of the United States in the Middle East is not hopeless.

Gen. Petraeus learned the hard way how our policy on the Palestine-Israel question hampered his ability to put down anti-US elements in Afghanistan. His military efforts, as he reported, were rendered all but impossible to bring to a successful end because US policies on the Palestine-Israel question negated what he was trying to achieve. If the United States were to mold its policies in the direction of promoting local aspirations, there is every reason to believe that support for acts of violence against the United States would diminish. A change in policies might well be more effective than missiles fired from drone aircraft.

NOTES

[1] Tina Susman, *Guilty Plea, and a Threat of More Attacks, From New York Bomber*, BALT. SUN, June 22, 2010, at 1A.

[2] Harold Hongju Koh, Legal Adviser, US Department of State, Annual Meeting of the American Society of International Law (March 25, 2010), *available at* www.state.gov/s/l/releases/remarks/139119.htm.

[3] Lawfulness of a Lethal Operation Directed Against a U.S. Citizen Who Is a Senior Operational Leader of Al-Qa'ida or An Associated Force, at 8-9 (Nov. 8, 2011), *see* Appendix A..

[4] UN Economic and Social Council, *Special Rapporteur for Extrajudicial, Summary or Arbitrary Executions, Civil and Political Rights, Including the questions of Disappearances or Summary Executions*, ¶ 39, UN Doc. E/CN.4/2003/3, 59th sess. (2003) (Asma Jahangir).

[5] Rob Crilly, *Imran Khan's anti-drone protest falls short of destination*, TELEGRAPH (October 7, 2012), www.telegraph.co.uk/news/worldnews/

asia/pakistan/9592632/Imran-Khans-anti-drone-protest-falls-short-of-destination.html.

6   Stanford Law Sch.& New York Univ. Sch. of Law, Living Under Drones:
    Death Injury, and Trauma to Civilians from US Drone Practices in
    Pakistan 15 (2012), available at www.livingunderdrones.org/wp-content/
    uploads/2012/10/Stanford-NYU-LIVING-UNDER-DRONES.pdf (hereafter
    Living under Drones).

7   Lawfulness of a Lethal Operation Directed Against a U.S. Citizen, *supra* note
    3, at 8.

8   *Living under Drones*, *supra* note 6, at 88-99.

9   *Id.* at 12-13.

10 Salman Masood & Pir Zubair Shah, *C.I.A. drones kill civilians in Pakistan*,
    N.Y. Times (Mar. 17, 2011), www.nytimes.com/2011/03/18/world/
    asia/18pakistan.html?_r=0.

11 *Living under Drones*, *supra* note 6, at 58, 61-62.

12 Mary Ellen O'Connell, *The International Law of Drones*, ASIL Insight (Nov.
    12, 2010), www.asil.org/insights101112.cfm.

13 Hakim Almasmari, *US makes a drone attack a day in Yemen*, The National
    (June 15, 2011), www.thenational.ae/news/world/middle-east/us-makes-a-
    drone-attack-a-day-in-yemen.

14 *Yemenis protest US drone attacks outside president's house*, Press TV
    (January 28, 2013), *available at* www.presstv.com/detail/2013/01/28/286057/
    yemenis-protest-us-drone-attacks/.

15 Natasha Lenard, *Yemen's human rights minister criticizes U.S. drone strikes*,
    Salon (Jan. 23, 2013), www.salon.com/2013/01/23/yemens_human_rights_
    minister_criticizes_us_drone_strikes/.

16 Scott Shane, Mark Mazzetti & Robert F. Worth, *Secret assault on terrorism
    widens on two continents*, N.Y. Times, Aug. 15, 2010, at A1.

17 Mark Mazzetti, Charlie Savage & Scott Shane, *A U.S. citizen, in America's
    cross hairs*, N.Y. Times, Mar. 10, 1013, at A1.

18 Robert F. Worth, Mark Mazzetti & Scott Shane, *Drone strikes' risks to get
    rare moment in the public eye*, N.Y. Times (Feb. 5, 2013), www.nytimes.
    com/2013/02/06/world/middleeast/with-brennan-pick-a-light-on-drone-
    strikes-hazards.html?pagewanted=all.

19 David Alexander, *Retired general cautions against overuse of "hated" drones*,
    Reuters (Jan. 7, 2013), www.reuters.com/article/2013/01/07/us-usa-
    afghanistan-mcchrystal-idUSBRE906O8O20130107.

20   Shashank Bengali & David S. Cloud, *U.S. drone strikes up sharply in Afghanistan*, L.A. Times (Feb. 21, 2013), articles.latimes.com/2013/feb/21/world/la-fg-afghanistan-drones-20130222.

21   Spencer Ackerman, *2012 was the year of the drone in Afghanistan*, Wired (Dec. 6, 2012), www.wired.com/dangerroom/2012/12/2012-drones-afghanistan/.

22   *See* AP, *More Afghan civilians killed by drones in 2012, U.N. Says*, CBS News (Feb. 19, 2013), www.cbsnews.com/8301-202_162-57570052/more-afghan-civilians-killed-by-drones-in-2012-u.n-says/.

23   Nick Hopkins, *UK to double number of drones in Afghanistan*, Guardian (Oct. 22, 2012), www.theguardian.com/world/2012/oct/22/uk-double-drones-afghanistan.

24   David Kilcullen & Andrew McDonald Exum, *Death From Above, Outrage Down Below*, N.Y. Times (May 16, 2009), www.nytimes.com/2009/05/17/opinion/17exum.html?pagewanted=all.

25   Peter Osborne, *It may seem painless, but drone war in Afghanistan is destroying the West's reputation*, Telegraph (May 30, 2012), www.telegraph.co.uk/news/worldnews/asia/afghanistan/9300187/It-may-seem-painless-but-drone-war-in-Afghanistan-is-destroying-the-Wests-reputation.html.

26   Kilcullen & Exum, *supra* note 24.

27   *US troops in Niger drone base*, Sydney Morning Herald (Feb. 24, 2013), www.smh.com.au/world/us-troops-in-niger-drone-base-20130223-2ey6e.html.

28   Kermit Roosevelt, Countercoup: The Struggle for Control of Iran 150-197 (McGraw-Hill 1979).

29   Jonathan Kwitny, Endless Enemies: The Making of an Unfriendly World 161-178 (St. Martin's Press 1984).

30   John F. Burns, *Bin Laden Stirs Struggle on Meaning of Jihad*, N.Y. Times, Jan. 27, 2002, at A1.

31   Wilbur Crane Eveland, Ropes of Sand: America's Failure in the Middle East 253-254 (W. W. Norton & Co. Inc. 1980).

32   *Syria Expelling 3 U.S. Diplomats*, N.Y. Times, Aug. 14, 1957, at A1.

33   Eveland, *supra* note 31, at 276.

34   Helena Cobban, The Making of Modern Lebanon 89 (Westview Press 1985).

35   Joint Resolution to Promote Peace and Stability in the Middle East, Pub.L. 85-7 Sec. 2 (1957).

36   Continuing coverage of terrorist attack on America, *CBS Special Report*, 12 Noon PM ET, Sept. 12, 2001.

37 George W. Bush, President, United States, President Bush's address to a joint session of Congress and the nation (Sept. 21, 2001), *available at* www.washingtonpost.com/wp-srv/nation/specials/attacked/transcripts/bushaddress_092001.html.

38 Jennifer Steinhauer, *Giuliani Says City Won't Accept $10 Million Check From Saudi*, N.Y. TIMES (Oct. 11, 2001), www.nytimes.com/2001/10/11/nyregion/11CND-PRIN.html.

39 Jennifer Steinhauer, *Citing Comments on Attack, Giuliani rejects Saudi's gift*, N.Y. TIMES, Oct. 12, 2001, at B13.

40 David Horovitz, *Editor's Notes: Crime and Punishment*, JERUSALEM POST, March 19, 2010, at 24, *available at* www.jpost.com/Opinion/Columnists/Editors-Notes-Crime-and-punishment; Jill Dougherty, *Clinton dismisses any crisis with Israel*, CNN (March 16, 2010), www.cnn.com/2010/POLITICS/03/16/israel.clinton/index.html.

41 Sarah Lyall, *Ex-Official Says Afghan and Iraq Wars Increased Threats to Britain*, N.Y. TIMES, July 21, 2010, at A10.

42 Maureen Dowd, *Seven Days in June*, N.Y. TIMES, June 23, 2010 at A27.

43 Interview With Imam Feisal Abdul (Sept. 8, 2010) (*transcript available at* transcripts.cnn.com/TRANSCRIPTS/1009/08/lkl.01.html*)*.

44 *Osama Bin Laden v. The U.S.: Edicts and Statements*, FRONTLINE (PBS Sept. 5, 2013, 9:09 PM), www.pbs.org/wgbh/pages/frontline/shows/binladen/who/edicts.html.

45 *Good Morning America*, ABC NEWS (Sept. 2, 2010).

46 Barack Obama, President, United States, Remarks by the President on a New Beginning Cairo University Cairo, Egypt (June 4, 2009), *available at* www.whitehouse.gov/the-press-office/remarks-president-cairo-university-6-04-09.

47 Jeffrey Fleishman, *Is graceful talk enough in Muslim world?*, CHI. TRIBUNE, June 5, 2009, at C1.

48 Alan Fram, *Worldwide, Muslims leery of Obama*, BOS. GLOBE, June 18, 2010, at 13.

49 G.A. Res. 67/19, 3, UN Doc. A/RES/67/19 (Nov. 29, 2012).

50 Neil MacFarquhar, *France breaks with Obama on Palestinian statehood issue*, N.Y. TIMES (Sept. 21, 20110), www.nytimes.com/2011/09/22/world/middleeast/france-breaks-with-obama-on-palestinian-statehood-issue.html.

51 *US pressure preventing us from getting nine UNSC votes - Palestinian minister*, BBC MONITORING MIDDLE EAST, Nov. 10, 2011.

52 Catrina Stewart, *UK and France vow to halt Palestinian UN bid*, INDEPENDENT (Nov. 5, 2011), www.independent.co.uk/news/world/middle-east/uk-and-france-vow-to-halt-palestinian-un-bid-6257576.html.

53 Shlomo Shamir & Reuters, *UN Security Council panel fails to agree on Palestinian statehood bid*, HA'ARETZ (Nov. 11, 2011), www.haaretz.com/news/diplomacy-defense/un-security-council-panel-fails-to-agree-on-palestinian-statehood-bid-1.395072.

54 S.C. Res 465, UN Doc. S/RES/465 (Mar. 1, 1980); Geneva Convention IV: Relative to the Protection of Civilian Persons in Time of War, art. 49, Aug. 12, 1949, 75 U.N.T.S. 288.

55 Herbert Hansell, *re International Law and Israeli settlement policy, in* Digest of United States Practice in International Law 1575-83 (1978).

56 *Excerpts from interview with President Reagan conducted by five reporters*, N.Y. TIMES, Feb. 3, 1981, at A14.

57 Obama, *supra* note 46.

58 CNN Wire Staff, *Fayyad: Peace talks may need stronger U.S. mediation role*, CNN (Dec. 12, 2010), www.cnn.com/2010/US/12/12/mideast.talks/index.html.

59 U.N. SCOR, 50th Sess., 3538th mtg. at 6, U.N. Doc. S/PV.3538 (May 17, 1995), *reported in* Barbara Crosette, *U.S. vetoes a condemnation in U.N. of Israeli land seizure*, N.Y. TIMES, May 18, 1995, at A10; U.N. SCOR, 52nd Sess., 3747th mtg. at 4, U.N. Doc. S/PV.3747 (Mar. 7, 1997), *reported in* Paul Lewis, *U.S. vetoes U.N. criticism of Israel's construction plan*, N.Y. TIMES, March 8, 1997, at A3.

60 MARJORIE COHN, COWBOY REPUBLIC: SIX WAYS THE BUSH GANG HAS DEFINED THE LAW 21–23 (Polipoint Press 2007).

61 *See Ross* chapter 7.

62 See Ivan Sascha Sheehan, *Has the War on Terrorism Changed the Terrorist Threat?*, 31 STUDIES IN CONFLICT AND TERRORISM, at 743 (2009).

13

SURVEILLANCE DRONES IN AMERICA

Jay Stanley

At the time of this writing, with the exception of our border regions, the use of drones within the United States is extremely limited. Under Federal Aviation Administration (FAA) rules, commercial use of drone technology is entirely banned. The few police agencies that are deploying them can only do so under very tight strictures: below 400 feet in altitude, line-of-sight only, during daylight hours only, not over densely populated areas, with a spotter present in addition to a pilot, and with both of those operators possessing certain certifications.[1] Most of the drones being used by police agencies are noisy and can only stay aloft for short periods of time (less than an hour).[2]

Nevertheless, the prospect of drones in US airspace has attracted an enormous amount of attention and concern over privacy issues from across the political spectrum. In fact, this issue has led to an outpouring of legislative activity unlike anything we've seen in the privacy area in years, if ever. Strong legislation to regulate this technology has been introduced in Congress[3] and in more than forty-two state legislatures in 2013—with eight states having enacted bills into law as of this writing.[4] Polls have found large majorities of Americans concerned over the privacy issues surrounding drones,[5] and the subject has attracted an enormous amount of media attention.

The significant gap between the amount of fuss that drones have generated and the limited nature of their current deployment has led some to suggest that concerns are based on paranoia and misinformation.

Nothing could be further from the truth. While there are undoubtedly many people who are not familiar with the details of just how limited drone use in the United States still is today, there are very good reasons for Americans to be concerned, even putting aside the large Predator drones that have been deployed at US border regions,[6] and which raise privacy questions on their own. The biggest danger is that drones will come to be used for routine, pervasive surveillance and tracking. That might seem far-fetched today, but there are good reasons for thinking that we may find ourselves living in such a reality.

Drones are an enormously powerful surveillance technology. Not only is the underlying technology evolving rapidly and almost certain to become even more powerful, but the legal strictures on their use will certainly loosen over time—perhaps radically. Congress has already ordered the FAA to begin loosening the rules. The FAA Modernization and Reform Act of 2012[7] requires the FAA to simplify and accelerate the process by which it issues licenses to government agencies to use drones. The act requires the FAA to integrate drones into the national airspace no later than September 2015, legalize the commercial use of drones, and allow any "government public safety agency" to operate any small (under 4.4 pound) drone as long as certain conditions are met.[8] It is far from certain that the FAA will actually meet this deadline, but the gears are in motion for a significant loosening of the rules surrounding the deployment of drones in American airspace.

Looking further into the future, it is possible that radical new approaches to air traffic management could eventually clear the way even further for the use of drones—for example through systems in which aircraft automatically alert one another to the other's presence and route around each other, like packets on the Internet.

Police and government agencies, meanwhile, are likely to seek to use this technology for pervasive, suspicionless mass surveillance. To begin with, there is a long history of government agencies seeking to engage in mass surveillance, from the Cold War spying abuses to today's deployment of license plate scanners and surveillance cameras in our public places, to the sweeping NSA programs that were revealed by Edward Snowden. And when it comes to drones, it is already clear that some agencies would leap at the chance to deploy pervasive aerial surveillance. In 2011, the city of Ogden, Utah, sought FAA permission to deploy an autonomous unmanned blimp as "a deterrent to crime when it is out and about."[9] Similarly, Hawaii took steps toward federal approval to fly drones for surveillance over its harbors.[10] In both cases, permission was ultimately denied by the FAA, but the desire is clearly there.

As the FAA loosens strictures on the use of drones, it is probable that more and more police departments will begin using them, as there is pent-up demand among police departments for cheap aerial surveillance. Ownership of drones could quickly become common among departments large and small. From there, it's not hard to envision how things may develop in the absence of strong privacy protections. Organizations of police drone operators would be formed to exchange tips and advice. We would begin to hear about their deployment by federal agencies (other than on the border) with increasing frequency. And we would start to hear more stories about how they're being used; most departments and agencies would be relatively careful at first, and we would hear of drones being put to use in specific, mostly unobjectionable police operations, such as raids, chases, and searches supported by warrants.

Fairly quickly, however, we would begin to hear that a few departments are deploying drones for broader, more general uses: drug surveillance, marches and rallies, and generalized monitoring of troubled neighborhoods. Meanwhile the technology for carrying out mass surveillance with drones will be improving.

Innovations will likely allow for drones to stay aloft for longer periods of time more cheaply—involving blimps, perhaps, or solar-powered flight—which could become key in permitting their use for persistent surveillance. They will develop the ability to mutually coordinate, so that multiple drones deployed over neighborhoods can be linked together (the technologies for doing this are already surprisingly advanced).[11] This could allow a swarm of craft to form a single, distributed wide-area surveillance system. Meanwhile, "wide-area surveillance" systems that can monitor a wide area from a single craft will also likely improve.

At the same time, drones and the computers behind them will become more intelligent and capable of analyzing the video feeds they are generating. Without privacy protections, what we could see is that drones could be used not only to track multiple vehicles and pedestrians as they move around a city or town, but also to store that data for an extended period of time. And increasingly, the data would be mined. With individuals' comings and goings routinely monitored, databases would build up records of where people live, work, and play; what friends they visit, bars they drink at, doctors they visit; and what houses of worship, political events, or sexually oriented establishments they attend—and who else is present at those places at the same time. Computers would comb through this data looking for "suspicious patterns." This could mean anything from looking for the extremely remote possibility that someone is planning a terrorist attack, to looking for someone planning a protest, to someone who, because of the places they've been, is suspected of having a higher-than-average possibility of driving under the influence. When the algorithms kick up the alarm that someone is "out of the ordinary," the person involved would become the subject of much more extensive surveillance.

"WIDE-AREA PERSISTENT SURVEILLANCE"

That's the nightmare scenario. But at least one important part of this scenario is already rapidly becoming reality: the technology that allows drones to engage in "wide-area persistent surveillance" is already here. The government has developed a system dubbed ARGUS-IS, which is basically a super-high, 1.8 gigapixel resolution camera that can be mounted on a drone. Gigapixel cameras have received attention through high resolution photographs created at Obama's first inauguration and at a Vancouver Canucks fan gathering where individual faces can be zoomed in on and made out in a crowd of many thousands of people.[12] ARGUS is basically a video version of such photographs, able to simultaneously photograph a 38-square-mile area with a resolution high enough to make out a pedestrian waving his arms. The technology, its developer boasted, is "equivalent to having up to a hundred Predators look at an area the size of a medium-sized city at once."[13]

ARGUS does not merely photograph a city. It also automatically detects moving vehicles and pedestrians and tracks their movements—where they start and finish each journey and the path they take in between. The surveillance potential of such a tracking algorithm attached to such powerful cameras should give us pause. To identify an individual, it is not necessary to use technologies such as face or license-plate recognition, cell phone tracking, or gait recognition. Even knowing where a set of moving pixels starts and finishes its day can reveal a lot, because even relatively rough location information about a person will often identify them uniquely. For example, according to one study, just knowing the zip code (actually census tract, which is basically equivalent) of where you work, and where you live, will uniquely identify five percent of the population. If you know the "census blocks" where somebody works and lives (an area roughly the size of a block in a city, but larger in rural areas), the accuracy is much higher, with at least half the population being uniquely identified.[14]

However, ARGUS-type tracking could be used to get more precise data than that. In many cases, it could determine a vehicle's home address, which most likely reveals who you are if you're in a single-family home, and narrows it down considerably even if you're in a large apartment building. Academic papers have been written about inferring home address from location data sets.[15] Add work address and that would most likely identify virtually anybody. And of course lodged in the data set would be not just where a particular vehicle starts and finishes its day, but all the places it stopped in between.

In fact, these kinds of capabilities have already been deployed in the United States. A company called "Persistent Surveillance Systems" is trying to sell a similar capability to domestic police agencies. The city of Dayton, Ohio, actually tested and considered deploying a system that is in many respects similar to ARGUS. And although it shares many of the features that are causing so much concern over drones, it has escaped all the limits placed on drones simply by using a manned aircraft rather than unmanned drones. Manned aircraft are more expensive than drones and so are unlikely to be used as widely as drones may eventually be, but this deployment shows the desire of some police departments for this capability and points toward what we could see in the future.

According to a Dayton Police Department slide presentation obtained by Ohio activists, the department is pursuing a program called "Trusted Situational Awareness." The slide show, entitled "2013 Aerial Surveillance Project,"[16] portrays a test of the system that was conducted for eight days in June 2012 during daylight hours over Sinclair Community College in Dayton.

The program is important, according to the slide show, because it "can be utilized to prevent and minimize acts of terrorism, crime and murder." A slide boasts, "Real-time and imagery technology allows Law Enforcement to: Identify and interrupt illegal activity while providing valuable forensic intelligence." "Forensic intelligence" usually means something like, "keeping records of everything everybody is doing so we can go back and carry out retroactive surveillance whenever we need it." The slide show describes how the police "selected 18 incidents for aerial surveillance," including a burglary in progress and a robbery spree at three commercial locations. "Analysts were able to track the primary suspect to all of these locations as well as to a Clark gas station prior to the robberies," the police boast.[17]

Of course it is a good thing to solve and prevent crime. But in the United States it does not accord with our tradition, law, or Constitution to allow the government to look over everybody's shoulders (literally or figuratively) *just in case* they engage in wrongdoing. We require the police to have individualized suspicion of wrongdoing before they invade our privacy in that way.[18] There is no question that there are some crimes the police will solve if we allow our country to turn into a total surveillance state, but that is a bad tradeoff. The police here want to "identify" illegal activity, which is fine, but not if that's accomplished by watching *all* activity.

A group of citizen activists assisted by the ACLU of Ohio pushed back against this program in Dayton, and eventually the police department decided to discontinue it. But companies that manufacture these technologies are still seeking domestic markets, including not only Persistent Surveillance Solutions but also other small companies, such as Logos Technologies, maker of the Kestrel surveillance system that has been extensively used in Afghanistan,[19] as well as defense giants such as BAE Systems, the contractor on ARGUS-IS.[20]

DRONES ON THE BORDER

In addition, the Kestrel system has been deployed on a test basis along the US-Mexico border.[21] It's important to note that the US government defines the "border" as extending 100 miles inland from the actual external boundaries of the United States—an area that, the ACLU once calculated, contains two-thirds of the entire American population.[22] As of this writing, Customs and Border Protection has not issued a Privacy Impact Assessment on its deployment of Predator drones in domestic border "regions" (although it is reportedly preparing one)[23] and has not established regulations to protect privacy, despite a formal call to do so from the privacy community. As a result, we do not know what the agency's current practices are, but it is possible that it is already carrying out persistent surveillance of large land areas within the United States.[24]

LOCATION TRACKING

One of the biggest problems with allowing wide-area persistent surveillance is the invasive nature of the location tracking it would enable. Location tracking represents a significant invasion of privacy. While the government has argued that because we have no "reasonable expectation of privacy" when we are in public, neither rational policy nor the Constitution offers any protection against the police or other government bodies carrying out extended tracking of individuals' locations. The government made this argument before the Supreme Court in the case *U.S. v. Jones*, in which two men were convicted of drug possession after the government followed one of their vehicles for nearly a month using a hidden GPS tracker without a warrant.[25]

There are two flaws with the government's argument. First, just because people who are in public are susceptible to being viewed by those in their immediate vicinity as they travel about does not mean they are susceptible to being viewed over an extended period of space and time. No one is surprised to encounter an occasional police officer or patrol car. But if that officer were to follow you around for weeks at a time, you would likely be uncomfortable and unhappy. If we are all followed 24/7 by our own personal police officer, elected officials would hear about it very quickly from angry constituents. Yet that is the equivalent of what tracking technologies do.

Second, when you encounter a police officer in public, the officer can, of course, observe you—but you can also observe the police officer, and so your sense of when and how you are being observed follows the ancient and well-known-to-all rules of human eye contact. That fundamental equity evaporates when you're watched through technologies such as GPS trackers or high-flying aircraft. The fact that most location tracking takes place silently and invisibly adds a significant element to the invasion of privacy.

And there should be no doubt that persistent tracking of location does constitute an enormous invasion of privacy, potentially revealing a deep array of information about people such as their political, religious, and sexual activities. As the D.C. Circuit explained in its ruling on the case that later went to the Supreme Court as *Jones*:

> A person who knows all of another's travels can deduce whether he is a weekly church goer, a heavy drinker, a regular at the gym, an unfaithful husband, an outpatient receiving medical treatment, an associate of particular individuals or political groups—and not just one such fact about a person, but all such facts.[26]

What would be the effect on our public spaces, and our society as a whole, if everyone felt the keen eye of the government on their backs whenever they ventured outdoors? Psychologists have repeatedly found that people who are being observed tend to behave differently, and make different decisions, than when they are not being watched. This effect is so great that a recent study noted that "merely hanging up posters of staring human eyes is enough to significantly change people's behavior."[27] Ultimately, the chilling effects of mass drone surveillance would lead to an oppressive atmosphere in which people learn to think twice about everything they do, knowing that it will be recorded, charted, scrutinized by increasingly intelligent computers, and possibly used to target them.

OTHER PRIVACY PROBLEMS

Mass surveillance is the biggest privacy concern created by drones, but it is not the only one. Drones also raise—often in intensified fashion—many of the same issues that pervasive video surveillance causes in other contexts. For example, video surveillance is susceptible to individual abuse, including voyeurism. In 2004, a couple making love at night on a pitch-black rooftop balcony in New York, where they had every reason to expect they enjoyed privacy, were filmed for nearly four minutes by a New York Police Department (NYPD) helicopter using night vision. This is the kind of abuse that could become commonplace if drone technology enters into widespread use. (Rather than apologize, NYPD officials flatly denied that this filming constituted an abuse, telling a television reporter, "[T]his is what police in helicopters are supposed to do, check out people to make sure no one is . . . doing anything illegal.")[28]

Discriminatory targeting poses another danger. Individuals operating surveillance systems bring to the job all their existing prejudices and biases. In Great Britain, which has embraced surveillance cameras more than any other country and where they have been intensively studied, camera operators have been found to focus disproportionately on people of color. According to a sociological study of how the systems were operated, "Black people were between one-and-a-half and two-and-a-half times more likely to be surveilled than one would expect from their presence in the population."[29]

In addition to abuse by what are arguably the inevitable "bad apples" within law enforcement, there is also the danger of institutional abuse. Sometimes, bad policies are set at the top, and an entire law enforcement agency is turned toward abusive ends. That is especially prone to happen in periods of social turmoil and intense political conflict. During the labor, civil rights, and anti-Vietnam War movements of the 20th century, the FBI and other security agencies engaged in systematic illegal behavior against those challenging the status quo. And once again today, we are seeing an upsurge in spying against peaceful political protesters across America.[30]

WHEN DRONES ARE ARMED

Finally, there is the prospect of armed drones. From their controversial deployment for targeted killings and other uses abroad, we know that armed drones can be incredibly powerful and dangerous weapons. When domestic law enforcement officers can use force from a distance, it may become too easy for them to do so. When it becomes easier to do surveillance, surveillance is used more, and when it becomes easier to use force, force will be used more. We have seen this dynamic with "less lethal" weapons such as Tasers. Between 2001 and August 2008, 334 people in the United States died after being tased, according to Amnesty International,[31] and Tasers are often used in clearly unnecessary situations—for example, in retaliation against nonviolent people who have angered a police officer. Force applied via drone may also be more likely to result in harm to innocent bystanders.

Efforts to arm domestic drones are widely seen as beyond the pale, and for the most part have not yet been seriously contemplated. The International Association of Chiefs of Police has recommended against arming Unmanned Aerial Vehicles, for example.[32] But exceptions have arisen. One sheriff in Texas mused about mounting less-lethal weapons like rubber bullets on unmanned aircraft.[33] The Electronic Frontier Foundation uncovered Customs and Border Protection documents suggesting possible future enhancements to its drone program including "non-lethal weapons designed to immobilize TOIs [targets of interest]."[34] Customs and Border Protection denied any plans to arm its drones with "weapons of any kind."[35] Still, there is good reason to think that, once current controversies subside and the spotlight of public attention shifts elsewhere, we will see a push for drones armed with lethal weapons.

Overall, it is clear that despite the limited nature of current police deployments of drones, the high levels of public anxiety over this technology are abundantly justified.

Supporters of surveillance drones sometimes ask why there should be such a fuss over drones, given that the police and federal government have used manned helicopters for aerial surveillance for decades. For one thing, drones erase the "natural limits" that have always applied to aerial surveillance using manned aircraft. Manned helicopters and fixed-wing aircraft are expensive to acquire, staff, and maintain. A police helicopter costs from $500,000 to $3 million to acquire, and $200–$400 an hour to fly. Manned aircraft are large, complex machines requiring expert ground crews, multiple shifts of pilots and co-pilots, and (unlike drones which can often be hand-launched) runways or helipads. Such expenses mean there are inevitably going to be far fewer of them—which in turn means the police are likely to use them only where they are most needed. With drones, on the other hand, it's easy to foresee a day when even a professional police drone could be acquired for less than a hundred dollars, including maintenance costs. And if technology and laws eventually reach the point where drones can fly autonomously, they would become even cheaper because police departments wouldn't even have to pay staff to control or monitor them.

In addition, police helicopters *do* raise privacy issues. Because of the expense of using manned police aircraft, privacy invasions have not risen to the level that our legal system has felt compelled to address them. But incidents do happen— such as the New York City rooftop voyeurism incident mentioned above. And any police helicopter that followed a citizen around town for no reason, or hovered over the backyard of an innocent homeowner whose daughter was sunbathing with her friends, would probably draw complaints. With drones, scenarios like those are bound to happen much more frequently because unmanned flight is so much less expensive. In addition, technologies like ARGUS have now emerged and could be attached to a helicopter; the nation simply hasn't had the chance yet to confront that possibility.

COMMERCIAL USE

The issues raised by the private use of drones are different and more complex than those raised by police and other government use. While a push by police and government agencies to use drones for broad surveillance purposes is entirely predictable and inevitable, it's probably too early to know to what extent drones will be used to invade privacy by the private sector, or how.

In addition, there are important countervailing values when it comes to private drones, such as the right to photography. We have seen photographers questioned, harassed, and arrested around the country for such activities as photographing bridges, trains, and government buildings, and for photographing police carrying out their public duties. Some photographers have had their cameras (or camera-phones) seized, and photographs destroyed.[36] The ACLU has challenged such interference with photographers, and the courts have all but unanimously held that photography of things visible from a public place where a photographer has a right to be is protected by the First Amendment.[37]

What happens when photographers—whether certified reporters or citizen photographers—seek to exploit drone technology for similar purposes? While we don't want the government watching citizens without suspicion of wrongdoing, it is important to preserve the right of citizens to watch their government, and such uses of drones implicate First Amendment rights.

Drones will certainly have positive uses on the government side—helping with search and rescue missions, wildfires, environmental or geological surveys, or disaster relief, for example—and they will have beneficial uses on the private-sector side as well. In fact, the technology is likely to become the subject of incredible innovation as thousands of hobbyists, tinkerers, and companies explore the technology and invent helpful and imaginative ways of exploiting it. Ideally we can protect our privacy without curbing such innovation or interfering with First Amendment-protected uses of the technology.

That said, there are several foreseeable ways in which drones could be used by private actors to invade privacy. Voyeurism is an obvious one; state "Peeping Tom laws" already exist in every state to prevent surveillance,[38] and trespass and nuisance laws may also be used to exclude low-flying drones from property. However, the language and scope of these laws varies widely from state to state.

Another privacy threat from private drones includes the persistent observation of landowners' back yards or other areas of private property. While the Supreme Court ruled in the 1986 case *California v. Ciraolo*[39] that police flying a fixed-wing aircraft did not need a warrant to look for marijuana plants in a private, fenced back yard because "any member of the public flying in this airspace who glanced down could have seen everything that these officers observed," it is not clear such logic would apply in the case of persistent, prolonged surveillance of private property. Many homeowners who don't think twice about having an occasional Cessna fly overhead would react strongly if they were to learn an aerial camera was trained on their yard for weeks at a time.

For that matter, private-sector persistent surveillance of public spaces would also raise many of the same privacy issues as public surveillance by the government. Imagine a live version of Google Earth. Location tracking by private companies would be just as serious an invasion of privacy as by the government, as would the simple act of blanket 24/7 aerial photography of all our public spaces.

But it's not clear that such uses will be realized, and given the important countervailing interests of the First Amendment and the benefits of protecting innovation, the bottom line is that because of the different issues they raise, private drones should be approached by policy makers separately.

A CROSSROADS

We're at a crossroads today. We are at a highly significant moment in the history of drones. This new technology is part of today's broader technology revolution, which has made it possible to monitor and record the smallest details of what we do—our every movement, our every purchase, and our every communication.

If we do nothing, there should be little doubt that these new technological capabilities will be exploited to the limit by government agencies. We have learned just how sweeping the National Security Agency's (NSA) surveillance programs are—for example, keeping records on the communications of every American. Many police departments are using automated license plate recognition cameras to record location information not just on wanted vehicles, but on everybody who drives a car.

It is in the context of these programs and others like them that drones will penetrate American life. We as a society must make a fundamental decision: whether we are to become a "collect it all" society, in which records of our activities are collected and stored by the government "just in case." This is the vision of those pushing for persistent wide-area surveillance, and we are now in the early stages of a broad debate over whether to allow such surveillance. If we accede to the "collect it all" vision in the context of drones or of the NSA, we should not be surprised when that same philosophy is extended to everything—to our financial transactions, hotel records, Internet searches, medical information, and every other possible source of data.

Throughout the history of our civilization, we have always limited the power of the authorities to intrude upon our private lives in the absence of evidence that we are involved in wrongdoing. But what we're seeing now is the argument that just because we have new technologies that make it easy, we should allow the government to build up a sea of information on everybody to have on hand just in case investigators want to "swim through it" for a particular investigation. Some also want to assign computers to sift through all of this information searching for signs of "suspicious" behavior. It may be computers that are watching us, but we'll be watched just the same—with all the same potential for bad consequences should some algorithm make an error, or reach a conclusion based on bad data, or misinterpret what we're doing.[40]

Storage of all this information also gives the government a frightening new power it has never had before: the power to hit "rewind" on our life and see the history of our movements, transactions, and communications—to turn our life into an open book. Such "retroactive surveillance" is an enormous power that no government has ever had or should have over its people.

As Justice John Harlan observed in 1971, words are "measured a good deal more carefully and communication inhibited" when we suspect we're being monitored, and if we allow such monitoring to become prevalent, "it might well smother that spontaneity—reflected in [the] frivolous, impetuous, sacrilegious, and defiant discourse—that liberates daily life."[41] If we allow ourselves to become a society in which our every move is recorded, we'll find ourselves living in another country, one that we might not much like.

Unfortunately, there are many uncertainties about how our Constitution will be applied by the courts to pervasive aerial surveillance. The legal system has always been slow to adapt to new technology. For example, it took the Supreme Court forty years to apply the Fourth Amendment to telephone calls. At first, the court found in a 1928 decision that because telephone surveillance did not require entering the home, the conversations that travel over telephone wires are not protected.[42] It was not until 1967 that this literal-minded hairsplitting about "constitutionally protected areas" was overturned, with the court declaring that the Constitution "protects people, not places."[43] Today, technology is moving much faster than it did in the telephone era—but the gears of justice turn just as slowly as they ever have, and maybe even slower.

Just as the new technology of the telephone broke the court's older categories of understanding, so too will drones with all their new capabilities create new situations that will not fit neatly within existing jurisprudential categories of analysis. For example, how will the courts view the use of drones for routine location tracking? The Supreme Court started to grapple with such questions in its recent decision in the *Jones* GPS case, but it is far from clear what the ultimate resolution will be. The court ruled in *Ciraolo* that the Fourth Amendment provides no protection from aerial surveillance, and while the new factors that drones bring to the equation could shift that judgment, we cannot be certain.

Legislators should not wait for cases to come before the courts; they should act to preserve our values now.

Ultimately, drones are but one technology we are now facing that confronts us with basic questions about whether we will act to preserve our fundamental privacy rights. If our Constitution is to protect the degree of privacy the framers envisioned, and which we still need today as much as ever, it will have to incorporate protection against such mass warrantless collection of information about Americans. And in case our courts do not interpret our Constitution broadly enough to provide that degree of privacy when faced with new technologies, we must insist that Congress and other policy makers protect that privacy through legislation.

NOTES

1   Federal Aviation Administration, Unmanned Aircraft Systems (UAS) Operational Approval [N 8900.227] (proposed July 30, 2013), *available at* www.faa.gov/documentLibrary/media/Notice/N_8900.227.pdf.

2   *See, e.g., Draganflyer X6 Helicopter Tech Specs*, DRAGANFLY INNOVATIONS INC. (last visted Sept. 22, 2013), www.draganfly.com/uav-helicopter/draganflyer-x6/specifications/.

3   *See Reps. Zoe Lofgren and Ted Poe Introduce Bipartisan Bill to Protect Americans' Privacy Rights from Domestic Drones*, CONGRESSWOMAN ZOE LOFGREN (last visted Sept. 22, 2013), lofgren.house.gov/index.php?option=com_content&view=article&id=785&Itemid=130.

4   Allie Bohm, *Status of Domestic Drone Legislation in the States*, ACLU FREE FUTURE BLOG (updated Sept. 25, 2013), www.aclu.org/blog/technology-and-liberty/status-domestic-drone-legislation-states.

5   *U.S. Supports Some Domestic Drone Use: But public registers concern about own privacy*, MONMOUTH UNIVERSITY POLL (June 12, 2012), *available at* www.monmouth.edu/assets/0/32212254770/32212254991/32212254992/32212254994/32212254995/30064771087/42e90ec6a27c40968b911ec51eca6000.pdf.

6   *Unmanned Aircraft System MQ-9 Predator B*, U.S. CUSTOMS AND BORDER PROTECTION (May 1, 2013), www.cbp.gov/linkhandler/cgov/border_security/am/documents/oam_fact_sheets/predator_b.ctt/predator_b.pdf.

7   FAA Modernization and Reform Act of 2012, Pub. L. No. 112-95, § 213, 126 Stat 11 (2012).

8   Jay Stanley, *Congress Trying to Fast-Track Domestic Drone Use, Sideline Privacy*, ACLU FREE FUTURE BLOG (Feb. 6, 2012, 2:39 PM), www.aclu.org/blog/technology-and-liberty-national-security/congress-trying-fast-track-domestic-drone-use-sideline.

9   James Nelson, *Utah city may use blimp as anti-crime spy in the sky*, REUTERS (Jan. 16, 2011), www.reuters.com/article/2011/01/16/us-crime-blimp-utah-idUSTRE70F1DJ20110116; Tim Gurrister, *Ogden blimp may be patrolling*

by *Christmas*, STANDARD-EXAMINER (Aug. 31, 2011), www.standard.net/stories/2011/08/29/ogden-blimp-may-be-patrolling-christmas; James Nelson, *Utah city may use blimp as anti-crime spy in the sky*, REUTERS (Jan. 16, 2011), www.reuters.com/article/2011/01/16/us-crime-blimp-utah-idUSTRE70F1DJ20110116.

10 Jim Dooley, *State Surveillance Drones 'Under Review'*, HAWAII REPORTER (Feb. 1, 2011), www.hawaiireporter.com/state-surveillance-drones-under-review/123.

11 *See, e.g.*, Rebecca Searles, *Flying Robots Called 'Nano Quadrotor' Drones Swarm Lab (Video)*, HUFFINGTON POST (Feb. 2, 2012), www.huffingtonpost.com/2012/02/02/flying-robots-nano-quadrotor-drones-swarm_n_1249442.html.

12 *See* David Bergman, *How I made a 1,474-Megapixel Photo During President Obama's Inagural Address*, DAVID BERGMAN (Jan. 22, 2009), www.davidbergman.net/blog/how-i-made-a-1474-megapixel-photo-during-president-obamas-inaugural-address/; *see* GIGAPIXEL.COM (last vistited Sept. 22, 2013, 5:35 PM), www.gigapixel.com/image/gigapan-canucks-g7.html; *see also Tokyo Tower Gigapixel Panorama*, 360 GIGAPIXELS.COM (last visited Sept. 22, 2013, 5:40 PM), 360gigapixels.com/tokyo-tower-panorama-photo/.

13 *NOVA: Rise of the Drones* (PBS television broadcast,Jan. 23, 2013), *available at* www.pbs.org/wgbh/nova/military/rise-of-the-drones.html; See also Jay Stanley, *Report Details Government's Ability to Analyze Massive Aerial Surveillance Video Streams*, ACLU FREE FUTURE blog (Apr. 5, 2013), www.aclu.org/blog/technology-and-liberty-free-speech-national-security/report-details-governments-ability-analyze.

14 Philippe Golle & Kurt Partridge, *On the Anonymity of Home/Work Location Pairs*, in PROCEEDING PERVASIVE '09 PROCEEDINGS OF THE 7TH INTERNATIONAL CONFERENCE ON PERVASIVE COMPUTING (2009), *available at* crypto.stanford.edu/~pgolle/papers/commute.pdf.

15 *See, e.g.*, John Krumm, *Inference Attacks on Location Tracks*, in in PROCEEDING PERVASIVE '07 PROCEEDINGS OF THE 5TH INTERNATIONAL CONFERENCE ON PERVASIVE COMPUTING (2007), *available at* research.microsoft.com/en-us/um/people/jckrumm/Publications%202007/inference%20attack%20refined02%20distribute.pdf.

16 *2013 Aerial Surveillance Project*, CITY OF DAYTON, OHIO, *available at* www.google.com/url?sa=t&rct=j&q=&esrc=s&frm=1&source=web&cd=2&cad=rja&sqi=2&ved=0CDQQFjAB&url=http%3A%2F%2Fwww.acluohio.org%2Fwp-content%2Fuploads%2F2013%2F04%2F2013_0206Aerial AirborneSurveillanceProgramPresentationToDaytonCityCommission.pdf&ei=hpo_UpbeHMTEigKlxoGIDA&usg=AFQjCNG3wxoGOaZ-CbIH9 DOakzzyFk6o3A&sig2=gzvvLrIDU7E962tUV9FNoQ.

17 *Id.* at 10.

18   "The right of the people to be secure in their persons, houses, papers, and effects, against unreasonable searches and seizures, shall not be violated, and no Warrants shall issue, but upon probable cause, supported by Oath or affirmation, and particularly describing the place to be searched, and the persons or things to be seized." U.S. CONST. amend. IV.

19   *Logos Technologies' Kestrel surveillance system surpasses 60,000 operational hours in Afghanistan*, LOGOS TECHNOLOGIES (Aug. 12, 2013), www.logos-technologies.com/news/08-12-2013.html.

20   Stew Magnuson, *Wide Area Surveillance Sensors Prove Value on Battlefields*, NAT'L DEFENSE MAGAZINE (Nov. 2012), www.nationaldefensemagazine.org/archive/2012/November/Pages/WideAreaSurveillanceSensorsProveValueonBattlefields.aspx.

21   *Id.*

22   *Fact Sheet on U.S. "Constitution Free Zone,"* ACLU (Oct. 22, 2008), www.aclu.org/technology-and-liberty/fact-sheet-us-constitution-free-zone.

23   Brian Bennett, *Senators examine domestic drones' effect on privacy*, L.A. TIMES (Mar. 20, 2013), articles.latimes.com/2013/mar/20/nation/la-na-drones-privacy-20130321.

24   Electronic Privacy Information Center, *Domestic Drones Petition*, EPIC (last visited Sept. 22, 2013), epic.org/drones_petition/.

25   132 S.Ct. 945, 946 (2012).

26   United States v. Maynard, 615 F.3d 544, 562 (D.C. Cir. 2010).

27   Sander van der Linden, *How the Illusion of Being Observed Can Make You a Better Person*, SCIENTIFIC AMERICAN (May 3, 2011), www.scientificamerican.com/article.cfm?id=how-the-illusion-of-being-observed-can-make-you-better-person; M. Ryan Calo, *People Can Be So Fake: A New Dimension to Privacy and Technology Scholarship*, 114 PENN ST. L. REV. 809, 836 (2010), *available at* www.pennstatelawreview.org/articles/114/114%20Penn%20St.%20L.%20Rev.%20809.pdf.

28   Jim Dwyer, *Police Video Caught a Couple's Intimate Moment on a Manhattan Rooftop*, N.Y. TIMES (Dec. 22, 2005), www.nytimes.com/2005/12/22/nyregion/22rooftop.html.

29   Clive Norris & Gary Armstrong, *The Unforgiving Eye: CCTV Surveillance in Public Spaces* (Centre for Criminology and Criminal Justice at Hull University 1998).

30   *See Spyfiles*, ACLU (last visited Sept. 22, 2013), www.aclu.org/spyfiles.

31   *Tasers – Potentially lethal and easy to abuse*, AMNESTY INTERNATIONAL (Dec. 16, 2008), www.amnesty.org/en/news-and-updates/report/tasers-potentially-lethal-and-easy-abuse-20081216.

32 Aviation Committee, *Recommended Guidelines for the use of Unmanned Aircraft*, Int'l Ass'n of Chiefs of Police 2 (Aug. 2012), *available at* www.theiacp.org/portals/0/pdfs/IACP_UAGuidelines.pdf.

33 *Groups Concerned Over Arming Of Domestic Drones*, CBS DC (May 23, 2012), washington.cbslocal.com/2012/05/23/groups-concerned-over-arming-of-domestic-drones/.

34 Philip Bump, *The Border Patrol Wants to Arm Drones*, Atlantic Wire Blog (July 2, 2013), www.theatlanticwire.com/national/2013/07/border-patrol-arm-drones/66793/.

35 *Id.*

36 *See* Jay Stanley, *You Have Every Right to Photograph That Cop*, ACLU (Sept. 7, 2011), www.aclu.org/free-speech/you-have-every-right-photograph-cop.

37 *E.g.*, Glik v. Cunniffe, 655 F.3d 78, 85 (1st Cir. 2011).

38 *See NDAA Voyeurism Compilation*, NDAA.org (updated July 2010), www.ndaa.org/pdf/Voyeurism%202010.pdf.

39 476 U.S. 207, 213-14 (1986).

40 *See* Jay Stanley, *Computers vs. Humans: What Constitutes a Privacy Invasion?*, ACLU Free Future Blog (July 2, 2012), www.aclu.org/blog/national-security-technology-and-liberty/computers-vs-humans-what-constitutes-privacy-invasion.

41 United States v. White, 401 U.S. 745, 787 (1971) (Harlan, J., dissenting).

42 Olmstead v. United States, 277 U.S. 438 (1928), *overruled by* Katz v. United States, 389 U.S. 347 (1967).

43 Katz v. United States, 389 U.S. 347, 351 (1967).

14
TO STOP THE DRONES?
Tom Hayden

Thanks largely to American public opinion, President Obama no longer has a Roman-style legion he can deploy to distant battlefields. Obama is currently engulfed in brinksmanship over Syria; while the future is uncertain, he has repeatedly pledged there will be no American "boots on the ground." Obama has withdrawn 100,000 US troops from Iraq, as promised, despite that country's volatile sectarian divisions. He is removing most, if not all, of the 100,000 US ground troops from Afghanistan on a 2014 timeline, with that country likely to spin out of US control in the years ahead. It is difficult to imagine him sending ground troops to either Iran or Egypt. Obama often emphasizes his hope to achieve "some nation-building at home," combined with a greater emphasis on diplomacy, or "soft power," abroad. That has been the demand of social justice movements for decades as the United States was committed to policies of military invasion and occupations.

Caught between the global military priorities of the national security state and the skepticism of the American people, Obama has found drones to be an expedient "solution" while he engages in his careful steps of disengagement. At least that was so until the drone controversy began to boil over in 2013 because of protests, critical news coverage, and opposition from an unusual source: the advocates of counterinsurgency.

The use of drones was a classified and relatively inexpensive way to retreat from Iraq and Afghanistan without appearing "soft" on terrorism to the generals and the American Right. That Obama used drones, cold-bloodedly, with kill lists and all, does not minimize his effort at strategic retreat and redeployment from these two ground wars and the overall "war on terrorism."

"What he needs is a strategy for getting out without turning a retreat into a rout," wrote Gideon Rose in the June 25, 2011, *New York Times*.[1] Rose, the editor of *Foreign Affairs*, is a key thinker in the security establishment and former Clinton-era official. His Machiavellian advice to Obama is based on the experience of President Richard Nixon and Secretary of State Henry Kissinger in de-escalating the Vietnam War before that one turned into a full-scale debacle amid the Watergate scandal in 1975.

The basic premise for Rose, shared as a virtual oath of admission to the national security establishment, is that the state should never appear to lose even when in fact it is losing. Reputation is everything for a superpower, especially when cutting its losses. The three rules of withdrawal [or "strategic redeployment"], according to Rose, are: first, deflect attention from the fact that you are doing so; second, "lay down suppressive fire so the enemy cannot rush into the gap you leave behind"; and third, remain engaged by providing "enough support to beleaguered local partners so they can fend off collapse for as long as possible." Rose defines withdrawal as "the removal of ground forces from direct combat, not the abandonment of the country in question."[2]

According to Rose, Nixon's mistake was using "brutal and ham-fisted" secret bombing raids along the Ho Chi Minh Trail to buy time for the "decent interval" of his strategic retreat. Similarly, "[D]rone attacks and raids against enemy targets in Pakistani sanctuaries today are a precision replay of actions in Cambodia and Laos, but more effective and less controversial."[3]

Declassified Oval Office cables from 1972 revealed that Kissinger told Nixon to blame the failures on "South Vietnamese incompetence," not the impotence of American power. "[W]e've got to find some formula that holds the thing together a year or two," Kissinger added, "after which . . . no one will give a damn," he told Nixon.[4] Obama should be able to accomplish the same in Afghanistan, Rose projects, apparently believing such an approach to be a brilliant prophylactic for the protection of empire. There were costs to Nixon's approach, Rose acknowledges, such as "charges of lying, escalation, and betrayal," which Rose believed, at least in 2011, Obama could avoid because of his effective secrecy and residual popularity at home.

For a brief historical moment, it appeared that these Machiavellian notions might work, especially after the killing of Osama bin Laden in May 2011 and the US escalation of drone attacks, especially over Pakistan's tribal areas where the Taliban are believed to take sanctuary.

But national security officials, who themselves never interact with voters in the public sphere, and whose deeds and budgets are shrouded in secrecy, underestimated the skeptical nature of the American public. Just as photos of burned and tortured Vietnamese seared into American consciousness during the first of our televised wars in the 1960s, so too, photos and images of civilian casualties would leak out even through the highly controlled news management during Iraq and Afghanistan. While investigative reporting was virtually born with the exposure of the My Lai massacre in 1969, the spirit of independent media became even more relentless in the Internet age. Dungeons, torture chambers, mass graves, and the human damage inflicted by drones could not be easily suppressed, much less defended.

A 2013 survey in Pakistan by the Pew Research Center found that only five percent of Pakistanis approved of US drone strikes targeting extremists, while 68 percent disapproved.[5] Civil liberties lawyers connected the drone policy to a litany of constitutional abuses since 9/11. Documentary filmmakers, including Jeremy Scahill and Robert Greenwald, circulated moving on-the-ground interviews with civilian victims. Whistleblowers emerged from unlikely spaces within the very architecture of the security state itself. The *Times* and others published front-page disclosures on the secret war that had been downloaded and sent to WikiLeaks by Private First Class Bradley (Chelsea) Manning. It began to seem like Watergate all over again, especially with revelations that Congress itself was being deceived.

Obama and others were mistaken if they thought that public opinion could be calmed by the disappearance of American casualties and budgetary costs, and the simultaneous rise of a secret war symbolized by drones.

While it took years for American opinion to turn against the wars in Iraq and Afghanistan, and while opinion is decidedly mixed over drones, there is little question that the drone policy is beginning to stall and flounder. Like mushrooms, drones simply cannot grow in the sunlight of a wired world.

Far from his hopes of a new foreign policy, Obama is in grave danger of leaving a new Imperial presidency as his legacy. Like the 1960s fear of an "international communist conspiracy," the 2001–2013 fear of an "international terrorist conspiracy" has taken precedence above all other priorities and threatens to become a cancer on his presidency. Like the "military-industrial complex" that President Dwight D. Eisenhower criticized in his farewell address, a broader national security complex has become the dominant force among competing elites, causing a growing drain on democracy, accountability, and budget priorities at home.

President John F. Kennedy realized the danger of unleashing these ultra-militaristic forces after his traumatic experiences during the Bay of Pigs in 1961 and the US-Soviet missile crisis over Cuba in 1962. In the aftermath, he began to embrace the domestic priorities symbolized in the 1963 March on Washington for Jobs and Freedom, and in his American University call that same summer to reverse the nuclear arms race with the Soviet Union. Credible evidence suggests that Kennedy planned to de-escalate in Vietnam after the 1964 election. At the very least, the record reveals that he opposed the sending of US ground troops just as he opposed their use in the Cuban invasion of 1961. The same history reveals the existence of what some have called "the deep state,"[6] a description of the permanent caste of elite decision-makers carrying out military strategies in favor of market-friendly regimes and opposed to even moderate progressives coming to power. In those days, their opposition was to anyone described as neutral, non-aligned, or open to coalitions with the Left. The same narrowness applies today toward any forces coexisting, for example, with the Muslim Brotherhood.

Kennedy was hated as virulently by the John Birch Society, right-wing generals, and white Southerners as Obama is hated by their descendants today in the Tea Party, the Koch brothers, Sheldon Adelson, and certain allies among the police and the military. Obama will face even greater anger as he tries to orchestrate the de-escalation of the war on terror. During the Cuban missile crisis, JFK had to conspire with his brother Bobby *against his own generals and security advisers* in order to avoid nuclear war with the Soviets. Obama no doubt faces parallel dangers today.

Interestingly, Obama himself is admitting the limited power of his office by frequently calling for Congress and public opinion to "rein in" his own presidency, a statement he first made in October 2012. There are those who may consider such calls, like his more recent "welcoming" of public debate on drones and secrecy, and his off-the-cuff comment that Medea Benjamin was "worth listening to" as she was dragged away from a public speech, as signs of Obama's chronic vacillations. Perhaps so, but Obama certainly was a man of steel during his unprecedented 2007–2008 presidential campaign against the Clinton Democrats and the mainstream establishment. What else might explain this appearance of presidential caution? Could it reflect a contending balance of forces within the executive branch?

What we are seeing, in my view, is a fierce antagonism among elements of the national elite behind the curtains of power. The fight is not about withdrawing from empire, but about attempting to realistically reform empire versus making a Custer-like last stand against the rest of the world, including the rising multiracial majority in the United States itself.

Obama appeared to reduce the drone attacks in response to the rising criticism, from 117 on Pakistan in 2010 as US troop levels peaked in Afghanistan, to 64 in 2011, 46 in 2012, and 20 as of September 2013.[7] He reversed himself suddenly in July 2013, showering nine drone strikes against Yemen for reasons that remain unclear. As the US-defined terrorism battlefields inevitably expand, Obama will resort to further use of drones if only as a temporary expedient in the absence of public support for US ground troops. In the process, he has learned that their price in public and media opinion, and potential blowback, is high, offsetting their original low-budget, low-visibility selling points. The blowback from his targeted drone assassinations of Anwar al-Aulaqi, al-Aulaqi's son, and others in Yemen continues to reverberate globally.[8] If the off-on diplomatic talks with the Taliban are to succeed at all, ending drone attacks on their sanctuaries will have to be part of any political settlement.

Obama also employed drones in overthrowing Libya's Muammar el-Qaddafi in 2011, helping sow chaos in Libya, precipitating the killing of American officials at Benghazi, and spreading the military conflict to Mali and the rest of North Africa. In Yemen, Libya, and North Africa, the use of drones appears to be a defensive tactic to fill a strategic policy vacuum.

In addition to reducing the drone attacks without admitting so publicly, Obama has struggled to formulate updated rules of warfare and accountability in the age of drones, cyber warfare, and the resumption of flagrantly secret wars by the CIA. He also wants to revisit the open-ended Authorization for the Use of Military Force that followed the 9/11 attacks. This would be a welcome step if a unified administration fought for it and if there were serious partners in Congress for democratic reform. So far there are few, with only two members of the Senate Intelligence Committee registering vocal complaints over the record of secret wars, kill lists, and the like. Amid revelations by Edward Snowden of "big data" spying on the American people, Congress did react with an opposing coalition made up of critics to the right and left of the national security state. That may be a harbinger of future efforts to reclaim foreign policy by Congress.

It should be noted that the Congress' own intelligence committees would not even exist but for the public outcry in the 1970's that led to Nixon's resignation and the Vietnam War's dismal end. Ever since, those committees have appeared to be steadily more complicit in secret CIA maneuverings than watchdogs for the public interest in transparency. Oversight has been hollowed out.

The question is whether the drone controversy will find its way into congressional debate, which is what occurred when the Vietnam and Watergate debates finally drove Congress to pass the War Powers Resolution in 1973 and cut funding for an earlier imperial presidency in 1975. So far, there is little evidence of the sort of congressional will that was asserted in that earlier time. In the recent behind-the-scenes power struggles—the darkness where the mushrooms grow—the CIA appears to be keeping control over its secret "Af-Pak" war machine, including the drone war in Pakistan, and Obama has appointed a CIA insider, John Brennan, to help "rein in" the agency's operatives. Far from reining in the horse, the problem is that the beast is out of the barn.

A sense of the crisis Obama faces may be gleaned from a parallel on the domestic front, the "war on gangs" of several past decades, which was theorized by neo-conservatives like James Q. Wilson, framed by Reagan Republicans like William Bennett, led by police chiefs like William Bratton, and ended in the greater incarceration of young prisoners than anywhere else in the world. Law and order worked in politics, but the inner cities still suffer from the domestic counterterrorism imposed by elite units of local police. Hundreds of thousands of people will be stigmatized by criminal records for life. Civil liberties were set aside for secret dossiers and databases. Street violence finally declined for multiple reasons, including the hard measures of law enforcement, but the violence only spread to the prisons, cycled back to the streets, and could flare up again at any moment. The same *mano duro* policies, often with the same advisers, were exported to Central America and beyond, where prisons remain choked with thousands of young people lacking all hope. Meanwhile, poverty in black communities has risen, even under Obama, and the neo-conservative trope about suppressing crime in order to create investment opportunities has proven to be absurd. If one thinks of the unconstitutional tactics imposed by the New York and (until recently) Los Angeles police, not to mention in hundreds of smaller cities, and project that level of domestic suppression into the villages of Afghanistan or Yemen, one might just begin to imagine the future of suffering and humiliation without alternatives that millions of young people face around the world.

The limitations of the drone war should be clear from any study of history and strategy. Wars cannot be won from secret aerial launches against unknown forces and figures on the ground. But since America is unlikely to relaunch ground troops any time soon, the power vacuums on the ground will expand and threaten American security officials. The lobbyists for the military and for drones in particular [yes, they have their very own lobby] go on making money off their failures, while the discretionary funds available continue to shrink. Public opposition to both drones and excessive secrecy is likely to expand indefinitely. The options are narrowing.

Opposition and protest are not enough, however, now that the drone protests have had a global effect. An articulate new vision of American security, with a blueprint to overhaul the policies on drones, cyber warfare and counterterrorism to bring them under much greater public scrutiny and congressional oversight, is desperately needed to avoid the drift. Kevin Martin, longtime director of the organization Peace Action, is right in declaring we need "a foreign policy for the 99 percent."[9] As the status quo disintegrates, that need will only grow.

NOTES

[1] Gideon Rose, *What Would Nixon Do?*, N.Y. TIMES (June 25, 2011), www.nytimes.com/2011/06/26/opinion/sunday/26afghan. html?pagewanted=all&_r=0.

[2] *Id.*

[3] *Id.*

[4] *Id.*

[5] *On Eve of Elections, a Dismal Public Mood in Pakistan*, PEW RESEARCH (last visited Sept. 20, 2013), www.pewglobal.org/2013/05/07/chapter-3-attitudes-toward-the-united-states-and-american-policies/#drones-pakistan.

[6] *See generally* PETER DALE SCOTT, The Road to 9/11: Wealth, Empire, and the Future of America (Univ. of Cal. Press, 2008).

[7] *Charting the Data for US Airstrikes in Pakistan, 2004-2013*, THE LONG WAR JOURNAL (last visited Sept. 19, 2013, 10:06 PM).

[8] *See generally* JEREMY SCAHILL, DIRTY WARS (Nation Books 2013).

[9] Kevin Martin, *Towards a Foreign Policy for the 99 Percent*, FOREIGN POLICY IN FOCUS (Dec. 18, 2012), fpif.org/towards_a_foreign_policy_for_the_99_percent/.

APPENDIX A
DEPARTMENT OF JUSTICE WHITE PAPER DRAFT
NOVEMBER 8, 2011

LAWFULNESS OF A LETHAL OPERATION DIRECTED AGAINST A U.S. CITIZEN WHO IS A SENIOR OPERATIONAL LEADER OF AL-QA'IDA OR AN ASSOCIATED FORCE

This white paper sets forth a legal framework for considering the circumstances in which the U.S. government could use lethal force in a foreign country outside the area of active hostilities against a U.S. citizen who is a senior operational leader of al-Qa'ida or an associated force[1] of al-Qa'ida-that is, an al-Qa'ida leader actively engaged in planning operations to kill Americans. The paper does not attempt to determine the minimum requirements necessary to render such an operation lawful; nor does it assess what might be required to render a lethal operation against a U.S. citizen lawful in other circumstances, including an operation against enemy forces on a traditional battlefield or an operation against a U.S. citizen who is not a senior operational leader of such forces. Here the Department of Justice concludes only that where the following three conditions are met, a U.S. operation using lethal force in a foreign country against a U.S. citizen who is a senior operational leader of al-Qa'ida or an associated force would be lawful: (1) an informed, high-level official of the U.S. government has determined that the targeted individual poses an imminent threat of violent attack against the United States; (2) capture is infeasible, and the United States continues to monitor whether capture becomes feasible; and (3) the operation would be conducted in a manner consistent with applicable law of war principles. This conclusion is reached with recognition of the extraordinary seriousness of a lethal operation by the United States against a U.S. citizen, and also of the extraordinary seriousness of the threat posed by senior operational al-Qa'ida members and the loss of life that would result were their operations successful.

The President has authority to respond to the imminent threat posed by al-Qa'ida and its associated forces, arising from his constitutional responsibility to protect the country, the inherent right of the United States to national self defense under international law, Congress's authorization of the use of all necessary and appropriate military force against this enemy, and the existence of an armed conflict with al-Qa'ida under international law. Based on these authorities, the President may use force against al-Qa'ida and its associated forces. As detailed in this white paper, in defined circumstances, a targeted killing of a U.S. citizen who has joined al-Qa'ida or its associated forces would be lawful under U.S. and international law. Targeting a member of an enemy force who poses an imminent threat of violent attack to the United States is not unlawful. It is a lawful act of national self defense. Nor would it violate otherwise applicable federal laws barring unlawful killings in Title 18 or the assassination ban in Executive Order No. 12333. Moreover, a lethal operation in a foreign nation would be consistent with international legal principles of sovereignty and neutrality if it were conducted, for example, with the consent of the host nation's government or after a determination that the host nation is unable or unwilling to suppress the threat posed by the individual targeted.

Were the target of a lethal operation a U.S. citizen who may have rights under the Due Process Clause and the Fourth Amendment, that individual's citizenship would not immunize him from a lethal operation. Under the traditional due process balancing analysis of *Mathews v. Eldridge,* we recognize that there is no private interest more weighty than a person's interest in his life. But that interest must be balanced against the United States' interest in forestalling the threat of violence and death to other Americans that arises from an individual who is a senior operational leader of al-Qa'ida or an associated force of al-Qa'ida and who is engaged in plotting against the United States.

The paper begins with a brief summary of the authority for the use of force in the situation described here, including the authority to target a U.S. citizen having the characteristics described above with lethal force outside the area of active hostilities. It continues with the constitutional questions, considering first whether a lethal operation against such a U.S. citizen would be consistent with the Fifth Amendment's Due Process Clause, U.S. Const. amend. V. As part of the due process analysis, the paper explains the concepts of "imminence," feasibility of capture, and compliance with applicable law of war principles. The paper then discusses whether such an operation would be consistent with the Fourth Amendment's prohibition on unreasonable seizures, U.S. Const. amend. IV. It concludes that where certain conditions are met, a lethal operation against a U.S. citizen who is a senior operational leader of al-Qa'ida or its associated forces—a terrorist organization engaged in constant plotting against the United States, as well as an enemy force with which the United States is in a congressionally authorized armed conflict—and who himself poses an imminent threat of violent attack against the United States, would not violate the Constitution. The paper also includes an analysis concluding that such an operation would not violate certain criminal provisions prohibiting the killing of U.S. nationals outside the United States; nor would it constitute either the commission of a war crime or an assassination prohibited by Executive Order 12333.

I.

The United States is in an armed conflict with al-Qa'ida and its associated forces, and Congress has authorized the President to use all necessary and appropriate force against those entities. *See* Authorization for Use of Military Force ("AUMF"), Pub. L. No. 107-40, § 2(a), 115 Stat. 224, 224 (2001). In addition to the authority arising from the AUMF, the President's use of force against al-Qa'ida and associated forces is lawful under other principles of U.S. and international law, including the President's constitutional responsibility to protect the nation and the inherent right to national self defense recognized in international law *(see, e.g.,* U.N. Charter art. 51). It was on these bases that the United States responded to the attacks of September 11, 2001, and "[t]hese domestic and international legal authorities continue to this day." Harold Hongju Koh, Legal Adviser, U.S. Department of State, Address to the Annual Meeting of the American Society of International Law: The Obama Administration and International Law (Mar. 25, 2010) ("2010 Koh ASIL Speech").

Any operation of the sort discussed here would be conducted in a foreign country against a senior operational leader of al-Qa'ida or its associated forces who poses an imminent threat of violent attack against the United States. A use of force under such circumstances would be justified as an act of national self-defense. In addition, such a person would be within the core of individuals against whom Congress has authorized the use of necessary and appropriate force. The fact that such a person would also be a U.S. citizen would not alter this conclusion. The Supreme Court has held that the military may constitutionally use force against a U.S. citizen who is a part of enemy forces. *See Hamdi,* 542 U.S. 507, 518 (2004) (plurality opinion); *id.* at 587, 597 (Thomas, J., dissenting); *Ex Parte Quirin,* 317 U.S. at 37-38. Like the imposition of military detention, the use of lethal force against such enemy forces is an "important incident of war." *Hamdi,* 542 U.S. at 518 (plurality opinion) (quotation omitted). *See, e.g.,* General Orders No. 100: *Instructions for the Government of Armies of the United States in the* Field~ 15 (Apr. 24, 1863) ("[m]ilitary necessity admits of all direct destruction of life or limb of armed enemies") (emphasis omitted); International Committee of the Red Cross, *Commentary on the Additional Protocols of 8 June 1977 to the Geneva Conventions of 12 Aug. 1949 and Relating to the Protection of Victims of Non-International Armed Conflicts* (Additional Protocol II) § 4789 (1987) ("Those who belong to armed forces or armed groups may be attacked at any time."); Yoram Dinstein, *The Conduct of Hostilities Under the Law of International Armed Conflict* 94 (2004) ("When a person takes up arms or merely dons a uniform as a member of the armed forces, he automatically exposes himself to enemy attack."). Accordingly, the Department does not believe that U.S. citizenship would immunize a senior operational leader of al-Qa'ida or its associated forces from a use of force abroad authorized by the AUMF or in national self-defense.

In addition, the United States retains its authority to use force against al-Qa'ida and associated forces outside the area of active hostilities when it targets a senior operational leader of the enemy forces who is actively engaged in planning operations to kill Americans. The United States is currently in a non-international armed conflict with al-Qa'ida and its associated forces. *See Hamdan v. Rumsfeld,* 548 U.S. 557, 628-31 (2006) (holding that a conflict between a nation and a transnational non-state actor, occurring outside the nation's territory, is an armed conflict "not of an international character" (quoting Common Article 3 of the Geneva Conventions) because it is not a "clash between nations"). Any U.S. operation would be part of this non-international armed conflict, even if it were to take place away from the zone of active hostilities. *See* John O. Brennan, Assistant to the President for Homeland Security and Counterterrorism, Remarks at the Program on Law and Security, Harvard Law School: Strengthening Our Security by Adhering to Our Values and Laws (Sept. 16, 2011) ("The United States does not view our authority to use military force against al-Qa'ida as being restricted solely to 'hot' battlefields like Afghanistan."). For example, the AUMF itself does not set forth an express geographic limitation on the use of force it authorizes. *See Hamdan,* 548 U.S. at 631 (Kennedy, J., concurring) (what makes a non-international armed conflict distinct from an international armed conflict is "the legal status of the entities opposing each other"). None of the three branches of the U.S. Government has identified a strict geographical limit on the permissible scope of the AUMF's authorization. *See, e.g.,* Letter for the Speaker of the House of Representatives and the President Pro Tempore of the Senate from the President (June 15, 2010) (reporting that the armed forces, with the assistance of numerous international partners, continue to conduct operations "against al-Qa'ida terrorists," and that the United States has "deployed combat-equipped forces to a number of locations in the U.S. Central ... Command area[] of operation in support of those [overseas counter-terrorist] operations"); *Bensayah v. Obama,* 610 F.3d 718, 720, 724-25, 727 (D.C. Cir. 2010) (concluding that an individual turned over to the United States in Bosnia could be detained if the government demonstrates he was part of al-Qa'ida); *al-Adahi v. Obama,* 613 F.3d 1102, 1003, 1111 (D.C. Cir. 2010) (noting authority under AUMF to detain individual apprehended by Pakistani authorities in Pakistan and then transferred to U.S. custody).

Claiming that for purposes of international law, an armed conflict generally exists only when there is "protracted armed violence between governmental authorities and organized armed groups," *Prosecutor v. Tadic,* Case No. IT-94-1AR72, Decision on the Defence Motion for Interlocutory Appeal on Jurisdiction,

,-r 70 (Int'l Crim. Trib. for the Former Yugoslavia, App. Chamber Oct. 2, 1995), some commenters have suggested that the conflict between the United States and al-Qa'ida cannot lawfully extend to nations outside Afghanistan in which the level of hostilities is less intense or prolonged than in Afghanistan itself. *See, e.g.,* Mary Ellen O'Connell, *Combatants and the Combat Zone,* 43 U. Rich. L. Rev. 845, 857-59 (2009). There is little judicial or other authoritative precedent that speaks directly to the question of the geographic scope of a non-international armed conflict in which one of the parties is a transnational, non-state actor and where the principal theater of operations is not within the territory of the nation that is a party to the conflict. Thus, in considering this potential issue, the Department looks to principles and statements from analogous contexts.

The Department has not found any authority for the proposition that when one of the parties to an armed conflict plans and executes operations from a base in a new nation, an operation to engage the enemy in that location cannot be part of the original armed conflict, and thus subject to the laws of war governing that conflict, unless the hostilities become sufficiently intense and protracted in the new location. That does not appear to be the rule of the historical practice, for instance, even in a traditional international conflict. *See* John R. Stevenson, Legal Adviser, Department of State, United States Military Action in Cambodia: Questions of International Law, Address before the Hammarskjold Forum of the Association of the Bar of the City of New York (May 28, 1970), *in* 3 *The Vietnam War and International Law: The Widening Context* 23, 28-30 (Richard A. Falk, ed. 1972) (arguing that in an international armed conflict, if a neutral state has been unable for any reason to prevent violations of its neutrality by the troops of one belligerent using its territory as a base of operations, the other belligerent has historically been justified in attacking those enemy forces in that state). Particularly in a non-international armed conflict, where terrorist organizations may move their base of operations from one country to another, the determination of whether a particular operation would be part of an ongoing armed conflict would require consideration of the particular facts and circumstances in each case, including the fact that transnational non-state organizations such as al-Qa'ida may have no single site serving as their base of operations. *See also, e.g.,* Geoffrey S. Com & Eric Talbot Jensen, *Untying the Gordian Knot: A Proposal for Determining Applicability of the Laws of War to the War on Terror,* 81 Temp. L. Rev. 787, 799 (2008) ("If ... the ultimate purpose of the drafters of the Geneva Conventions was to prevent 'law avoidance' by developing de facto law triggers—a purpose consistent with the humanitarian foundation of the treaties—then the myopic focus on the geographic nature of an armed conflict in the context of transnational counterterrorist combat operations serves to frustrate that purpose.").[2]

If an operation of the kind discussed in this paper were to occur in a location where al-Qa'ida or an associated force has a significant and organized presence and from which al-Qa'ida or an associated force, including its senior operational leaders, plan attacks against U.S. persons and interests, the operation would be part of the non-international armed conflict between the United States and al-Qa'ida that the Supreme Court recognized in *Hamdan*. Moreover, such an operation would be consistent with international legal principles of sovereignty and neutrality if it were conducted, for example, with the consent of the host nation's government or after a determination that the host nation is unable or unwilling to suppress the threat posed by the individual targeted. In such circumstances, targeting a U.S. citizen of the kind described in this paper would be authorized under the AUMF and the inherent right to national self-defense. Given this authority, the question becomes whether and what further restrictions may limit its exercise.

II.

The Department assumes that the rights afforded by Fifth Amendment's Due Process Clause, as well as the Fourth Amendment, attach to a U.S. citizen even while he is abroad. *See Reid v. Covert*, 354 U.S. 1, 5-6 (1957) (plurality opinion); *United States v. Verdugo-Urquidez*, 494 U.S. 259,269-70 (1990); *see also In re Terrorist Bombings of US. Embassies in East Africa*, 552 F.3d 157, 170 n.7 (2d Cir. 2008). The U.S. citizenship of a leader of al-Qa'ida or its associated forces, however, does not give that person constitutional immunity from attack. This paper next considers whether and in what circumstances a lethal operation would violate any possible constitutional protections of a U.S. citizen.

A.

The Due Process Clause would not prohibit a lethal operation of the sort contemplated here. In *Hamdi*, a plurality of the Supreme Court used the *Mathews v. Eldridge* balancing test to analyze the Fifth Amendment due process rights of a U.S. citizen who had been captured on the battlefield in Afghanistan and detained in the United States, and who wished to challenge the government's assertion that he was part of enemy forces. The Court explained that the "process due in any given instance is determined by weighing 'the private interest that will be affected by the official action' against the Government's asserted interest, 'including the function involved' and the burdens the Government would face in providing greater process." *Hamdi*, 542 U.S. at 529 (plurality opinion) (quoting *Mathews v. Eldridge*, 424 U.S. 319, 335 (1976). The due process balancing analysis applied to determine the Fifth Amendment rights of a U.S. citizen with respect to law-of-war detention supplies the framework for assessing the process due a U.S. citizen who is a senior operational leader of an enemy force planning violent attacks against Americans before he is subjected to lethal targeting.

In the circumstances considered here, the interests on both sides would be weighty. *See Hamdi,* 542 U.S. at 529 (plurality opinion) ("It is beyond question that substantial interests lie on both sides of the scale in this case."). An individual's interest in avoiding erroneous deprivation of his life is "uniquely compelling." *See Ake v. Oklahoma,* 470 U.S. 68, 178 (1985) ("The private interest in the accuracy of a criminal proceeding that places an individual's life or liberty at risk is almost uniquely compelling."). No private interest is more substantial. At the same time, the government's interest in waging war, protecting its citizens, and removing the threat posed by members of enemy forces is also compelling. *Cf Hamdi,* 542 US at 531 (plurality opinion) ("On the other side of the scale are the weighty and sensitive governmental interests in ensuring that those who have in fact fought with the enemy during a war do not return to battle against the United States."). As the *Hamdi* plurality observed, in the "circumstances of war," "the risk of erroneous deprivation of a citizen's liberty in the absence of sufficient process ... is very real," *id.* at 530 (plurality opinion), and, of course, the risk of an erroneous deprivation of a citizen's life is even more significant. But, "the realities of combat" render certain uses of force "necessary and appropriate," including force against U.S. citizens who have joined enemy forces in the armed conflict against the United States and whose activities pose an imminent threat of violent attack against the United States-and "due process analysis need not blink at those realities." *Id.* at 531 (plurality opinion). These same realities must also be considered in assessing "the burdens the Government would face in providing greater process" to a member of enemy forces. *Id.* at 529, 531 (plurality opinion).

In view of these interests and practical considerations, the United States would be able to use lethal force against a U.S. citizen, who is located outside the United States and is an operational leader continually planning attacks against U.S. persons and interests, in at least the following circumstances: (1) where an informed, high-level official of the U.S. government has determined that the targeted individual poses an imminent threat of violent attack against the United States; (2) where a capture operation would be infeasible-and where those conducting the operation continue to monitor whether capture becomes feasible; and (3) where such an operation would be conducted consistent with applicable law of war principles. In these circumstances, the "realities" of the conflict and the weight of the government's interest in protecting its citizens from an imminent attack are such that the Constitution would not require the government to provide further process to such a U.S. citizen before using lethal force. *Cf Hamdi,* 542 6 U.S. at 535 (plurality opinion) (noting that the Court "accord[s] the greatest respect and consideration to the judgments of military authorities in matters relating to the actual prosecution of war, and ... the scope of that discretion necessarily is wide"); *id.* at 534 (plurality opinion) ("The parties agree that initial captures on the battlefield need not receive the process we have discussed here; that process is due only when the determination is made to continue to hold those who have been seized.") (emphasis omitted).

Certain aspects of this legal framework require additional explication. *First,* the condition that an operational leader present an "imminent" threat of violent attack against the United States does not require the United States to have clear evidence that a specific attack on U.S. persons and interests will take place in the immediate future. Given the nature of, for example, the terrorist attacks on September 11, in which civilian airliners were hijacked to strike the World Trade Center and the Pentagon, this definition of imminence, which would require the United States to refrain from action until preparations for an attack are concluded, would not allow the United States sufficient time to defend itself. The defensive options available to the United States may be reduced or eliminated if al-Qa'ida operatives disappear and cannot be found when the time of their attack approaches. Consequently, with respect to al-Qa'ida leaders who are continually planning attacks, the United States is likely to have only a limited window of opportunity within which to defend Americans in a manner that has both a high likelihood of success and sufficiently reduces the probabilities of civilian causalities. *See* Michael N. Schmitt, *State-Sponsored Assassination in International and Domestic Law,* 17 Yale J. Int'l L. 609, 648 (1992). Furthermore, a "terrorist 'war' does not consist of a massive attack across an international border, nor does it consist of one isolated incident that occurs and is then past. It is a drawn out, patient, sporadic pattern of attacks. It is very difficult to know when or where the next incident will occur." Gregory M. Travalio, *Terrorism, International Law, and the Use of Military Force,* 18 Wis. Int'l L.J. 145, 173 (2000); *see also* Testimony of Attorney-General Lord Goldsmith, 660 Hansard. H.L. (April21, 2004) 370 (U.K.), *available at* http://www. publications.parliament.uk/pa/ld200304/ldhansrd/vo0404 21/text/40421-07.htm (what constitutes an imminent threat "will develop to meet new circumstances and new threats . . . . It must be right that states are able to act in self-defense in circumstances where there is evidence of further imminent attacks by terrorist groups, even if there is no specific evidence of where such an attack will take place or of the precise nature of the attack."). Delaying action against individuals continually planning to kill Americans until some theoretical end stage of the planning for a particular plot would create an unacceptably high risk that the action would fail and that American casualties would result.

By its nature, therefore, the threat posed by al-Qa'ida and its associated forces demands a broader concept of imminence in judging when a person continually planning terror attacks presents an imminent threat, making the use of force appropriate. In this context, imminence must incorporate considerations of the relevant window of opportunity, the possibility of reducing collateral damage to civilians, and the likelihood of heading off future disastrous attacks on Americans. Thus, a decision maker determining whether an al-Qa'ida operational leader presents an imminent threat of violent attack against the United States must take into account that certain members of al-Qa'ida (including any potential target of lethal force) are continually plotting attacks against the United States; that al-Qa'ida would engage in such attacks regularly to the extent it were able to do so; that the U.S. government may not be aware of all al-Qa'ida plots as they are developing and thus cannot be confident that none is about to occur; and that, in light of these predicates, the nation may have a limited window of opportunity within which to strike in a manner that both has a high likelihood of success and reduces the probability of American casualties.

With this understanding, a high-level official could conclude, for example, that an individual poses an "imminent threat" of violent attack against the United States where he is an operational leader of al-Qa'ida or an associated force and is personally and continually involved in planning terrorist attacks against the United States. Moreover, where the al-Qa'ida member in question has recently been involved in activities posing an imminent threat of violent attack against the United States, and there is no evidence suggesting that he has renounced or abandoned such activities, that member's involvement in al-Qa'ida's continuing terrorist campaign against the United States would support the conclusion that the member poses an imminent threat.

Second, regarding the feasibility of capture, capture would not be feasible if it could not be physically effectuated during the relevant window of opportunity or if the relevant country were to decline to consent to a capture operation. Other factors such as undue risk to U.S. personnel conducting a potential capture operation also could be relevant. Feasibility would be a highly fact-specific and potentially time-sensitive inquiry.

Third, it is a premise here that any such lethal operation by the United States would comply with the four fundamental law-of-war principles governing the use of force: necessity, distinction, proportionality, and humanity (the avoidance of unnecessary suffering). *See, e.g.,* United States Air Force, Targeting, Air Force Doctrine Document 2-1.9, at 88 (June 8, 2006); Dinstein, *Conduct of Hostilities* at 16-20, 115-16, 119-23; *see also 2010 Koh ASIL Speech.* For example, it would not be consistent with those principles to continue an operation if anticipated civilian casualties would be excessive in relation to the anticipated military advantage.

Chairman of the Joint Chiefs of Staff Instruction 5810.01D, Implementation of the DoD Law of War Program~ 4.a, at 1 (Apr. 30, 2010). An operation consistent with the laws of war could not violate the prohibitions against treachery and perfidy, which address a breach of confidence by the assailant. *See, e.g.,* Hague Convention IV, Annex, art. 23(b), Oct. 18, 1907, 36 Stat. 2277, 2301-02 ("[I]t is especially forbidden ... [t]o kill or wound treacherously individuals belonging to the hostile nation or army . . . ."). These prohibitions do not, however, categorically forbid the use of stealth or surprise, nor forbid attacks on identified individual soldiers or officers. *See* U.S. Army Field Manual 27-10, *The Law of Land* Warfare,¶ 31 (1956) (article 23(b) of the Annex to the Hague Convention IV does not "preclude attacks on individual soldiers or officers of the enemy whether in the zone of hostilities, occupied territory, or else-where"). And the Department is not aware of any other law-of-war grounds precluding use of such tactics. *See* Dinstein, *Conduct of Hostilities* at 94-95, 199; Abraham D. Sofaer, *Terrorism, the Law, and the National Defense,* 126 Mil. L. Rev. 89, 120-21 (1989). Relatedly, "there is no prohibition under the laws of war on the use of technologically advanced weapons systems in armed conflict-such as pilotless aircraft or so-called smart bombs—as long as they are employed in conformity with applicable laws of war." *2010 Koh ASIL Speech.* Further, under this framework, the United States would also be required to accept a surrender if it were feasible to do so.

In sum, an operation in the circumstances and under the constraints described above would not result in a violation of any due process rights.

B.

Similarly, assuming that a lethal operation targeting a U.S. citizen abroad who is planning attacks against the United States would result in a "seizure" under the Fourth Amendment, such an operation would not violate that Amendment in the circumstances posited here. The Supreme Court has made clear that the constitutionality of a seizure is determined by "balanc[ing] the nature and quality of the intrusion on the individual's Fourth Amendment interests against the importance of the governmental interests alleged to justify the intrusion." *Tennessee v. Garner,* 471 US. 1; 8 (1985) (internal quotation marks omitted); *accord Scott v. Harris,* 550 U.S. 372, 383 (2007). Even in domestic law enforcement operations, the Court has noted that "[w]here the officer has probable cause to believe that the suspect poses a threat of serious physical harm, either to the officer or to others, it is not constitutionally unreasonable to prevent escape by using deadly force." *Garner,* 4 71 U.S. at 11. Thus, "if the suspect threatens the officer with a weapon or there is probable cause to believe that he has committed a crime involving the infliction or threatened infliction of serious physical harm, deadly force may be used if necessary to prevent escape, and if, where feasible, some warning has been given." *Id.* at 11-12.

The Fourth Amendment "reasonableness" test is situation-dependent. *Cf Scott*, 550 U.S. at 382 (*"Garner* did not establish a magical on/off switch that triggers rigid preconditions whenever an officer's actions constitute 'deadly force.'"). What would constitute a reasonable use of lethal force for purposes of domestic law enforcement operations differs substantially from what would be reasonable in the situation and circumstances discussed in this white paper. But at least in circumstances where the targeted person is an operational leader of an enemy force and an informed, high-level government official has determined that he poses an imminent threat of violent attack against the United States, and those conducting the operation would carry out the operation only if capture were infeasible, the use of lethal force would not violate the Fourth Amendment. Under such circumstances, the intrusion on any Fourth Amendment interests would be outweighed by the "importance of the governmental interests [that] justify the intrusion," *Garner*, 471 U.S. at 8-the interests in protecting the lives of Americans.

C.

Finally, the Department notes that under the circumstances described in this paper, there exists no appropriate judicial forum to evaluate these constitutional considerations. It is well-established that "[m]atters intimately related to foreign policy and national security are rarely proper subjects for judicial intervention," *Haig v. Agee*, 453 U.S. 280, 292 (1981), because such matters "frequently turn on standards that defy judicial application," or "involve the exercise of a discretion demonstrably committed to the executive or legislature," *Baker v. Carr*, 369 U.S. 186, 211 (1962). Were a court to intervene here, it might be required inappropriately to issue an ex ante command to the President and officials responsible for operations with respect to their specific tactical judgment to mount a potential lethal operation against a senior operational leader of al-Qa'ida or its associated forces. And judicial enforcement of such orders would require the Court to supervise inherently predictive judgments by the President and his national security advisors as to when and how to use force against a member of an enemy force against which Congress has authorized the use of force.

III.

Section 1119(b) of title 18 provides that a "person who, being a national of the United States, kills or attempts to kill a national of the United States while such national is outside the United States but within the jurisdiction of another country shall be punished as provided under sections 1111, 1112, and 1113." 18 U.S.C. § 1119(b) (2006).[3] Because the person who would be the target of the kind of operation discussed here would be a US citizen, it might be suggested that section 1119(b) would prohibit such an operation. Section 1119, however, incorporates the federal murder and manslaughter statutes, and thus its prohibition extends only to "unlawful killing[s]," 18 U.S.C. §§ 1111(a), 1112(a) (2006). Section 1119 is best construed to incorporate the "public authority" justification, which renders lethal action carried out by a government official lawful in some circumstances. As this paper explains below, a lethal operation of the kind discussed here would fall within the public authority exception under the circumstances and conditions posited because it would be conducted in a manner consistent with applicable law of war principles governing the non-international conflict between the United States and al-Qa'ida and its associated forces. It therefore would not result in an unlawful killing.[4]

A.

Although section 1119(b) refers only to the "punish[ments]" provided under sections 1111, 1112, and 1113, courts have held that section 1119(b) incorporates the substantive elements of those cross-referenced provisions of title 18. *See, e.g., United States v. Wharton,* 320 F.3d 526, 533 (5th Cir. 2003); *United States v. White,* 51 F. Supp. 2d 1008, 1013-14 (E.D. Cal. 1997). Section 1111 of title 18 sets forth criminal penalties for "murder," and provides that "[m]urder is the unlawful killing of a human being with malice aforethought." 18 U.S.C. § 1111(a). Section 1112 similarly provides criminal sanctions for "[m]anslaughter," and states that "[m]anslaughter is the unlawful killing of a human being without malice." *Id.* § 1112(a). Section 1113 provides criminal penalties for "attempts to commit murder or manslaughter." *Id.* § 1113. It is therefore clear that section 1119(b) bars only "unlawful killing."

Guidance as to the meaning of the phrase "unlawful killing" in sections 1111 and 1112—and thus for purposes of section 1119(b)—can be found in the historical understandings of murder and manslaughter. That history shows that states have long recognized justifications and excuses to statutes criminalizing "unlawful" killings."[5] One state court, for example, in construing that state's murder statute, explained that "the word 'unlawful' is a term of art" that "connotes a homicide with the absence of factors of excuse or justification." *People v. Frye,* 10 Cal. Rptr. 2d 217, 221 (Cal. Ct. App. 1992). That court further explained that the factors of excuse or justification in question include those that have traditionally been recognized. *Id.* at 221 n.2. Other authorities support the same conclusion. *See, e.g., Mullaney v. Wilbur,* 421 U.S. 684, 685 (1975) (requirement of "unlawful" killing in Maine murder statute meant that killing was "neither justifiable nor excusable"); *cf also* Rollin M. Perkins & Ronald N. Boyce, *Criminal Law* 56 (3d ed. 1982) ("Innocent homicide is of two kinds, (1) justifiable and (2) excusable."). Accordingly, section 1119 does not proscribe killings covered by a justification traditionally recognized under the common law or state and federal murder statutes. "Congress did not intend [section 1119] to criminalize justifiable or excusable killings." *White,* 51 F. Supp. 2d at 1013.

B.

The public authority justification is well-accepted, and it may be available even in cases where the particular criminal statute at issue does not expressly refer to a public authority justification. Prosecutions where such a "public authority" justification is invoked are understandably rare, *see* American Law Institute Model Penal Code and Commentaries§ 3.03 Comment 1, at 23-24 (1985); *cf Visa Fraud Investigation,* 8 Op. O.L.C. 284,285 n.2, 286 (1984), and thus there is little case law in which courts have analyzed the scope of the justification with respect to the conduct of government officials. Nonetheless, discussions in the leading treatises and in the Model Penal Code demonstrate its legitimacy. *See* 2 Wayne R. LaFave, *Substantive Criminal Law* § 10.2(b), at 135 (2d ed. 2003); Perkins & Boyce, *Criminal Law* at 1093 ("Deeds which otherwise would be criminal, such as taking or destroying property, taking hold of a person by force and against his will, placing him in confinement, or even taking his life, are not crimes if done with proper public authority."); *see also* Model Penal Code § 3.03(1)(a), (d), (e), at 22-23 (proposing codification of justification where conduct is "required or authorized by," *inter alia,* "the law defining the duties or functions of a public officer," "the law governing the armed services or the lawful conduct of war," or "any other provision of law imposing a public duty"); National Commission on Reform of Federal Criminal Laws, *A Proposed New Federal Criminal Code*§ 602(1) (1971) ("Conduct engaged in by a public servant in the course of his official duties is justified when it is required or authorized by law."). And the Department's Office of Legal Counsel ("OLC") has invoked analogous rationales when it has analyzed whether Congress intended a particular criminal statute to prohibit specific conduct that otherwise falls within a government agency's authorities. *See, e.g., Visa Fraud Investigation,* 8 Op. O.L.C. at 287-88 (concluding that a civil statute prohibiting issuance of visa to an alien known to be ineligible did not prohibit State Department from issuing such a visa where "necessary" to facilitate an important Immigration and Naturalization Service undercover operation carried out in a "reasonable" fashion).

The public authority justification would not excuse all conduct of public officials from all criminal prohibitions. The legislature may design some criminal prohibitions to place bounds on the kinds of governmental conduct that can be authorized by the Executive. Or the legislature may enact a criminal prohibition in order to limit the scope of the conduct that the legislature has otherwise authorized the Executive to undertake pursuant to another statute. *See, e.g., Nardone v. United States,* 302 U.S. 379, 384 (1937) (federal statute proscribed government wiretapping). But the generally recognized public authority justification reflects that it would not make sense to attribute to Congress the intent to criminalize all covered activities undertaken by public officials in the legitimate exercise of their otherwise lawful authorities, even if Congress clearly intends to make those same actions a crime when committed by persons not acting pursuant to public authority. In some instances, therefore, the best interpretation of a criminal prohibition is that Congress intended to distinguish persons who are acting pursuant to public authority from those who are not, even if the statute does not make that distinction express. *Cf id.* at 384 (federal criminal statutes should be construed to exclude authorized conduct of public officers where such a reading "would work obvious absurdity as, for example, the application of a speed law to a policeman pursuing a criminal or the driver of a fire engine responding to an alarm").[6]

The touchstone for the analysis whether section 1119 incorporates not only justifications generally, but also the public authority justification in particular, is the legislative intent underlying this statute. Here, the statute should be read to exclude from its prohibitory scope killings that are encompassed by traditional justifications, which include the public authority justification. The statutory incorporation of two other criminal statutes expressly referencing "unlawful" killings is one indication. *See supra* at 19-22. Moreover, there are no indications that Congress had a contrary intention. Nothing in the text or legislative history of sections 1111-1113 of title 18 suggests that Congress intended to exclude the established public authority justification from those justifications that Congress otherwise must be understood to have imported through the use of the modifier "unlawful" in those statutes. Nor is there anything in the text or legislative history of section 1119 itself to suggest that Congress intended to abrogate or otherwise affect the availability of this traditional justification for killings. On the contrary, the relevant legislative materials indicate that, in enacting section 1119, Congress was merely closing a gap in a field dealing with entirely different kinds of conduct from that at issue here.[7]

The Department thus concludes that section 1119 incorporates the public authority justification.[8] This paper turns next to the question whether a lethal operation could be encompassed by that justification and, in particular, whether that justification would apply when the target is a U.S. citizen. The analysis here leads to the conclusion that it would.

C.

A lethal operation against an enemy leader undertaken in national self-defense or during an armed conflict that is authorized by an informed, high-level official and carried out in a manner that accords with applicable law of war principles would fall within a well established variant of the public authority justification and therefore would not be murder. *See, e.g.,* 2 Paul H. Robinson, *Criminal Law Defenses*§ 148(a), at 208 (1984) (conduct that would violate a criminal statute is justified and thus not unlawful "[w]here the exercise of military authority relies upon the law governing the armed forces or upon the conduct of war"); 2 LaFave, *Substantive Criminal Law* § 10.2(c) at 136 ("another aspect of the public duty defense is where the conduct was required or authorized by 'the law governing the armed services or the lawful conduct of war'"); Perkins & Boyce, *Criminal Law* at 1 093 (noting that a "typical instance[] in which even the extreme act of taking human life is done by public authority" involves "the killing of an enemy as an act of war and within the rules of war").[9]

The United States is currently in the midst of a congressionally authorized armed conflict with al-Qa'ida and associated forces, and may act in national self-defense to protect U.S. persons and interests who are under continual threat of violent attack by certain al-Qa'ida operatives planning operations against them. The public authority justification would apply to a lethal operation of the kind discussed in this paper if it were conducted in accord with applicable law of war principles. As one legal commentator has explained, "if a soldier intentionally kills an enemy combatant in time of war and within the rules of warfare, he is not guilty of murder," whereas, for example, if that soldier intentionally kills a prisoner of war—a violation of the laws of war—"then he commits murder." 2 LaFave, *Substantive Criminal Law* § 10.2(c), at 136; *see also State v. Gut,* 13 Minn. 341, 357 (1868) ("That it is legal to kill an alien enemy in the heat and exercise of war, is undeniable; but to kill such an enemy after he has laid down his arms, and especially when he is confined in prison, is murder."); Perkins & Boyce, *Criminal Law* at 1093 ("Even in time of war an alien enemy may not be killed needlessly after he has been disarmed and securely imprisoned…"). Moreover, without invoking the public authority justification by its terms, this Department's OLC has relied on the same notion in an opinion addressing the intended scope of a federal criminal statute that concerned the use of potentially lethal force. *See United States Assistance to Countries that Shoot Down Civil Aircraft Involved in Drug Trafficking,* 18 Op. O.L.C. 148, 164 (1994) (concluding that the Aircraft Sabotage Act of 1984, 18 U.S.C. § 32(b)(2) (2006), which prohibits the willful destruction of a civil aircraft and otherwise applies to U.S. government conduct, should not be construed to have "the surprising and almost certainly unintended effect of criminalizing actions by military personnel that are lawful under international law and the laws of armed conflict").

The fact that an operation may target a U.S. citizen does not alter this conclusion. As explained above, *see supra* at 5, the Supreme Court has held that the military may constitutionally use force against a U.S. citizen who is part of enemy forces. *See Hamdi,* 542 U.S. at 518 (plurality opinion); *id.* at 587, 597 (Thomas, J., dissenting); *Ex parte Quirin,* 317 U.S. at 37-38 ("Citizens who associate themselves with the military arm of the enemy government, and with its aid, guidance and direction enter [the United States] bent on hostile acts," may be treated as "enemy belligerents" under the law of war.). Similarly, under the Constitution and the inherent right to national self-defense recognized in international law, the President may authorize the use of force against a U.S. citizen who is a member of al-Qa'ida or its associated forces and who poses an imminent threat of violent attack against the United States.

In light of these precedents, the Department believes that the use of lethal force addressed in this white paper would constitute a lawful killing under the public authority doctrine if conducted in a manner consistent with the fundamental law of war principles governing the use of force in a non-international armed conflict. Such an operation would not violate the assassination ban in Executive Order No. 12333. Section 2.11 of Executive Order No. 12333 provides that "[n]o person employed by or acting on behalf of the United States Government shall engage in, or conspire to engage in, assassination." 46 Fed. Reg. 59,941, 59, 952 (Dec. 4, 1981). A lawful killing in self-defense is not an assassination. In the Department's view, a lethal operation conducted against a U.S. citizen whose conduct poses an imminent threat of violent attack against the United States would be a legitimate act of national self-defense that would not violate the assassination ban. Similarly, the use of lethal force, consistent with the laws of war, against an individual who is a legitimate military target would be lawful and would not violate the assassination ban.

IV.

The War Crimes Act, 18 U.S.C. § 2441 (2006) makes it a federal crime for a member of the Armed Forces or a national of the United States to "commit[] a war crime." *Id.* § 2441 (a). The only potentially applicable provision of section 2441 to operations of the type discussed herein makes it a war crime to commit a "grave breach" of Common Article 3 of the Geneva Conventions when that breach is committed "in the context of and in association with an armed conflict not of an international character." [10] *Id.* § 2441(c)(3). As defined by the statute, a "grave breach" of Common Article 3 includes "[m]urder," described in pertinent part as "[t]he act of a person who intentionally kills, or conspires or attempts to kill ... one or more persons taking no active part in the hostilities, including those placed out of combat by sickness, wounds, detention, or any other cause." *Id.* § 2441(d)(1)(D).

Whatever might be the outer bounds of this category of covered persons, Common Article 3 does not alter the fundamental law of war principle concerning a belligerent party's right in an armed conflict to target individuals who are part of an enemy's armed forces or eliminate a nation's authority to take legitimate action in national self-defense. The language of Common Article 3 "makes clear that members of such armed forces [of both the state and non,-state parties to the conflict] ... are considered as 'taking no active part in the hostilities' only once they have disengaged from their fighting function ('have laid down their arms') or are placed *hors de combat;* mere suspension of combat is insufficient." International Committee of the Red Cross, *Interpretive Guidance on the Notion of Direct Participation in Hostilities Under International Humanitarian Law* 28 (2009). An operation against a senior operational leader of al-Qa'ida or its associated forces who poses an imminent threat of violent attack against the United States would target a person who is taking "an active part in hostilities" and therefore would not constitute a "grave breach" of Common Article 3.

V.

In conclusion, it would be lawful for the United States to conduct a lethal operation outside the United States against a U.S. citizen who is a senior, operational leader of al-Qa'ida or an associated force of al-Qa'ida without violating the Constitution or the federal statutes discussed in this white paper under the following conditions: (1) an informed, high-level official of the U.S. government has determined that the targeted individual poses an imminent threat of violent attack against the United States; (2) capture is infeasible, and the United States continues to monitor whether capture becomes feasible; and (3) the operation is conducted in a manner consistent with the four fundamental principles of the laws of war governing the use of force. As stated earlier, this paper does not attempt to determine the minimum requirements necessary to render such an operation lawful, nor does it assess what might be required to render a lethal operation against a U.S. citizen lawful in other circumstances. It concludes only that the stated conditions would be sufficient to make lawful a lethal operation in a foreign country directed against a U.S. citizen with the characteristics described above.

NOTES

[1] An associated force of al-Qa'ida includes a group that would qualify as a co-belligerent under the laws of war. *See Hamlily v. Obama,* 616 F. Supp. 2d 63, 74-75 (D.D.C. 2009) (authority to detain extends to "'associated forces,'"which "mean 'co-belligerents' as that term is understood under the laws of war").

[2] *See Prosecutor v. Tadic,* Case No. IT-94-1AR72, Submission of the Government of the United States of America Concerning Certain Arguments Made by Counsel for the Accused, at 27-28 (Int'l Crim. Trib. For the Former Yugoslavia, App. Chamber July 17, 1995) (in determining which body of law applies in a particular conflict, "the conflict must be considered as a whole, and "it is artificial and improper to attempt to divide it into isolated segments, either geographically or chronologically").

3   *See also* 18 U.S.C. § 1119(a) (2006) (providing that "'national of the United States' has the meaning stated in section 101(a)(22) of the Immigration and Nationality Act," 8 U.S.C. § 1101(a)(22) (2006)).

4   In light of the conclusion that section 1119 and the statutes it cross-references incorporate this justification, and that the justification would cover an operation of the sort discussed here, this discussion does not address whether an operation of this sort could be lawful on any other grounds.

5   The same is true with respect to other statutes, including federal laws, that modify a prohibited act other than murder or manslaughter with the term "unlawfully." *See, e.g., Territory v. Gonzales,* 89 P. 250, 252 (N.M. 1907) (construing the term "unlawful" in statute criminalizing assault with a deadly weapon as "clearly equivalent" to "without excuse or justification"). For example, 18 U.S.C. § 2339C(a)(1) (2006) makes it unlawful, *inter alia,* to "unlawfully and willfully provide[] or collect[] funds" with the intention that they may be used (or knowledge they are to be used) to carry out an act that is an offense within certain specified treaties, or to engage in certain other terrorist acts. The legislative history of section 2339C makes clear that "[t]he term 'unlawfully' is intended to embody common law defenses." H.R. Rep. No. 107-307, at 12 (2001).

6   Each potentially applicable statute must be carefully and separately examined to discern Congress's intent in this respect. *See generally, e.g., Nardone,* 302 U.S. 379; *United States Assistance to Countries that Shoot Down Civil Aircraft Involved in Drug Trafficking,* 18 Op. O.L.C. 148 (1994); *Application of Neutrality Act to Official Government Activities,* 8 Op. O.L.C. 58 (1984).

7   Section 1119 was designed to close a jurisdictional loophole-exposed by a murder that had been committed abroad by a private individual-to ensure the possibility of prosecuting U.S. nationals who murdered other U.S. nationals in certain foreign countries that lacked the ability to lawfully secure the perpetrator's appearance at trial. *See* 137 Cong. Rec. 8675-76 (1991) (statement of Sen. Thurmond). This loophole is unrelated to the sort of authorized operation at issue here. Indeed, prior to the enactment of section 1119, the only federal statute expressly making it a crime to kill U.S. nationals abroad (outside the United States' special and maritime jurisdiction) reflected what appears to have been a particular concern with the protection of Americans from terrorist attacks. *See* 18 U.S.C. § 2332(a), (d) (2006) (criminalizing unlawful killings of U.S. nationals abroad where the Attorney General or his subordinate certifies that the "offense was intended to coerce, intimidate, or retaliate against a government or a civilian population").

8   18 U.S.C. § 956(a)(l) (2006) makes it a crime to conspire within the jurisdiction of the United States "to commit at any place outside the United

States an act that would constitute the offense of murder, kidnapping, or maiming if committed in the special maritime and territorial jurisdiction of the United States" if any conspirator acts within the United States to effect any object of the conspiracy. Like section 1119(b), section 956(a) incorporates the public authority justification. In addition, the legislative history of section 956(a) indicates that the provision was "not intended to apply to duly authorized actions undertaken on behalf of the United States Government." 141 Cong. Rec. 4491,4507 (1995) (section-by-section analysis of bill submitted by Sen. Biden, who introduced the provision at the behest of the President); *see also id.* at 11,960 (section-by-section analysis of bill submitted by Sen. Daschle, who introduced the identical provision in a different version of the anti-terrorism legislation a few months later). Thus, for the reasons that section 1119(b) does not prohibit the United States from conducting a lethal operation against a U.S. citizen, section 956(a) also does not prohibit such an operation.

[9] *See also Frye,* 10 Cal. Rptr. 2d at 221 n.2 (identifying "homicide done under a valid public authority, such as execution of a death sentence or killing an enemy in a time of war," as examples of justifiable killing that would not be "unlawful" under the California statute describing murder as an "unlawful" killing); Model Penal Code § 3 .03(2)(b), at 22 (proposing that criminal statutes expressly recognize a public authority justification for a killing that "occurs in the lawful conduct of war" notwithstanding the Code recommendation that the use of deadly force generally should be justified only if expressly prescribed by law).

[10] The statute also defines "war crime" to include any conduct that is defined as a grave breach in any of the Geneva Conventions (or any Geneva protocol to which the United States is a party); that is prohibited by four specified articles of the Fourth Hague Convention of 1907; or that is a willful killing or infliction of serious injury in violation of the 1996 Protocol on Prohibitions or Restrictions on the Use of Mines, Booby-Traps and Other Devices. 18 U.S.C. § 2441(c).

APPENDIX B

May 23, 2013

FACT SHEET: US POLICY STANDARDS AND PROCEDURES FOR THE USE OF FORCE IN COUNTERTERRORISM OPERATIONS OUTSIDE THE UNITED STATES AND AREAS OF ACTIVE HOSTILITIES

Since his first day in office, President Obama has been clear that the United States will use all available tools of national power to protect the American people from the terrorist threat posed by al-Qa'ida and its associated forces. The President has also made clear that, in carrying on this fight, we will uphold our laws and values and will share as much information as possible with the American people and the Congress, consistent with our national security needs and the proper functioning of the Executive Branch. To these ends, the President has approved, and senior members of the Executive Branch have briefed to the Congress, written policy standards and procedures that formalize and strengthen the Administration's rigorous process for reviewing and approving operations to capture or employ lethal force against terrorist targets outside the United States and outside areas of active hostilities. Additionally, the President has decided to share, in this document, certain key elements of these standards and procedures with the American people so that they can make informed judgments and hold the Executive Branch accountable.

This document provides information regarding counterterrorism policy standards and procedures that are either already in place or will be transitioned into place over time. As Administration officials have stated publicly on numerous occasions, we are continually working to refine, clarify, and strengthen our standards and processes for using force to keep the nation safe from the terrorist threat. One constant is our commitment to conducting counterterrorism operations lawfully. In addition, we consider the separate question of whether force should be used as a matter of policy. The most important policy consideration, particularly when the United States contemplates using lethal force, is whether our actions protect American lives.

Preference for Capture

The policy of the United States is not to use lethal force when it is feasible to capture a terrorist suspect, because capturing a terrorist offers the best opportunity to gather meaningful intelligence and to mitigate and disrupt terrorist plots. Capture operations are conducted only against suspects who may lawfully be captured or otherwise taken into custody by the United States and only when the operation can be conducted in accordance with all applicable law and consistent with our obligations to other sovereign states.

Standards for the Use of Lethal Force

Any decision to use force abroad – even when our adversaries are terrorists dedicated to killing American citizens – is a significant one. Lethal force will not be proposed or pursued as punishment or as a substitute for prosecuting a terrorist suspect in a civilian court or a military commission. Lethal force will be used only to prevent or stop attacks against U.S. persons, and even then, only when capture is not feasible and no other reasonable alternatives exist to address the threat effectively. In particular, lethal force will be used outside areas of active hostilities only when the following preconditions are met:

First, there must be a legal basis for using lethal force, whether it is against a senior operational leader of a terrorist organization or the forces that organization is using or intends to use to conduct terrorist attacks.

Second, the United States will use lethal force only against a target that poses a continuing, imminent threat to U.S. persons. It is simply not the case that all terrorists pose a continuing, imminent threat to U.S. persons; if a terrorist does not pose such a threat, the United States will not use lethal force.

Third, the following criteria must be met before lethal action may be taken:

1. Near certainty that the terrorist target is present;

2. Near certainty that non-combatants[1] will not be injured or killed;

3. An assessment that capture is not feasible at the time of the operation;

4. An assessment that the relevant governmental authorities in the country where action is contemplated cannot or will not effectively address the threat to U.S. persons; and

5. An assessment that no other reasonable alternatives exist to effectively address the threat to U.S. persons.

Finally, whenever the United States uses force in foreign territories, international legal principles, including respect for sovereignty and the law of armed conflict, impose important constraints on the ability of the United States to act unilaterally – and on the way in which the United States can use force. The United States respects national sovereignty and international law.

U.S. Government Coordination and Review

Decisions to capture or otherwise use force against individual terrorists outside the United States and areas of active hostilities are made at the most senior levels of the U.S. Government, informed by departments and agencies with relevant expertise and institutional roles. Senior national security officials – including the deputies and heads of key departments and agencies – will consider proposals to make sure that our policy standards are met, and attorneys – including the senior lawyers of key departments and agencies – will review and determine the legality of proposals.

These decisions will be informed by a broad analysis of an intended target's current and past role in plots threatening U.S. persons; relevant intelligence information the individual could provide; and the potential impact of the operation on ongoing terrorism plotting, on the capabilities of terrorist organizations, on U.S. foreign relations, and on U.S. intelligence collection. Such analysis will inform consideration of whether the individual meets both the legal and policy standards for the operation.

Other Key Elements

U.S. Persons. If the United States considers an operation against a terrorist identified as a U.S. person, the Department of Justice will conduct an additional legal analysis to ensure that such action may be conducted against the individual consistent with the Constitution and laws of the United States.

Reservation of Authority. These new standards and procedures do not limit the President's authority to take action in extraordinary circumstances when doing so is both lawful and necessary to protect the United States or its allies.

Congressional Notification. Since entering office, the President has made certain that the appropriate Members of Congress have been kept fully informed about our counterterrorism operations. Consistent with this strong and continuing commitment to congressional oversight, appropriate Members of the Congress will be regularly provided with updates identifying any individuals against whom lethal force has been approved. In addition, the appropriate committees of Congress will be notified whenever a counterterrorism operation covered by these standards and procedures has been conducted.

NOTES

[1] Non-combatants are individuals who may not be made the object of attack under applicable international law. The term "non-combatant" does not include an individual who is part of a belligerent party to an armed conflict, an individual who is taking a direct part in hostilities, or an individual who

is targetable in the exercise of national self-defense. Males of military age may be non-combatants; it is <u>not</u> the case that all military-aged males in the vicinity of a target are deemed to be combatants.

ABOUT THE CONTRIBUTORS

Marjorie Cohn is a professor at Thomas Jefferson School of Law in San Diego, former president of the National Lawyers Guild, and deputy secretary general of the International Association of Democratic Lawyers. Her books include *Cowboy Republic: Six Ways the Bush Gang Has Defied the Law*; *Rules of Disengagement: The Politics and Honor of Military Dissent* (with Kathleen Gilberd); and the edited volume, *The United States and Torture: Interrogation, Incarceration and Abuse*. Cohn is a recipient of the Peace Scholar of the Year Award from the Peace and Justice Studies Association. She testified before Congress about the Bush torture policy.

Medea Benjamin is a cofounder of CODEPINK and Global Exchange. She was described as "one of America's most committed—and most effective—fighters for human rights" by *New York Newsday*, and called "one of the high profile leaders of the peace movement" by the *Los Angeles Times*. In 2005, Benjamin was one of 1,000 exemplary women from 140 countries nominated to receive the Nobel Peace Prize. Benjamin is the author of ten books, including *Drone Warfare: Killing by Remote Control*.

Phyllis Bennis is a fellow of the Institute for Policy Studies, where she directs the New Internationalism project. She is also a fellow of the Transnational Institute in Amsterdam. Her books include *Ending the US War in Afghanistan: A Primer*, and *Before & After: US Foreign Policy and the War on Terror*. She writes for *The Nation* and is a frequent commentator on MSNBC and C-SPAN.

Richard Falk is Albert G. Milbank Professor of International Law Emeritus at Princeton University. He is currently research professor at Orfalea Center for Global & International Studies at the University of California-Santa Barbara. Falk was the Special Rapporteur on Occupied Palestine for the UN Human Rights Council from 2008 to 2014. He was also appointed expert advisor to the president of the UN General Assembly. Falk has published more than fifty books, most recently *Legality and Legitimacy in Global Affairs*, *Global Parliament* (with Andrew Strauss), and *Path to Zero: Dialogues on Nuclear Dangers*.

Tom Hayden is an author, teacher, and editor of *The Nation*. He has taught at UCLA, Pitzer College, Scripps College, and Occidental College. Hayden has covered US military policies in Iraq, Afghanistan, and the underlying "Long War" doctrine for a decade. Hayden combines fifty years of activism, beginning with civil rights and opposition to the Vietnam War, with nearly twenty years as an elected legislator in California.

Pardiss Kebriaei is a senior staff attorney at the Center for Constitutional Rights. She is lead counsel for CCR in *Al-Aulaqi v. Panetta,* which seeks accountability for the killing of three American citizens in US drone strikes in Yemen, and was counsel in *Al-Aulaqi v. Obama,* which challenged the authorization for the targeting of an American citizen placed on government "kill lists." Kebriaei represents men currently and formerly detained at Guantánamo in their efforts for release and reintegration, and represented the families of two men who died at the prison in their lawsuit for accountability in *Al-Zahrani v. Rumsfeld.*

Jane Mayer is a staff writer for *The New Yorker.* She covers politics, national security, and Washington for the magazine. She has also authored one book, *The Dark Side: How the War on Terror Turned into a War on American Ideals,* and has co-authored two others, *Strange Justice,* and *Landslide. The Dark Side* and *Strange Justice* were finalists for the National Book Award. All three were *New York Times* best sellers.

Ishai Menuchin is the 2003 Laurent of the Rothko Chapel "Oscar Romero Award for Commitment to Truth and Freedom." He is executive director of the Public Committee Against Torture in Israel (PCATI), and chair of the board of directors of Amnesty International Israel. Menuchin was one of the first "Refusniks" of the Lebanon war in 1982, and was also the spokesperson of Yesh Gvul (There is a limit)—a soldiers' refusal movement—for more than two decades. He currently lectures in the departments of social work and political science at Ben-Gurion University. His books include *Activism and Social Change.*

Jeanne Mirer has practiced civil and human rights law throughout her career, specializing in developing theories to interpret US law consistent with international human rights law. She is currently co-chair of the International Committee of the National Lawyers Guild and president of the International Association of Democratic Lawyers. She has written several articles and white papers as well as a chapter in Marjorie Cohn's anthology, *The United States and Torture: Interrogation, Incarceration, and Abuse.*

John Quigley is President's Club Professor of Law, Moritz College of Law, Ohio State University. He is the author of books and articles, and serves as an expert in domestic and international courts on the topics of international law, law of war, and human rights. His most recent books include *The Statehood of Palestine: International Law in the Middle East Conflict* and *The Six-Day War and Israeli Self-Defense: Questioning the Legal Basis for Preventive War.*

Tom Reifer is associate professor of sociology and affiliated faculty in ethnic studies and women's and gender studies at the University of San Diego, and associate fellow at the Transnational Institute. Dr. Reifer was formerly associate director of the Institute for Research on World-Systems, and the Program on Global Studies, a branch of the Institute for Global Conflict and Cooperation. Dr. Reifer has written extensively on human rights, torture, related issues of war and peace, and US foreign policy.

Alice K. Ross has worked at the Bureau of Investigative Journalism since the drones project's inception. She is a graduate of City University's investigative journalism master's program and previously worked as a features writer and editor for magazines in the UK and Spain.

Jay Stanley is Senior Policy Analyst with the ACLU's Speech, Privacy and Technology Project, where he researches, writes, and speaks about technology-related privacy and civil liberties issues and their future. He writes for, and serves as editor of, the ACLU's technology policy blog, *Free Future*. Stanley has authored and co-authored influential ACLU reports on a variety of topics, including a December 2011 report on domestic drones. Before joining the ACLU in 2001, Stanley was an analyst at the technology research firm Forrester, where he focused on Internet policy issues.

Archbishop Desmond Tutu won the Nobel Peace Prize in 1984, the US Presidential Medal of Freedom in 2009, and the Templeton Prize in 2013. In 1986, he was elected Archbishop of Cape Town, the highest position in the Anglican Church in South Africa, and in 1994, Tutu was appointed as chair of South Africa's Truth and Reconciliation Commission, where he pioneered a new way for countries to move forward after experiencing civil strife and countless atrocities. He is the author of many books, including *God Has a Dream*, and *The Book of Forgiving*, co-authored with his daughter, the Rev. Mpho Tutu.

Harry van der Linden is professor of philosophy at Butler University. He is the author of *Kantian Ethics and Socialism* (1988) and other writings on Kant, Marx, and Marburg neo-Kantianism. He coedited *Philosophy Against Empire* (2006), *Democracy, Racism, and Prisons* (2007), and *Rethinking the Just War Tradition* (2007). His most recent articles analyze the concept and justification of violence, humanitarian intervention, preventive war, US military hegemony, and just military preparedness as a new category of just war theory. He is the executive editor of the *Radical Philosophy Review*.

INDEX